THE GYPSY 'MENACE'

MICHAEL STEWART
(*editor*)

THE GYPSY 'MENACE'

Populism and the New Anti-Gypsy Politics

HURST & COMPANY, LONDON

First published in the United Kingdom in 2012 by
C. Hurst & Co. (Publishers) Ltd.,
41 Great Russell Street, London, WC1B 3PL
© Organization for Security and Co-operation in Europe (OSCE), 2012
This publication was published with the support of the OSCE Office for
Democratic Institutions and Human Rights (ODIHR). The opinions
and information it contains do not necessarily reflect the policy and
position of ODIHR.
Printed in the United Kingdom

A Cataloguing-in-Publication data record for this book is available
from the British Library.

This book is printed using paper from registered sustainable
and managed sources.

ISBN: 978-184904-2192 (hardback)
       978-184904-2208 (paperback)

www.hurstpub.co.uk

CONTENTS

CONTENTS

PART 3
COMBATING EXTREMISM

PREFACE

Misha Glenny

'Do you have problems with people from Central and Eastern Europe? Have you lost your job to a Pole, Bulgarian, Romanian or other Eastern European? We want to know'. This is the Dutch Freedom Party's latest initiative, providing frustrated followers with a forum to share their negative experiences of eastern Europeans in the Netherlands. Site visitors are asked to click one or more boxes, each representing a particular 'problem' presented by eastern Europeans: drunkenness, double parking, degradation and noisiness.

Petty, you might think, but this kind of challenge to social tolerance is symptomatic of the way many people in Europe are coming to think about the cultural and social diversity that is, from another point of view, the very foundation of our continent's strength. And among the primary victims of this change in both public attitudes and in politicians' rhetoric have been the Roma or Gypsy peoples.

The publication of *The Gypsy Menace*, identifying a deeply disturbing trend in European politics in countries as diverse as Bulgaria, Italy and France, comes at a specific and ominous historical moment. As the authors here show, there has been a huge rise in cultural discrimination against Gypsies in various parts of Europe since the early 1990s—and this trend is now about to combine with what we know is going to be a truly terrible five to ten year trough in the European and world economy. The wider nationalist turn of the main parties in a country like Bulgaria has already merged with the activities of more extreme parties to infuse 'the Roma question' with a national-redemptive quality. Such a shift of the frame within which Roma are seen may yet find an echo in other countries of the region.

So, in a sense, the issue of the Gypsies becomes a sensitive touchstone to see how Europe is going to deal with itself at this moment of challenge. Does it have the maturity to do the right thing? 'Never again' was carved into the stones thrown into the foundations of the European Union. Never again would the terror that Nazi Germany and its allies brought to European minorities be allowed to stalk our lands. These words were easily uttered in the years of confidence when politicians felt they had the answers to the challenges Europe faced. Harder to say and mean them today.

It all comes down to what it means to be European. For the past fifty years Europe's values have had huge status and carried such clout that they swept all before them. Everyone wanted to be judged a European in their values—even the Soviet Union joined up to a 'European' Organisation for Security and Cooperation. There was, of course, something touchy feely about all this—wiping away the history that had stained the continent sixty years ago with a gentle unction of those enlightenment values: tolerance, civilisation and reason. But there was also a robust rigour to the doctrine, articulated perhaps most vigorously by the German philosopher and public intellectual, Jürgen Habermas, that modern European institutions would allow citizens to use their capacity to deliberate and pursue rational interests and to expand the community of reason. What Habermas called 'rational-critical communication' would allow us to deal, even at trans-national levels of deliberation, with real and deep conflicts of interest without reviving the spectres of the past.

But that uplifting hope that we might manage to create a common, European space of calmly purposeful, post-national negotiation and compromise, looks ever more illusory. In February 2012, one of the French presidential candidates, had this to say about the Romanian Roma living in France in ad hoc camps by the side of towns: 'The origin of the problem, that is to say the movement of a population that is nowhere accepted and lives in abject conditions, is that we did not establish a European regulation (*une règle européenne*) to keep that population where it ought to live, in Romania'.[1] The shocking nature of Hollande's stance was not his further proposal that state controlled camps should be built to contain these restless foreigners, but the taken for granted nature of his observation that amongst the European peoples some should be more equal than others—that there are some to whom the founding principle of the Union, the free movement of persons, should not apply. For François Hollande the task is 'to regulate this problem at the European level' so that 'we are not confronted with the repeated circulation of this population'. Now we know what the French Socialists hope from the European Union's much vaunted 'European Roma Strategy' which is being composed as this book goes to press.

It does all come down to what it means to be European.

At the current moment, as this book demonstrates, the radicalisation of anti-Roma politics has gone furthest in Hungary, with the staggering successes of the Jobbik party (the Movement for a Better Hungary) in those parts of the country where a large, impoverished Romany minority shares their misery with economically-distressed Magyars. Looking to the years ahead, I fear for the Balkan basin as a whole, the home to many millions of Roma. Just as in the 1930s, south-eastern Europe remains especially vulnerable to recession or depression. Then this region was hardest hit of Europe because the agricultural bias of their economies produced the notorious 'price scissors' that drastically reduced their purchasing power. Today the price scissors may have different causes but their effects remain as powerful as in the past. Furthermore, with all the money held in and managed by German and Austrian banks, control over their own economies is once again slipping out of the grasp of national governments.

Such economic collapse and political impotence was the background to the violence of south-eastern Europe in the 1930s. As Greece staggers now towards collapse and given that Greece has played a crucial political role in countries like Bulgaria, former Yugoslavia, Europe and even, to some extent, economically, the subterranean rumble of economic-political instability travelling along the regional level fault-lines is once again all*too audible. More than anywhere in our continent it is clear here that European integration has only partially succeeded—and that there is a real danger of social instability. How this might manifest itself is anyone's guess. Privately, many political leaders in central and eastern Europe can still do the anti-Semitic talk, larded with the old international conspiracy nonsense—but this has almost no political credibility and there is no political or propaganda gain to be made from promoting political anti-semitism. And this is for one main reason: there aren't many Jews left in this part of the world—and we all know why that is: the peoples of this region collaborated in their removal first under the Nazis and then in the repeated waves of anti-semitic posturing under their Soviet rulers. And in the current context, where a right-wing shift in the US and Europe promotes Israel as a critical ally, there is even less reason to play with this poison. And so, in this part of the world, only the Roma are left.

The point is that with a looming economic catastrophe that will particularly affect central and south-eastern Europe, breaking up the social and economic compromises of the past twenty-five years, vigilance against violence of any sort is critical. But, given European history, vigilance about violence directed against minority groups is even more essential. Today, in Bulgaria, Kosova and Macedonia, issues around Romany poverty and ethnic allegiance loom large. In October 2011, there were mass demonstrations in Sofia and other Bulgarian cities calling for 'An End to the State of Gypsyness' and t-shirts sporting the slogan 'I don't want to live in a Gypsy country' appeared in huge numbers all over the country. Interestingly, those demonstrations arose out of a non-ethnic conflict (the driver of a car belonging to a Romany criminal boss mowed down and killed a nineteen-year-old non-Roma Bulgarian) but it was then ethnicised by a familiar constellation of failings. The unsuccessful integration of minorities in Bulgaria should only be seen as the starting point. Corruption, organised crime and an ineffective justice system (the crime boss had long benefitted from a notorious impunity) combined with a lack of social justice, an absence of broad political legitimacy and a general crisis of representation, led thousands of outraged Bulgarians to take violently to the streets and terrify Romany families who had nothing to do with 'Tsar Kiro', as the head of the accused's family is known. What began as a wave of public sympathy with the victims of a crime was then infused with outrage at state corruption and failure to protect and, ultimately, took the form of anti-minority protests.

This book deals with the Roma but one of its strengths is that while it charts the rise of anti-Romany politics on a continental scale, its agenda-setting first two chapters make clear that this kind of xenophobic populism is part of a much wider change to what the book's editor calls 'the social weight of difference'. In countries of north-western Europe, where Romany populations are traditionally minuscule and totally marginal to political life, the really grating issue is immigration and, within that, 'Muslim immigration and integration'. But the same sort of rhetoric, the same focus on the inadaptability of the stranger, the same recourse to a cultural absolutism that justifies radically exclusionary policies crops up.

As Michael Stewart makes clear, there are many complex roots of the mainstreaming of xenophobic politics, but one important and commonly overlooked factor includes the failure of the post-Maastricht politics of

Europeanisation. It is true that this project, which has set in chain an extremely complex model of integration of national economies and polities, cannot constantly be derailed by the vagaries of twenty-seven regional electorates. But the extraordinary failure of elites to even pretend to consult populations about where this strategy is going—and the underlying failure to think through and articulate what a trans-national political structure would look like and how it would operate with democratic legitimacy—renders the whole project extraordinarily fragile. Fragile in itself, and maddening to ever larger sections of the European electorates. As François Hollande intimates, for the ordinary resident of Marseille, Europe no longer stands for a growing concert of interests and cultures, but now signifies macro-economic chaos and illegal squatters on the doorstep.

And so the European crisis is not simply an economic calamity. It is a crisis of governance and identity that strikes at the very heart of the postwar European project. A little further down the line, the threats facing the Roma will be a threat facing all of us.

FOREWORD

NEW FORMS OF ANTI-GYPSY POLITICS: A CHALLENGE FOR EUROPE

Michael Stewart[1]

This book addresses the way widespread anxieties and fears about Roma and Gypsy 'neighbours', 'migrants', 'welfare claimants', 'squatters', 'nomads', 'beggars', and so on, become the source of an anger that can be and is, in the right circumstances, being mobilised politically with unexpected and potentially frightening consequences.

Beginning sometime around the end of 2005, in many countries of Europe, there began a rather rapid shift in political discourse regarding Roma. Changes in the standards of the acceptable—a far clearer articulation of racist and exclusionary ideas than was considered permissible at the turn of this century—have gone hand in hand with significant changes in the official treatment meted out to this, the largest, European minority. There has been a measurable increase in inter-ethnic violence and hate crimes against the Roma in a number of countries, a raft of new policies and initiatives have been introduced that more or less explicitly target this ethnic minority and a deteriorating language of public discourse on Roma across the continent has become part of a disturbing reformulation of populist politics in a number of countries. It is this threefold combination that makes this change noteworthy and worrying. These phenomena have arrived un-announced and remain under-analysed.[2]

The contributors to this volume, who all have years of experience working with Romany populations in different parts of Europe, provide the detailed evidence for these claims—but let me lay out the case in brief here.

Since 2008, in the Czech Republic, Hungary and Italy, anti-Romany violence has been a serious and even an increasing problem; Roma in other countries have also been affected.

As Andrzej Mirga, the Senior Adviser on Roma and Sinti Affairs at the Organisation of Security and Cooperation in Europe's Office of Democratic Integration and Human Rights office, summarised,

Arson attacks on Romani houses, physical assaults, racist slurs, property destruction and police violence are the dominant types of crimes reported. Among the reported incidents, some have resulted in death. Attackers often target whole families in their homes (Hungary, Czech Republic) or whole communities in isolated settlements (Italy, Czech Republic) (2009:6).[3]

In Hungary, observers registered at least forty-eight violent attacks against Roma, including nine fatalities (two of them minors) between January 2008 and July 2010. According to research by the European Roma Rights Centre, only one perpetrator has been found guilty to date (and he is appealing). Dozens of Roma people have been injured, ten of whom have suffered life-threatening harm. Firearms and Molotov cocktails were used in twelve incidents, hand grenades in two, and property was vandalised in at least nine. The victims have included political representatives, like officials of local Roma minority councils but also random Romany citizens. There have also been violent clashes between groups of Roma and members of the banned, extremist Magyar Garda (Hungarian Guard), the uniformed militia of the Jobbik party. After the Garda was banned, for two months starting 1 March 2011 an organisation calling itself the Civil Guard Association for a Better Future (Szebb Jövőért Polgárőr Egyesület), identical in all but name to the Garda, roamed the streets of the north Hungarian village Gyöngyöspata, terrifying its Romany inhabitants with bellicose marches and war crys against the minority. In April 2011 Jobbik won the local election and took over the municipal council.

In the Czech Republic, at least sixteen attacks against Roma have been reported in the same period, most employing Molotov cocktails, but there were also several cases of mob violence and large neo-Nazi marches that resulted in anti-Romany aggression. In one Molotov cocktail attack on a Roma home, a two-year-old girl suffered extensive burns and nearly died. If there have not been worse casualties this appears to be a matter of chance.

Vigilante hate crime against the Roma is rampant in Italy and has been committed with total impunity. Between 2006 and May 2009, at least six arsons were perpetrated against camps housing hundreds of Roma people in Livorno, Milan, Naples and Rome. Many of these people are immigrants from Romania. In Milan one Roma camp was burned to the ground in May 2008 and five camps near Naples were attacked with Molotov cocktails two days later. The Ponticelli camp in that city was set on fire once each month between May and July 2008. A settlement of Roma in Sicily was also set on fire in June 2008. In November 2009, a mob of as many as 300 people vandalised Roma homes in Alba Adriatica.

In April 2009, YouTube hosted for a few days a film of Slovak police officers abusing and humiliating six young Romany boys in detention. There are a dozen or so other cases of violence in Slovakia involving Romany victims, including shootings, group attacks and police violence. At the time of writing, in early 2011, none of the identified perpetrators has yet been sentenced to prison. Such incidents have not been confined to eastern Europe, home to the vast majority of Europe's Roma. In June 2009, in Northern Ireland (UK) a group of Romany families were subjected to a series of violent attacks on their homes in Belfast by so-called 'loyalist' gangs; the church in which they sought shelter was also attacked. Six months later, in Turkey, around 1000 people attacked Romany neighbourhoods in Manisa's Selendi suburb in January 2010.

In some countries (Czech Republic, Hungary, Italy, Slovakia) this violence is perpetrated by extremist, sometimes neo-Nazi, groups, but it is not committed on an ideological basis alone. Non-Roma locals have engaged more or less spontaneously in vigilante violence against Roma and Travellers since at least 2004, and individuals motivated simply by racist hatred (absent of any particular political ideology) have also committed anti-Roma attacks. The tactic of setting Roma and Traveller dwellings on fire, usually at night while people are sleeping in them, is prevalent. Firearms have been used in incidents in Hungary, the Russian Federation and Slovakia. In Bulgaria and Romania, racist attacks against Roma are sometimes publicly perpetrated by skinheads before or after football matches.

There is also evidence that the authorities take these sorts of attacks with less seriousness than they would if similar violence were being carried out against another group. Even though the Czech riot in Litvínov in 2008 resulted in sixteen injuries (half of them to police), and even though police outnumbered the rioters by two to one, no one has yet been successfully prosecuted for the violence committed there.[4] During a spate of murders of Hungarian Roma it took the police many months before they even considered the possibility of a racial motivation, despite a pattern of attacks that bore no resemblance to the 'gangland killings' of which they insisted these were a part. In Italy, too, in the three months after extremists claimed responsibility for the arson in Livorno, an attack in which several children died, the Italian authorities announced that the case was closed without prosecutions.[5] And so on.

But is there anything truly new here, the sceptic might ask? Some observers have compared the situation now to that of the mid-1990s, when violence prompted Roma emigration from central Europe to countries such as Canada; indeed, a spike in emigration from the Czech Republic in early 2009 (following the November 2008 Litvínov riot) prompted the Canadian authorities to re-impose a visa requirement for Czech citizens later that year. But, it is our sense, that the context was radically different then, when the violence was often driven by local conflicts over resources and socio-political dominance in the newly opened, democratic space of villages and small towns. Today, the violence takes place against the background of longstanding, unresolved tensions in relation to the integration of Romany communities. Indeed, in many of the countries we discuss, the socio-economic conditions of the Roma have deteriorated in recent years with a loss of urban employment, an increase in residential and educational segregation and, consequently, greater dependency on the public purse. At the same time, the Roma have been the apparent beneficiaries of large scale EU funded programmes for economic and social inclusion—all to little or no avail.[6] This changes the context in which the violence has erupted.

In 2010 the OSCE-ODIHR produced a field assessment of violent incidents against the Roma in Hungary. We would argue that these conclusions of theirs can be applied generally across the region:

… hate crimes do not occur in a vacuum; they are violent manifestations of prejudice, which can be pervasive in the wider community… the continued lack of integration of Roma… makes them vulnerable to prejudice and intolerance and, ultimately, to racially-motivated violence…

Unaddressed conflicts not only threaten to disturb social peace but also hinder the constructive resolution of socio-economic problems. In situations where relations between ethnic groups are already sensitive, hate crimes can exacerbate tensions and have an explosive impact.

Social acceptance of discrimination against particular groups is an important factor behind hate crimes.

So the significance and indeed, to some extent, the source of these attacks derives from the broader context in which they occur. A particular significance must be given to the change in the way politicians and public figures feel it is appropriate to discuss the Roma. Since 2005–6, and intensifying during and after 2008, extremist political parties and politicians in many EU countries have sharpened their anti-Romany rhetoric and actions, creating a climate in which rights violations are more likely to occur with impunity. In Hungary, the Magyar Garda, a paramilitary organisation with an explicitly racist agenda, continues to operate openly despite a decision by the Supreme Court to ban it in 2009. That same year, Jobbik, an extremist party with an explicit anti-Romany platform, won four seats in European Parliamentary elections. In Italy, the government has used anti-Romany rhetoric to harden public opinion against Roma and Sinti while strengthening a state of emergency explicitly aimed at Roma, moving aggressively to evict Roma from their homes and herd them into controlled camps. In Slovakia, in 2010, the far-right Ludova Strana Nase Slovensko (Our Slovakia People's Party) was increasingly active with rhetoric specifically referring to 'Gypsy criminality'. In November 2008, the Czech Workers' Party (DS) organised the rally in Litvinov, referred to above, when 500 neo-Nazis attempted to march on a Romany settlement before being stopped by police after violent clashes. Such incidents have since recurred. In February 2010 the Romanian Foreign Minister suggested in a speech that Roma are genetically predisposed to criminality and the media reported that the president defended his minister. During the controversy over the summer concerning Roma in France, both Bulgarian Prime Minister Borisov and Romanian President Băsescu erroneously referred to the Roma—who were exercising their right as citizens of an EU member to free movement in the Union—as nomads who need to travel. Violent conflicts between Roma and non-Roma have also arisen here (see Toma, this volume).

The transformation in the range of acceptable public speech is even more transparent in local politics. In September 2010, the Czech Social Democratic Party (ČSSD) group in the city of Most decided to continue a billboard campaign running the xenophobic slogan: 'Why should I regret being the majority nationality in my homeland? One state, one set of rules!' They had received a request from the acting chair of the national party to take down the controversial election advertisements but unanimously rejected his suggestion. They defended their stance with reference to supposedly shadowy figures pulling the strings behind the scenes; the leader of the local list claimed that the party chair 'probably has some advisor telling him it's not completely kosher, that Social Democrats shouldn't be saying something like this'.[7]

In Hungary, concerns about the Roma are even more clearly spoken. The mayor of a poor, north Hungarian village explained his attitude towards his Roma constituents as follows:

I just don't understand this question about who is a Gypsy. It is quite clear, isn't it? Everyone who is a Gypsy is a Gypsy. You can smell them from a kilometre. There is no definition for this—I can't find one. You have to accept that a person who was born a Gypsy has a different temperament; they live differently and behave differently. I grew up among Gypsy children. Everyone who is a Gypsy has remained a Gypsy. It makes no difference if they have a bath every night, the smell remains, just like with horses. There is a specific Gypsy smell. And they can smell the smell of the Peasants on us.

All these claims and assertions from elected public officials bring clearly into view the broader political context in which violent acts against Roma have to be seen. Across eastern Europe and, to a growing extent, in other countries of Europe where 'anti-Roma politics' has political currency— either at a local level as in the United Kingdom, or at a national level, as in Italy and to some extent France—it remains acceptable to articulate unapologetically racist comments about this particular minority.

Once again, some will say that there is nothing particularly new about this. There is clearly great continuity in the stereotypes of anti-Romany xenophobia and in the forms of hostility directed to this minority. Representations of Roma as thieves, as asocial, as unable to fit into mainstream society, ineducable, and so on, are decades if not centuries old. The dominant myths are also remarkably resistant to correction. In the past year the eminent French historian, Henriette Asséo, has published a number of high-profile, coruscating assaults on the idea of the Roma of Europe and France as nomads (see, e.g., *Le Monde*, 6 September 2010) but this notion resurfaces whenever 'the Roma' are discussed in French political circles.[8] In eastern Europe it is more common that the Roma's supposed laziness and work-shy disposition is the source of commentary—even though 90 per cent of the Roma worked in socialist industry and on the collective farms just like their non-Roma neighbours in the full-employment world of the planned economy.

We maintain, following the evidence collected here, that we are now witnessing at least a dangerous permutation in the political salience of such language. There are now elected officials, parties and civic movements for whom 'problems with the Gypsies' lie at the heart of their grievances. This is something wholly new on the European political scene. Traditional European anti-Gypsy politics talked of Roma as 'nuisances', as a 'public scandal', even as 'a plague descended on the hardworking citizens' but never, not even in the 1930s, as a fundamental source of national woe.[9] Parties have now emerged in Bulgaria and Hungary with significant public support, and which use a language of absolute cultural difference to place 'the Gypsy menace' at the centre of their politics. These parties are able to take diverse popular grievances and sentiments of threat and loss—many of which are linked rhetorically to the presence of 'burdensome Gypsies'—and reframe them in a nationalist-populist discourse that offers a persuasive, indeed compelling, re-imagination of society. In Hungary, the main party concerned, 'Jobbik Magyarországért Mozgalom' (The Movement for a Better Hungary, commonly known simply as Jobbik), came third in national elections held in April 2010 and narrowly failed to outstrip the outgoing Socialist Party. In Bulgaria such ideas have transformed the electoral fortunes of the two parties who adopted them (see Efremova, below).

The argument of the book

This book derives from a small conference organised and funded by the OSCE's Office for Democratic Institutions and Human Rights held at University College London in September of 2009 and subsequent online discussions. It was not possible there, nor is it in a book of this length, to provide country by country coverage. Statistical surveys, like the Demand for Extreme Right Wing Index, DEREX, which uses the European Social Survey Round (1–4) for data, can provide a continental bird's eye-view over the medium term,[10] but they do so at the cost of loss of detail and specificity. Since the rise of the new populist, anti-Gypsy forces has been much more dramatic in some countries than in others—in Hungary voter intentions shifted from 10 per cent to 21 per cent in the years 2002–09—we have given particular prominence to some cases, allowing more than one chapter to explore the nature of anti-Romany sentiment in these instances. This book is divided into three sections, with a series of national overviews, followed by a set of detailed case studies and a final section dealing with ways in which the current situation can be addressed by citizens and government actors alike. In the first five chapters, our authors examine the contours of the new forms of social and political exclusion of Roma in Hungary, Bulgaria, the Czech Republic, France and Italy. They focus in particular on understanding the complex relationship between state policy, democratic public culture and the rise of anti-Roma sentiment—demonstrating the local specificity of anti-Romany politics but also pointing to underlying continuities.

In my own paper, I argue that the rise of a new form of populism that targets Roma has to be understood as part of a broader shift in European politics. Indeed, it can best be seen as the counterpart of the emergence of a strong anti-Muslim discourse in 'western' countries of immigration (and in Italy occasionally merges into this). In contrast to other authors, who tend to stress the role of immigration in creating the ground for populism to flourish, I focus rather on the unintended impacts of European integration. The institutional reconfiguration of economies and polities across the continent, which has proceeded without democratic legitimacy and without an adequate debate over the nature of our transnational project, has provoked the rise of cultural politics—populisms that focus less on economic issues than cultural differences between peoples. The Roma, like the Muslims, are above all victims of a growing difficulty over difference.

The substantive country studies begin with Bulgaria for two reasons. First, in certain respects, we have witnessed on the Bulgarian political scene as radical a remodelling and mobilisation of anti-Roma sentiments as in any other country. Two political formations in Bulgaria developed, since 2005, and for the first time I believe in Europe, a 'redemptive' attitude to 'solving the Gypsy question'. For Ataka and the Bulgarian National Guard, the depredations lain at the doors of 'the Gypsies' are the cause of national decline, and the repackaging of traditional anti-Romany prejudices as well as their homogenisation has allowed their integration into this novel form of populist, protest politics. If in the past Roma were a mere 'nuisance', now they are the great stain on the nation. Renewal and rebirth can only come about through purging the nation of this unwanted flotsam. As Efremova puts it, 'Roma thus become central in the project for the remodelling of the nation'. Two great points of interest emerge in this article: we learn, firstly, how the popular base and support for these positions comes as much if not more from the young, university educated intelligentsia as from poorer sections of society; and, secondly, we see how parties like these appropriate the fashionable and now hegemonic language of rights, culture, identity and respect and cast them in an entirely new light—and to quite different political ends than those who coined the idiom of modern political claims. These parties are thus unlike old styles of populist or extremist politics and cannot be countered by the old sloganising of a tired-out left-wing with its wooden-tongued talk of 'Nazis' and 'fascists'.[11]

Ataka at first, and later the National Guard as well, stood more or less alone in Europe when they reframed traditional anti-Gypsy prejudices into their noxious vision of criminality, corruption and moral decay sapping the nation's moral health. But events in Hungary under the last socialist government, when a new populist party (led by a former equal opportunities campaigner and human rights lawyer) rose to such prominence that it nearly knocked the Socialists into third place in parliamentary elections in 2010, suggest that there are other countries where a similar reformulation of the political game can and may take place. The rise of Jobbik has involved a complete rewriting of the range of the polite and the permissible in Hungary with one of its mayoral candidates in municipal elections in autumn 2010 proposing the permanent internment of Romany petty criminals and investigations as to the possibility of 'returning' Roma to India. Jobbik has achieved this by drawing on the particular features and frustrations of the Hungarian political landscape that János Zolnay characterises in his chapter. It has also—as I shall discuss later—drawn on an inspired understanding of the nature of modern political campaigns which has allowed them to turn 'the Gypsy problem' of the past (in which one element was petty criminal behaviour) into a single-issue of 'criminality'.[12]

In this country, János Zolnay argues, it is above all the local dynamic of politics that has fostered the conditions in which Roma as a whole can be criminalised in so much public speech. It is local mayors, more than national political leaders, who have found themselves in the front line of antagonisms and conflicts, and have often been responsible for introducing aggressive, racist and exclusionary language into the public sphere. This derives, if we follow Zolnay, from the concatenation of three forces: firstly, local public culture in Hungarian communities is traditionally 'permissive' of abuse, slander and mockery of Roma. It has been so for an awfully long time—and throughout the communist period, even if on the national stage the expression of such sentiments was forbidden. Secondly, there is great pressure on the local communal purse in Hungary since many welfare payments are distributed locally—so the municipality is the object of voters' frustration when their own claims cannot be met. In response, we find mayors adopting what Gregory Bateson would have identified as self-reinforcing schismogenetic behaviour, which are practices that increase local tension in the name of dealing with it. Thus, in many localities, in order to humiliate the Roma claimants, mayors who also wish to display their own reluctance at supporting these 'work-shy' citizens insist that Romany welfare recipients stand in a queue outside their offices on the morning of payment. Elderly Magyars who are equally dependent on state hand-outs are given individual appointments (Thelen et al., forthcoming). This strategy, which is formally designed to show to the 'working Magyars' that payments are not made casually to Roma, does nothing but inflame tensions and resentment.[13] Finally, thanks to the radically decentralising Hungarian constitution, localities are also responsible for crucial public institutions around which there have long been fierce political and social struggles—especially schools. In fact, ever since the 1960s when the communist Hungarian state announced an intention to integrate Roma into mainstream schools there have been more or less constant efforts, led mostly by the teaching body as well as many parents of non-Romany children, to resist this. Today, as Zolnay demonstrates, mayors across Hungary coordinate initiatives to ensure the reproduction of segregation in novel, concealed forms.

All this is fertile ground for the populist Jobbik with their discourse of speaking unpalatable truth to the elite and to power, articulating the concerns of the local, talking for all those who are not heard in (supposedly Jewish dominated) Budapest and so on. How far Jobbik will be able to take their mobilisation we cannot yet know. However it does appear clear that anti-Roma rhetoric will remain central to their politics. After a collapse of support during the local elections in late 2010, they started the year 2011 with a renewed emphasis on this issue.[14] This said, it has been the historic role of the current governing party's leader since 1989 to salami-slice all those Hungarian conservative formations not within his party until they feel so isolated that the only place still offering political life seems to be his own Federation of Young Democrats. It may well be—and many will hope—that Prime Minister Orbán achieves this task once again, dismantling Jobbik in the process. His task will only really be accomplished, however, if he simultaneously addresses the sources of frustration, rage and impotence that are generated by the current Hungarian distribution of power and resources between centre and periphery and which Zolnay characterises so effectively here.

The Hungarian case is rendered particularly tense by the stasis in which the economy of Hungary slipped into in the late 1990s. While neighbouring countries ploughed ahead with structural reforms and entered periods of sustained growth, Hungary, which had done so much to liberalise the economy until 1989, trod water and then slid back. Rates of unemployment amongst Roma (at least the official ones) have remained more or less constant since the end of the 1990s and this, naturally, has lead to tension over the effectiveness of welfare policy—a source of ethnic tension in any modern democracy. There is no question that the sense of frustration, of living in a world without a future, that is widely felt in countries like Bulgaria and Hungary is fertile ground for the kind of scapegoating end emotive rejection of 'the other' that Efremova and Zolnay demonstrate. But there is more to anti-Romany politics today than economic crisis and fears of insecurity.

The data presented by Gwendolyn Albert indicates complex and enduring sources of anti-Romany sentiment in a neighbouring ex-communist country. The Czech Republic has not suffered in anything like the same way as Hungary from poor macro-economic management and a failure of the political class to reform public institutions and procedures. It is quite likely that this Czech willingness to push ahead with painful change has had the positive impact of keeping support for extremist parties at the barely registerable level (less than 3 per cent)—compared to a national 17 per cent for the Hungarian Jobbik. It is also perhaps important that Roma constitute a far smaller percentage in the Czech population (c. 2.5 per cent) than in neighbouring Slovakia or Hungary (where they make up between 5 and 8 per cent of the population). They are also among the most 'assimilated' Roma in eastern Europe in many respects. However, as Albert and later Cada show, this does not mean that there has been any significant slackening of tension about the presence of these unwanted 'outsiders' in the Czech Republic. In other words, and to be absolutely blunt, the prosperous Czech Republic is as much a hotbed of xenophobic sentiment as its struggling southern neighbour. Indeed, though the results of an ongoing series of arson attacks have been far less deadly than the Hungarian killing spree of 2008–9, this is in Albert's view as much a matter of chance as of design.

Crucially, from the point of view of outsiders or Czechs trying to work out how to challenge the prejudice that runs so wide and deep, Albert argues that

while the Czech Republic has long been criticised internationally for its systemic discrimination of the Roma … such criticism [is] rarely discussed or analysed in detail in the Czech media. Rather, inside the Czech world, such international criticism is interpreted as part of an ongoing narrative in which the Czechs are alone against the world, the perpetually misunderstood victims. The rest of the world is simply not to be trusted....

She relates this to the public culture in the Czech Republic in which the dissolution of the nation by its more powerful neighbours is always imagined as imminent.

In 'old Europe', just as in the new, the contours of anti-Romany prejudice can only be drawn accurately if we see that these ideas are part of a broader ideological field including the forms that national identity takes and the local history of dealing with Romany social and cultural difference. In the first chapter, dealing with western Europe, a young Italian scholar, Giovanni Picker, explains the apparent paradox that in Italy it has been left-wing mayors who have initiated and pursued some of the most radical, exclusionary agendas against Roma. Tracing recent policy initiatives in Rome and other cities like Bologna and Florence back to what he characterises as a current of 'non-inclusionary multiculturalism' in the Italian left, Picker shows how a very old and specifically Italian conception of Roma as 'nomads' (and so foreigners) feeds current attacks on Romanian (migrant) Roma (see About, 2004).

Concluding this first part of the book, the historian Ilsen About explains how the sudden eruption of an anti-Romany republican politics in France in the summer of 2010 can only be understood in the terms of the history of treatment of Roma by republican institutions over the past century. His careful reading of the way administrative procedures operated shows that when the law defines a sub-category of resident non-citizens, on the basis of nationality, ethnic identification or way of life, then the theoretical possibility of becoming an outlaw moves from being a risk to part of the normal order of things. In this way, the history of the French legal categorisation of the Gypsy population demonstrates the intense and progressive involvement of the state apparatus and its role in creating an underclass community, repeatedly excluded and rejected by the authorities of the national community.

In each of these chapters, the authors present global overviews of the development of particular anti-Romany policies, currents in public opinion or political platforms that shape national policy and practice. In the next section, five authors present case studies from Northern Ireland, Romania, Italy, Hungary and the Czech Republic, demonstrating the range of conflicts that have emerged recently between Roma and majority populations but also the convergence of political rhetoric around these.

We open with the first of two papers by anthropologists Kata Horváth and Cecilia Kovai discussing the transformation of Gypsy/Hungarian relations in one Hungarian village over the course of the past ten years. It has been said that anthropologists act as psychoanalysts of the social order and this article, which is one of the most important pieces of ethnographic reporting about Roma to have emerged from eastern Europe in the past twenty years, demonstrates just what that means. With detailed observation of the habits of everyday interaction in a small town, these authors lay bare the process by which a formally assimilationist (but *de facto* semi-exclusionary) cultural politics of the communist period has been replaced by a radically exclusionary and separatist practice. According to Hováth and Kovai, even though in the past the Gypsy/Hungarian distinction provided the basis of all social interaction between members of these two categories in Hungarian villages, this fact was never named and so no one was ever called 'a Gypsy' to their face. This meant that Gypsies lived in the village under a constant pressure that they should not behave in such a way as would force someone to call them 'a Gypsy'. They lived with the false promise that if they became educated, acquired wealth, lived like 'normal people' (read Hungarian peasants) then they would be treated as such. But the promise was illusory. Now, however, thanks to economic, demographic and, above all, political changes, the promise of assimilation has been taken back and 'the Gypsy' is constantly named and the Gypsies more or less happily bring their 'Gypsiness' to the public space. And, in consequence, the majority feels (quite unreasonably in many respects) that they are engaged in a battle for territory with this newly named presence, 'the Gypsies' who are taking over their institutions (the school, the bars, economic life). They feel 'their' space constantly encroached upon by this previously unnameable but ever present social force.[15]

This paper does not discuss in any detail the rise of Jobbik or the voting proclivities of those who appear in the discussion—instead it provides a uniquely intimate vision of the world in which Jobbik, or its equivalents elsewhere, appear to provide solutions to aching social problems. Although the paper draws on immensely detailed knowledge of social interactions in one small community, its findings can be generalised far beyond the northeast region of Hungary, and beyond this country's borders, since all the communist countries followed fundamentally similar policies towards their Romany minority, denying their cultural identity and encouraging a kind of forced assimilation (cf. Kaminski, 1983). It explains, for instance, the enormous resonance of the uniformed Hungarian Guard marches in Hungarian villages as a form of reclaiming the territory that, it appears, has been 'lost' to the Roma minority.

In the next chapter, we return to the Czech Republic, a country which shared a rather similar policy of forceful assimilation and full employment for Roma in the communist period, but where anti-Romany sentiment diverges now from the Hungarian patter. Which is not to say that this case is much less worrying. As Albert has already argued, there is no clear link between anti-Gypsy feelings and economic crisis here, and yet we find—in Cada's presentation—a deep and very widely shared hostility to the Roma, with 80 per cent or more associating themselves with points of view that would be seen as extremist in any other country. At the same time Cada demonstrates the continuity in anti-Romany prejudice from east to west. The idiom of exclusionary talk in this civilised country is neither exactly race, nor ethnicity—but the inadaptability of people who are, with Czech humour, commonly known as 'our fellow citizens'. No one mentions skin colour, few mention Indian origins, but 'otherness' in terms of attitudes to work and welfare is exaggerated and then seen as a quasi-biological attribute of the culture of this minority. This is, of course, that familiar form of modern racism, 'cultural racism', first identified by Paul Gilroy in his commentaries on post-imperial Britain (1979) in which the inflammatory image of skin and physiognomy—so irremediably associated with Nazism—is displaced in favour of behavioural attributes that are biologised (large families, lack of disposition to work hard, criminal proclivities, etc.). Cada correctly labels this racism, but it is important to remember that this is an analyst's interpretation and is not the surface appearance. His survey method, however, allows him to demonstrate that when asked to make explicit judgments a full 80 per cent of Czechs believe that because Roma belong to another sort of people they are unable to adapt or change.

This notion of inadaptability is central to much populist discourse in Europe today and Cada points to the peculiar paradox at its heart, the Catch 22 of this kind of anti-Romany prejudice: those people who are fiercest in demanding the total social and cultural assimilation of this minority are also those who tend to choose an ethno-racial (biological) interpretation of cultural and social difference. The paradox, however, is that, as Cada puts it, 'they demand full assimilation from members of other ethnic groups while believing that the Roma are unable to assimilate due to their otherness'. It appears, then, as if the Czech Republic has become the home of that version of the old sociological theory, 'the culture of poverty' that radically blames the poor for their own condition and declares the pointlessness of doing anything to change things since in a sense they live in 'ghettos'/are unemployed, fail at school, etc., 'because this suits their cultural proclivities'.[16]

One of the ways in which anti-Romany politics has taken shape in western Europe since 2000 is through representing increased Romany labour mobility—an inevitable consequence of integration of eastern European countries into the European Union—as 'migration' in the popular media. Several of our authors deal with this (including Picker in Italy and Benedik et al. in Austria) but from the western fringe of the European continent, Clark and Rice bring a particularly vivid case study of conflict between Romany migrant workers and indigenous 'hosts'. Taking off from Slavoj Žižek's discussion of the uncomfortable and intrusive 'proximity of the Neighbour', they note that for the anxious and fearful loyalists of Belfast no matter how far away the Roma could have been, they would always be 'too close'. Like Benedik and Horváth, but more explicitly perhaps, they are working with an anthropological notion of 'the political' as referring to that dimension of antagonism that is, in Chantal Mouffe's resonant phrase, inherent in human society. They are interested, therefore, less in the formal politics of the evictions and threats the Roma faced, than in the underlying assumptions and fears inspired in part by the gestures of everyday life (dress, style, manners and customs) that inspired and motivated the attacks. And for this reason, though it emerges that Loyalist ex-paramilitary organisations were involved in coordinating the evictions, the authors are wary of conceding to the line promoted in the British press that 'racism is the new sectarianism'. We would particularly like to commend their strategy that simultaneously tries to find the general in the local and holds on to the goal of grasping the specificity of this conflict, refusing to allow it to be 'reduced' to one phenomenal form of a general and rather abstract 'anti-Gypsy prejudice'.

This interpretative approach, which explicitly owes something to Paul Brass's pioneering work on Indian riot systems and the difficulties of classifying social action in those contexts, is also employed by Toma in her powerful discussion of the preconditions for establishing an effective and sustainable conflict mediation service in Romania. Like Clark and Rice, Toma is interested in the way events are represented. Toma's concern is with the idea of the 'last drop' that sends the liquid of conflict pouring over the rim of social control. She attempts to build a systematic comparison of situ-

ations in which local conflicts have become violent and are simultaneously
represented as 'ethnic'. She finds that after the event there is, in newspaper
reports and other media, a systematic reference to a supposed 'last drop'.
As Toma says, in one case this involved:

> a quarrel between a Hungarian and a Roma person in a local bar …; in another, in
> the neighbouring village, a Roma person was caught in the act, stealing from the
> agricultural property of a local Hungarian. Neither of these situations are singular
> or so spectacular as to merit a community based conflict. In fact, such events hap-
> pen regularly without consequence, in these very localities too. But in both cases,
> these 'last drop' events were considered as appropriate occasions to recall old-new
> grievances against Roma…

with the 'consequence' that violence broke out. But from the point of view
of actors wishing to intervene and take steps to calm things down, it is
essential to understand that the 'last drop' is rather a part of the representation of the conflict than its cause—it is simply an expression of an already
existing, underlying tension. With first hand experience of such situations,
Toma is well placed to comment that it is typical of bodies who rush in
immediately after conflict breaks out that they confuse the cause of the
conflict with its consequence (the last drop) because of their lack of local
knowledge and under the influence of whatever stereotypes are prevalent in
society at the time. Toma is, therefore, in effect proposing a conflict mediation service inspired by the sort of ethnographic understanding of local
everyday life demonstrated by many of the other authors in this volume.

Toma's concern to link scholarship to professional activity takes us
straight into the last part of the book where five chapters examine ways in
which social actors can act to defuse and de-ethnicise social antagonisms.

In 'Cucumbers Fighting Migrations' the reader will find a fascinating
study that illustrates the enormous complexity of social and political intervention in this field and the often tragic lack of serious local knowledge
among activists and others. The material covers nearly two decades of interactions and shows the kinds of confusions engendered when both well
meaning and more hostile citizens of the city of Graz tried to deal with an
influx of Romany beggars, first from Yugoslavia and then from the Slovak
Republic. As Benedik and his co-authors argue, the combination of temporary migration, poverty, images of 'the east' appearing on people's doorsteps
and Romany cultural strategies in Graz produced a 'cocktail that was hard
to deal with for a medium-sized Catholic town in Austria'.

Central to their account is the demonstration of how a small number of
beggars came to be construed as a danger or hazard threatening the town.

It takes a peculiarly fragile and insecure public culture in a prosperous city like this to respond as the citizens of Graz did. So intense was the fear and hostility to begging Romany women and children in 1996 that a specific local by-law was passed forbidding their 'aggressive mendiancy'. Once again, we are dealing here with forms of xenophobia that can only partially be referred back to economic insecurity. Culture (which is to say, politics in another guise) plays as prominent a role when the image of a woman, a migrant woman (who being from the east is presumed to have 'backward ideas'), taking an economically active role for her family, on the streets of a foreign city comes to challenge and violate basic socio-cultural regulations so strongly as to provoke legal initiatives.

This chapter points to another important aspect of these conflicts today. The efforts of a sympathetic local Catholic priest and an NGO to both 'give a name' to the beggars and link them to the fate of the Austrian and, even more, the local, Burgenland *Zigeuner*, almost all of whom died in the Second World War, had paradoxical results. In particular it enabled the local tabloid and conservative press to make the link between these new 'Yugoslavs' or 'Slovak citizens' (who till then had not been explicitly ethnicised) and the highly denigrated local notion of *'Zigeuner'*. Though that term was rapidly tabooed in debates about beggars, it floated in the public space long enough to tar the word Roma effectively. Here, again, the local history of Roma/non-Roma relations plays a crucial role in the way relations and interactions are shaped and the way 'Roma' come to be represented as unwanted intruders. The fact that so little is known about Roma makes interventions particularly tricky; but the difficulties are only compounded in a case like this where so few of the activists or investigators (journalists, public officials) are willing to actually talk to the Roma themselves and find out what they are up to.

Lidia Balogh, who prefaces her work with a brief but crucial overview of the activity of the Magyar Garda in the past few years, picks up a point that Toma stressed—the critical role of the local authorities and political elites in framing conflicts. As Zolnay argues earlier, the local level of political competence has both great autonomy and therefore decisive importance in the negotiation and treatment of antagonisms and conflicts. Balogh demonstrates just how this works by contrasting the way two Hungarian villages with superficially similar ethnic conflicts responded to an 'offer' from the Hungarian Guard to provide a show of force. It has become a common part of the Guard's strategy to arrive in villages with simmering conflicts, where they can claim that their presence is needed to restrain 'the criminal Roma' because of the lack of proper policing and a strong municipal hand. In fact, of course, their presence contributes decisively to further undermining the authority of official governing bodies. Interestingly, in both of Balogh's cases the village leaderships chose to avoid the disruption and terror that a visit from the semi-militarised Guard usually brings. In the first case a series of local considerations, including the effect such an event might have on the reputation of the village as a safe tourist resort—as well as a number of ongoing cross-community initiatives—enabled the mayor to see the invitation off. In the other case—in a village which is in many ways heavily identified with a culturally conservative, irredentist and nostalgic Magyar nationalism—a mayor who actively rejects racial or ethnic distinctions in his treatment of his voters makes the village an unwelcome place for the Guard. He does so even though there is more than one ongoing local conflict between certain Hungarians and their Romany neighbours. Cases like this would clearly merit deeper consideration for they demonstrate the decisive role that political decisions and choices play in the negotiation of genuine and trying social problems and conflicts.

While Balogh focuses on the role of local actors in hindering the appeal of populist movements, Britta Schellenberg, drawing on eleven separate country reports, provides a road map for policies that will help preserve a pluralist and humane Europe by dealing with such politics at the level of the whole continent. She does not argue that one strategy will meet all situations, but offers a timely concoction of mostly long-term measures that are all easily implementable. Schellenberg does not have an answer as to how to reduce the electoral pull of populist parties but notes that existing parliamentary strategies (especially incorporation or partnership as in Italy or Holland) have not had their desired outcome. Schellenberg also wisely emphasises the need to analyse and recognise different manifestations of extremism outside of formal politics. In many countries such views emerge on internet sites and in virtual social networks—often located on north American servers and so hiding behind the USA's first amendment protection barriers—but they too need to be challenged if they are not to shift the terrain of public culture.

Schellenberg also points pertinently to certain 'touchy' topics where the radical right sometimes manages to acquire defenders in the mainstream— such as around questions of 'free speech'. Her recommendation that training be provided to journalists, politicians, opinion formers in all their guises, in how to deal with such 'tricky' issues seems most timely. In former communist countries these issues of 'free speech' have, for obvious historical reasons, a particular complexity. András Pap provides a detailed examination of the ways constitutional lawyers and human rights activists have, in one jurisdiction, tied themselves in knots, much to the amusement of the populists who are adept at using the language of constitutionality to promote their deeply anti-constitutional vision of a state and nation purged of unwanted citizens. It is clear to anyone watching both the Hungarian and the Czech political scene—where there are strong legacies of human rights opposition to communist dictatorship—that efficient legal action to combat both discrimination and hate crimes are being disarmed or even undermined by tendentious extensions of certain human rights principles. It will take at least one more generation to rise through the ranks of officialdom before people trained wholly out of the shadow of the Marxian state are in positions of power, and so it is no exaggeration of Pap to note that these kinds of mistakes seriously threaten aspects of the still fragile democracies in the region.

To conclude, we move away from the issue of anti-Romany sentiments and politics and consider the basis on which Roma themselves might begin to mobilise in self defence and self assertion. The extent to which Roma have not organised themselves and have not sought representation is one of the most striking features of the east European political scene. It is, furthermore, a notorious feature of most bottom up Romany NGOs that they are family fiefs and have great difficulty branching out to a 'common Roma' people. Kovai wonders if at least one of the reasons for this is the legacy of what she and Horváth call 'the order of not naming the Gypsy'. In the old order world, family and kinship remained the only social space where a positive sense of Gypsiness could be articulated, where all the negative stereotypes associated with 'Gypsies' (which led the word to be tabooed in the first place in interactions with the Magyars) can be inverted or denied. But family is, of course, as much a source of division in a community as of unity. Now that 'the Gypsy' is openly spoken of in the public space, now that individual Roma are labelled 'Gypsy' by their non-Roma neighbours, now that there are 'Roma' organisations and institutions, there are signs that a new sense of 'shared Gypsiness' may emerge. This study raises the question therefore of whether the potential now exists for creating a civil rights type defensive movement among the Roma. If Roma do move from being weak political actors, it would be an ironic product of the social processes that have also produced such rabid hostility and aggression as has rarely been seen in these countries for many decades.

Can we talk of eastern and western Europe in one breath?

This book raises a number of questions about the comparability of the phenomena discussed in its various chapters. Is the flaring up of violence against Romanian migrant Roma in Belfast really a symptom of the same feelings as led the burghers of Graz to ban begging by Romany women? Is there some deeper connection between these and the feelings of loss, uncertainty and permanent crisis with no future that make Bulgarian middle classes so receptive to the ideas of parties like Ataka and the National Guard? Or, to put this another way, does the rise of anti-Gypsy politics in different parts of Europe demonstrate a converging evolution of 'public culture' in eastern and western Europe? Simply put, is it coherent to talk about intensifying anti-Roma politics on a European scale?

In my own chapter I argue that there are underlying features of current European public cultures that create conditions of receptivity for a politics based around fear and hostility targeting a clearly defined enemy population in the midst of the nation. Some of the cultural material that this politics draws on has, of course, a far longer history, but the fact that these old prejudices have been reworked in rather similar forms and with such ferocity in the past few years in different parts of our continent deserves further reflection. I use the term 'public culture' here to refer to 'the public space in which a society and its constituent individuals and communities imagine, represent and recognise themselves through political discourse, commercial and cultural expressions, and representations of state and civic organisations' (Hansen, 1999: 4). I use this term rather than 'political culture' in order to stress the multiple sources of political understandings that are not accessible to analysts through the traditional tools of political science (public opinion surveys, analyses of voter behaviour, party programmes and the like), to depict that sense of the political, captured by Chantal Mouffe, as rooted in the habits and practices of everyday life, and in the collective identifications embedded in our daily 'culture'.

Changes in public culture have diverse sources but there are four ways in which I think we can draw parallels between the two parts of the continent. The first concerns the rise of what we might call a newly legitimised xenophobia. In western Europe the changing character of migration has had a profound impact on public culture, with countries that had previously been sending countries becoming host countries for non-European migrants and refugees (Italy and Spain, for instance). In this process, the shift to non-European migration made religion a salient issue in some countries. Elsewhere increasing rates of immigration are commonly linked with declining fertility and birth rates among the native-born. Declining birth rates combined with ageing population are now understood to threaten the economic foundation of the European welfare state (Berezin, 32).[17] In eastern Europe, by contrast, concerns around the indigenous Romany minority are also linked to fears of demographic decline among the 'white' majority and so push very similar 'issues' onto the populist agenda.[18]

The precise play of issues here can be complex and specific. Berezin makes the important argument that xenophobia and anti-immigrant stances, albeit part of the picture, cannot accurately capture the broader dynamics of populist politics. Illegal immigration, rather than immigration *sui generis*, was in the early 2000s a pressing transnational issue. And likewise it could be argued that it is not 'the Gypsy issue' *per se* which is driving radical politics in central and eastern Europe, but irregularities and illegalities symbolically (and unfairly) associated with this minority—criminality, abuse of the welfare system, etc., and the kind of issues over control of public space identified by Horváth and Kovai. The enduringly ambivalent status of Romanian migrant workers in states like the UK is itself probably a source of the (unfair) sense that Romanians are not entirely legitimate migrant workers—as Clark and Rice demonstrate for Belfast.

A second way in which public culture across our continent has shifted concerns, as I argue in my own chapter, the transformation and threatened disappearance of the postwar 'world of security' as represented by the model of 'social (i.e. welfare) Europe'. In the west, ordinary citizens experienced a period of greater social security and spreading affluence between 1945 and 1980 and (with the exception of certain industrial areas) beyond that time too; the social contract forged during those years, the so-called 'postwar settlement', guaranteed social welfare, lowering retirement ages etc., increasing social protection. Something parallel, albeit it at a slower pace and from a lower starting point, took place within the authoritarian structures of the 'Peoples' Democracies' in the east. In both east and west, then, there is now a sense that the old order of social security is under threat. Ethnic minorities that can be represented as indigent provide an obvious target for outrage from the dispossessed and all those threatened by the new global order.

A third context concerns the impact of Europeanisation as a force shaping public culture and the sense of where citizenship and belonging lie. In opposition to the common claim that these effects are shallower in the east, because of late accession, it can be argued that the much faster pace of reforms there in the last two decades have helped produce a sharper sense that people there now live in a 'pseudo democracy' ruled by privileged minorities, which siphon off wealth, power and resources to both the 'above' and the 'below'. It is, then, the hard-working, long-suffering 'ordinary' middle that is the victim of this new European order. This is the classic condition for an explosive type of populist revolt.[19] Recent research points to an increase in nationalist resentment at the European Project in countries as differently placed as Hungary and Poland, and this can be seen to be paralleled by similar developments in the west (Charles, 2010).

Finally, we find a parallel disillusionment with politics and a growing lack of confidence in the political and party system in general. It could be said that this started happening in central and east Europe first, with universal disillusion with communism in the late 1970s and 1980s, followed by withdrawal into private lives; and once again in the late 1990s, after the euphoria of democracy and its (unfulfilled) promises had passed. Such disillusion feeds into that classic trope of populism—the distance of elites from the people and their presumed (and in many cases actual) corruption. In this context the populist political call to the nation, to awaken the slumbering folk, arouses certain moral sensibilities in voters, a feeling of a world that is in need of defence from various corrupt and criminal classes—another fertile breeding ground for parties like Jobbik or the Bulgarian National Guard to sow their seed in.

In all this, we have to remember, paraphrasing Hansen on post-colonial India, that democracy provides not just a form of government, but modifies social practices and institutions. Eastern Europeans became involved in new forms of civic organisation; participated in campaigns, in claim-making activities within everyday life, in all the 'trivia' of public engagement in a society which tries to operate as if all citizens are equal before the law. And all these activities lead to new ways of imagining society. Thus democracy makes new claims possible. Today, because of the objectification and codification of cultural difference in pluralist and multicultural politics enshrined in discourses circulating around and down from the European Union, when citizens do feel empowered or compelled to make claims these characteristically take a cultural form. In this sense the framing of populist claims around cultural collectivities represents not a deformity with respect to liberal models but rather a 'vernacularisation' of democratic discourses and procedures in the new Europe.[20]

This is not, let me hasten to add, to say that eastern and western public cultures are one and the same and that the evidence of this book suggests the treatment of Roma is likely to converge. Far from it. The diverse forms of Romany integration in different parts of Europe mean that problems arising between Roma and non-Roma vary hugely. This is even true within regions. Hungary and Bulgaria are the countries where 'redemptive' anti-Romany politics are strongest because of the sense citizens have in both those countries that they are living in a permanent and unending state of crisis—this kind of sentiment is not found in the Czech Republic and though anti-Gypsy feelings are vicious there too, they do not provide the basis for significant political mobilisation at the moment.

In 2012 the EU is moving to finalise some kind of European Roma Strategy or Framework and greater integration of initiative in the wake of President Sarkozy's varied interventions in the summer of 2010 and the Hungarian Presidency of the Union in the first months of 2011. But it is inconceivable that this will produce a complete homogenisation of the field. In the east, for instance, integration into the EU, and the increasingly global horizon that opened up when the Iron Curtain came down, has prompted eastern elites to seek recognition at an international level. At the same time, they feel a kind of anxiety from below, of being 'encroached upon' by the Roma and the poor. These distinctive, regional pressures are likely to impact on the way local elites deal with populist reformulations of enduring social issues.[21]

If there are direct parallels to be drawn between eastern and western Europe these rather concern the form of politics and the way populist parties mobilise new constituencies. In particular the cases in this book suggest that what some political scientists have recently called 'events' play a crucial role for the ability of certain political forces to shift the ground of public culture through building around these implicit or explicit campaigns. Let me explain with an example.

On 16 October 2006, in a now notorious incident, a Hungarian school teacher, Lajos Szögi, driving home through the north Hungarian village of Olaszliska, stopped his car after fearing that he had knocked down a child. In the next few minutes, in front of his children, he was lynched by a group of Roma. This appalling tragedy has since become an 'event', taken up for months, indeed years, afterwards and represented on each and every occasion, a Jobbik spokesperson who made a pronouncement. Indeed it became a central motif of Jobbik's propaganda. This allowed these frankly extremist forces to construct a powerful and persuasive narrative to which many more subscribe than support the party which has put so much effort into circulating it.[22] As a result of Jobbik's campaigning and the media coverage around 'Olaszliszka', the trial itself was followed by a huge section of the Hungarian public and Lajos Szögi has become a heroic-martyr figure in populist rhetoric.[23]

The effect of all this has been that, ever since, alarmist and stereotyped reporting on instances of crimes associated with Roma individuals has proliferated in the mainstream media and in some private channels, like the extremist Hír TV.[24] According to the 2008 report of the Hungarian National Security agency: 'Several years of a more or less consolidated status ended with the crime committed in Olaszliszka, which also resulted in a greater focus in the media on conflicts connected to Roma, which were previously often treated as local phenomena'.[25]

The point I wish to stress here is the role this single incident has played in populist anti-Gypsy mobilisation. The lynching was clearly reframed inside a compelling narrative and so became the basis for a more or less openly announced campaign. And this campaign, which picked up subsequent 'similar' events (there was a barely related gang-land killing in a bar in Veszprém in western Hungary, in which Roma were implicated in 2009, for example) and re-interpreted earlier, otherwise long-forgotten incidents, opened a space for a movement like Jobbik to alter the conditions of receptivity for certain nationalist and, in this case, anti-Roma articulations.

At the conference held to launch the discussions that led to this book, Andrzej Mirga suggested that the Olaszliszka case, and the later one in Veszprém, had been a catalyst for all that happened later in Hungary, including the wave of violence against the Roma there. The feeling of that part of society attracted to anti-Roma and populist politics was captured, he felt, by the columnist Zsolt Bayer in the daily *Magyar Hírlap*, who had written: 'Everyone in the whole wide world knows that those murderous animals were Gypsies… A huge number of Gypsies have given up on coexistence and given up on their humanity'.[26] Olaszliszka was the proof of this. As Mirga indicated, 'events' recast into political narratives like 'the lynching in Olaszliszka' play a crucial role for organisations and parties, allowing them to reshape and homogenise myriad local grievances into communal subjectivities and thus underpin a new nationalist project. It is in just such ways that Roma can come to be seen by more and more 'nationally oriented souls' (of whom there are many more than support extremist politics) not just as the traditional 'thief' or law-breaker but as an enemy, as the unbearable thorn in the side of the struggling nation.

What has happened, it might be said, is that a mere occurrence has been turned into an 'event' by the collective evaluation generated by Jobbik and its allies in the media; the emotional resonance of this evaluation in turn distinguished the event from the myriad narratives that float in public space (Sewell, 956). To adapt an argument of the political scientist Mabel Berezin, public narratives that emerge in response to chance 'events' can be used by the analyst to reveal a public conversation about institutional change in the European nation state and the relationship between those changes and its citizens (Berezin, 2009: 57).[27] What started as a private tragedy thus becomes a 'public political event' which 'engages the collective imagination and has the capacity to alter public perception, and so also *may* in the future alter political actions' (2009, 56). In the United Kingdom, immigration has been turned into such an 'event', in large part by an organisation called 'Migration Watch'—and this clearly impacts on the development of conflicts like that in Belfast. Likewise, the Regiani case in Italy initiated a series of developments, including instances of mob violence against the Roma, and led to changes in government policy (see Picker). Benedik also illustrates this process at a local level in the city of Graz.

It might, however, be said that the French president attempted and failed, at least in part, to turn a riot on 19 July 2010 in the Loire valley into an 'event' that would truly justify his subsequent actions and the demand to clear all illegal camps of Gens de Voyage and Roma alike. This outcome suggests that it may be easier for oppositional populist movements to achieve this kind of transformation—because of the role 'campaigns' play in turning occurrences into events. In Hungary, the Olaszliska murder allowed Jobbik's uniformed sister organisation the pretext of demonstrating in any and every village where it could claim that the 'Hungarian' (read non-Roma) population was under threat from the 'criminals' (read Roma). Jobbik's display of quasi-paramilitary strength allowed a further radicalisation of opinions, generating (like the violence they evoke) social situations in which citizens had to 'take sides'. They establish a form of politics in which there is only 'friend' and 'foe' and thus create the conditions of receptivity for a radical alteration of people's vision of their neighbours, of their fellow local citizens and of the broader society to which they belong. It is this that is at stake, I believe, in the creation of 'events' with Roma as their subjects.

In conclusion, the lesson of this volume is that there is a broad shared context in which anti-Romany politics and ideas are circulating today. This is determined by the fact that across Europe polities face: a rising tide of xenophobia; a feeling of loss of sovereignty and democratic oversight; disillusionment with existing political elites; and having to confront the challenges posed by the culturisation of political collectivities. These all enable, nay promote, a wave of anxieties that will, in certain circumstances be used to turn the Roma into a suitable 'target population' to which fears and frustrations can be attached. In those countries with large Romany minorities and politico-economic lethargy such sentiments may become the basis of significant political programmes and formations. Elsewhere, as in Italy, France or Northern Ireland these sentiments feed into momentary conflagrations.

Whether or not the reader follows me in this analysis, the longer term concern, for all of us who have the welfare of the Roma and the wellbeing of our continent at heart, is that the conditions which place the Roma at the centre of both xenophobic movements and gestures, as well as the underlying marginalisation of the Roma that renders them such ready targets for resentment and scapegoating, be effectively addressed in all their manifest complexity.

PART 1

ANTI-GYPSYISM: NEW CONTOURS OF SOCIAL AND POLITICAL EXCLUSIONS

1

POPULISM, ROMA AND THE EUROPEAN POLITICS OF CULTURAL DIFFERENCE

Michael Stewart

This collection of essays examines a wide range of phenomena found in different European countries, putting the case that, for the first time on a continental scale, Roma are becoming a central focus of radical, xenophobic politics. In order to understand these developments better, it will help to place them in a broader context. I argue that the way in which, over the past six or seven years, Roma and Gypsies have increasingly been treated in an intolerant and hostile fashion, reflects broader and deeply disturbing trends in European politics which have made anxiety, resentment and hostility towards 'strangers in our midst' increasingly prominent features of public life. In each of the cases discussed in this book, under various structural and social pressures, we see European actors testing the limits of the 'social imaginary' and beginning to flesh out new ways of thinking about the ties that bind and connect citizens in modern Europe. In this chapter, I focus on three forces that feed this new boundary making: the unintended impact of the European Project which, paradoxically, creates the broad conditions of receptivity to xenophobic politics across the whole continent; changes in European social and economic structures which threaten traditional redistributive systems and place poor 'others' in an unflattering spotlight; and, finally, alterations to the way citizens are linked to polity which

3

seem to render populist formations peculiarly attractive at the outset of what may prove to be a long-lasting, conservative cultural mood.

In this broader context, hostility to the Roma is, *mutatis mutandi*, the counterpart of various forms of hostility to Muslim immigrant minorities in other countries. In both cases the social problems associated with the presence of a reasonably easily identifiable 'other' are being re-presented as the consequence of inherent, unchangeable features of an alien, 'non-' or 'un-European' culture. Like its mainly western counterpart, anti-Gypsy politics has largely left behind the crude 'colour' racism of the middle of the twentieth century, replacing it with a form of culture conflict modelled on popular versions of Huntingdon's 'clash of civilisations'. It is no accident, as we shall see, that it is the image of 'criminal Roma' or 'workshy Roma'— rather than Roma *per se*—that provides one of the clarion calls of the new xenophobic politics.

Europe and its unexpected others

The European Project—that grand conception of an economic union and growing political coordination alongside some kind of cultural marriage of the ever feuding nations of Europe—was conceived, in the years just after the Second World War, as a space of cosmopolitan democracy and a well-spring of toleration. The writings of the German philosopher, Jürgen Habermas, provided perhaps the most compelling, if always critical, exegesis of this project. But times have changed. Sixty years on, at the start of the second decade of the new millennium, this project is profoundly challenged. All readers of this book will be familiar with the profound institutional difficulties thrown up by the adoption of a single currency as well as by painful issues around (the tragically now all-but-forgotten) enlargement. This collection focuses instead on a less visible challenge that arises in the form of a recurrent and widespread transformation of 'the social weight of difference' (Berezin, 2009)—a transformation that, it can be argued, derives in large part from the inachieved and hesitant nature of the European Project.[1]

Differences in 'race', 'ethnicity', religion and nationality are always more or less present in modern societies. Sometimes these have historical roots, as in eastern European states where the legacy of imperial collapse and the ethnic division of labour in early modern society have produced large, territorial patchworks of cultural difference. In western Europe such differences derive either from the history of colonialism and withdrawal or, more recently, under the weight of impending demographic collapse, with coun-tries compelled to bring in migrant labour to meet the demands of the local labour market. The free movement of persons and labour, which is one of the fundamental planks of the European Project, also encourages new forms of ethnic mixing within EU Member States. Now, under a series of endog-enous and exogenous shocks to both the European Project and the nation states that constitute it, the tendency to categorise these various 'others' not just as different, but as agents of disorder or bearers of an unspecified 'threat' to national identity is gaining cultural and political momentum.[2]

An alteration in 'the social weight of difference' poses of course a dissi-pate challenge to a programme of restructuring as vast and apparently robust as 'the European Project'. But because of the power of electoral revolts, changes of tide in the currents of public opinion have a nasty habit of producing sudden and unexpected political shifts, as Europe's political leaders discovered to their embarrassment (if not any real cost) with the systematic rejection by their peoples of the 2005 European Constitution. Moreover, this change in the way difference is experienced, these new ways of thinking about society and reciprocal social bonds, acquire compelling force because they appear to offer one way of seeing off the huge social changes being driven by the tectonic shifts in the global economic and political order since the 1980s. The result is that the conceptual space for thinking about tolerance and co-existence has radically changed since the boom years of postwar Europe, when the European Project emerged. I will, shortly, explain why I place Europe at the centre of the problem, but first let me establish the evidential case that the conditions in which we deal with 'difference' are truly shifting.

Data in support of this claim are multifarious and the changing attitudes towards Roma and Gypsies—some of which I discussed in the introduction and which is, with the exception of Italy, perhaps more visible in eastern and southern Europe than in the north and west—are just one small part of this. In many western European countries, in the wake of the, historically speaking, recent immigration of religiously distinct populations to a num-ber of north European countries, Muslim minorities have been brought into the political spotlight. In Belgium, as a result, we have had the stupefy-ing example of the Members of Parliament, who, in May 2010, while allow-ing their country to totter one more step towards dissolution, were willing to take time out from staring into the political abyss to pass a law that would affect less than a hundred women in their country, by banning them from wearing what might, in jollier times, be plausibly glossed as a fashion accessory promoted by a tiny group of mullahs in the Persian gulf. Likewise, in the midst of the greatest international financial crisis since the 1930s, the Swiss population thought it a proper moment to outlaw further constructions of minarets in their country. In the Netherlands, a party that brilliantly combines paternalist and xenophobic discourses about religious others with a democratic rhetoric of rights and entitlements has managed to reshape the national political field and, in September 2010, threatened to enter government as a junior coalition partner. In each case, the idiom of hostility and exclusion varies—anything that challenges the French totem of secularism is the enemy in the Hexagon, while in their mountain fastness the Swiss appear to be overcome by a true form of Islamophobia—but in all these cases the mere fact of cultural diversity is deemed to present an unacceptable challenge to peace, order and the good life.[3]

In Italy, we see just how far a regional government is willing to put its Roma in a 'state of exception' where the standard considerations from which full citizens benefit no longer apply (Giovanni Picker, this volume). In May 2008 Italian Prime Minister Silvio Berlusconi signed a decree declaring a 'state of emergency in relation to settlements of communities of nomads'.[4] An ordinance followed, ordering identification (including fingerprints) of people 'also of minor age' living in the 'nomad camps'.[5] The European Parliament condemned the decree, stating, 'collecting fingerprints of Roma [...] would clearly constitute an act of direct discrimination based on race and ethnic origin'.[6] Nevertheless, the Italian government continued to collect personal data and, on 27 July, the Minister of Interior, Roberto Maroni, gave a justificatory speech to the Italian Parliament claiming in a moment of inspired cynicism that he was merely providing legal identities to those nomads whose lifestyle had prevented their acquisition through more regular channels. As Mr Sarkozy has learnt at his cost, and as the Czechs have long known, the essential move is formally to de-ethnicise in order to avoid accusations of racism. So, Mr Maroni pointed out that 'in the ordinance we never speak about Roma, but only about nomad camps. Therefore, this is not an ethnicity-based measure, but one which deals with a *de facto* situation [*situazione di fatto*], meaning the unauthorised nomad camps'.[7]

This series of events in spring and summer 2008 has become the standard of everyday national politics vis-à-vis Roma in contemporary Italy; since the Berlusconi election of 2008 the government seems to have been carrying out a consistent boundary-making process separating 'us' from 'them'

(Wimmer, 2002: 52). Frequent forced evictions, a political rhetoric blaming Roma for creating insecurity, and intolerance in political speeches, characterise the political discourse in this country.

In Hungary, the Movement for a Better Hungary, Jobbik for short, has successfully colonised 'the Gypsy question' (as this has long been known). It draws on and reinforces a series of widespread myths and genuine conflicts. Hungarian public culture has long been concerned with a purported demographic collapse of the Magyar people and this has for two or more generations fed fears about 'swamping' by the Roma. In 1981, Hungarians believed (wrongly) that Roma made up over 12 per cent of the population (researchers reliably estimated 5 per cent). In 2001 respondents claimed that Roma were nearly 23 per cent of the population and estimated that by 2021 they would be over 35 per cent of the Hungarian citizenship (they remain, in reality, c. 7 per cent).[8] Jobbik politicians link this phantasmagorical demographic explosion to fears of welfare dependency and the collapse of the Hungarian welfare state. At the same time, by focusing on high levels of petty criminality among the long-term poor and battling to get the label 'Gypsy crime' accepted for this, Jobbik has managed to run an extraordinarily successful campaign. Often they have simply argued that 'Gypsy crime exists'[9] and by doing so aim at a double target: the Roma who, they (falsely) say are responsible for most violent crime and the political elite, NGOs, liberals, ex-communists, etc., who want to cover this truth up and lie to the people.

In Slovakia, the governing authorities seem to have accepted that all Roma-related initiatives have so far yielded little result and have considered adopting more radical solutions, including separating Roma children from their families and placing them in boarding schools. In the words of the Slovak Prime Minister, the relevant programme would 'gradually put as many Roma children as possible into boarding schools and gradually separate them from the life they live in the settlements'.[10] The problem here is not so much the idea of providing collegium for children of impoverished families, but the tone of the proposal which is entirely cast as an assault on the 'inadaptables', the Roma.

In Bulgaria these days one does not need to go far to encounter the strands of intensely negative discourse towards Roma—in 2009, the nation's most popular politician (the former mayor of Sofia) Boyko Borisov pleaded to a large Bulgarian immigrant meeting in Chicago for expatriates to return to their country to help deal with the problem of the 'bad human capital', that is the 1 million Roma, 700,000 Turks and 2.5 million retirees.[11] Contrary to the media's immediate assessment that Borisov had committed political suicide, the message resonated with deeply held sentiments in Bulgaria. Borisov was elected Prime Minister a few months later. Once it was the Turkish speaking and Muslim minority—as cross-border kin of the neighbouring Turkish state (and behind that as symbolic embodiments of the Ottoman behemoth)—that were the national enemy. How times change. As Efremova shows (this volume) the young, passionate, educated, and patriotic members of the flourishing 'National Guard' see their organisation as 'the guardian of Bulgarians against Gypsy terror'.[12]

Several of the authors in this book point to the role of political elites, who use the 'Gypsy issue' to reframe broader policy areas like welfare and security (see, e.g., Picker and Zolnay). But none of these changes can be laid simply at the door of politicians who take possession of an issue to whip up an obfuscating nationalist fervour and draw clear lines around a constituency of voters. Politicians, of course, have a central role in disseminating ideas—both those who adopt this powerful form of rhetoric and, those on the other side, who in their feeble and mealy-mouthed manner fail to make a case for the benefits of cultural diversity and avoid confronting xenophobic discourse head-on—but they are feeding upon fears, anxieties and discourses that arise independently of their activities. We can see this in the way the newfound fear of otherness bursts out in the lives of 'ordinary' individuals. On Saturday 15 May 2010, in a shop in Trignac, in northwestern France, a sixty-year-old lawyer, aided by her daughter, ripped the veil of a younger Muslim customer, after making remarks about her 'black burqa'.[13] And in the same month, after a shoot out between two local families of Serbian descent in the sleepy Swiss town of Martigny, locals called for all 'criminal foreigners' to be expelled. A motion to this effect was put before the Swiss federal parliament by the Democratic Union of the Centre.[14] So when figures like President Sarkozy attack the presence of Roma migrants living in shanty towns under bridges, alongside motorways and in other lost spaces of the urban jungle, though he is attempting to legitimise a hyperbolically exaggerated policy initiative, he is also drawing on widespread concern, disquiet and even revulsion at these living conditions and those who appear to bring them into being.

From suburban fisticuffs, through 'radical policy initiatives' in the speeches of mayoral candidates, to parliamentary antics and the speeches of Prime Ministers-in-waiting or presidents in polling trouble, there lies a common thread: with respect to culturally or religiously different minorities, the norms of reciprocal respect and trust among peoples who live alongside each other in European countries are coming under threat. Difference is being reframed as incompatibility and purportedly culturally distinct behaviour is being used to justify radical demands for 'root and branch' reform of educational, welfare and, in extreme cases, citizenship regimes. And it is often the mere fact of persistent 'otherness' that is given social value in these diverse claims and assertions.

As this cultural politics of difference widens its scope throughout Europe what is at stake is a debate over the very nature of society—a debate the proponents of the new politics are both able and ready to 'colonize politically' (Holmes, 2000: 36). And they are able to do so rather effectively because of the new (intended and unintended) possibilities for coordination of events across the EU. So, at the very moment of increased migration of Roma to the west from countries like Romania and Bulgaria (giving rise to new tensions in western European countries at the end of a long period of increased labour mobility) we have witnessed a rise in populist fury at economic and political stagnation in countries of the east (Hungary and Bulgaria in particular). Local populists did not miss the opportunity to capitalise domestically on the role of the migrant Roma in giving their country a poor name abroad. This way of bringing together events in different parts of our continent to political advantage may harbinger a longer term danger. The very fora designed to enable European integration, such as the European Parliament, may in time be turned by the forces of populism—so often divided by the national particularism inherent in this political style—into a space where they can discover the echo of each other's contempt for 'the Roma' and achieve further and more frightening metamorphoses of anti-Roma politics.[15]

Anti-Roma politics in the context of the new populist and integralist politics

Drawing on the research brought together in this volume I have come to the conclusion that the increasing salience of anti-Roma politics today is not only not simply, but is only barely the product of economic crisis and 'structural adjustment'. While such forces do drive the engines of pessimism, disillusion and a receptivity to radical politics, the idioms and framing of anti-Roma politics have much deeper roots than this and are best seen as but one expression of a wider phenomenon in which the European social imaginary is mutating.[16] Across the continent, the idioms, concerns and stakes that define political practices in their everyday, localised forms are altering in such a way that ethnic or religious others come to have a newfound political prominence (see Hansen, 1999: 14). In the former communist countries of central and eastern Europe, as democratic discourses and procedures are 'vernacularised', we find processes that closely parallel a slightly older phenomenon in western Europe where far too many politicians now claim that they are able and willing to defend national culture against immigrant groups, 'foreign values', or even the unwanted influence of their neighbouring states in domestic affairs.

In order to specify these general roots of the new anti-Roma politics and to demonstrate why I believe that this phenomenon is here to stay we need to take a look into the nature and the social bases of what one might, hitching together the work of two social scientists, call the new populist-integralist politics. I have found the works of Douglas Holmes and Mabel Berezin—both of whom view Europe from a distant vantage, transatlantically—particularly inspiring. In a wide-ranging investigation, Douglas Holmes argues that the novelty of 'integralist' politics today lies in the attempt to link the search for lost or disappearing socio-cultural solidarities with a new way of imagining society. He calls this project integralism, perhaps because of its use of rich and distinctive local life-worlds to model and indeed provide the institutional scaffolding for socio-cultural integration at regional or state level. Mabel Berezin, for her part, has focused on the disruptions imposed on the traditional order of national citizenship as a result of pan-European transformations and the anxieties these engender. Taken together, Holmes and Berezin's work provides a compelling basis for understanding the rise in a politicised anti-Romany sentiment.

The nature of the populist-integralist programme and its European context

Following Douglas Holmes, we can see that the movements that have recently promulgated anti-Roma politics draw on a long tradition of European political thought that Isaiah Berlin once identified as 'the counter-Enlightenment' and that also came to be known in the early twentieth century as 'populism'. Populism is understood here, following Berlin, as based less on a set of political assumptions than on postulates about the essence of human nature. Populism is, in brief, the belief in the political and social value of belonging to a group or culture. It is, therefore, inextricably linked with the threat of alienation—the uprooting of persons, their deracination and cultural estrangement—all themes that provide vivid imagery to modern populist-integralisms.[17]

Populism takes what are, in reality, the dispersed and hugely diverse human practices and beliefs of a population in a territory (mostly a national territory) and endows them with a collective significance, creating in this way distinctive political possibilities for reframing the image of a society.[18] In order to do so it draws, according to Berlin, on a number of different strands or styles of thought. One of these is a tradition of expressionism, according to which all human creations have a 'voice', which, in effect, articulates a deeper, and more real, 'inner truth' and ideal. The institutions, and all the creations of a people, at least when the people is free, give voice to its inner nature. In this way all the nation's acts can be seen as expressions of a collective will. The concomitant of this is, of course, that the people's voice can be smothered (by a small powerful clique of 'foreigners' or, as today, by masses of impoverished, pampered 'aliens').

Populism also draws on a strand of pluralism that rests on a belief in the multiplicity and, above all, the incommensurability of the values of different cultures and societies. Resistance to all forces that can be represented as threatening the unique culture of a people is thus built into such movements. In this way, populists appear to offer a means for circumventing the, supposedly, alienating and homogenising forces of modernity, by calling on the aid of culturally based solidarities. The duty, then, of the populist politician is to preserve cultural distinctions among 'an enduring plurality of different groups' and this provides the rationale for discriminatory practices of inclusion and exclusion that we see popping up in Czech towns (Albert, this volume) and Italian cities alike (Picker, this volume).

But there are crucial new features to the politics that Holmes analyses and that lead him to give them the 'integralist' moniker. The recent populist realignment has used incongruent aspects of the European Project to rethink the very terms of reference of what a European agenda might mean and, in so doing, built an anti-European and anti-cosmopolitan politics. Just as President Sarkozy, in the aftermath of the French 'no' to the new constitution in 2005, ended a tradition of denouncing nationalism as the enemy of Europeanism by declaring Europe to be the best means of defending national interests (see Fassin, 2011: 515) so, in a more systematic fashion, have the populists taken up and transformed to their own ends quasi-theoretical, quasi-administrative schemas that have operated in this institutional setting for some fifty years. Modern populist-integralism's love affair with the strong state and its promotion of cultural plurality derives as much from the use of this model by the EU as from this oppositional movement's own historical-intellectual roots. It thereby, as we shall see, ties itself into dominant socio-cultural models of what a modern Europe should look like, even as it effectively drastically limits and undermines central tenets of those models.

The European Project has been based in a broad societal theory that blends a complex moral vision and technocratic practice, but lacks a formal constitutional theory or philosophy of its own (Judt, 2005: 100–129). Holmes' survey of the treaties that serve as constitutional instruments uncovers a highly pragmatic organisational emphasis but a lack of any overarching, openly articulated, theoretically grounded vision of where Europe is headed and on what basis. Discrepancies between the administrative agenda and national practice have been historically resolved, at least within the bureaucratic elite that sits in the European driving seat, through merging two discursive frameworks: Catholic social doctrine and French social modernism. These have served, albeit not as official doctrines or policies of the EU, as conceptual approaches that underpin a loose European federalism.

The EU's model of technocratic governance appears to have been inspired by French social modernism's concept of society as 'a field of human interdependence susceptible to planning and administration through the application of scientific norms and principles' (Holmes, 2000: 29). Though drawing on the works of de Tocqueville, Le Play, Proudhon and Durkheim, in its ultimate expression it envisages a highly pragmatic, state-led social project coalescing around what Holmes calls 'a school of solidarity'. The state is to be led by societal technicians seeking to create a distinctive social order through administrative interventions in infrastructures, industry, public services and social welfare. Thus, what Paul Rabinow once termed the 'middling modernism' that was imposed in France since the 1950s, became the basis of the technocratic practice of the EU, which drew its method of 'convergent action' as well as the paradigm of institutional decision-making from this model.

The second strand of European technocratic thought derives from German Social Catholicism which, like the above, also has its roots in ideas that emerged coterminous with industrial societies in the late nineteenth century. This too seeks to create an intricate moral discourse connecting society and the individual, providing an account of the conditions of individual autonomy and its source in social interdependencies. According to this doctrine, man is a social person who achieves perfection only in society; the state exists to help the persons who live in society, by providing the complex conditions that enable people to live in groups ('the common good'); and allows individuals to take care of their own needs (Mulcahy, cited in Holmes, 2000: 48).[19]

For their part, integralist politicians have an ambivalent relationship with these ideological legacies—for, just like progressive resistance, its populist counterpart is constrained to follow the contours of power. So, while the populists resist the radical restructuring of the social order that French social modernism has sought, haltingly, to impose since 1980 or so, they dream still of a strong state that will defend the people and its nation. Likewise, they reject the extensive social solidarity of the Catholic doctrines—rejecting its application to immigrants in the west and the Roma in the east—but they still draw on the ideas of subsidiarity, the protection of cultural groups and state intervention to sustain the cultural diversity that is at the root of their objection to the modernist social project.[20]

The integralists are thus part and parcel of fierce debates around what Europe might stand for. Holmes identified three sub-strands of 'cultural' discourse that jostle for attention and hegemony in current discussions about what a modern Europe should look like. Each of these is imbued with varying intensities of emotion and conceptual rigour and each of them impacts on attitudes towards poor minorities, like the Roma. We need to assess them all briefly as these strands of discourse are to a limited, but important, extent mutually constitutive, and help shape what is fast becoming the fourth strand in European debates, populist-integralism itself.

The first strand is a version of cultural pluralism rooted in an idealised view of European civilisation and results in a vision of cultural diversity transcended by religion: 'Europe unified by Christendom'. This is probably a rather widely held and certainly rarely debated view uniting politicians as distinct as Valéry Giscard d'Estaing, *burqa* banning Belgians, anti-Muslim Bulgarians, Hungarian and Polish conservatives, as well as Popes past and present.

Holmes describes the second strand, as pursuing 'a pluralism manifest institutionally in a decentralized and socially progressive 'Europe of regions' in which ethnic, religious and cultural distinctions could be preserved, if not enhanced' (34).[21] Central to this view is the Catholic concept of subsidiarity, which is the devolution of power as a constitutional guarantee protecting fundamental cultural rights.

Now, up to quite recently, an equally important third strand in European 'moral thought' kept the implications of these various pluralisms in check: a profound opposition to racism, xenophobia, anti-semitism and neo-fascism— that is, all the forces that appear most hostile to a humane and tolerant Europe and against which Europe was built in the aftermath of the Second World War. This is also connected to the deep rejection of nationalism (ever since the 1951 Schumann Plan) within the European technocratic elite.[22]

The drawback, however, of this way of tackling the logical implications of pluralism is that by constantly and solely invoking the horrors of the Second World War and the Holocaust as the moral basis of the European Project, it obscures potentially more potent and relevant contemporary models of European unity in plurality and thereby restricts a defence of cultural diversity as a political agenda in its own right, preventing such a defence from finding terms and idioms relevant to the world we live in today (see also Holmes, 1999: 35).

Holmes reached the conclusion that (populist-) integralism now represents the fourth strand in this European socio-moral discourse. This strand is very sceptical of the whole European Project, as currently conceived, and believes that the universalist metaphysics and practices that have provided its foundational architecture, have at every step ridden roughshod over basic facts of human nature and society. For integralists, the European Project should be radically transformed, redirected towards the emergent cultural imperatives, which have been articulated so well by authors in the populist, expressionist and pluralist counter-Enlightenment tradition.

It is this discourse, I would argue, that provides the foundation and strength of modern anti-Romany political strategies and that transforms what were old, stereotyping and oppressive prejudices about Gypsies that had no political import beyond the local level into a national (transnational?) political agenda that could, in the not too distant future, pose very serious threats to Europe's Romany minority.

Populism as pathological normalcy in Europe?

Various academic labels have been attached to the resurgent populist-integralisms, many of which imply this political phenomenon occupies a specific temporality or temporal position: the 'populist moment' (Berezin) or 'zeitgeist' (Mudde), 'neo-nationalism' (Gingrich and Banks) and a 'silent counter revolution' (Ignazi). Questions inevitably arise then as to how enduring this mood that promotes anti-Roma and anti-migrant politics is likely to be; how deep and wide does it run?

The evidence suggests that there are large electoral bases for a politics of this sort. These include, of course, all or many of those people who have lost out over the past thirty years. In different ways, in different regions of Europe, a profound socio-economic reconfiguration has taken place since the mid 1970s, gaining strength particularly after the end of the Cold War. Fundamental transformations have occurred in the structure of the economy and society: the collapse of Russo-Soviet domination of eastern Europe and the communist economies that went with this; rapid integration of European markets; and new regulations and financial structures and wholesale economic restructuring. All these are compounded by the dawning realisation of the impending and radical transformation of the European demographic profile, which, in turn, has led to a widespread movement of labour into Europe as citizens and states try to cope with demographic imbalance. These have helped produce what Ignazi calls a 'conservative cultural mood'; together all this has made possible the reinterpretation, or new imagining of 'society', that is now generating a redefinition of our political culture.

Specifically, at the level of lived experience, traditional, local orders of distinction and privilege have collapsed, and pre-existing frameworks of social meaning (the value of particular sorts of manual labour, for instance, in Hungarian, Bulgarian or Czech steel towns or Italian alpine villages) have been impoverished. And the moral claims, from communities that sustained such life worlds, to support from the central state, have evaporated. These people form 'the new poor', identified by Holmes and Berezin, as a whole category marked less by the loss of socio-economic status as by their sense of 'expulsion from the public sphere'. These all-round losers feel that relationships binding them 'to a wider social nexus' have been nullified and, as a result, they find it difficult if not impossible to achieve an all encompassing conception of society. In many places of Europe we find these people struggling to resist change, and hoping to reinsert themselves in a social order by creating what Holmes calls 'integral lives'. These lives are sustained by an inner cultural logic, enabling people to retain and even develop cultural practices that they see as defying the deracinating and homogenising effects of EU integration and rapid economic transformation.

But beyond those who have lost out over the past thirty-five years, there seem to be broader electorates that are attracted by a politics built on the integralist skeleton. Populist-integralists provide a language and practice of identification and, thereby, a living model of an alternative social order in which many of the most threatening social forces appear to have been neutered—and this gives their discursive programme a wide appeal. Where do we find these electorates? A traditional answer would be among those we have just discussed, the most disillusioned and 'the losers from globalisation' or in central and eastern Europe those who perceive themselves as 'the losers of the transition'. But in eastern Europe, in essence, this is the majority of the population, as demonstrated by numerous sociological studies.[23] In any event, it is not possible to draw a firm line between the haves and have-nots, for perception plays a critical role in such social positioning.

Georgia Efremova's paper in this volume demonstrates the wide range of audiences and participants at Bulgarian National Guard events. Her fellow marchers during her participant observational research were students from the university—not the lumpen proletariat. Douglas Holmes made a similar point in his earlier research, remarking on the plurality of audiences he saw at Le Pen events in France (and likewise for the other integralist politicians he studied, including the British National Party). Various sections of society attend these events that see their moral frameworks of meaning eroded and are drawn to 'the politics of loss and dissatisfaction'—including farmers, conservative Catholics, pensioners and schoolteachers, factory workers, owner of small shops and businesses, university students, youth organisations, and police.[24] As far as these people are concerned, the current populism is the rebellion of the 'silent majority'. The populist followers today (of Geert Wilders in Holland, the National Front in France and Gabor Vona in Hungary) include the hardworking, slightly conservative, law abiding citizen, who in silence but with growing anger, sees his world being 'perverted' by progressives, criminals and aliens.

And so, though populism, like the charismatic authority of its most characteristic leaders, has a reputation as an unstable, episodic political force with a cyclical dynamic, this new populist-integralism may present a different kind of beast. In the traditional model, drawn of course from Weber's foundational discussions, when an explicitly populist, outsider group gains prominence, parts of the establishment react with a combined strategy of preventing them from gaining a toehold in the system, and including populist themes and rhetoric in their own discourse and policies. It was this dynamic that led Mudde to talk of a 'populist Zeitgeist' (2004) when the political atmosphere is clouded by populist concerns and rhetoric. As soon as the populist challenge seems to have peaked, the zeitgeist evaporates. But, today, in part because of the structural challenges discussed below in the nature of European polities, it may be that populism will prove to be a more regular feature in liberal democracies, erupting whenever significant sections of the 'silent majority' feel that the governing elite no longer represents them (Mudde, 2004: 563). In other words, we may be dealing with a new ideological concoction that represents a profound and lasting change in the political culture, rather than a social programme expressing a purely local and temporary pathology. Or, as Mudde puts it, we may be witnessing a paradigmatic shift from populism as a 'normal pathology' to populism as a 'pathological normalcy'.[25]

So what are the characteristic and distinctive features of this new politics and its context that may render it troublingly enduring? First, it is crucial to understand that this phenomenon is novel. In the period 1950–94 or so, with the memory of the 1930s so present and with (until the mid-1970s), the living example of dictatorships in the Iberian peninsula, extremist politics remained marginalised in European societies. Radicalism represented a savage exception to mainstream national politics and only managed to garner very limited support, with movements of resurgence being snuffed out as rapidly as they emerged (Goodwin, 2011: 1). It appeared then as if these 'normal' circumstances would last forever. However, since the mid-1990s, when, for the first time since 1945, an extreme right-wing party entered a democratic government (in Italy), a range of new parties and political actors have entrenched themselves in the European political scene (Berezin, 2009).[26]

Second, the kind of cultural solutions to enduring socio-economic problems that populist-integralisms promote—the recasting of social solidarity in a culturally particularistic framework in order to undermine the idea of a pluralist Europe—is also ideologically novel in the sense that it is not a replaying of the politics of the 1930s, however familiar certain of its (mainly symbolic) gestures appear to be. Its modern features include targeting those beneath (welfare claimants) not those above (financiers, lawyers, Jews) apart from the ever-loathed 'establishment'; its lack of interest in militaristic expansionism and rewriting past injustice and its far more rigorous adherence to democratic forms and electoral legitimacy. The focus in eastern Europe on criminal and workshy Roma and on immigration and religion in western Europe are even clearer examples of the way culture rather than race has been politicised by these movements.[27]

Third, the truly radical nature of the European Project and the ways in which the policy momentum of European integration has disrupted local life-worlds have provided a peculiarly potent and, commonly, infuriating image of a political elite divorced from the concerns of ordinary (national) citizens, which plays straight into the traditional hinterland of populism.[28] As Holmes argues, structurally, the EU is a political project concealed as a series of technical tweakings of European economic arrangements, a point its founder, Jean Monnet, once conceded.[29] As a result, the European Project appears to involve a multiplicity of layers of informal, inter-governmental agreements that rarely come under public scrutiny—that are not subject to any obvious democratic scrutiny at the voting urns. Notoriously, Europeans cannot name their MEPs and have minimal understanding of the workings of the Brussels/Strasbourg machine. At the same time those 'technical tweakings' emanating from the Leviathan have very tangible consequences in peoples' lives from the trivial—like the type and shape of bananas that Europeans were able to eat in the early 1990s—to the hugely significant—like the number of hours Europeans are allowed to (declare to) work each week or the imminent and potentially permanent destruction of European fish stocks, or, for members of the Eurozone, the fiscal framework within which nationally elected governments have to operate.

Furthermore, as Mabel Berezin points out, on a macro level, European integration has disequilibrated the mix of national cultural practice and legal norms that have governed European nation states. For instance, national constitutions have had to be changed in order to adapt to EU law, or, as in France, the constitution was altered in order to be able to call a referendum on the EU constitution. Perhaps even more pertinently, on a micro level, integration violates longstanding habits of collective national attachment and national experience through regulatory harmonisation amongst other things (Berezin, 2009: 195). So, the accelerated process of integration produces a combination of macro and micro disequilibration; it threatens to make the nation space 'unfamiliar' to many citizens and this opens the door to contestation; hence we find national identities and nation-ness are reasserted across the political spectrum as a consequence.[30] As Berezin puts this, Europeanisation disaggregates and reaggregates established national political space, but never resolves the central tension inherent in its attempt to reconceptualise the polity while retaining the territorial nation state as its primary building bloc (2009: 194).

Like it or not, the nation state has been and still is the cultural compromise of modernity (Wimmer, 2002). As a political form it is not just geographically situated and territorially bounded, and as such a material entity, but it is also an experiential entity, because it gives 'cultural form to collective interpretations of the past and evaluations of the future' (Berezin, 2009: 46). As Andreas Wimmer has argued, national experience is the collective experience of living on a territory with a distinct set of cultural and legal norms which produces attachments (based on national security, individual enfranchisement and shared language/culture) and it is this national experience, which demonstrates and confirms that passion for the nation is not an isolated emotion held by political extremists, but something much wider and deeply seated. The force of such attachments were manifested, by way of example, in the multiple 'nos' to the European constitution. As this book goes to press they are being asserted even more fiercely in the diverse responses to the crisis of the euro. In this way we see, following Benedict Anderson's pioneering study (1983/1991), that nations are not only political categories, but they are also constituted as moral ontologies, or collectively defined ways of being in the world. As Berezin puts it, 'national experience is a committed and committing phenomenon, a part of daily life that lies dormant with the collective and individual consciousness, until an internal or external force threatens that experience and makes it manifest' (Berezin, 2009: 49).

And this is precisely what Europeanisation has done: threatened national experience and made it manifest as well as simultaneously failing to provide a plausible cultural explanation of what will replace the 'moral ontology' of the nation.[31] This is the same point that Douglas Holmes has been making for some time: the consolidation of a vast multicultural and multiracial Europe is a central dimension of the emerging social order but remains unmatched by a fundamental constitutional philosophy, let alone political structures that could underpin this kind of integration.[32] Europe as a cultural concept and project (neither a 'melting pot' nor nation-building) remains undefined, the language of its descriptions in various treaties elliptical. And the very real damage done by leaving this central ambiguity becomes obvious when it is the negation of Europe (what it is 'not') that is the only category available to define Europe's terms of reference. Thus, for example, the terms 'non-EC nationals', 'third countries', and 'non-Europeans', all of which are categories of administrative action, serving as organising principles at the borders and boundaries of the new twenty-seven state Europe, have come to shape core understandings of 'Europe'. And this, in turn, provides one of the sources for integralist politics of exclusion in our case too—Roma as non-Europeans.

But it is not just the way the European Union has operated and the unintended consequences of the impact of its bureaucracy that lies behind the success of populist-integralism. There are other pan-continental forces at work as well.

Mabel Berezin points to some of the further sources of these peoples' dissatisfaction with the existing structures and their search for 'a new European political, social and cultural space' (2009: 29) and, in particular, points to the changing nature of the relationship of the people to the polity that has left many feeling that they have no public voice. Until recently, European party structures have been, in the *longue durée* since the end of the nineteenth century, remarkably stable. This is not to say that individual parties have been long lived, but that the type of parties, the style of their politics and their typical constituencies, have been so. In the past thirty years or so, however, this has begun to alter. Signs of emerging disconnections have included the appearance of fringe and new parties, voter apathy ('the disappearing voter') and electoral instability—unprecedented rates of abstention on the local, national and European level have produced electoral fluctuations on an unprecedented scale (2009: 29). Whereas party affiliation used to be rooted in a whole way of life, and loyalties were transmitted in the workplace, the café or the kitchen, now the much greater role media plays in the dissemination of political information contributes to the shift away from the ideological commitments of old-style European politics.[33]

Much the same holds, *mutatis mutandis*, for eastern Europe, where the emergence of new political forces after the end of Soviet occupation, and the failure of almost all the historical (pre-1949) parties to re-establish themselves, has produced a rather similar result. In general then, if Berezin is correct that one of the functions of political parties in European democracies has been to mediate the relationship between people and polity, then there is analytic work to be done in capturing how the 'folk' can today be linked to the state. The emergence of new forms of 'civic engagement' especially around the integralist agendas is surely one sign of such structural adjustment. This is the reason, it seems to me, that Hungarian and Bulgarian students can join with such abandon populist movements (Jobbik and the Bulgarian National Guard or its successors) that have uniformed wings attached to them. At least in the Hungarian case the uniform's design is brilliantly ambivalent—you would say it was a Hungarian folk dancer's suit, until the insignia of the militia and the armbands are attached. It is as if, in a strange way, the presence of this kind of semi-militaristic force acts as a guarantee of a form of representation that has, as I argued above, been lost along with the life-world of labour, welfare and social security for life.

Integralist politicians address a wide range of groups, who are deeply dissatisfied with and distrustful of the political system, and feel almost wholly unrepresented on their own terms. They reassure them that they do not need 'to divest themselves of their idiosyncratic identities'; on the contrary, the only way they can guarantee themselves meaningful social participation is from the standpoint of their own particular sensibilities and consciousness (Holmes, 2009: 59).

The strong focus on family, gender and sexual policy in many of these movements—from Bulgaria where Romany prostitution and transvestism provides a rich source of outrage, through to Denmark and Holland where the pressure from the opponents of multicultural tolerance impose tests on non-western migrants to ensure, for instance, that they understand that tolerance of nude bathing is a part of the national way of life, provides another way in which the new populism successfully links the normative practices of the everyday and domestic to the national and the political. Eric Fassin talks of 'sexualised democracy' to refer to these forms of sexualised nationalisms and Douglas Holmes of 'experimental identity projects', but at its simplest the politics of exclusion, through enforcing gender and kinship codes, looks very like traditional politics—establishing order through controlling the types of families and sexual relations people may legitimately enter into. This is, of course, immediately recognisable to anyone familiar with the literature on South Asian nationalisms where conflicts over veiling and purdah go back as long as the life of nationalist movements. The novelty lies less, then, in the content or form of such politics, than in the intensity with which such concerns are felt today in Europe and the extent to which, therefore, populist-integralists are able to mobilise support around the defence of 'our way of life'. It is, as anthropologists teach their students in Kinship 101, the apparent naturalness of our way of doing family that makes it such a powerful tool for justifying, in democratic terms, the exclusion of others.

Taking an eagle-eye, then, to the rise of populist politics, we find changes in public culture that favour radicalisation and system polarisation—that is to say the rise of a neo-conservative cultural mood and a tendency towards radicalisation and polarisation in response to the emergence of issues not treated by the mainstream parties (of left or right), including, especially, immigration or Roma, and security issues; all of this leads to the presence of an underground and mounting legitimacy crisis of the political and party system.[34]

This has a crucial consequence for minorities in European states and the Roma in particular. As Holmes insists, populist-integralism presents political meaning as expressed in collective experiences and forms of solidarity rooted in town, class, community or nation. This doctrine leads integralist audiences straight back to questioning current, dominant conceptions of human collectivity as rooted in shared humanity, and towards experimental identity projects which aim to fill the perceived 'gaps' in today's public culture.[35] And since nationalism is the main 'cultural compromise' of modernity, and the drawing of group boundaries occurs invariably along national and ethnic lines (with the nation state as the primary form of social closure even today), it is more or less inevitable that populism will use ethnic and ethno-religious markers to define who is in and who is out of the new society. So, one way integralism offers its constituency a 'way back in' is through removing the symbolically offending and wounding 'other' (be they Muslims or Roma) who are imagined to have unjustly occupied the public space from which such constituencies feel excluded (see Horváth, this volume).[36] And it is for this reason that integralists are so emotionally violated by everyday practices that try to institute a cosmopolitan and tolerant space, such as the much maligned 'politically correct' language, or monitoring of public spending (and appointments) for evidence of discrimination. This is why their supporters take such visceral pleasure when their leaders theatrically violate the conventions of political discourse with self-consciously 'outrageous' comments. They are, in such gestures, taking back the space they feel has been lost to them.

If all this is correct, anti-Romany politics will require a rich and complex cultural-political response. It will, in fact, require a careful rethinking of the nature of the political and social community that is Europe and its constituent states—one that will, in my view, inevitably and quite correctly have to deal with (and in some sense integrate) the culturalist challenge thrown down by the integralists. The populist voters and, far beyond them, all those who find an echo of their feeling of cultural threat in the rhetoric of the populist parties, need to be joined in conversation about these 'threats'. In that conversation the case for cultural diversity in its modern forms, the understanding that otherness in our midst is the inevitable, irreducible condition of human culture (what else is gender and kinship, at base, than a means of establishing difference between 'us' and 'them') and the additional understanding that diversity is the great source of dynamism in human history, have to be argued carefully and constructively. The dangers of not doing so (as well as the possibility of achieving this) are beautifully illustrated by two of the Hungarian papers in this volume. In Hungary, the communist political regime from 1958 till 1986 denied Roma their cultural-historical status as a minority and produced, as Horváth and Kovai show, horrific torsions in the lives of Roma in consequence. Now, Hungary faces the challenge of acknowledging and integrating Romany presence, rather than denying it as in the past or trying to violently suppress and exclude it as the integralists wish. But this cannot be done without arguing the case that diversity breeds cultural strength, not vice versa.

This may seem like a daunting task in a Europe that is fracturing politically but there are, I would argue, some grounds for optimism. Take the fact that the issues at stake are not confined to Roma—Muslim minorities in immigrant-receiving countries are as much a source of populist fury. Lessons learnt in dealing with the populist-integralists in one part of Europe can, I suspect, be applied, *mutatis mutandis*, in other parts too.[37] This is, perhaps, one of the upsides of European integration.

But we will also require a new 'elite' discourse of what Europe is 'for'. In response to the serial 'nos' to the Treaty of Maastricht, politicians like Nicolas Sarkozy (who was then only a candidate for president) proclaimed that the solution was to return to a 'Europe of Nations', to reassure voters that Europe was constituted by and acted in the interest of 'nations'. This 'quick fix' (which worked electorally) left, of course, no space for the numerous minorities of our continent (religious, ethnic, regional, etc.) but worse, it is a strategy that simply postpones the problems inherent in the European Project to later and, meanwhile, provides legitimacy to all those populist-integralists who oppose the transnational, trans-community solidarity and polity that Europe has to try and build in the century ahead. To create a Europe which strengthens the rights of its citizens, that offers new freedoms and pleasures to its inhabitants, that offers a vision of social life that is more attractive than the return to the fictive ethnic-communal cradle offered by the new populists, will require a return to our roots and a reconception of what this grand political project might offer to its people and the world beyond. In this sense, the plight of the Roma is truly Europe's plight and successfully combating the populist drive to exclude them may contribute centrally to a positive reformulation and reconstruction of the overall European political project.

2

ABUSIVE LANGUAGE AND DISCRIMINATORY MEASURES IN HUNGARIAN LOCAL POLICY

János Zolnay

In the latest European parliamentary election, held in June 2009, a far-rightist party, Jobbik (Movement for a better Hungary), won 14.77 per cent of the votes cast, and then sent three representatives to the European Parliament. In the economically depressed north-eastern region, where the proportion of Roma population is much higher than average, 20–22 per cent of voters supported the party.

A year later, in the first round of the parliamentary elections held in April 2010, Jobbik gained third place with 16.88 per cent of votes and won forty-seven out of 386 seats.[1] In the individual constituencies in the north-east regions, 27–34 per cent of voters supported its candidates in the first round of the elections. Undoubtedly, this extreme rightist party had gained support in the political vacuum that had emerged after the socialist government lost its legitimacy in autumn 2006. But the party also exploited a tragic incident that had brought about a change in general attitudes towards the Roma community in Hungarian society: in October 2006 a teacher was lynched, in front of his children, by a group of Roma men and women in a village after he had accidentally hit a Roma girl with his car. (The girl was slightly injured.) The incident triggered a 'moral panic'. Extreme and moderate rightist media, as well as the then ex-parliamentary Jobbik party, blamed the government for having mismanaged its policy towards the Roma, and these arguments found willing ears in the public. Jobbik in particular consistently focused on this incident, holding it in front of the Hungarian public for the following four years. In this way the party managed to unite traditional extremist supporters of the anti-Semitic far right (who used to support the now moribund MIEP party) and the racist anti-Roma far right. Except for a tiny group of MPs who sat from 1998 to 2008, Hungary had no extremist party in the democratically elected parliament before 2010.

In this paper I argue that one of the most important sources of this shift in the Hungarian political scene derives from the dynamics of local politics. Local politicians have largely been responsible for introducing aggressive racist terms into public discourse, finding that the local political sphere was a fertile ground for hate speech targeted at Roma communities. Inciting terms and statements of mayors have strongly shaped the topics of public political discussion during the last two or three years. This has fed into the rise of political extremism, as the hate speech of the extremist politicians targeting Roma seems to grow logically out of local politicians' prejudices and their discriminatory measures.

Moreover, the norms of local public discourse in Hungary are largely 'permissive' to the generation of hatred and incitement against Roma communities (see Pap, this volume). Using abusive language, slander, and terms of mockery when talking about individual Roma, or the Roma community as a whole, is generally accepted in local political communication, even in full, public meetings of the local councils. Mayors, local councillors, legal or police officers unhesitatingly state that Roma children are genetically inclined to become criminals; that Roma families have more children than non-Roma families (as they say, 'Roma women give birth to the "strategic child"') in order to maximise the amount of child care allowance and social benefit; and that the increasing number of Roma threatens national security since the (non-Roma) Hungarians will lose their homeland within a few decades, and so on.

My aim, then, here is to assess factors behind these discriminatory discourses and the escalation in incitement in local political life. I will illustrate how policy conflicts over welfare, education and anti-discriminatory measures are used by local politicians to move the ground of political discourse. But first a word on the Hungarian administrative system which gives such importance to the local.

A fragmented system of governance

Hungarian local politicians are frustrated for several reasons. They are necessarily incapable of managing the problems of enduring low employment, poverty, increasing educational segregation of Roma pupils caused by 'white flight' of non-Roma, middle class families, or the development of ethnic ghettos in certain micro-regions. In the face of these challenges, they tend to scapegoat Roma for social problems which are in fact non-Roma specific. The employment of Roma was radically disrupted soon after political transition, and nowadays just 28 per cent of economically active male Roma are employed. Nevertheless, the majority of those who are excluded *en permanence* from the labour market are not Roma (Havas, 2008). Nor is poverty a Roma specific problem. The immiseration of groups of several villages and small regions is more intense than the scale of residential segregation of Roma there, which arises from the above mentioned 'white flight' of the local middle class families.

The Hungarian municipal system is radically fragmented and decentralised (I. Pálné Kovács, 2001).[2] Every settlement, even the smallest village, has its own elected municipal council and mayor. Soon after the political transition, the immense stock of formerly state-owned assets were devolved to local municipalities, including the vast majority of the communal housing stock. Local municipal councils were assigned responsibility for public education and local welfare; they have the right to define catchment areas and the institutional structure of the elementary and secondary school system, local pedagogical programmes and curricula (Horváth, 2000). The national government has no decentralised administrative offices entitled to regulate such conditions attached to the payment of welfare, nor are there are any procedures within the regulations governing education that can restrict local political decision-making.

All this is, to some extent, an unintended consequence of the attempt to create a truly democratic system in 1990. The original aim of creating the fragmented and decentralised municipal model was to revitalise villages ruined by development policies that had displayed strongly politicised preferences in previous decades.[3] In addition, legislators expected that local municipalities would be able to assess communities' needs more accurately and design measures to meet local needs more effectively than higher levels of the state. However, the central budget finances the municipalities' public activities through non-earmarked transfers, the total of which is set according to various statistical criteria. As a result, local politicians are allowed to re-allocate resources among the sectors for which they are responsible, and target particular categories of those in need of local welfare or particular institutions. This means that local decision-makers always re-allocate resources in favour of the middle class (Szalai, 1995, 2004).

Poverty and exclusion from the labour market

Average income levels of the Roma have continuously worsened in the post-transition era, while poverty in society at large has decreased slightly over the past ten years or so. Relying on the data of TÁRKI, the Social Research Institute, which considers 'poor' anyone whose income is half of the median income, then 31.9 per cent of the Roma were poor in 1991, increasing to 61.5 per cent in 2001. If we take those in poverty to be all those with less than half the average income, then 48.9 per cent of the Roma were poor in 1991, and 68 per cent in 2001. Another measure reinforces the sense of structural inequality: in 1991, 61.6 per cent of the Roma belonged to the bottom fifth income group, while in 2002 the figure was 75.1 per cent.

Income-related deep poverty is closely connected with exclusion from the labour market. There are poor people amongst those who receive regular income from a job, but the cause of permanent and hopeless deep poverty is, in the first place, the long-term loss of contact with employment. In the post-transition years in Hungary, during the 'transition crisis', the decrease in employment had more serious effects on the population than the general effects of the economic recession or the decline in real income. The employment crisis in Hungary reached its nadir in 1997. Overall, there had been a decrease of 26 per cent in the rate of employment in comparison with the period before transition, due to collapse of the mining industry, heavy industry, the food industry and extensive agriculture.[4] During the next two years there was a moderate increase, but then the growth faltered. In any case, however, the growth in employment had not reached former unskilled workers and under-educated groups. And overall, in spite of the considerable economic growth, the number of individuals in employment stayed at a relatively low level in comparison with neighbouring states.

The situation of the Roma in the labour market became catastrophic during the first years of the transition period, both in comparison to their previous level of employment and to society at large. In 1993, almost half of working-age Roma were registered jobless in contrast with 13 per cent in society at large. Less than one third (28 per cent) of Roma men between the ages of fifteen and fifty-nine years were in employment against 64 per cent of the total population. (In the years before the transition 85 per cent of Roma men of work-age were employed.) When it comes to female employment, the gap is even wider: in 1993, 15 per cent of Roma women were in regular employment against 66 per cent of women in the total population.

Ten years later, in 2003, a repeat survey found no essential change in the employment situation of the Roma. In 2003, formal employment provided the primary source of livelihood for only 28.1 per cent of Roma men—in contrast with the 56.5 per cent of the total male population. Furthermore, Roma men who had income from informal or casual employment usually merely did irregular, odd jobs. Only 15.1 per cent of Roma women had income from some kind of formal employment—in contrast with the 43.7 per cent of the total female population. Today it is fair to say that the exclusion of the Roma from the labour market has a history of three decades and affects at least two generations (Kertesi, 2005).

In fact, the low level of employment remains the weakest point of Hungarian society. There are a number of reasons for this, some policy based, and deriving from a wide ranging belief that the unskilled, unemployed will never be able to re-integrate into the labour market. Government policy was, therefore, to have them absorbed by the pension system, maternity and child care provisions so that a dramatic decline in the number of the employed did not result in even more serious unemployment figures (Köllő, 2009). Thus, at the beginning of the 1990s, a special pension scheme was created for those who were near to retirement age, making it possible for them to 'escape unemployment', at least on paper. Many other people tried to avoid unemployment by getting themselves put on disability pensions (Ékes, 2007). Social benefit schemes, especially maternity pay that is provided for three years, were also an alternative to unemployment, although the amount given has lost its purchasing power since political transition in a drastic fashion. Underlying these schemes lay the belief that the uneducated, unemployed were unemployable and unusable economically—a fact which has led Hungary to have among the lowest employment rates in the EU,[5] and especially low among those with an education of only eight grades of elementary school, into which category many Roma fall.[6]

Unpaid labour and welfare

In 2008 the mayor of a small village, Monok in north-east Hungary, decided that henceforth the local municipal council would only provide the long-term unemployed with social benefit on condition that they perform unpaid, public works. This local regulation, which was patently unlawful within the terms of existing welfare legislation, promptly became well publicised by the media and popular throughout the country. Dozens of local municipalities applauded and introduced similar measures after the 'Monok model'. In press interviews, as well as in petitions addressed to the Minister of Welfare, the 'rebellious' mayors made it clear that long-term unemployed Roma were parasites, freeloaders, lazy, alcoholic, irresponsible and had only themselves to blame for their fate. Local politicians stated that taxpayers were fed up with supporting the unemployed Roma. The 'Monok model' had an unprecedented effect on public political discourse. The parliamentary opposition promised that they would legalise the 'Monok model' when they took over the government, and the then Minister of Welfare reacted considerately, took none of the mayors to court, and initiated a modification of welfare legislation to legalise this practice. But none of the parliamentary parties could compete with the extreme rightist Jobbik party which claimed, with good reason, that the mayors had wholeheartedly taken over the terms and arguments which Jobbik had introduced.

It was striking that the mayors did not simply blame the unemployed Roma for social and financial problems but suggested that Roma communities violate national security. The mayor of Monok contextualised his actions in an interview:

The Hungarian population is decreasing while the number of Roma is increasing. I inherited my homeland from my grandfather and I'm obliged to leave it to my grandchildren, but due to demographic trends this seems to be difficult. At last we have to speak our mind: that Roma families have one child after the other just because they regard children as a source of social income, that is to say, as a means of subsistence. In twenty years the Roma population may became dominant in Hungary and perhaps they will oust us from our ancestral homeland as the Albanians did with the Serbs in Kosovo.

His colleague, the mayor of Edelény, another small town in north-east Hungary, stated at a full council meeting, in front of local television cameras, that 'pregnant Roma women in the neighbouring villages intentionally poison themselves and hit their abdomen so as to give birth to mentally retarded babies in the hope of a higher family allowance'. The Jobbik party immediately spoke up for the mayor, saying that he had been brave enough to disclose problems instead of sweeping them under the carpet.

Anti-segregational education policy

The Hungarian public educational system is based on a number of basic principles: the free choice of syllabus by the schools who also determine the educational targets and qualifications to be offered; central funding, the quantity of which is regulated statistically according to various 'norms'; and allowance for a diversified school system (with a range of providers permitted, including municipal councils, churches, endowments, or colleges, and even universities). Right after 1990 the state abandoned its control over the content (and accuracy) of the syllabus and indeed all attempts to control public education directly and exclusively. Local municipal councils became basically responsible for maintaining public education. In practice, each school's programme is approved by whichever body manages it. This body decides what sort of programmes its schools provide and how many pupils to enrol. And all of them are entitled to demand the same per capita grant (known as 'normative funding') according to their pupil numbers and to any special programmes they run. (Church-run schools are given additional grants from the state budget.) Though the funding itself comes from the central state budget and is determined according to an overall assessment of the school's needs, it is not earmarked—which means that the managing body (most commonly the local authority) is not obliged to transfer the full amount to the school.

Per capita funding is linked structurally to free choice of school. Freedom of choice, however, means mutual freedom of choice. All parents can put their childrens' names down for any school they want, but enrolment is only bound to be granted by schools to children who live within their catchment area. Beyond that, however, it is up to the school and the extent of their free places to decide to accept children from outside their area. This becomes an important issue in regions of Hungary with schools in several nearby villages, where one tends to become 'the Gypsy school' and one a 'whites only school'.

The mutual choice of schools and parents has led to an extremely unequal distribution of educational goods and services. An exceptionally telling index of school selection and equal opportunities in public education is that while in the OECD, on average, the differences in performance of reading and comprehension are due to differences between schools in 36 per cent of children, in Hungary this accounts for 71 per cent of the variation in children's literacy abilities. In other words, the performance of children at school and their chances for further education is determined by early school choice to a much greater extent in Hungary than in most OECD countries.

The effects of early school selection are enhanced by diversification of the school system. As early as 1985, the preconditions for liberalisation of the system of eight years of primary and four years of secondary school were created by a law on public education. But it was not until the first Act on Public Education of the democratic regime, in 1993, that the specialised authority was created which allowed actual modifications and reforms to the system. After this date, the managers of any school, in most cases the local authority, could decide if they would maintain six class or eight class secondary schools (i.e. with 'secondary transfer' at ten or twelve). As a result of this, the existing differences in quality among secondary schools (some of which prepared children for university and some for vocational training) were pushed earlier 'up' the system: selection now begins at an earlier point, in fact when parents decide to send their children to primary schools that offer the eight or only six years—the latter tending to provide the more attractive option for the academically ambitious. And now the six and eight year secondary schools effectively select among the applying children, aged twelve and ten respectively, by imposing an early and difficult, although entirely legitimate, entrance exam. Roma children rarely make it into the better schools in these selections.

Furthermore, the over-representation of Roma pupils in 'catch-up' groups and classes for children with learning disabilities and behavioural disorders can be regarded as a form of deliberate separation. Alongside more or less explicit practices of ethnic segregation, the exodus of non-Roma children from schools once the Roma reach a certain percentage, plays a crucial role in separating pupils: non-Roma parents, who have the choice, will take their children into schools where the proportion of Roma pupils is lower, whereas Roma parents do not have such a choice—and this is done with the explicit knowledge and connivance of the local school directors (whose funding, of course, increases to meet the demand).

According to studies carried out by the Hungarian Institute for Education in 2000, approximately 10 per cent of all Roma elementary school pupils attended homogeneous Roma classes while an additional 25 per cent attended classes where Roma children were in the majority. Ethnic segregation has been increasing rapidly since that survey and the tendency appears to be unstoppable.

Two elements of the public education act's amendment in 2005 have further affected the basic structure of Hungarian public education.

- *Rules referring to establishing catchment areas* were amended so that if more than one primary school operates in a settlement, overlapping catchment areas should be established so that the proportion of severely disadvantaged pupils to be enrolled would not differ between catchment areas by more than by 25 per cent.
- *Rules referring to the admission of children from outside the catchment area* were amended so that if a primary school—once it has accepted applications from its own catchment area—takes further applications, it should give preference to children whose domicile or, failing that, place of official residence is in the village or town where the school is. And at this stage the admission of a severely disadvantaged child may be refused only if there is a lack of space. If there are too many applications for places at this stage a lottery is held attended by all interested parties. Severely disadvantaged or special needs children may be admitted at this stage with priority and without taking their chance in the lottery. (Special conditions for this may be set by the local council.)

Both amendments notably restrict the schools' opportunity to select and limit the municipalities' practice of pursuing educational policies that reinforce segregation.

It remains the case that the Ministry of Education cannot prevent municipal councils from circumventing anti-segregation regulations by merely administratively merging schools, thus formally eliminating inter-institutional disparities and segregation. Councils can also merge schools leaving the borders of catchment areas untouched, or permit highly successful schools to cream off non-Roma pupils by enrolling them in classes with special curricula and ignoring catchment zones entirely.

As far as was possible, the ministry had tried to avoid addressing policies explicitly geared to solving problems of Roma pupils. Two target groups were named instead: 'severely disadvantaged children' and 'children with special education needs' and objective criteria were established for the category of 'severely disadvantaged': these involved families where the educational level of the parents was not higher than eight grades of primary school, and where, due to their low per capita income, they were entitled for regular, extra so-called 'child protection' welfare support.

The integration programme of the ministry used categories that could be clearly defined and applied, assuming a benevolent will. However, cases of misuse could never be entirely prevented; and, of course, those whom the programme targeted were highly motivated to evade the rules. So, for instance, one of the criteria for 'severely disadvantaged' is that the parents' educational level must not be higher than eight grades of primary school—but this data was qualified as 'sensitive' by the Data Protection and Freedom of Information Commissioner. Referring to this fact, schools are able to modify the data on composition of the parental cohort when entering a funding competition or asking to join an integration programme. Experience shows that precisely this was done by many schools and municipal councils.[7] Another solution was devised in northern Hungary. No sooner had the anti-segregation regulation been published than Salgótarján, a medium sized city in the northern region, immediately merged all of its elementary schools into a single administrative unit so as to circumvent the law.

The ability of a local council that manages schools in its area to influence segregation depends on its size and position in the local educational market, within which, in practice, a 'distribution trade' of pupils is conducted. Thus villages and small towns, or the school directors working in these, can be literally incapable of implementing governmental measures aiming to provide more equal opportunities because they are at the mercy of parental decisions to choose schools for their children outside the settlement. To describe the nature of the challenge today, let me refer to a former legal institution, the 'virilist' representation system that existed in the era of the Habsburg Monarchy. In the councils of larger cities and counties, 50 per cent of representatives were elected and the rest of them were delegated from among the payers of the highest taxes.[8] This method was undoubtedly profoundly anti-democratic, but nevertheless ensured that groups of gentry, aristocrats, factory owners, shareholders, merchants, wholesalers and so on became interested in improving public services (Vörös, 1979).

This conceptual comparison helps us to understand the current dilemma of the small settlements (Zolnay, 2008). According to nationwide sociological surveys on Roma conducted in 1993 and in 2003, 40 per cent of the Roma population lives in small villages, inhabited by less then 2000 persons. Ghettoisation of several neighbouring villages and small regions is intense due to 'white flight' and the phenomenon which I would call the inverse 'virilist' model: elite groups sentence a village to 'social death' by abandoning it and so set a trend that seems to be irreversible. The old, the poor and, most of all, the Roma are trapped in those settlements and the institutions that serve them.

Nowadays, in small settlements, it is a crucial point whether influential groups in the village use local public institutions or not; whether they are beneficiaries of local welfare services or not; and whether they have their children enrolled in local schools or in schools somewhere else.

- In the standard 'virilist' model, the village's influential elite groups, that is, entrepreneurs, farmers, intellectuals, civil servants, officials etc., are equally interested in improving public service, maintaining social institutions, kindergartens, and high standard schools. The distribution of financial resources might be unequal but the public sphere is, at least, not under-financed.
- If, however, elite groups' interests are selective, some sectors remain under-financed, non-earmarked state transfers are redistributed in favour of improving infrastructure, servicing debt or supporting entrepreneurs. A proportion of non-earmarked state transfers that are supposed to finance social and welfare allowances are redistributed up to a point in almost every settlement in Hungary: they end up being spent on public education, urban development, services department etc.
- In villages characterised by an inverse 'virilist' model, the local elite groups have absolutely no interest in providing public service and maintaining institutions. They may decide to close or under-finance kindergartens and schools, and social institutions. As the Mayor of Sárpilis (Tolna County) said in an interview: 'What next! We are not willing to maintain and finance schools exclusively for Roma kids! Let them go to school somewhere else—whoever will have them'.[9]

The clearest example was that of the village of Jászladány, inhabited by not more than 6000 persons. The mayor made up his mind to take radical measures to stop and reverse 'white flight' and the consequent ghettoisation of the single elementary school. The local municipal council took advantage of the fact that central finance for schools makes no distinction between state schools run directly by the ministry and 'independent' or 'foundation' schools, as they are known in Hungary. So, the municipality 'doubled' the number of local elementary schools by establishing a foundation which then created a 'foundation school', and then rented the main school building to its own foundation. The basic purpose was to make the 'foundation school' attractive for non-Roma families by excluding Roma pupils. The Roma pupils continued going to the old ministry controlled local school.

Much was at stake in this settlement: would it prove possible, using this approach to institute a new legal model for segregating Roma children within the state educational system, and so halt 'white flight'. The educational minister also was aware that a lot was at stake: the credibility of his entire integration (or anti-Segregation) policy. However, the local gypsy (Roma) self government was constitutionally entitled to exercise its veto on such a 'doubling' of the number of local elementary schools and, in this way, for two years it successfully hindered the project. The government was confident that the constitutional guaranties of cultural autonomy for national and ethnic minorities would, this time (and as a rare exception), be effective and that the municipal council would, sooner or later, yield to the opposition of the minority self government. But the mayor and the councillors were determined enough to follow their policies through to completion and mobilized the ethnic Magyar voters to take part in the next local election for the minority self-government—a possibility allowed in the original law since it was assumed that no one would cheat the system in this way. Thus the majority managed to 'hijack' the gypsy (Roma) minority self government and elected four non-Roma members to the five members' body, including the mayor's wife.

After this 'hijacking' of the minority government the Ministry of Education had no other choice than to grant a licence to the 'foundation school'. The case was regarded as an unparalleled abuse of law by the ombudsman for minority rights who has also been concluded that it was improper to grant the 'foundation school' license as the very basis on which the school was brought into being was fundamentally unconstitutional. Nevertheless, the project to separate Roma and non-Roma pupils was successfully accomplished here. The non-Roma pupils were enrolled to the 'foundation school', and the vast majority of Roma pupils were not admitted; they had no choice other than to accept places at the rump elementary school situated in a shabby and poorly equipped building.

'It is not me who is segregating, it is life that segregates', the mayor said on television. 'I'm protecting the children who wish to learn and I'm creating an opportunity for them to stay here in Jászladány'. He argued that by creating an alternative educational framework, the municipal council wished merely to stop the village's non-Roma pupils being enrolled elsewhere.

Contrary to all those who worried, or hoped, that this model of ethnic segregation which had proved so successful in Jászladány, would become precedent for other small settlements with a single, ethnically shared elementary school, nothing of the sort happened. This was presumably because the scandal and ill publicity around this incident had made the name of Jászladány infamous.

Instead, mayors of small regions often agree informally on allocating Roma and non-Roma pupils among each other's elementary schools and catchment areas in a way that is acceptable to the non-Roma parents. The goal of such agreements is, again, to curb 'white flight' from a given micro region as a whole. In order to prevent middle class pupils being enrolled in schools somewhere outside the micro region, some villages where non Roma are in the majority are willing to maintain homogeneous Roma elementary schools: Roma pupils living in the neighbouring villages are admitted, while non-Roma parents choose elementary schools for their children somewhere else, but inside the micro region. Many local municipal councils transport non-Roma pupils by bus to schools designated informally as attractive elementary schools with the proportion of Roma pupils not higher than tolerated by the influential parents. In extreme cases, a 100 per cent exchange of pupils can be observed between two neighbouring villages.

Paradoxically, Roma pupils' chances might be better in villages characterised by inverse 'virilist' models than those where pupils are allocated places informally by mayors. This is because in this case, when ghettoised elementary schools are closed due to lack of funding, the pupils have to be admitted by other schools in the surrounding settlements. However, an incident occurred in 2007 when thirty Roma pupils were not admitted by a single elementary school in their area. Two villages that had been administratively merged, against local wishes, thirty years before they were officially separated again after political transition. The one village (Sződ) didn't have a Roma population, while the other village (Csörög) had a high population of Roma families. The school remained in Sződ, but the two municipal councils hadn't been able to agree on asset sharing. On the pretext that one of their school buildings had to be closed, the municipal council of Sződ refused to admit pupils from Csörög. The real motive of refusal was the debate on asset sharing. But it was a well known fact that non-Roma pupils were willingly admitted by schools situated in Vác, a town nearby, and the refusal of Sződ's municipal council only affected Roma pupils. The mayor of Sződ said on television: 'Frankly speaking, if the concerned pupils were not Roma, the problem wouldn't have emerged, because they could be enrolled without any difficulties'.

Meanwhile, the municipal council of Vác blackmailed the mayor of Csörög. The waste depot that treats Vác refuse is situated within the administrative boundary of Csörög and for many years the Csörög mayor had striven to get rid of it. The mayor of Vác recognised that he was in a position to exert some pressure and made it known that the affected thirty Roma pupils would be enrolled to any of his town's public schools so long as the village gave unlimited permission for the waste depot to remain in its current location. The mayor of Vác said publicly: 'Otherwise the kids can forget about our schools and go to the hell'.

Finally the ministry intervened and the pupils were enrolled at several schools in the surrounding settlements. But the dilemma has not been solved: the children living in that village still do not belong to any school's catchment area. They are simply missing from the educational map.

Testing the Equal Opportunity Act

The Equal Opportunity Act has a special section on school segregation, emphasising that a violation of the requirement of equal treatment has occurred if:

- children are unlawfully segregated in an educational institution, or in a separate section within a class or group
- an education or training system, or the institutional standards of such, do not achieve certain technical requirements or do not meet professional standards, and thus do not ensure a reasonable expectation of being able to prepare for state exams (Iványi, 2006)

However, the parts of the act prohibiting negative discrimination ignore the principles of the public education system established in various Educational Acts. Parental free choice of school excludes the possibility that Roma children's increasing separation could be qualified as deliberate, administratively organised segregation. The distribution of pupils among schools and the distribution of goods and services among pupils are determined first of all by the mutual selection of parents and schools. Municipalities that maintain schools with attractive and magnetic curricula contribute significantly to the creation and preservation of inequalities, as well as to ethnic segregation within their education catchment area. They have the right to define their catchment areas and the institutional structure of school systems, as well as local pedagogical programmes and curricula. They are also empowered to distribute financial resources among schools. As a result, in most cases, it cannot be proven that municipal councils maintaining segregated schools are themselves actively organising segregated education.

And, in reality, because of parental free choice, ethnic segregation is not created by the municipal councils. The proportion of Roma children in a school is one of the most important considerations when parents choose a school for their children. The average tolerated proportion of Roma in a school varies from one area of the country to another, but if a municipality tried to change the distribution of public education resources, or that of Roma and non-Roma pupils beyond that regarded by local elite groups as desirable, then migration between schools or even relocation between settlements would start immediately and remain until the proportion accepted by parents was re-established.

A test case rooted in the two laws—the Equal Opportunity Act and the Public Education Act—first took place in the autumn of 2005. A foundation, called the 'Chances for Children Foundation', referring to the Equal Opportunity Act, took up legal proceedings against the municipality of Miskolc.[10] The foundation was established explicitly with an aim to launch test cases on discrimination in education. The foundation claimed that the city had violated the requirement of equal treatment as the municipal council had administratively merged two elementary schools both of which were *de facto* segregated, leaving the borders of each school's catchment area untouched.[11] The foundation was established explicitly with an aim to launch test cases on discrimination in education against municipalities maintaining schools.

It was appropriate that the city of Miskolc in Borsod county (north-east Hungary) was among the first municipalities to be taken to court, since the municipal council had decided to reduce its expenditure by merging thirty-two schools into half that number—but had not taken the opportunity implied in the Act on Equal Opportunity to change their enrolment practices. This school reorganisation generated tension in the city, especially in the cases where a school with a majority of Roma children was united with a neighbouring institution of much higher reputation and a minority of Roma. The leaders of the city's education policy were eager to calm the anxious parents that unification of the institutions wouldn't affect enrolments—it was in this way, however, that the municipal council unintentionally exposed itself to being sued.

The test case in Miskolc had great importance regarding education policy. Beyond the actual case, the issue was whether it is possible to describe and analyse the phenomena of inequality of opportunities in public education and ethnic segregation with the legal formulation of 'equal treatment', 'negative discrimination' and 'illegal separation', and whether it is possible to identify municipalities as active responsible subject for the process. If it is possible, then it is also conceivable that the courts enforce alterations to local education policy. But the case also proved that municipal councils are at the mercy of the choices made by influential parents and the enrolment strategies adopted by elite schools.

The foundation won the suit in the final instance. The verdict obliged the city's municipal council to correct its policy, however the city leadership ignored it. The enforcement of the verdict would have jeopardised the fragile system that had been constructed by the council. The primary aim of the city's education policy was to keep school migration under control in the long run. In the city there was one homogeneous Roma elementary school, three additional schools with a Roma majority, nine elementary schools with an increasing number of Roma students, and six elite schools.

Schools with an increasing number of Roma students—the 'buffer schools'—played a crucial role from the point of view of controlling school migration. The decision-makers recognised that they can only control school migration and segregation among schools if segregation within schools is such that certain groups in 'buffer schools' can be offered an attractive enough curriculum. In Miskolc the most important means of internal selection was bilingual teaching, where schools teach core subjects in two chosen languages. The management of the city has, therefore, issued permits allowing bilingual groups to be formed in a number of 'buffer schools' which are in a critical situation from the point of view of 'ethnic' proportions. There are several reasons why bilingual teaching tends to be an efficient means to achieve internal segregation within a school. The catchment area of bilingual classes is the whole city. The evidence suggests that parents consider bilingual classes to form attractive elite cohorts independent of the number and proportion of Roma pupils in the rest of the classes in the same school. Formal entrance exam for admission to such classes is prohibited, but schools can select their pupils for bilingual classes through 'informal conversations' with six- to seven-year-old applicants. There is an informal consent in the city that Roma pupils are not admitted to bilingual classes (Zolnay, 2006). On the other hand, the municipal council is genuinely convinced that Roma pupils, excluded from bilingual classes but who attend other classes in the same school, can also benefit from the system which effectively retains the Hungarian majority pupils within the same school. The municipal council was aware that if the court's verdicts were enforced, the existing balance would be upset, the high degree of within-school segregation would convert to segregation between schools, and Roma pupils' access to a normal or expected standard of education would be even more unequal then it is now.

In the last decade, local public discourse had a stronger effect on governmental political decision-making than vice versa. The Ministry of Education was not able to enforce crucial elements of its anti-segregation policy and did not manage to force municipal councils to implement anti-segregation regulations in educational policy and school management. Key politicians often gave out hints that they agreed with the abusive, inciting language used by local mayors against Roma communities, and regret they can't afford to utter the same publicly. No one dares pick a quarrel with local politicians.

In terms of the overall argument of this book, this chapter demonstrates the nature of the conflicts, and the institutional fault-lines along which they run, that populist politics draws upon to mobilise its purported 'silent majority'. It is no accident that it has been in cities like Miskolc, with a recent history of economic decline and political marginalisation, that Jobbik has gained greatest support. The Hungarian institutional and legal infrastructure plays its own role here, channelling social conflicts over access to scarce local resources along ethnic lines. The language of rights, used by those who seek to provide greater access for Roma to resources that are supposedly equally distributed, inadvertently feeds into the discourse of their opponents. The strategy of the local municipality, to muddle through, ignore the law and hope that time is on their side, seems to work in the very short term. It is inconceivable that it will provide a long term remedy to the underlying social conflicts.

3

INTEGRALIST NARRATIVES AND REDEMPTIVE ANTI-GYPSY POLITICS IN BULGARIA

Georgia Efremova

In his recent book, *The Geopolitics of Emotion*, French thinker and political scientist Dominique Moisi stresses the paramount role of emotions in shaping and defining civilisations and the people inside them, as well as in guiding political conflict. Hope leads humanity forward, humiliation—backward, while fear immobilises it, he writes. Fear of the other and confusion over national identity have long been some of the key emotions characterising many Western societies. At the formal European level of the EU, the recent Roma controversy brought the issue forcefully to the table of the seemingly tired architects of integration. In the months since France announced and began undertaking its plans to liquidate more than 300 illegal Roma settlements across its territory and the repatriation of their inhabitants to Bulgaria and Romania, the Roma issue has acquired urgency, once more being reinserted into priority agendas, such as the programme of the 2011 Hungarian presidency. The fierce exchanges between member countries which Sarkozy's statements provoked (witnessed rarely, if ever, before in European Union politics), along with the dominant stance, which could be summed up as 'not in my backyard', have provided a powerful sign

43

of the fear that is one of the primary characteristic emotions found across the EU today.

In the context of the widespread indignation against discrimination, hypocrisy and populist 'vote catching' following the French defence of its policy in terms of national security, the prolonged official silence of Bulgaria, one of the countries destined to receive back its Roma, has not passed unnoticed. Some commentators have seen here a tactic to de-dramatise the situation resulting from fears about the country's Schengen perspectives. Others criticised the government's policy for allowing the country to be accused of 'exporting its problems' to Europe, as a result of discrimination suffered by its minorities who then flee to more affluent states. A second, less recognised and more dangerous, ramification of this silence was that it opened a space for various strands of explosive rhetoric in the domestic field questioning both Europe's double standards and the Bulgarian leaders' hesitation to follow suit and eliminate the breeding grounds of 'criminality, disease and incapacitating dirt'.

'Let them sue them, if they break the law. Why do they send them back to us? They are their problem now', characterised a common stance aired during the first month after Sarkozy's policy was announced. This pointed to the not so uncommon rhetorical strategy through which the problems of one country are repackaged as a common European issue and packed off to Brussels to be solved. A further strand of such rhetoric suggests that in reality many of the repatriated Gypsies are being sent back to places where they never came from, which in turn undermines the very concept of repatriation.

An important shift in public culture can be observed from the above. The forefront question surrounding the internal conflicts and debates around the returning Roma was not about those particular 'Gypsies' *per se* but about 'Gypsyness' (*ciganiia*) and the 'Gypsyfication' (*ciganizaciia*) of policy approaches and institutions. This rhetorical strategy poses a challenge to dominant notions of integration, and calls for a complete reinterpretation of questions of legitimacy, the role of the state, and the proper place of the nation and its constituents in policy goals. If at some point in the past the word '*ciganiia*' was used locally to refer to something dirty or disorderly in a very loose as well as a rather practical/physical sense, in the current climate the term's use has been radically extended to imply perversion, immoral and unprincipled practice and a civilisational regression (in Elias' sense, implying a regression from 'European' standards of shame and repugnance) with sharp implications for society at large. Today, in Bulgaria, 'Gypsyness' has become a signifier for a wide range of references in the form and practice of politics. Thus we find talk of the unfulfilled promises and disorder of democratic *ciganiia*, the falsification of votes in the electoral *ciganiia* or the *ciganiia* of conniving Brussels lobbyists and corrupt politicians at home.

At this particular moment in Bulgaria's democratic trajectory and integration into the European Project, new social distinctions and forms of sociability are emerging, new quests for collective self-interpretation and new political imaginaries arise in response to what are experienced as the corrosive and alienating effects of deep and rapid Euro-integration. These political imaginaries are at once particular to the country (in their local matrices of uses and meanings, as the example of *ciganiia* above shows) but are also related to the wider European process of integration and the dissonant impacts this has created, permitting a renewed political combination of the counter-Enlightenment strands of populism, expressionism and pluralism—a phenomenon that Douglas Holmes has termed 'integralism'.

The most recent instances of the repatriation of Roma to Bulgaria can be considered as one vivid example of the processes at play here. The uncertainties of social life and the conditions of economic deprivation in Bulgaria have, in the past decade and more, set some people on the move. Their 'return to the homeland' has sent moral shocks through the national space and given rise to renewed anxieties in which culture has been placed in the centre of political debate. This chapter focuses on integralist dynamics flaring up in Bulgaria, where widespread anti-Roma sentiments are now being mobilised, gradually repackaged and homogenised, and more widely distributed. This process has started in the last five years, and today it largely underpins the success of integralist populist/nationalist parties and organisations in Bulgaria.

In trying to make sense of this phenomenon in this chapter, I make several interrelated arguments: first, that in order to understand the reconfiguration of the political field today, in which we have seen the crumbling of the so-called 'Bulgarian ethnic model' and the rise of nationalist organisations, we need to think beyond simple explanations of politicians exploiting constantly available and always present ethnic hatreds and give thought to the role of emotions in political life and the organisation of movements. I want to suggest that a heightened emotionality has increased receptivity in some levels to the current calls for 'protecting the nation' and 'punishing the criminals'. This has gradually built up and has been organised around the complex interweaving of issues in compelling integralist narratives anchored in certain 'turning points' and 'events'. So, following Mabel Berezin, I adopt an approach that uses 'events' as a methodology to study populist-integralist rhetoric. This allows us to balance the analysis and account for both the emotional and cognitive range of stances and practices. I would argue that this is critical for understanding the salience of anti-Gypsy politics today in the broader context, as well as more specifically in the Bulgarian case on which I focus.

Second, I have labelled the particular form of anti-Gypsy politics I find in Bulgaria 'redemptive' because in its logic Roma are presented both as cause and manifestation of state weakness and are in turn placed at the centre of national/cultural decline and the need for salvation. Whereas previously the Roma were treated as a nuisance, unpleasant to the eye, in the new integralist discourse the forging of the new Bulgarian identity seems to be imagined as passing through a purge of the Roma from Bulgarian society. Roma thus become central in the project for the remodelling of the nation.

Third, the strong invocation of the state by these parties is connected to a language of rights and entitlements. Indeed I would argue that the successful combination of democratic discourse of rights and entitlements with nationalist rhetoric lies at the basis of the legitimacy of this discourse in the ears and hearts of integralist publics.

Finally, I try to show how some of this works on a local level through focusing on one often overlooked actor in the Bulgarian nationalist scene—the Bulgarian National Union and National Guard (hereinafter BNS/NG or NG used interchangeably).

Since its emergence in 2007, the NG has styled itself as 'the guardian of Bulgarians against Gypsy terror' and has actively participated in the creation of a 'national discourse'. The national discourse, following Todorova (2006), could be conceptualised as an arena of competing views of nationalism. I argue that the NG has effectively engaged the academic community as well as politicians (nationalists and non-nationalists) in a negotiation of values and ideas about the nation—a negotiation of a new 'cultural compromise' (Wimmer, 2002). It has done so through a series of activities and, most importantly, through a weekly television show aired, for more than two years, on one of the primary channels in Bulgaria,[1] part of which I analyse below. Before I attempt to present and unwrap some of these narratives, I want to quickly go back to what was perhaps the 'turning point' for Bulgarian anti-Gypsy politics and nationalism more generally.

The opening up of integralist spaces: The unmaking of an ethnic model

Years before the National Guard came on the scene there was the Ataka party. The great reconfiguration in the Bulgarian political field within the last five years was marked by the emergence of this party in 2005—a phenomenon that many labelled as 'a big surprise in Bulgarian politics'. The rise to political prominence of Ataka was facilitated by opportunities which had long been in the making, but Ataka decisively overturned an established trend in academic studies that glorified the concept of the 'Bulgarian ethnic model', relating to the formation and successful integration into the political life of the country of the Movement for Rights and Freedoms (MRF), the *de facto* ethnic Turkish party in Bulgaria that has been active since the beginning of the transition (for instance, Bakalova, 2000; Ragaru, 2001; Vassilev, 2002). Post-Ataka, a number of studies have discussed the changing political field (Kovalski, 2007; Rechel, 2007), but mostly from within the 'ethnic model' metaphor and so continue to conceal underlying and unresolved ethnic tensions. These authors posit that the ethnic tensions and differences which have always been there (during communism, and in the first decade of transition) have been gradually aggravated and amplified by a number of economic factors (increased poverty, and economic marginalisation that have disproportionately consumed the ethnic minorities, and particularly the Roma) leading to the ethnicisation of certain socio-economic problems, notably welfare and social security (Petkov, 2006).

The academic interpretation is mirrored in political life, where politicians continue to cling to and lean on the metaphor of the ethnic model to guard against the use of ethnicity to gain political capital (accusing each other of 'playing the ethnic card').[2] However, the reality they confront has decisively changed; what was previously unspeakable has today become a mainstream political language and mode of expression. Most Bulgarians can today recall a notorious statement by the current Prime Minister, Boyko Borisov. Speaking in front of the largest Bulgarian community abroad, in Chicago, Borisov, who was not yet Prime Minister but had already been mayor of Sofia, begged Bulgarian expatriates to return to their country which now can only draw on 'bad human capital' to constitute the governing class in the face of 1 million Roma, 700,000 Turks and 2.5 million retirees.[3] Contrary to the immediate assessment of the experts, Borisov's statement was far from political suicide: the message obviously resonated with otherwise deeply held sentiments in Bulgaria, where he was elected Prime Minister a few months later.[4]

As suggested, the ethnicisation of social difference has had an overwhelmingly threatening impact on one minority: the Roma. This was most notable when Ataka emerged in the 2005 election campaigning almost exclusively on anti-Roma slogans. Taken to court after its first appearances it won its appeal and then gained electoral advantage from exploiting a number of brawls immediately prior to the elections (Krasteva, 2005). Since then there have been important additions and switches of rhetoric.

As a political party Ataka was formed only months before the 2005 parliamentary elections and its quick success was then credited to the slogan of its leader, Volen Siderov, 'The Gypsies to Saturn' (a word play with the Bulgarian word for soap—*sapun*')[5] that, in the context of the ethnic brawls immediately preceding the party's formation, was treated by political commentators as a cheap instrumentalisation of ethnic prejudices, an exploitation of voters' sentiments for quick political effect. But how are prejudices instrumentalised? How is emotion invoked, and how are these (integralist) sentiments triggered?

Ghodsee has analysed most comprehensively the party platform—pointing to the combination of strands from left and right, such that their rhetoric appeals not only to 'single-focus ethnocentrics but also to the disenfranchised' (2009: 28). Ataka invented a political pattern that Hungary's Jobbik was later to adopt: its political programme includes modern leftist ideas: a strong nation state as a bulwark against global capitalist forces and against European integration, placing the working man at the centre of policy instead of money, profit and market, higher taxation for the rich, and a return to public ownership especially of industries 'threatened' by foreign acquisition (Magyari, 2009; Halasz, 2009). The combination of such leftist elements (working peoples' values and social solidarity) with rightist xenophobia and demands for order is precisely what underpins the concept of 'integralism' used to discuss the various manifestations of anti-Gypsy politics in this volume—the political attempt to place the search for values and solidarities which are felt to have been subverted and eroded by the reconfiguration of economic and political space at the centre of politics. The political programme thus orients around a new imagination of society, aiming to redraw the boundaries of national identity and belonging and leave outside those who are simply 'too different'.

Taking stock of emotion in the analysis of radical politics

Recognising this deeper structural underpinning and strong cultural long-ing is imperative to understanding these new phenomena—otherwise our analysis is bound to stay on the surface. The statement that 'Attaka strategi-cally *deploys a discourse of ethnic and religious intolerance to garner popular support* on the far-right for what is essentially a far-left political agenda' (Ghodsee, 2009: 28) assumes too eagerly that there is a ready made pool of voters who would immediately react to the slogan, 'The Gypsies to Saturn'. It is not enough to say that populist or nationalist leaders today exploit people's feelings, play on their anger and win votes, for such politicians are finding new ways of constructing difference, rendering it more offensive and explosive through understanding the anxieties it has triggered. What is required is to penetrate the logic of integralist politics, to understand the search for cultural solutions to socio-economic problems. We need to explore how the play on emotions occurs and what makes is so success-ful—how annoyance and nuisance are converted into moral outrage and indignation; how loose fears turn into a sense of an impending threat. To my mind, the key move is to realise that cognition and emotion are bundled together, making certain convictions powerful. We cannot, in other words, approach electoral support for right-wing parties in terms of (purely rational) voter preferences; and we cannot treat it as cheap exploitation of emotions which will soon die off—we need to go deeper.

In this paper I attempt to present an initial step towards this end by following writings on social movements which explore how emotional disposition intersects with other kinds of organisational and strategic dynamics (Goodwin et al.). These authors argue that emotions are socially and culturally constructed, and demonstrate how some of those construc-tions—outrage, indignation, shame, pride—are related to moral institu-tions, felt obligations and rights, and information about expected events. This analytic strategy dovetails with my use of the concept of 'events', conceived of as 'templates of possibilities' (following Berezin), in which collective emotions and interpretations are evoked; events contain moments of recognition (turning points) and thus have the potential to give rise to new collective imaginations and alter public perception in important ways. The conceptualisation of events as both emotionally and cognitively powerful allows us to locate important moments of recognition and shifts of perception. In this way we can begin to understand how loose and diverse sentiments of fear and anxiety are homogenised and packaged into new collective subjectivities forming in the face of 'criminality' and the 'imposing threat' of *ciganiia*.

Why is this important? First of all because this is a significant strand of a wider public conversation which is taking place today in Bulgaria as well as across Europe. This rhetoric participates in the present renegotiation of the dominant 'cultural compromise' and, as such, it is part of an emerging public culture that it is also reshaping in important ways. Public culture is understood here, following Hansen, as 'the public space in which a society and its constituent individuals and communities imagine, represent and recognize themselves through political discourse, political and cultural expressions, and representations of state and civic organizations' (1999: 4).

But, above all, in my mind, this is tremendously important because these political imaginaries are in many cases stronger than and outlive the movement or party in whose organisation or structure they emerge. In other words, it may be that Ataka, BNS/Guardia in Bulgaria, or Jobbik in Hungary disintegrate or see their political influence wane after incorporation into government or simply with time, yet many of their ideas will live on as part of the public culture they have shaped, and will be there to be picked up again by the new spark of integralist flames in the future. Today, the construction of crime as a cultural trait of the Roma is particularly dangerous because this representation of difference will live on. It already reshapes and guides social relations in multiple local political communities across Europe, but it could also become part of other cultural nationalist projects in the future—when it will have the advantage of being 'recognized as one of the available repertoires', to use Wimmer's terminology again.

The flaring up of integralist imaginaries: BNS/NG and redemptive anti-Gypsy politics

I choose to focus on one particular strand of the integralist narratives of redemptive anti-Gypsy politics in Bulgaria that has been overlooked and escaped analysis to date, despite its prominence for a significant period: the Bulgarian National Guard/NG. While Ataka is particularly well remembered for its strong anti-Gypsy slogans around elections, the National Guard was the first to construct and inject an integralist concoction—a narrative combining social and cultural aversion to the Roma with issues of national identity—into the political field and public space. In a way it laid the foundation for much of what we hear or notice today in Bulgaria.

The origins of the National Guard go back to 2001, when the Bulgarian National Union was established as a civil organisation for the protection and furthering of Bulgarian culture and spirit. Its two sub-units are the 'Humanitarian corpus' (organising social welfare actions)[6] and the sports organisation 'Edelweis' (now organising NG's training activities). Several years later, at its inception in 2007, the National Guard caught the head-lines as it presented itself as a response to lawlessness and rising Gypsy criminality. The NG thus became the uniformed wing of the BNS, its members participating in special training that also involved simulation of military conditions. Anyone applying to the National Guard had to become a member of BNS first, but only some made it into the NG—having proven their consistency, dedication to the cause and taken the Guard's oath.[7] The (then) leader and founder of BNS/NG, Boyan Rasate, played a crucial role in inspiring pride in national heritage, in focusing the young-sters' bounding energy into careful action, as well as acting as a knowledge-able interlocutor and host of a weekly NG television show.[8]

An avid lover of study, at thirty-seven Boyan Rasate is still a student of political sciences at Sofia University. At the same time, he is a man of action; he has faced multiple legal charges, been fined for his anti-Roma statements and was, at the time of writing, on probation. Boyan inspired his followers through his own actions, his leadership of the NG taken on as much more than a mere 'day job'. Both his wife and his four-year-old girl were part of many NG initiatives. Having probably learned first to parade and then to walk, his daughter proudly marched next to her parents and did not complain of freezing weather, mud or long climbs to reach the tomb of a fallen Second World War Bulgarian general who deserved to be honoured. On their way there, they will have repeated time and again, shouting them with the full force of their lungs, the three mottos: 'freedom or death', 'long live Bulgaria' and 'free, social, national'.[9]

A crucial note that is worth stressing is that for all the demonisation they are subjected to, the BNS/NG members are young, passionate, educated, and patriotic. Paradoxically, they are not what one expects to see after hav-ing read their publications and website, filled with aggressive slating of the Roma. It is the educated, the literate and not necessarily economically dis-advantaged Bulgarian youth which forms the base core of the BNS/NG. Many of them are well-to-do young professionals. This presents an interest-ing sign for the development of the democratic process and extremism, overturning common assumptions that education, literacy and economic prosperity somehow by default counteract the recurrent constructions of ethnic majoritarianism (as Hansen has also argued in this discussion of the rise of Indian nationalism), or that democracy, once established and consolidated, is self-sustaining since it produces a more rational form of organisation of interests. In my short field research among members of the movement and organisation, I came to see the NG also as an avenue/opportunity for social interaction and as offering a way 'to belong' that many young people seek. I found genuine emotion in their love for their country and search for a lost pride and something to believe in, and this led me to talk of their 'noble' nationalism (Efremova, 2008). Indeed, for many of them, what is at stake is a defence of the nation and their own identity, and a struggle to bring justice to the Bulgarian population. They are, in a way, engaged in a 'struggle for recognition'—only this happens to concern 'the majority' of society.

In its circular dynamics, the functioning of this integralist and redemptive discourse is such that a) all privileges accorded to Roma and alleged degradations/perversions committed by them reveal that the state is corrupt and weak; b) Roma are conceived of as both a cause of state weakness (that Roma are intrinsically perverted, a 'disease' that has contaminated the state and nurtures a culture of crime, chaos and anarchy) and a manifestation of it—the fact that Roma enjoy immunity from punishment for criminal acts; are protected by anti-hate crime legislation, by international human rights organisations and Bulgarian political incumbents' own misconceived humanism and enslavement to foreign values; are financially privileged with the innumerable Roma projects and funding—and all this points again to the incapacity and degradation of the state; c) as a consequence, the only way out of the ensuing decline of the nation is payback and redemption. Redemptive anti-Gypsy politics is therefore based on turning a social/political issue into one of national survival. In other words, Roma cease to be just an eye sore for Bulgarian society, they are situated at the centre of the political stage and turned into the primary scapegoat for all national ills and diseases.

Legitimating integralism: The particular resonance of redemptive anti-Gypsy politics

An important consideration is how and why certain discourses come to be widely seen as legitimate. In a seminal study on nationalism, Andreas Wimmer has argued that in order to be recognised, a discourse has to be viewed as legitimate, as operating within legitimate boundaries delineated by the 'cultural compromise'[10]—that is to say, the existing cultural compromise limits the field of recognisable and the legitimate arguments. In similar reasoning, in a study of an earlier instance of a successful nationalist public mobilisation at the start of the Bulgarian transition in 1989, Peter Stamatov has argued that the success of this movement was contingent upon the ability of a nationalist public to connect persuasively its own claims to values and ideals that lay at the foundation of public space.[11] The particular idiom of post-communist Bulgarian nationalism was successful because it integrated itself with universalist and democratic ideals in the 'discursive ideology' of public reasoning that was dominant during these early years of transition (Stamatov, 2000).

In a similar mode, I argue that the present nationalist discourse in Bulgaria (as currently projected by both NG and increasingly by Ataka) is successful because it manages to combine a nationalist rhetoric of protection by exclusion with democratic and universalist discourses on rights and entitlements; such a combination manages to successfully articulate the integralist 'desires, anxieties and fractured subjectivities' of Bulgarians today (Hansen, 1999: 4) within a democratically legitimate and powerful discourse.

Integralist sensibilities are awakened by the undermining of social solidarity and security. Both aspects of security—welfare (as a community of solidarity based on sameness) and physical security—are implicated in the current integralist claims that call for a strong state, a state which provides its deserving subjects with various entitlements—including access to resources, but also protection from arbitrary violence/crime. The 'Gypsy issue' becomes implicated in both respects—Gypsies are seen as the lazy, undeserving recipients of welfare who also engage unpunished in criminal acts, some of which are allegedly of a 'distinctly Gypsy' character. It is precisely these two elements (undeserving provision of welfare and criminality) that provide the strongest premise for the process of 'othering' Roma.

This discourse is recognised as legitimate by integralist publics because, on the one hand, the two elements (welfare and criminality) are strongly connected to the democratic discourse of 'rights and entitlements' implicit in the democratic space (every individual entitled to equal rights and desires). On the other hand, the call to the nation is appealing because, as Wimmer has argued, the main institutions of modern society are structured along national or ethnic lines; its appeal is also generated by the peculiar dislocations of the nation state dyad that integration is producing in a multiracial, multiethnic Europe, in the absence of an overarching and compelling vision of society (Holmes; Berezin).

Integralist narratives: Events in the analysis of redemptive anti-Gypsyism

The following presentation and analysis is based on the integralist narratives aired through the weekly BNS/Guardia television show broadcast on one of the major channels, as well as the available issues of the NG newspaper. I suggest that the television programmes function as 'spectacular events', defined as experience building events, since the open articulation of such rhetoric serves as a reconfirmation in the ears of integralist publics (Berezin, 2009). Extending the line of argument further, the TV shows themselves can be conceptualised as 'campaigns' that use 'sequential events', which Berezin has defined as 'building events'. These are events which 'interrogate the past and imagine the future' by moving forward in time and building new experiences (ibid). Importantly, much of the success of these campaigns depends on the careful selection and interweaving of issues, which the host of the programme, the organisation's leader, Boyan Rasate, carefully managed over the course of the two years in which the programme ran.

Programmes included studio guests—various experts or politicians or more 'ordinary' citizens (Bulgarian families, typically 'victims of the Gypsy terror'). An effective discursive strategy was employed. The discussions were always made to appear balanced and as presenting both sides/perspectives; guests in the studio included people with different (sometimes opposing) views—yet somehow a nicely packaged message always emerged at the end through a carefully layered progression. Viewers' calls were also taken throughout the programme, presenting different views and posing provocative questions to host and the guests. This illustrates the somewhat populist approach—debating the national questions 'with you, the nation' constitutes further 'proof' of the host's alleged commitment to openness, the value of democracy and, ultimately, democracy itself.

Privileged citizens: The conspicuous consumption of rights

There are many strands subsumed into this issue which form part of the larger campaign, and multiple ways in which integralist sensibilities are offended, leading to the reframing of the issue as discrimination of the majority/'ordinary' Bulgarians and manifesting 'Gypsy privilege'. The second NG programme was fully dedicated to the issue of 'privilege' (7 May 2007)[12] where a big focus point was the 'Decade of Roma Inclusion', which the programme explained was 'initiated amid escalating Gypsy crime and violent acts perpetrated with impunity, and will end this way, in an even greater disintegration, unless there is a change in government policy'. The following is an illustrative excerpt for the rich and interweaving thematic of Gypsy privilege:

The Bulgarian state is unjust towards its citizens; it privileges one of its minorities at the expense of the rest of the citizens—and this cannot be called integration. Despite all the care, the majority of Gypsies do not wish to get an education, and notwithstanding the existence of special employment programs, they refuse to work as well. The state in its turn builds houses for them, which they destroy. Such care for the young Bulgarian families does not yet exist. This integrative government strategy is wrong because it instils a sense of privilege and impunity, which in turn, very logically, implants a sense of resentment in Bulgarians. If this doesn't change, Gypsies will continue to loot, build their houses illegally (including ram shacks on top of gas pipelines), travel without tickets in city transportations, and get state assistance coming out of the pockets of Bulgarian taxpayers. They will continue to trade with their children abroad, and in Bulgaria become criminals, beggars, and prostitutes. The only ones taking advantage of these programs [i.e. Roma-related state-supported programmes] are neither Bulgarians nor Gypsies themselves, but the so-called human rights organizations and the countless scribblers of integration projects. The Bulgarian state must stop this, and provide care only for those who are truly socially engaged and socially productive—because to work is not only a right but an obligation as well, of every good citizen.

What can be seen here is the complex intertwining of different issues into one single large problematic, so condensed at present that the invocation of one single aspect triggers the outpouring of various other emotionalities. Perhaps this is how 'ideological fantasies work' as Žižek has suggested; but what we could see through it is the certain continuation of values. Articulations and aspirations to the decent life—an honourable wage, the centrality of work to one's goals and self-expression, realisation in life, and productive labour at the basis of the moral universe—which are central to integralist rhetoric, are, as some have argued, an expression of surviving peasant values, or what Buzalka has termed 'post peasant populism'. Importantly, the reference to honest and productive labour and, as its opposite, the 'reward without effort', are at the basis of today's criticism against both elites and minorities—corrupt politicians and lazy Gypsies share in taking something without offering or producing anything in return.

To a large extent the strength of appeal of this articulation of images is precisely that—painting pictures through details—'ram shacks on top of gas pipes', as well as giving everyday examples close to people's experiences—'travelling without bus tickets'. Despite the many elements of articulation, however, most important is that in the final analysis, the blame for today's problems is placed largely on the state and its weakness. In this context, the Roma are simultaneously a cause and a manifestation of this weakness. Although at the first reading the issue is about Roma being 'genetically predisposed' to criminality (the cause), on the second reading the issue supersedes it—ultimately, the real culprit is the state which, by not being able to counter such behaviour, breeds it, since 'the Gypsy measures its jumps according to the stick' (a Bulgarian saying, here substituted with Gypsy as a metaphor for dog). The fact that Gypsies are thus left unpunished creates a climate of disorder and chaos (the manifestation) to the detriment of 'true', law-abiding Bulgarians. Central to this frame, the call is thus about ensuring equality before the law, and the search for justice and order, echoing the sense of instability and uncertainty produced by the two successive transitions. Tellingly, one of the main slogans the NG carried on placards on all marches for the first year read: 'When law turns to lawlessness, resistance is mandatory'.

Important to note is also the direction of criticism towards the Roma NGOs, which is not completely off the mark—the need for accountability and taking responsibility, by both Roma NGOs and Roma leaders, has been highlighted[13] and reflects a wider concern, not a simple NG accusation or general finger pointing. To go further, the fact that NG rhetoric bases a large part of its argument on already existing and identified issues among the larger community (what following Hansen would constitute part of 'political culture' organised around 'legitimate problematics') helps to explain, in part, the more general appeal of its claims.

Free speech under threat: The political correctness disease

The issue of free speech is another issue belonging to the arena of 'legitimate problematics', one which integralist discourse is able to skilfully repackage in arguing that at present it is Bulgarians who are discriminated against in this country, and that it is their freedom of speech which is restricted by what the NG has resentfully labelled 'the Bulgarian political-correctness-masochist-project'. NG has declared itself against the use of the word 'Roma' and insists on using 'Gypsy', which it claims is part of the Bulgarian language, 'for as long as it is not criminalized'. At the advent of human rights organisations racing to file discrimination claims against Bulgarians and thus 'interrupt the very principle of our supposed advances into liberal democracy', NG members frequently invoke Article 2 of the discrimination law to remind the public of the provision for each individual to a guaranteed right to equality in front of the law; equality in treatment and opportunity for participation in public life; and effective defence against discrimination.

The threat to freedom of speech participates in both frames—a) both as excessive immunity granted to Roma (protected by anti-hate speech legislation) and as such conferring them privilege—of being 'the protected group' and thus distinct from and above Bulgarians; and b) because it weakens the state—by eroding it from inside (the reverse discrimination of Roma towards Bulgarians) while being imposed from outside (and thus constituting a foreign value). An important 'event' is associated with the issue:

Gypsy criminal culture: 'It's in their blood'

What is now commonly referred to as the 'Sisters Delneiski case', until today an open investigation, involved the rape and brutal killing of two little girls (deadly head injuries suffered through beating with stones). An important turning point in the mediation of the event, as well as the interpretations it gave rise to, occurred when several months later Dr Plamen Tsokov, professor of psychology in the University of Plovdiv and expert on court psychology, made a presentation of his study stating that this sort of crime answers to a specific perpetrators' crime (of minority descent). The expert's public statement announcing the conclusions that the killers of the sisters Delneiski are surely of a minority background was widely reported in the media and became a controversial issue in the Bulgarian public space.[14] A case against the doctor was eventually filed with the commission for discrimination on the charge of inciting ethnic hatred and a fine of 250 leva. This was an important turning point, a moment of recognition. It became an important 'event' after the doctor's appearance of the NG programme. And it became an event precisely because it provoked important changes in the imaginable, by providing the space for NG to ask: 'What are the implications for the democratically protected free speech, stamped over by the overriding political incorrectness? For stating a hypothesis, you are found guilty right away; whereas after two years, the murder against Bulgarians has seen no convictions or detentions'. This is one of the many allusions to the 'political umbrella' over Gypsy crimes and thus privilege—and the state inciting impunity among this ethnos.

The following exchange is an excerpt from the 14 January 2008 'Gypsy Crime: Myth or Reality' programme. Further, as an illustration of the previously identified discursive strategy employed by Rasate—posing of questions seemingly 'in defence' of Roma in order to make the opposite argument. This is what could be attributed to Rasate's charisma—the argumentative style rather than the body language (which is usually connected to populist rhetoric and could be a valid argument for Boyko Borisov's style, for example). Ultimately it is what makes for the success of NG rhetoric—arguing on the part of Roma, taking (if only for argument's sake) the opposite side to one's own, then logically arguing back to his point (aided by his good use of language but also by simple call to reason), and not being afraid of putting one's ideas to the test.

Rasate turns to Tsokov: 'Don't you think that this is an instance of media purposefully trying to create a distorted image of this minority and to place them under bad spotlight in front of society? […] As a psychologist, what do you think this lack of respect for the law is owed to?'

Tsokov: 'Education in the first place—but not as in the failure of society (we are not to transfer blame/responsibility "from the sick head to the healthy head"). They marry very early (and are then eligible for state aid)—the state has not done its job—early marriages have to be done away with'.

Rasate: 'Yes but these are cultural specifics of this ethnos—and if we start impeding these we would in effect discriminate against them and we would endanger their cultural identity'.

This provided a stepping stone in the campaign, a sequential event in its building. The issue was revisited before the year's close with MRF's bill for amendment of the penal code and harsher sentences for crimes of ethnic and religious discrimination (8 December 2008, 'MRF's new bills and the threats for freedom of speech').[15] Rasate presents himself as baffled at the lack of any proposal to change the law and penalise the buying of votes, or making sexual advances to the under-aged etc. He suggests this leaves hate crimes to be punished more severely than these truly serious offences. A discussion follows on the concept of 'hate crimes' (dismissed as vague, not useful, discriminatory against the majority). As the concluding remarks point out:

Twenty years after the beginning of the so-called transition, the freedom of press and speech are again challenged; liberal and humanitarian facades from everywhere, talk of democracy and human rights, as Bulgarians become hostages to such vague and abstracted concepts. A new dictatorship is coming to Bulgaria, hidden under the mask of intended freedom. In the country we find corruption, perversion, poverty and destruction, but instead of dealing with these open wounds, the power-holders start a chasing of ghosts and prepare the evening of accounts with their political opponents. For us, nationalists, however, freedom is the utmost highest value, and we will fight for it till the end. Bulgaria above everything.

The cultural arguments which establish an inherent connection and inviolability as to the nature of Gypsies, and present certain traits as normalised are, needless to say, very dangerous as they further serve the process of social habituation among the majority. One of the ways of establishing the cultural connection with criminality is simply posing the question as integralist nationalist rhetoric does: 'Is crime a Gypsy culture? Could lack of respect of the laws of state of this ethnic group be attributed to culture? Could it be that parasitism as a way of life is a basic priority for a given ethnic group—and could it be that group's 'copyright'?' And indeed it can, according to NG rhetoric—'in the case of Gypsies, it is a 'trade mark'; what one needs is no more but to remember the case of Plovdiv's neighbourhood Stolipinovo—of the unpaid electricity bills of Roma, but their paid cell phone bills!'

The appeal to experiences common to Bulgarians is very powerful: 'Ever wondered why there are no Gypsies when you go to pay your electricity bill?'; 'Ever wonder why your bill often looks inflated?' It is powerful precisely because this is a generally heartfelt popular complaint—that inflated electricity bills are one way the (now) private energy companies compensate for those 'customers' who do not pay for their electricity at all—and is very evocative, especially in a context of large energy price increases. The conclusion which logically emerges then is that this is indeed 'the Gypsy way': 'Gypsies take but do not give; in turn for us who have worked so hard and give money to state—the resources are being distributed back unequally'— and this constitutes a basic transgression of the law of equality, bringing us back to the need for a new force to restore the justice and order.

Importantly, with regard to anti-Gypsy politics, the notions and ideas fuelling resentment today are much the same as the popular discourses of the economy during communism (Stewart). Much more is attributed to culture: for example, in the same show, the cultural custom of marrying early, hence becoming eligible for social assistance and thus a burden to society; as well as the recasting of the habits of garbage disposal as a peculiar element of Roma culture (which they therefore lack). The supposed lack of family culture is also said to impede Gypsies from sending their children to school—unless they are beneficiaries of the '*kifla i mliako*' (milk and crois- sant) programme—the biggest educational incentive scheme run nationally. What has changed today is the connection of such ideas to culture (as evinced in the increasingly popular perceptions that there are certain kinds of crime particular to the Gypsy culture, that criminality is in Gypsy blood). Culture also underpins the solutions offered.

Further underpinning integralist anxieties of uncertainties and disorder, one of the most important way in which the NG has attempted to position Gypsies as a menace for state integrity, law and order is through forging links between Gypsies and anarchism. Illustrative of these links is the following excerpt from an NG newspaper titled 'Most Authentic Anarchists at Home': 'Under the shadow of the chaos and the mask of petty crime, Gypsies are preparing a massive future anarcho-revolution! This was discovered by a team of young experts, conducting analysis on the consecutive actions on the principle of direct action carried out by autonomous groups of Gypsy anarchists, as well as the sensational connection between the Bulgarian Anar- chist Federation and the Gypsy NGO "There is, there isn't"'[16]. The article postulates the existence of a pact of cooperation between the two for several years—evidence for which is also provided by the 'free rider' argument, applicable to both. The squatting and denial of private property by Gypsies, free love, going through garbage cans and so forth are other links the article creates to cast Roma as anarchists. From there, the menace to the political body and state structure of the Bulgarian nation becomes automatic.

Not far away is the issue of how to counter this. The 15 December 2008 show, titled 'Criminality, anarchy, chaos—the vices of contemporary soci- ety' treated the question of reintroducing the death penalty in response to anarchism. 'Certainly, there were many crimes punishable by death sentence before [under communist rule]; abolished with the liberalization of the judicial system, this has created a scene of corruption and criminality in the last 20 years'. This is also illustrative of the NG's position with regards to the communist state—ideologically wrong as it was, there was order and a strong state, but 'Now there is only progressive chaos'. The December 2008 show was placed in the context of the December student protests and anar- chy in Greece, which became an event in its own right in the Bulgarian political field, transcribed into the domestic context as directly linked with the source of deviance and disorder at home: the Gypsies. The question raised by the particular reformulation of this event was, could there be a similar outbreak in Bulgaria? The students invited as guests posited that it is highly possible, also considering the funding from abroad of such anarchist organisations.

The integralist political campaign for putting an end to impunity had been gaining speed for a year. The need for tougher crime laws and 'fast and strict justice' was debated extensively previously and given prominence in NG programming. To the question 'Who should be sentenced to the death penalty?' posed in the 2 July 2007 'Death Penalty' show, the high administrator from the Commission for Research in Criminality, Ministry of Justice, and guest in the studio, Mr Boyan Kairov, gave the following pronouncement: 'The killer, the rapist, drug trafficker, the robbers, who are in front of the eyes of everyone; [...] and especially the people who have robbed the state in a harsh manner—they have in essence robbed each citizen [...]'. This was an important turning point in NG discourse and a strong call to return to normalcy and a re-establishment of the collective solidarities under threat—and to safeguard society. Here is where quotes from the national heroes from nineteenth century Bulgarian liberation wars find particular resonance. Among them, Levski is frequently quoted: 'for those who take away from society, the traitors and national enemies—only death, death and death'.

National catastrophe: The cultural anxieties of a nation

But the primary integralist anxiety revolving around what is seen as the impending national catastrophe, involves socio-cultural issues and the state's inability to form a protective policy to preserve national cultural heritage, the Bulgarian family and language, and the patriotic spirit of state, society, and youth. Particularly with regard to the latter, one important aspect is the perceived moral youth degradation—expressed in the degradation of education and the absence of patriotic spirit, on the one hand, compared with the lure of sex, drugs, internet, discos and chalga music, on the other, and all this acting as a psychological manipulation, pushing the youth further toward sexual perversion.[17] The former is especially salient as an issue in the broader society and the common critique goes along the line of: 'The Turks did not manage to Turkify us for 500 years while the Gypsies got us dancing *kyuchek* in only ten'.

The theme about perversion—criminal as described above, but also sexual and cultural—is central to NG discourse and fundamental to linking the Roma to Bulgaria's great national decline. The main topic of NG's third programme (14 May 2007) was 'transvestites in Bulgaria'—i.e., 'who becomes a transvestite and why? How should we treat them? How does the state treat this minority?' To highlight the issue at hand, one of the guests invited to the programme was a 'real transvestite from the Sofia streets', Milena, a Gypsy transvestite, working in front of the Ministry of Agriculture, twenty-four-years-old with a 2nd grade education. This show combines the main rhetorical elements of NG discourse: the Gypsy minority, which is criminal, yet protected, as transvestites are (the introduction of the sexual thematic); they are protected both by state (through its inactivity or unwillingness to punish those who break the law) and by international organisations.

This also introduces another novel way to talk about the corrupted nature of Bulgarian politics—that is, their 'perverted nature'.[18] This could be said to have become a 'code word' in the new nationalist vocabulary, and is present in some form in almost every other show or public statement; additionally a separate show on 17 December 2007 was dedicated to 'The sexual perversions in Bulgarian political life'. The show ends with the conclusion that in Bulgaria, both transvestites and Gypsies are above the law and 'untouchable'. And while they both find protectors in the form of politicians, lobbies in parliament and human rights protection organisations, they pose a threat to culture and society and the erosion of the nation.

Rodolubie *vs. Gypsy racism (who loves and who hates in our nation)*

Equally important in manifesting the 'rift' between Roma and Bulgarians, in contesting the basic principles of social membership and identity, and in constructing a fundamental divide of 'us vs. them', is achieved by going one step further and accusing Roma themselves of reverse discrimination. Resentment is directed against the 'obvious' 'Gypsy racism'. As Stoyan Nikolov, BNS member and author of the article 'Gypsy racism', writes: 'Crimes are committed by Gypsies out of ethnic hatred. Gypsy racism is rooted in Gypsies' identity. They divide all people to good and bad, clean and not clean, Gypsy and *gadje* (according to Nikolov, meaning 'savage'). Gypsies have a special word for Bulgarians, '*daz*' meaning 'slave'—thus Bulgarians are for Gypsies savages and slaves…'

Urgent action to save the nation from the hatred and conspiracies of Roma against Bulgarians is to be achieved under the banner of *rodolubie* ('love for the nation'). It is the most central belief/sentiment for NG members, and is used as a basis for calls to transcend divisions; for unity and integration of the nation. Interesting here is the theme of integration and its construction as two completely opposite meanings with emotive powers. Whereas integration is considered almost a perverse term in the context of Roma issues (as being 'the wrong project of integration'),[19] once the offending minority is excluded the focus transfers to the need for integration, for unity. Thus, remarkably, the NG message also becomes one of inclusion,[20] with NG projecting itself not as a promoter of negative and sterile hatred but of the noble *rodolubie*, or love for the country.

Multiple viewer calls were received on the NG expressing various anxieties: a concern over a sprawling Gypsy ghetto on the outskirts of one viewer's neighbourhood—'they are illegal, dirty, throwing their garbage outside of the containers positioned there for the purpose'. Another caller voiced their resentment at the impossibility of even policing such ghettos, in fear of the over 500 organisations in Bulgaria campaigning for Roma rights, 'whose sole mission is trying Bulgarians committing wrongdoings over Gypsies, with the result that today no policeman could afford to enter the Gypsy ghettos, fearing accusations in abuse and discrimination; not to talk of electric company regulators...' Next, a viewer tells of a Bulgarian cemetery nearby that is 'frequently desecrated by Gypsies' and of 'people being afraid of even going there to light a candle', driving the point further—'it seems that not only living but also dead Bulgarians are suffering at the hand of Gypsies'.

Thus, the media stories of desecrated cemeteries and torn national flags, which are reprinted, reread and rearticulated through this important channel of anti-Gypsy politics in Bulgaria, show the dangers of such campaigns. Each times a new layer is added, each emotional strand is accompanied by a cognitive shift. My hope is that the above exposition has made at least one step in the understanding of this dynamic. The fundamental importance of it lies in the realisation that stories have a life of their own, and public narratives have lasting impacts—they frequently survive their original designers. Or as a popular Bulgarian saying goes, every spoken word is a thrown stone.[21] This points to the certain irreversibility of popular narratives and imaginaries, once created; and, fittingly here, metaphorically it suggests that all too often, the distance from words of aggression to acts of aggression is rather short.

What next? A question of Gypsyness

Following several years of a fight 'on the street' and one unsuccessful attempt to march through the front doors of parliament (unsurprisingly in retrospect attributed by the party to the 'electoral *ciganiia*' characteristic of Bulgarian political life and democratic politics more broadly), the BNS finds itself in a weakened position. It has lost its charismatic 'general', its mouthpiece, and some of its members. The year 2009 proved decisive for the Bulgarian National Guard Movement—after two years of broadcasting, its established television show was discontinued in early summer following the change of ownership of the new channel to a new media holding run by NG's political opponents. With a public statement, Boyan Rasate withdrew himself from the organisation several months later, invoking his higher dedication to the cause and decision not to endanger the movement's chances by his presence. Not so publicly, but with important repercussions, several of the NG members reportedly split up earlier this year and became founding members of a new organisation called 'National Resistance' which fashions itself as a grassroots 'leaderless resistance' and has been increasingly active in the public and media space. The behind-the-scenes manoeuvring which gave rise to these developments remains obscure.

Yet even if the NG appears to have receded from the active position of performance in the political field today, its campaign and the production of anti-Gypsy politics are at present continued by various actors, among which is once more the Ataka party. Siderov's provocative anti-Gypsy slogans in landing the victorious 9 per cent for the party in 2005 were interpreted as a cheap shot precisely because they lasted only that long. After setting foot in parliament, however, the rhetoric was largely softened—interpreted by the politician himself as a metaphor: 'I am not against Gypsies and Turks, just against the Gypsyfication and Turkicisation, chalgaisation of Bulgaria; I have used this metaphorically'. The hand raised in Nazi salute was explained away as simply stretching. The immediate change in Ataka rhetoric post-elections has been towards slogans like 'Out of NATO', 'Out of IMF', 'Revision of the privatization process', etc., and has been interpreted as an attempt to 'wipe the extremist traces'.[22] And, in the years since, when it did indulge in anti-minority slogans, it linked the images of death of the nation primarily to MRF and the Turkish minority, and religious issues in Bulgaria.[23]

In the last three years, and up until recently, there seemed to be a clear delineation in the division of labour associated with the production of anti-minority rhetoric and experimentation with integralist imaginaries. Thus, while the NG took up the task of collecting integralist anxieties and embodying them in the compelling narrative characterising redemptive anti-Gypsyism, Ataka campaigned against the construction of mosques and EU bureaucracy. This delineation is presently shifting, as Ataka has now decisively launched into the new terrain of anti-Gypsy politics opened by the receding of the NG, and is able to do so from the position of a party currently securely asserted in political prominence through its 'advisory role' to Borisov's new centre-right government since the parliamentary elections in June 2009. Furthermore, the integralist campaign which has placed anti-Gypsy politics in centre stage, which Ataka could now swiftly and easily take over upon, is given another boost and further legitimacy by recent developments beyond Bulgaria's borders, creating new issues which integralist forces at home interweave in existing public narratives of danger, criminality and perversion in public space.

'Europe is Liquidating its Gypsy Camps, When Will Bulgaria Follow?' asks the title of a long exposition on 'the Gypsy issue' presented in a recent issue of the Ataka newspaper.[24] In this sense the current actions of the French government are another important 'event' in the European political field and public culture. They have put on the table and brought under the spotlight the tensions enveloping one of the central tenets of European policy—the concept of integration. What has had resonance among Bulgarian integralist publics is the 'quick and decisive reaction of a state which takes measures to protect the security of its citizens, disregarding the always present accusations of "rights defenders" profiteering from propaganda of the human rights of the Roma tribe'—'a state which understands that 'integration' could happen only with the submission of the Roma to the law and to the national reference' (ibid.).

This forces us to consider of the complex overlap and interplay between the various integralist strands of anti-Gypsy politics across Europe today, and the mutations and/or convergence of issues and imaginaries and their mutual legitimation. To date, the vernacularisation of what Hansen has called 'conceptual grammars'—a range of meanings of concepts and discourses—into the 'connotative domains' of specific local and national contexts, remains an open field of contestation (Hansen, 1999: 25). The controversy stirred by the recent demonstrations of this 'strong and decisive French state' is undeniably stretching the range of meanings of the concepts and notions of Gypsyness, integration, and the European Project itself.

How those may further ignite new integralist imaginaries in the Bulgarian context remains to be seen.

As the editorial piece in the daily edition of what could be regarded as the most authoritative public media in Bulgaria, Economedia, presented it, the problem 'is not one of Gypsies, but of Gypsiness'. It further asked 'whether Bulgarians would manage to integrate the Roma minority to the basic principles of civilized life, or the minority will pull the majority towards itself [...] Whether we will gradually civilize the ghetto or the ghetto will be expanding toward the centre'.[25] The insertion of Gypsyness into a narrative of civilisational values and a creation of a palpable dichotomy between the two (civilisation vs. Gypsyfication) I think gives a sense of what really is at stake in the new 'event' created by French actions, provoking emotional resonance and in turn giving rise to new collective interpretations. Once again, as Moisi writes, every civilisation is driven not only by political and cultural factors but also by the emotions guiding people inside it: propelling hope, regressive humiliation, and immobilising fear. In the Bulgarian context, the balance between these emotions, and their inextricable impact on political conflict, is still unfolding.

4

SOCIAL EXCLUSION OF THE ROMA
AND CZECH SOCIETY

Karel Čada

Introduction

The text presents an analysis of the opinions and stances among Czechs on the issue of social exclusion of the Roma and evaluates possible solutions and possibilities for overcoming existing and adverse developments. The text summarizes in a broader context results of the research 'The key to supporting of integrational policies of municipalities' conducted by Ivan Gabal Analysis & Consulting Company in 2008. Available public opinion polls have mostly focused on a single dimension of this problem and fail to gauge public perceptions of the urgency and salience of the co-existence with the Roma as a topic, and the solutions most widely supported by the public. This study focuses on the structural differences between regions and the number of socially excluded Roma localities situated in their territory. While the creation of such localities is mostly a regional matter, particularly exclusion from the labour market and from the structures of mainstream society, the public perceives ethnic exclusiveness very forcefully. And while the ability to understand these problems varies according to the degree of direct experience of them, the identification of inhabitants of excluded localities by ethnicity means that the public perceives these people as being different and treats them accordingly.

A literature review of radical right parties and voter behaviour by Jens Rydgren developed the following list of conditions that help to explain the emergence of contemporary radical right parties:

1. A post-industrial economy;
2. Dissolution of established identities, fragmentation of culture, multi-culturalisation;
3. The emergence or growing salience of socio-cultural cleavages;
4. Widespread political discontent and disenchantment;
5. Convergence between the established parties in a political space;
6. Popular xenophobia and racism;
7. Economic crisis and unemployment;
8. Reaction against the emergence of New Left and/or Green parties and movements;
9. A proportional voting system;
10. Experience of a referendum that cuts across the old party cleavages. (Rydgren, 2002)

I follow some of this reasoning in my text, especially the focus on the growing salience of socio-cultural cleavages, the ideological convergence between established parties, economic crisis and unemployment. I start by describing the activities of the extreme right-wing in the Czech Republic and analysing the results of the European Parliamentary election (EP) in June 2009, in order to identify the main changes in the Czech far right-wing scene and the regions where the activities of these groups enjoy the strongest support. I focus on the roots and context of attitudes towards the Roma and the possibility for abuse of these attitudes by far right-wing parties.

Methodology

An analysis of the ways mainstream society sees its co-existence with the Roma and of issues relating to socially excluded Roma localities requires a deeper insight into the structure of Czech public opinion, particularly as it has developed over time and how it is regionally differentiated. In my view, the key element in defining and analysing public opinions is the question of how 'the ethnic climate' in Czech society has been developing and in which direction. A further key issue relates to the difference in the number and size of Roma localities in different regions of the Czech Republic and whether the ethnic climate has changed as a result of the deepening social exclusion of the past decade. Change in the ethnic climate and its variation across regions of the Czech Republic are so significant that they had to be taken into account both in the determination of the survey's methodology and in the analysis of results. The data analysed in the text come from the survey designed by Ivan Gabal Analysis & Consulting Company in collaboration with Open Society Prague. I was a part of the research team. The survey aimed, at least in some areas, to compare current attitudes with results obtained in the 1990s. We formulated questions and determined their order in the questionnaire on the basis of similar surveys which we had carried out in 1994 and 1996.[1]

The activities of the extreme right-wing in the Czech Republic

After 1989 the first extreme right-wing party was the Republican Party of Czechoslovakia (Sdružení pro republiku—Republikánská strana Ceskoslovenská) established by Miroslav Sládek, who was repeatedly described in the media as a charismatic leader. The party was represented in Parliament in 1992–98, during which time its election results increased from 1.0 per cent in 1990 to 5.98 per cent two years later, and 8.01 per cent in 1996. For the next two years it dropped to 3.9 per cent which was insufficient for entry to the Czech Parliament. There has been no extreme right-wing in the Czech Parliament since the Republican Party of Czechoslovakia lost its seats.

Financial problems resulted in the party's slide into bankruptcy. In 2001 the Republican Party of Miroslav Sládek (Republikáni Miroslava Sládka) was established, which gained less than 1 per cent in the parliamentary elections in 2002. In 2002, the Workers' Party (Dělnická strana)[2] split off from the Republican Party of Miroslav Sládek. The Workers' Party increasingly won support from neo-Nazis. The Czech political scientist, Jan Charvat, argues that: 'Until 1998, the Czech neo-Nazis were against any cooperation with political parties. Conversely, they distanced themselves from politics and held revolution as the only way, until they realized the unexpected dynamics this link provided' (Čopjaková, 2009). Until 2008 the Workers' Party received minimal media coverage and remained unknown to the broader public. The situation has changed since. The activities of extremists have moved from the closed spaces of pubs or clubs into the streets and political discourse. Furthermore these activities meet with public support, especially in several regions where respondents to surveys say that co-existence with Roma is problematic.

THE GYPSY 'MENACE'

According to the Czech Security Information Service (BIS, 2009) the year 2008 represented a breakthrough for Czech right-wing extremists. The number of extremist actions suddenly increased and they were able to spread materials and opinions outside the range of their supporters. For some years the Czech neo-Nazis had been getting more and more professional and radical, but 2008 represented a true shift, 'mainly in terms of quality, which are likely to influence developments in the next years' (BIS, 2009). Most striking was the change in the structure of the neo-Nazi scene. Although extremists kept their unofficial groupings such as 'National Resistance' (Národní odpor)[3] and 'Autonomous Nationalists' (Autonomní nacionalisté),[4] they complemented the activities of these with political representation, i.e. the Workers' Party started seriously addressing voters in the first half of 2008. In connection with events in the autumn of that year in Litvinov, north Bohemia—when a Workers' Party march tried to divert 'spontaneously' to march through and presumably attack the Roma-dominated housing estate in the suburb of Janov—right-wing extremists began to enjoy a degree of support for the first time from ordinary voters. The extremists claimed after these events that the newfound willingness among locals to offer help, their open support and sometimes active cooperation, was the main sign of the success of their anti-Romany actions. The secret services noted also that the model of action was 'inspired by the German right-wing extremist scene', hence 'they staged several so-called spontaneous events which they had not announced beforehand' (BIS, 2009).

In the first half of 2009 extremist actions, mostly organised by the Workers' Party, achieved intense media coverage. A march of neo-Nazis through Ustí nad Labem (a large city in the former Sudetenland of northern Bohemia with a large Roma population) in April 2009 raised the biggest media attention. The national media also reported extensively on marches in Brno, Přerov and Pilsen. Although more than two-thirds of all the reportage was negative, the publicity of events organised by right-wing groups generally increased, especially during April 2009. According to an analysis made by the Newton Media company, such events were up to seven times more likely to be publicised in the mass media than protest actions organised by their opponents.

In the European parliamentary elections the Workers' Party won more than twenty-five thousand votes and passed the 1 per cent necessary for the payment of state contribution. Probably the majority of European radical right-wing populist parties tend to hold strong anti-statist positions. They articulate these in sharp criticism of high levels of taxation, of the bureau-cratic state in general, and of welfare costs (Betz, 1993). Undoubtedly, a very important part of the electoral success of right-wing parties is the abil-ity to mobilise voters who have not been interested in politics before. Regionally speaking, the Workers' Party was more successful in the under-developed regions of northern Bohemia that are characterised by high proportions of socially excluded Roma,[5] high unemployment rates, and low levels of education and GDP per capita. These regions are also characterised by a weak turnout in EP elections.

Correlation of support for the Workers' Party with characteristics of regions

Characteristics	Coefficients of correlation	
Number of socially excluded Roma people per capita[6]	0,860159	▲
Level of education	−0,819244	▼
Turnout in the European Parliament elections 2009	−0,78958	▼
Registered unemployment rate	0,64184	▲
GDP per capita	−0,34572	▼

This industrial region of Bohemia bears a strong legacy of the communist era, belonging to the most intensely exploited territories of the Czech Republic. Open-cast brown coal mining and corresponding activities (espe-cially coal-fired plants) resulted in large scale environmental degradation, affecting the system of settlement and harming the health of the popula-tion. Then, the reduction of mining in the 1990s produced high unemploy-ment which aggravated the social crisis. Within this area, the Workers' Party was the most successful in the Ustecky region where it won 4101 votes (2.76 per cent). More than 2 per cent voted in support of the Workers' Party also in the Karlovarsky region.

We can explain the increasing popularity of radical right parties with reference to new forms of political cleavages. The traditional cleavages described by Seymour Martin Lipset and Stein Rokkan (1967) are class, religion, centre-periphery, and urban-rural distinctions. Typical of the new forms of cleavage is the co-existence of a centre-periphery axis with a new axis based on attitudes to the nation (on one side stand the proponents of internationalism—European Union, multiculturalism, etc.—and on the other, the proponents of national sovereignty who are hostile to immigrants and different ethnic groups). In the areas with a high support for the radical right parties we can see a combination of perceived peripherality with an emphasis on the role of the nation in promoting well-being. Because the number of immigrants in the Czech Republic is low, the hostility of supporters of extreme right is mostly oriented to the Roma population.

Attitudes towards Roma in the context of regional differences

Co-existence with the Roma is considered to be problematic on a national level by 66 per cent of the Czech citizens interviewed. This proportion of responses has not changed significantly over the long term. The same share of respondents gave this answer in 1996. Although the number of persons who perceive co-existence with the Roma as a very urgent or a somewhat urgent problem has decreased by 7 per cent since 1994, it may be said that in general two thirds of the adult population perceive co-existence with the Roma as a problem on a long term and immutable basis. Moreover, the issue of co-existence with the Roma cannot be understood—as far as the public are concerned—solely as a social or economic issue.

In the whole field of acknowledged problems that are picked up in our surveys, we can distinguish four categories: compliance with the law and with the rules—quality of public administration and justice (this includes crime, corruption, bureaucracy and compliance with the law); ethnic and racial tensions, i.e. elements weakening cultural homogeneity and uniformity of the Czech society (this includes racism and racial conflicts, co-existence with the Roma, influx of foreigners into the Czech Republic and terrorism); the standard of civilisation and related problems (state debt, the environment, level of political culture and situation in the health care sector) and social problems (unemployment, shortage of funds for serious social problems and the economic and social situation).[7] A primary prism of evaluation is ethnic and cultural dissimilarity, where the public view the Roma with the same logic that they apply to issues around co-existence with immigrants and foreigners. However, while Czech society is more open to co-existence with foreigners than eleven years ago, views about co-existence with the Roma have not changed fundamentally over the last ten years.

Prevailing attitudes to Roma in Czech society are still negative and, according to a majority, the cause of this lies on the side of the Roma. The public generally takes the Roma as people who abuse the social system and refuse to integrate into the labour market. Viewing the inhabitants of excluded localities as people who do not deserve help and who have themselves caused their plight diminishes the willingness of the public to spend public funds on integration policies, and indirectly confirms an acceptance of the social exclusion of the Roma as a solution to a situation in which the Roma live outside of the labour market and reject a way of life based on employment and wages. More than 90 per cent of the respondents believe that the Roma do not want to work, and abuse welfare allowances. The same opinion held in 1994 and 1996, although the numbers have slightly declined (by 3 per cent in comparison with 1996). The opinion that the root of the problem is not to be found in the social system or the labour market, but on the side of the Roma, still prevails and represents an important factor which has to be taken into account. It may be expected that mainstream society will ask why help should be provided to someone who is not seen as a victim of the system but who is viewed as profiting from it.

Co-existence with the Roma and the existence of socially excluded Roma localities gain importance, particularly, in various regional contexts. This fact is reflected in the differing emphasis ascribed to this issue by regional and national politicians. Thus it became an important driving force during pre-election struggles in municipal and even Senate elections, which have a specifically regional character stemming from the nature of two-round electoral systems with single winners. The public's declared sense of urgency that the problem of socially excluded localities must be resolved is clearly linked with the number of excluded in the area as well as with a general feeling of the structural backwardness of a region, in particular its economic and social dynamic and the state of its infrastructure. The highest overall level of dissatisfaction regarding the resolution of such regional problems appears among inhabitants of the Ústí and Karlovy Vary regions, with an above-average number of socially excluded Roma localities and a higher concentration of Roma inhabitants. The resolution of issues around structural shortcomings of the regions is declared to be as urgent as those associated with the presence of excluded localities. Although socially excluded Roma localities are seen as the predominant problem here, the inhabitants of this region also perceive the shortage or poor quality of schools, health care and social services and the shortage of job opportunities as an urgent problem—and to a greater extent than the other inhabitants of the Czech Republic. At the same time, this region is the one most often referred to as the preferred destination for Roma moving from other parts of the Czech Republic. This form of migration (mainly from Prague and Central Bohemia) results in a further deepening of structural backwardness of the socially excluded localities.

It is the combination of these conditions that probably led to the success of the Workers' Party in the last election. The general form of structural under-development within a region, which is linked to the existence of excluded localities and a below-average level of belief in the possibility of major changes in these areas, creates a complicated public environment for the implementation of programmes. This applies all the more so in regions with a high concentration of excluded localities. On the other hand, these regions are characterised by clear public awareness of the need to resolve this problem. In other words, despite the fact that proximity to or experience of excluded Roma localities increases the percentage of sceptics as to the possibility for fundamental change in the life of their inhabitants, these experiences also augment the demands for the local and regional administrative authorities to find solutions to this problem.

In summary, the existence of socially excluded Roma localities represents a key issue in those regions where they are found. The greater the sense of urgency surrounding problems connected with these localities, the greater the expectations from the political bodies. Because the mainstream political parties were not able to cope with this issue, a part of the population is seeking new alternatives. The parties of the radical right represent such an option.

The vicious circle of Czech discourse on Roma

In principle, the Czech public distinguishes two main explanations of the source of the problems of co-existence with the Roma minority: racial or ethnic dissimilarity and social differences.

Racial and ethnic explanations mainly accentuate the insurmountable impact of racial origin. These explanations describe the Roma as lazy by nature, with a tendency to abuse opportunities. In addition to the ethnic and nationalist frame, this range of views also extends to include an explicit biological-racial discourse used by respondents to explain the incompatibility of the life of the Roma with the style and rules of mainstream society. However, such racial interpretations do not necessarily entail support of strictly racist political methods, nor of political extremism, to solve this problem. Considering those who firmly and totally emphasise incompatibility, it may be presumed that they will also be inclined towards restrictive and segregationist policies.

Explanations which stress the social roots of the problems refer mainly to the shortage of opportunities for the Roma and also to the relationship of the mainstream population to this minority. Those who are firmly wedded to this interpretation are more likely to admit the disadvantageous set-up of the educational system in relation to Roma boys and girls and the closed nature of the labour market. Adherents of this type of explanation also acknowledge that there are issues around the activities of state bodies and the public administration.

Interestingly, the proportion of respondents who choose the ethnic and racial interpretation of the problem has not changed over the last ten years. The word 'racial' does not reflect an externally imputed extremism here, but was adopted in response to respondents who expressly consider the Roma as a diametrically different group. This opinion is best illustrated by the high level of support for the statement that the Roma are another race and will not adapt themselves or change. The share of respondents who agree with this interpretation has fluctuated at around 80 per cent over the long term. However, the share of those inclined to adopt nationalist views (the Roma do not behave as responsible citizens because they are not Czechs) has increased in comparison with ten years ago. The numbers of those agreeing that the Roma face discrimination in education and at the point of joining the labour market has slightly increased, though to a mere one third of the Czech population. The final report on the first two surveys, carried out in 1994 and 1996, on the ethnic climate, described the degree of racialised opinion as massive and alarming. The situation has not improved at all almost ten years later. This may be related to the fact that over this time Czech society has built a more defined symbolic border separating itself from the Roma, closing itself off from the Roma world, or at least squeezing it out to the peripheries of vision. Only a minority see the blame for this situation lying on the side of attitudes among the majority and many more claim the cause of this increased separation is the Roma, their ethnic identity and ethnic character.

This, the most widespread explanation of problems with the Roma minority, is connected with the way that Czechs imagine their relations with all other ethnic groups—which is based on the notion of racial and ethnic dissimilarity. People who are willing to be more accommodating of minority lifestyles[8] tend to see the source of conflicts in social background and circumstances. However, those people represent a tiny minority—approximately 5 per cent of Czech society. More than 40 per cent of respondents assert that members of different ethnic groups should adapt fully to the lifestyle and culture of mainstream society. Ironically, those who demand full adaptation to Czech culture and society also tend to emphasise the racial and ethnic interpretation of differences.[9] Thus they demand full assimilation from members of other ethnic groups while believing that the Roma are unable to assimilate due to their otherness. This is one of the paradoxes that emerge out of the prevailing cultural and social impenetrability of Czech society and out of its strong and long-lasting inclination towards demanding cultural and linguistic homogeneity, and a uniform lifestyle among its citizens.

This is, once again, an area where broader views impact on attitudes to the Roma. The promotion of cultural and social homogenisation dominated the entire communist period, when these were not only doctrines but practical policies enforced across the board, beginning with basic social arrangements and ending with petty issues of everyday life. Political and cultural diversity were, in brief, anathema. A certain role was played here by the long term inclination of Czech policy towards segregationist solutions for national tensions and conflicts, tendencies which resulted in the dissolution of the federal state with the Slovaks.

As we saw earlier, most of those who consider problems of co-existence with the Roma in terms of racial dissimilarity also consider the existence of socially excluded Roma localities as a serious problem in their region or municipality. These people also very clearly distinguish the world of mainstream society from the world of the Roma minority and are more likely to believe that the Roma can never fully adapt. Fifty per cent of those who rated Roma localities as a serious problem in their region definitely believe that the Roma are another race and are incapable of change or adaptation. Among that small section of the population (15 per cent) who do not believe that the Roma are a serious local/regional problem, this racial/inadaptable viewpoint is held by only 35 per cent of the respondents.

This variation in racial explanation found in our surveys reflects everyday discourse. Mainstream Czech anti-Gypsy expression does not make use of ethnic or racial terms at all but uses instead certain code-words, like 'inadaptables' and 'fellow citizens'. Thus, if a Czech refers to 'our fellow citizens' in a conversation, everyone knows to whom he/she refers. Note that though these words themselves are racially neutral and sound objective, the content of these expressions is strongly racial. This is a case of old ethno-racial wine in a new bottle with a formally ethnically-neutral vignette.

Furthermore, the emphasis in such discourse on the inadaptability of 'fellow citizens' extends and deepens the existing rupture between the majority and the Roma by stressing the impossibility of change.

The situation here corresponds to Gregory Bateson's concept of the double bind, which refers to a paradoxical form of communication in which an individual (or group) receives two or more conflicting messages, with one message negating the other. The Czech political discourse is thus trapped into a kind of schizophrenic loop composed of these contradictory signals. And as Gregory Bateson warns, 'almost any part of a double bind sequence may then be sufficient to precipitate panic or rage' (Bateson, 1972). This is a crucial point if one wishes to enter the deeper layers of the Czech integration debate. Discourse like this limits public trust in the possibility of integration at the same time as preparing the ground on which a new radical rhetoric can grow, a rhetoric which rejects this schizoid loop and describes the problems of co-existence with the Roma in a straightforward and 'convincing' racial fashion.

Conclusions

Czech public opinion perceives co-existence with the Roma as a problem resulting from the presence of an ethnically dissimilar and un-adapted population within mainstream society, not simply as a problem resulting from the presence of an extremely poverty-stricken social layer within society. While Czech society has become more open to co-existence with foreigners over the past ten years, ideas about co-existence with the Roma have not changed fundamentally. The more intensely respondents perceive the existence of Roma localities as posing an urgent social problem, the more they consider co-existence with the Roma in terms of ethnic and racial dissimilarity. Direct contact with the localities (through neighbourhood relations) makes people more sceptical of proposals for overcoming differences.

Whether or not people are able to admit the social dimension and not just focus on its ethnic aspects is particularly significant. This is crucial in determining opinions as to which institutions should play a role in dealing with the socially excluded localities and whether respondents support being offered to encourage the participation of the Roma themselves. The more people admit a social dimension to the problem, the more likely they are to agree that state bodies have a role to play in the resolution of these problems and should provide support for activities performed by Roma. At the same time such respondents express more optimism that the inhabitants of socially excluded localities may change their lives and living conditions. However, only a tiny minority of Czechs are willing to countenance a social dimension of these problems.

The popularity of the extreme right-wing Workers' Party increased in regions where inhabitants are more receptive to racial explanations of problems between Roma and other Czechs. A significant proportion of these regions perceives Roma localities in the first place as a security risk. On the other hand, structural shortcomings of these regions are perceived as of the same order of political urgency as the presence of 'excluded localities'. These views are very often combined with a higher level of dissatisfaction with aspects of regional and municipal policies than the national average—especially as concerns the shortage or poor quality of schools, health care, social services and job opportunities. The situation is aggravated by the fact that the public in these regions also have greater expectations of political bodies. There is then a genuine danger that if they feel frustrated by the inactivity of these bodies, they will be willing to move to alternative political voices outside the mainstream. In terms of Rydgren's list we find here the combination of socio-cultural cleavages, post-industrial decline and a strong feeling of political discontent (Rydgren, 2002). The combination of perceived structural shortcomings, dissatisfaction with economic development and hostility to a distinct ethnic group presents a breeding ground for the popularity of extreme right-wing rhetoric to grow.

Even though conditions in northern Bohemia might help to increase the popularity of radical right parties, the number of their voters is still relatively low compared with other European countries. Why? Firstly, the radical right parties lack a charismatic leader—a figure like Wilders, Haider or even Le Pen. Secondly, there is the relatively low number of immigrants in the Czech Republic. The Czech radical right parties define themselves only against Roma. And the proportion of Roma is not as high as in Hungary, for example. Moreover in the regions where the radical right does appeal to voters, anti-Roma rhetoric is part of the discourse of mainstream parties already. For example, in 2008, Jiří Šulc, former governor of the Usti region, from the Civic Democracy Party (ODS) put up three large-scale banners displaying the slogan 'Work, gadjos, for our better future'.[10] More generally, anti-Roma attitudes are not connected in Czech discourse only with extremist political parties, and they are very often hidden behind formally ethnic-neutral statements. As we have seen, anti-Roma attitudes are shared by the majority of Czech citizens and mainstream parties rely on this. But they play a double game. Even though their discourse is racially neutral and sounds objective on first consideration, its content is in essence strongly racial. This fact limits the opening for the radical right to gain broad public support at present, but it probably constitutes a potential for broader support in the future, if current government policy fails to improve conditions in north Bohemia and other such regions. Last but not least, in other European countries radical right parties have proven successful on a national level after a period of registered gains in local municipalities. The current Czech radical right parties have yet to share this experience. In the last election to local municipalities, in autumn 2010, the Workers' Party won 0.22 per cent.

The data presented above shows that the increasing popularity of far right-wing parties cannot be explained merely by the existence of socially excluded localities with different ethnic backgrounds. Equally important factors are the structural under-development of certain regions, the activity of political bodies and the broad contours of political discourse in the Czech Republic. All integration policies have to overcome deep-rooted beliefs that the life of the socially excluded and residence in these enclaves is, in truth, somewhat convenient for the Roma and in a sense 'corresponds' to their cultural or ethnic nature. Breaking this barrier is a prerequisite for changing the ethnic climate as regards the possibility for overcoming social exclusion and developing collective and individual solutions to Romany poverty, unemployment and under-education. A strategy of promoting individual achievements and finding exceptions may help weaken this prevailing opinion. Understanding and acceptance of the fact that a considerable proportion of the Roma do not like life in these enclaves will increase the urgency of finding a solution to this situation. On the other hand, a strengthening of attitudes and beliefs that emphasise racial differences may result in the strengthening of far-right parties or far-right rhetoric in the political arena. There is much still to be fought for in this field.

5

LEFT-WING PROGRESS?

NEO-NATIONALISM AND THE CASE
OF ROMANY MIGRANTS IN ITALY

Giovanni Picker

Introduction

In May 2008 Italian Prime Minister Silvio Berlusconi signed a decree declaring the 'state of emergency in relation to settlements of communities of nomads'.[1] Within nine days, an ordinance was issued by the government ordering identification (including fingerprints) of people 'also of minor age' living in the 'nomad camps'.[2] Five weeks later this decree was condemned by a European Parliament resolution stating, 'collecting fingerprints of Roma [...] would clearly constitute an act of direct discrimination based on race and ethnic origin'.[3] Nevertheless, the Italian government continued collecting personal data, and on 27 July 2008 the Minister of Interior, Roberto Maroni, gave a justificatory speech to the Parliament that led to numerous heated criticisms. Maroni's explicit rhetorical rationale was that the salutary goal of the emergency status was to give identity to those living in the nomad camps lacking ID cards. His clear concern during the speech was to work around the potential accusation of racism by stressing that 'in the ordinance we never speak about Roma, but only about nomad camps. Therefore, this is not an ethnicity-based measure, but one which deals with a *de facto* situation [situazione di fatto], meaning the unauthorised nomad camps'.[4]

This series of events in spring and summer 2008 was part of everyday national politics vis-à-vis Roma in contemporary Italy; after the Berlusconi election of 2008 the government seemed to carry out a consistent 'boundary-making process separating "us" from "them"'. Frequent forced evictions, political rhetoric blaming Roma for creating insecurity, and intolerance in political speeches, characterise the political discourse (Loy, 2009; Tavani, 2005).[5] Due to its relevance and its rather grave character, this discourse merits close and critical attention.

The four major topics in such discourse were almost identical to the main themes in Maroni's speech, namely:

1. Deviance: Roma are said to be dangerous, and often criminals.
2. Nomadism: Roma are said to be vagrants, and for this reason hardly able to adapt to a modern sedentary way of life.
3. Security and legality: Roma are a threat for urban and national security, and the citizenry must be protected in everyday life with substantial policy measures.
4. The necessity of social policies and assistance coordinated between national and local authorities: Roma need to be assisted by social policies that can guarantee social integration in order to prevent deviance from spreading amongst them.

This discourse and its associated policies were part of a deep-rooted xenophobic tradition against Roma in Italy (Colacicchi, 2008; Piasere, 2005) but contained two key innovations that make an analysis of its constitutive elements rather difficult. First, this was one of the first occasions when a usually locality-based issue, i.e. the 'Gypsy problem' (Sigona, 2005), became a national issue, paving the way for national measures. Second, the definition of those four major issues cannot be easily identified as deriving from a particular political culture, being neither clearly centre-left or centre right-wing. In other words, this is not simply another instance of a typical right-wing exclusionary idiom opposed to the social integration and multiculturalism traditionally associated with left-wing politics.

Beyond the problematic intersection of anti-immigration sentiments and the anti-Roma legacy in Italian policies, a central feature of approaches to Roma in Italy has been the trope of nomadism.[6] Nando Sigona (2003) has shown how the assumption of nomadism underpinning regional policies was used to label Roma fleeing Kosovo in the 1990s as nomads and 'keep them as "enemies", not "strangers"' (ibid, 76), secluding them into camps.[7] Migration is thus, in reference to the Roma, reframed as a putatively cultural practice: nomadism.

In this chapter I will analyse a specific case of the relationship between migration and the political left: the management by the Tuscan council of the immigration of Roma. My question is the following: to what extent since the arrival of Romany migrants has the left-wing regional council been able to recognise Roma difference while treating them equally and granting them equal rights? I will show how the legacy of radically exclusionary policies concerning Romany migrants by the Italian and, to a certain extent, the European left, has been accompanied by a 'merciful' ethno-nationalist idiom. In this way, the current nationalist idiom, which consists of two overlapping discourses—of social integration and deviance—can be seen to rest on a hazy and incoherent category of 'nomads'.

The left and the Roma in Italy

Studies focusing on the material living conditions of the Roma and their position in the symbolic social hierarchy in the cities of Bologna (Però, 1999), Rome (Clough Marinaro, 2003) and Florence (Colacicchi, 1996; Szente, 1997) demonstrate a familiar pattern from the end of the 1980s—the creation of a permanent status of segregation and fear of Roma induced by city authorities. Police actions of various kinds, both authorised and arbitrary, such as evictions, controls and stopping and searching cars driven by Roma, have occurred frequently. Interestingly, Bologna, Rome and Florence all have a long history of left-wing politics, and the studies just mentioned were carried out when each of them was governed by a left-wing mayor,[8] under whose administrations Romany migrants were given 'nomad camps' as a solution to their housing problems. This involvement of left-wing local governments in the exclusionary management of Romany migrants continues as I write.

In 2007, the left-wing mayor of Rome, Valter Weltroni, became the leader of the Democratic Party (Partito Democratico), which was the only opposition to the Berlusconi coalition, House of Liberty (Casa della Libertà'), in the 2008 election. In the aftermath of the so-called 'Mailat case', in which a Romanian citizen, Mr Mailat, temporarily staying in a shanty, was the only person accused of the murder of an Italian citizen, Ms Reggiani,[9] Veltroni declared:

We have to begin sending people back [to their country of origin] otherwise it won't be possible to cope with the issue [of security] in Turin, Rome and Milan. […] If one country wants to stay in Europe, it has to respect the rules. It [Europe] cannot open all our doors (*boccaporti*) and send people from one country to the other. ('Sicurezza: Veltroni carica I sindaci: via al rimpatrio o nessuno ce la fa', *La Repubblica*, 31 Ottobre 2007).

These kinds of extraordinary statements from a left-wing mayor have to be understood in the long-term development of policies towards Roma.

The first significant modern influx of Roma to Italy occurred in the second half of the 1970s, when the crisis of the Yugoslav economic model began to be evident. Just a few years previously the first attempts to regulate immigration had been implemented at a local level.[10] Due to the novelty of this phenomenon, and the related lack of institutional experience to face it, there has never been an integrated national policy vis-à-vis Roma. Instead, since the mid 1980s, a number of regional laws have been passed.[11] Almost always these the laws have been designed to incorporate knowledge of Romany social life provided by 'experts', i.e. civil society groups working with Roma, more often referred to as 'Gypsies' (Zingari) and 'nomads'.

These organisations draw on a culture of dealing with the Roma that has a long history in Italy. In the introduction to his social history of the education of Roma in Italy, historian Luca Bravi (2009) argues that 'today, the old stereotypes about Roma are still the same of those that brought Roma into the perimeter of Auschwitz: many "Gypsies" are still viewed as strangers characterized by nomadism, by asocial behaviours, and by theft considered as a way of life' (ibid: 17). The Italian system of education has historically reserved a special position for Roma and Sinti, with a mixture of inclusionary and exclusionary policies (ibid). Indeed, while education has traditionally been one of the most important grounds of dispute between the two major political forces, i.e. the Christian Democrats (DC party— Democrazia Cristiana) and the Communists (PCI party—Partito Communista Italiano), traditionally the education of Roma and Sinti has been inspired by ideologies drawn from both political forces. This may explain why educational policies for the Roma have never been completely inclusionary nor completely exclusionary activities.

It is within such a well-rooted tradition—positioned equidistantly between left-wing and Christian Democrat politics—that the most influential organisation on the education of Roma and Sinti, Opera Nomadi (Charitable Organisation for Nomads—ON), operated. In particular, as the major consultant of regional councils for drafting regional laws on Roma, it contributed significantly to coining the idiom with which Roma were viewed and which circulated in the first legislative texts on them. The first efforts of ON aimed to provide a place where 'nomads' could live and regularly attend classes in schools. These places, called '*aree sosta*' (stop areas) or '*centri sosta*' (stop centres), started to appear in the peripheries of big cities in the late 1960s. They were conceived as places where 'nomads' could come to a halt anywhere in the country during their travels, and in doing so not lose their own 'culture'. 'Culture' was viewed by ON as:

A set of rites, customs, uses, elaborated within an idealised past. These elements [were] considered at risk of extinction in industrial and capitalist society. This was a culture-tradition which [could be seen] to be either the cause of the 'delay' [in the process of development] of Roma or as a system from which to choose which elements to preserve and which to reject (Bravi and Sigona, 2007: 865; my translation).

To dig deeper into the links between left-wing politics and Romany migrants, I will narrow my focus here to Tuscany and its main city Florence, where the camp population of Roma in 1994 was about 1100, but had declined to about 600 in 2006. Since 1970, the year when Italian regions became governed by elected administrative bodies, Tuscany has been constantly ruled by the left (Socialists—PSI, Communists—PCI, and, later, Social Democrats—PDS/DS).[12]

The end of the 1980s: Tuscany and its 'nomads'

As far as Tuscany is concerned, the 'social Catholicism' within which ON's activities were carried out was also one of the main ideological references of the first policies concerning Roma. The major leader of the 'Tuscan' declination of 'social Catholicism' is Ernesto La Pira, who has twice been mayor of Florence, from 1950 to 1956, and from 1960 to 1964, and a prominent figure in the Italian constituent assembly (*assemblea costituente*).[13] His approach was based on political values such as non-violence, internationalism, social policy for the poor and ecumenism, and his political affiliation has always been the Christian Democrats. It is within this tradition, which can be called 'social Catholicism',[14] that the first attempts to face the '*problema Zingari*' in Tuscany were carried out.

In April 1987, a regional councillor, Giancarlo Niccolai, belonging to the 'Lapirian' current, proposed a law (17/88), which was entitled 'Interventions for the Protection (*tutela*) of Roma Ethnie (*etnia Rom*)',[15] and which received unanimous approval from the left-wing regional council. During his speech to the regional council, the councillor justified the bill by explicitly referring to the 'protection of nomads' as an ethnic and linguistic minority whose needs were currently absent from the national and regional agenda. According to Niccolai, the 'nomads' faced a range of difficult problems:

[1] We see, also in big cities like Florence, informal camps without essential services such as water, hygienic utilities, with repercussions for the health conditions of the inhabitants. [2] In addition to these disadvantages, difficulties stemming from the lack of work are also present, [3] illiteracy, as a consequence of lack of education [...] and this situation represents a risk for young people and their behaviour which sometimes reaches the margins of the legal framework. (Regione Toscana 1987: 1; my translation)

He further explained the goals of the law:

1. To promote the implementation of the camps (*campi sosta*) for sedentary people (*sedentatizzati*) and transit areas (*aree di transito*) [for those who travel], and set up health and social services for the guests who are staying.
2. To safeguard the positive values of the nomadic culture, and especially folk arts and crafts, through:
   – Ad hoc initiatives aimed at the development and production of handmade goods;
   – Financial support for the creation of handicraft work within the camp.
3. To provide school education for persons below eighteen-years-old, and combat illiteracy.

After defining the problems and declaring the intention to solve them, Niccolai concluded his speech by alluding to 'the civic tradition which has always characterised Tuscany', underlining the importance of 'reception' (*accoglienza*) as a distinctive value of their tradition (quoted in Rossa 1995: 43; my translation). In the text it was never mentioned that the Roma were migrants and foreigners. Rather, the law was framed within a discourse on 'nomadism'. It is important to analyse this discourse and its political context, considering both the particular text of the law and the debates around its approval.

Before proposing the bill, and in order to improve the proposed text, the regional council commission dealing with 'Health and Social Care' held consultations with some civil society organisations that were experienced in the field, having dealt previously with problems involving 'nomads'. The whole discussion was articulated in view of a clear goal: to allow the cultural preservation of this 'ethnie', through 1. Education, 2. Housing and 3. Social services (Regione Toscana, 1987). The rationale of the discussion was to reinforce the legitimacy of the incommensurable dichotomy between a sedentary culture or way of life and a nomadic culture, between us/Tuscans and them/nomads. That such a dichotomy existed was taken as unquestioned conventional wisdom by all participants in the meeting. The following dialogue between one of the consultants, who criticises the text of the law for not underlining the difference between our and their lifestyles, and the president of the commission, is instructive:

CONSULTANT: One of the fundamental dimensions of the Gypsy way of life is a nomadic style. It is important to state this, because […] there are [in the text of the law] some elements in favour of those who decide not to be nomadic any more, and in this way it fails to give enough guarantees to those who are still nomadic. The latter do not carry out a nomadic way of life just because they have not reached a higher degree of maturity, but because this lifestyle belongs to a fundamental dimension [of their persons] (ibid: 14).

The commission president then attempted to clarify what the consultant had just said:

PRESIDENT OF THE COMMISSION: This law is a product of our culture, and it could not be otherwise. Thus, drawing on this consideration we can say that the fact that it is a product of our culture does not mean that it should overwhelm other cultures which are currently in our region (ibid: 28).

This dialogue suggests a deep irreconcilable difference in patterns of behaviour between Roma and non-Roma. It could thus be argued that what was being represented was an 'insurmountable barrier to do what comes naturally to humans, in principle, namely, communicating' (Stolcke, 1995: 8). A further element of such a 'barrier' is its sense of a privileged position, of distance; Roma were not consulted beforehand, nor were they present during these discussions.

And nor did the law provide any real help for the Roma. In the autumn of 1987, a roadblock was organised by some of the inhabitants of Castello, a neighbourhood on the outskirts of Florence. The protest was against about a hundred people who were driving around without a fixed place to stay, just living in damaged caravans (Colacicchi, 1996). On 13 October 1987, the local authorities ordered 'the transfer of those nomads to an open-air area owned by the local council located in Olmatello Street, at the very edge of the city'.[16] A few months later, the us/them idiom was concretised when the municipality began to enclose the area with a thick, high permanent wall, and caravans and containers started to appear inside. All this was done on the basis of the 1987 law.

The 1990s: Time of crisis

The political crisis that began after Tito died in 1980 and finally brought Yugoslavia to its collapse in the early 1990s had a significant impact on the Florentine camps. Many Roma fleeing persecution in both the Bosnian and the Kosovo war entered Italy in order to join their relatives who had migrated westward since the mid-1970s.[17] Those who arrived in Florence found a shelter in the Poderaccio area, the only non-fenced place in the city in which they could stay, although in very precarious material conditions. This migration led to a new attempt to legislate for Romany difference, with a law designed on the basis of dedicated empirical investigations carried out by an influential think-tank, the Fondazione Michelucci,[18] a major consult-ant of the regional council who were employed at this time to investigate conditions in the Roma camps. Michelucci's key finding was that the Roma in Florence were not in fact nomads. Only a handful of the Roma in Tus-cany were still pursuing a nomadic way of life (Marcetti et al., 1993), and as a result a new bill concerning Roma should be proposed.

The 75/1995 regional law, abrogating the previous one, was entitled 'Interventions for the Roma and Sinti Peoples'. The most important differ-ence with the previous law was the linguistic shift from places of transit ('camps' or 'furnished transit areas') to places of permanent residence ('equipped residential areas') (*Aree attrezzate per il transito* and *Aree attrezzate residenziali*). Councillors began to ask for a census of the population living in the camps. A group of them decided to go and visit the camps in order to 'concretely implement projects which could answer to the needs of the inhabitants of the camps' (Rossa, 1996:94).[19]

The Michelucci research was an incisive critique of the camp as a housing solution for the Roma. The entire document was organised around a bino-mial principle: on one side there is 'Romany culture' (*cultura rom*), and on the other there is 'urbanism', which can either draw on a refusal (*rifiuto*) or reception (*accoglienza*) by the city's inhabitants. The researchers' agenda was to demonstrate empirically that the camps were not an appropriate housing solution, because they did not fit 'Romany culture'.[20] Stemming from this analysis the researchers proposed that little houses be constructed for the Roma, not at the margins of urban areas but within them. Different patterns of houses were proposed according to the exigencies of the local host society and the 'Romany culture'. The research represented the first attempt to authentically understand the Roma's requests and claims; and, in effect, the 75/1995 law partially removed the barrier between Romany immigrants and regional authorities: although the idiom of nomadism was used in the first law it is not the only one used in the new law. However, the text of the 1995 law did not shift the idiom away from the culturalist one of the 1987 law, and this was the most fundamental element of continuity between the first and the second law. A closer look at the 1995 law will illustrate this point in detail.

The preamble to law 75/1995 states in its first article:

This law dictates the norms for the preservation of Romany cultural patrimony and of Roma and Sinti identity, in order to facilitate the communication between cultures, to grant the right to a nomadic life, to religious practice, to stop and to stay within the regional territory. Moreover the right to enjoy access to social, health and school services is granted.

Since the influential Michelucci Foundation stressed the importance of adequate housing solutions for 'Gypsy culture', this element can be seen as attaching a new importance to the territorial dimension. Therefore, in the political construction of the Romany issue 'culture' assumes a strictly territory-based meaning. In other words, while the 1987 law was wrong in identifying all Roma as nomads (as the Michelucci research revealed), in the 1995 law it is still upon differences of territorial and housing habits from the majority population that the 'Romany culture' is assumed to be based.

In sum, the passage between the first and the second law shows that the idiom with which Romany migrants were framed by the left-wing Tuscan authorities remained predicated upon 'culturalist fundamentalism' (Stolcke, 1995). In the first law (17/1988), the culturalist idiom was exclusively related to nomadism, and in the second law (75/1995) it was still related to the link between people and territory, specifically housing habits recognised as somehow peculiar and partially different from the ones of the local society/culture.

And such official discourse, of course, had its vernacular concomitant. The Florentine media discourse of that period was mainly focused on the increased number of Roma fleeing the Yugoslav conflicts and settling in the Florentine camps. In particular, local committees of citizens protesting against the presence of the camps were a recurrent and predominant topic in the local press.[21] The idiom deployed in newspapers to define the presence of Roma and the reasons for the necessity of evicting them from the municipal territory was very close to that used in the two regional laws. While the law said 'they are different, therefore their culture should be protected', the citizens' committees appeared to be simply citing the law in their own terms, saying 'they are different, therefore they should either adapt to our rules or leave our land'.

Left-wing policy and its legacy: 'exclusive inclusion'?

In this way, the rigid cultural boundaries drawn by the first and second laws can be seen as the major sources of today's popular understanding of social integration of Romany migrants in Florence. In 2000 a new law was passed (2/2000) which aimed at:

safeguarding identity and the social development of Roma and Sinti in order to facilitate communication between cultures, to grant the right of nomadism, of religion, as well as the right to stop and to stay within the regional territory accessing social, healthcare and school services.

The 2000 law allowed Roma to access social housing, and 'to be part of a social integration project which has provided a way to autonomy and recognition to about 110 Roma within the regional territory' (Scioscia, 2009: 157). This law became the major framework within which to carry out publication. Yet what happened to the camps? On the basis of the new law, on 25 September 2001, an order was approved planning the restructuring of Poderaccio in order to relocate some families living in the shanty nearby to the new site. Relocation had to happen according to three main criteria: 'historic' factors, i.e. the presence of individual Roma at certain key moments of the area's social life; holding a permit of residence (valid so long as a majority of each household had this), and sending children to school. In addition, there were other, less formal, criteria, which were raised once placement interviews with families started to be held.

In order to illustrate the logic by which the authorities operated, I transcribe here parts of a long meeting I had with Marco in spring 2007, a district-level civil servant responsible for Romany issues, amongst other matters. Marco is an active member of the Democratic Party (PD), the major left-wing national party and the most powerful in Florence. During our meeting, Marco explained to me the ways in which he managed the relocation of the people from Poderaccio.

The last census, carried out in 2002, reported 147 people living there. At the moment of filling-up the new wooden houses, I found in front of me 190 people. So, our decisions have been the following three:

1. To fill up the thirty available houses with thirty families.
2. To ask the regional council to help, with its other projects of social inclusion and reception. This allowed us to place six families in houses.
3. We decided not to host three families, to whom we offered a financial donation. One of them refused our donation.

We took these three interventions without any ethnic discrimination (we didn't care whether they were Ashkaljia, Sinti, Roma, Macedonians…).[22] I don't care about all that. I operate with administrative criteria.

I operated a very analytical analysis of the single families, exactly because there were surplus people, almost forty surplus people. In November 2005 there was the transfer of people to the new second village. I am for multiculturalism: I don't have cultural prejudices, but I am severe in the imposition of rules. I have to say that some cultural approaches arrive at providing an excess of assistance (*posizioni assistenzialistiche*). Many associations hurt the Roma. A university professor was telling me that Roma understand rights but don't understand duties. There is no human being who understands rights without understanding duties. That professor was yelling at me because I was treating them [Roma] as citizens. But are they B-series citizens?

Marco continues with his position regarding general principles, and introduces a category that will subsequently be important in the analysis, i.e. 'unequal right'.

There is a certain cultural resistance by Roma to accept the rules. I explain[ed] [to] them that rules are universal: 'You are citizens just like the others'. But I believe in the unequal right, I don't think like Veltroni [the mayor of Rome] who draws on the principle of equality of possibilities. Yes, I agree, but according to my view there are subjects who don't start from where the others start, but from a much lower stage—due to their biographies, due to abandon. Therefore, they should have different treatment than other citizens, not in a discriminatory sense, but in a positive one.

Here, Marco is talking about rights and duties which, together with national identification, are the other pillars of belonging in the nation state. Rights and duties are, in the civil servant's point of view, the logical reason behind the different treatment of Roma in comparison with any other subjects with whom local authorities deal or have dealt. This treatment is considered by Marco not to be discriminatory [i.e. exclusionary]. However, when our conversation shifts from ideals and principles to practice, he clarifies what, a minute before, he called 'unequal rights':

If a civil servant follows a family for twelve years [follows in terms of providing social care], after which that family does not do anything, and the result of those twelve years is that the family sits down and waits for help, I come and I say: 'Stop!' I say 'No!' to the excess of assistance: people must act by themselves [*darsi da fare*]. This is real welfare [i.e. when people act by themselves]. I give you an example. The assistance period lasts one year, and then we propose […] a project […] well, Roma too must do something! I found you [i.e. Roma] a job, and what do you do? You abandon it only because you live at ten km [away] from your workplace? You cannot do this!! Some of them [Roma] abandon their jobs. Of course, I understand, they are nomad people! I do understand this. But there are also such great workers among Roma.

As is explicit in the last two excerpts, my interlocutor was following a particular reasoning: Roma are disadvantaged for reasons that do not come from them; therefore they must be helped. And if they don't do anything to help themselves this is because of their way of life: they are nomads. Yet, they also have to do something [*devono darsi da fare*]. The logic goes from inclusionary statements to exclusionary ones with a rather surprising simplicity, as if its reasoning—which he told me in a very relaxed atmosphere and as if he had explained it to many people before me—was regarded as self-evident.

It is noteworthy that this 'exclusive inclusion'—i.e. the logic of making Roma part of the society only until the point that cultural barriers become too great—was the leitmotiv of every interview I carried out. To universal civic rights, civil servants impose particularistic cultural barriers. And this logic is at work to keep, maintain, and perpetuate housing isolation and marginalisation. Marco's inclusionary principle therefore did not overcome 'cultural fundamentalism' and the 'culturalist' stance, 'which stresses that the culture to which I am said or claim to belong defines my essence. Cultures (static, finite and bounded ethnolinguistic blocs labelled "French", "Nuer" and so on) determine individual and collective identities, and the subject's place in social and political schemas' (Grillo, 2003: 160).

In 2007 Olmatello camp hosted 137 persons, and Poderaccio about 500 persons. All the inhabitants of the camp I regularly met told me about the excessive heat in summer and the excessive cold in winter; about their continuous fear of being evicted, especially families with little children, who had been told by state and local police that 'eviction might happen in the next few days'. The Olmatello camp had not been the object of intervention—not even after the 2000 law. Notwithstanding the materially precarious conditions there, the major concern of my interlocutors in the local council was the Roma's unbelievable difference. As Clara, a social educator working in the camps for the local council, told me:

Once I was stuck by something a Roma living in a camp told me. He said: 'if I don't get a job, I will go away', and he left for Germany. I would never be able to leave like that, from one day to the next. This is the point: maybe they have this travelling sense (*senso girovago*) in their blood, according to which they can easily travel.

Conclusion: Neo-nationalism and the left in Europe

Studies on the cultural basis of the European Union project have revealed a strong process of othering that is predicated on nationalist premises. In particular, commenting on the efforts carried out by EU officers to create a European symbolism in order to bring the activities of Brussels offices closer to the citizens of the Member States, Shore (2006) writes:

What is striking about these EU culture-building initiatives is the way they echo many of the techniques and methods used by nationalist elites in the nineteenth and twentieth centuries to forge Europe's existing Nation States [...]—precisely the model that EU advocates claim they are seeking to transcend. (2006: 711–12).

Within the more general context of transnationalism and globalisation, Gingrich and Banks (2006) argue that 'it is the EU's own systematic ambivalence of partially being a protective barrier against, as much as partially being a tool for and product of globalisation that therefore sets the systemic and structural standards for neo-nationalist's agency' (2006: 20). This new phenomenon is rather miscellaneous, and does not necessarily combine state and nation as the zone of homogeneity, as was the case in the classic definition of nationalism proposed by Gellner (1983). Rather than a new ideology, neo-nationalism is a social phenomenon involving new forms of community-making along national or regional lines, predicated on a reformulation of the idioms for identifications against the background of uncertainties caused by globalisation.

Studies focusing on the political right have shown a rise of racist stances vis-à-vis migrants that are imbued with the language of culture (Stolcke, 1995; Holmes, 2000; Stacul, 2006). Research on the other side of the political spectrum, i.e. the left, has so far been less intense. However Però (2006) uncovered the presence of a 'non-integrating multiculturalism' (Brah, 1996) in the mainstream left's attitudes towards migrants in Europe. In a later work, the author suggests that 'even so-called progressive forces are largely operating within an exclusionary logic, failing to extend what remains of their egalitarian and universalist principles beyond the narrow boundaries of their own national "imagined community"' (Però, 2007: 142). By setting his ethnography in the 'red city' of Bologna, the author set his study in a privileged context, Italy, in which to analyse the changes in the egalitarian side of the political spectrum.[23] What happened that brought the powerful Italian Left to adopt exclusionary policies appears to be that, historically, the European left has shifted from class-based definitions of migrants (in the 1960s and 1970s) to culture- or ethnicity-based definitions (Però, 2006; 2007). Certainly, notwithstanding the long tradition of political participation and class-based political struggles of the Florentine left, with the arrival of 'new immigrants' at the end of the 1980s this sense of class belonging lost its appeal. This was accompanied by a backlash against a serious politics of equality of socio-economic conditions and political rights, and an uncritical embrace of a neo-liberal agenda.

By making Roma objects whose culture was to be protected, the left-wing Tuscan regional council since the late 1980s planned and brought into being two areas at the extreme periphery of the town in which Romany migrants lived and some still live. This analysis has attempted to unmask the unstated and implicit ethno-nationalist stance underpinning these social policies: relegating people to such places is the material reflection of thinking about them as intrinsically outsiders vis-à-vis 'our own culture', be that Christianity, sedentary habits, or 'the civic tradition of Tuscany'. This reinforces intra-national boundaries that seem to be a common trope in Italian society—the 'neo-localism' that anthropologist Jaro Stacul (2006) has identified as the local main source of modern populist politics.

And if this is correct, responsibility for the popularity and persuasive force of the Berlusconi government's initiatives with which I began this paper lies in places unexpected and formally opposed to his conservative forces.

6

UNDERCLASS GYPSIES

AN HISTORICAL APPROACH ON CATEGORISATION AND EXCLUSION IN FRANCE IN THE NINETEENTH AND TWENTIETH CENTURIES

Ilsen About

On Friday 16 July 2010, a member of the 'Gens du Voyage' ('Travelling People') community was killed by a *gendarme* near Saint-Romain-sur-Cher, a small town in the *département* of Loir-et-Cher. During the next few days, relatives of the young man vented their resentment in the neighbouring town of Saint-Aignan-sur-Cher, where the police unit is stationed. A fifty-strong mob stoned the Gendarmerie's buildings, burned down cars and pieces of street furniture, and hacked down trees on the village square. A several hundred-strong military force was immediately dispatched to restore public order. This unusual midsummer series of events aroused considerable interest in the media, sparking reactions at the highest level of state. Amid growing hostility towards Roma people throughout Europe, these events were quickly hailed as the outcome of the ongoing logic of exclusion of Gypsies in France, reactivating ancient forms of anti-Gypsyism (Filhol, 2010; André, 2010). A few days later, at the other end of the country, gunfire was exchanged between the police and several men trying to escape after robbing a casino in a populous neigbourhood of Grenoble. One *gendarme* was wounded and one robber killed by the police.

Such was the context of the speech given by Nicolas Sarkozy in Grenoble on 30 July 2010, successively alluding to—and linking—crime and immigration, mentioning the 'failure of a fifty-year period of unregulated immigration', and suggesting that 'foreign-born French nationals' convicted of killing a police officer should be stripped of their French citizenship. Moreover, as a response to the riots in Saint-Aignan-sur-Cher, he promised to dismantle all illegal Roma camps (numbering an estimated 500 in France). Simultaneously, a special meeting was convened at the Élysée palace, featuring the Ministers of the Interior, Justice, Immigration, European Affairs, and Housing, as well as the heads of the police forces, the Police nationale and the Gendarmerie. Sarkozy's announcement sparked a heated row between the government and opposition parties and the various human rights organisations defending the 'Travellers', who denounced a two-pronged conflation whereby 'Travelling people/Roma' were linked to 'immigration/crime'.[1] Commentators were quick to recall the existence of the hardly-enforced Besson Act of 31 May 1990, theoretically making it compulsory for towns of more than 5,000 inhabitants to establish facilities for non-sedentary populations. The March 2003 Act on Interior Security, restricting the rights to occupy land, had then led to many barely legal situations, further undermining the daily life of communities (Moffen, 2010).

Around mid-August, about a hundred vehicles blocked the Aquitaine Bridge near Bordeaux to protest the evacuation of a sizeable camp, thus effectively preventing access to the city. After a round of negotiation, with the national media extensively covering this new episode, the city council finally decided to grant them access to another council-owned area. In the early days of September, several newspapers disclosed a presidential circular, dated 5 August 2010, suggesting the 'evacuation of unauthorised camps' in no uncertain terms: 'The President of the Republic, on the 28th of July, has assigned precise objectives for the evacuation of unauthorised camps: 300 illegal camps or settlements must be evacuated within three months time, Roma camps being given priority'.[2] This text, openly targeting the Gypsies (*Tsiganes*) as an ethnic community, was stigmatised by a united opposition front against government policies which seemed to merit the numerous criticisms voiced through the summer of 2010. Mid-September declarations by the European Commissioner for Justice, Fundamental Rights and Citizenship, Viviane Reding, were mainly focused on the necessity of maintaining freedom of circulation for European citizens, and condemning discrimination against Gypsy ethnic minorities, as witnessed in France.

After Viviane Reding's words had been relayed by the press, a particularly fierce exchange took place with the French president.

In October 2010, the press revealed the existence of MENS (French acronym for Non-Sedentary Ethnic Minorities), a database built and maintained by the 'Interministerial task force against travelling crime' ('Cellule interministérielle de lutte contre la délinquance itinérante') and used by the Gendarmerie. This database is said to store information pertaining to three categories of people in particular: 'Travelling people (Gypsies…)'; 'teams from rough urban areas'; 'travelling criminals from Eastern Europe (Roma…)'. One top official in the group explained that it had been created in 1997 to 'provide a new response to manifestations of travelling crime that were incompatible with how both forces, police and Gendarmerie, were organized and articulated, since travelling criminals simply do not abide to administrative and legal borders', although he denied the existence of any 'ethnic' database (Martin, 2010). These revelations, however, revived the debate about the attitude of French authorities towards Roma, in spite of denials from both the national headquarters of the Gendarmerie and the Ministry of the Interior. A formal complaint was subsequently lodged by several human rights groups to condemn the use of an ethnic, illegal and undeclared database.

During the summer of 2010, in an unpredictable succession of events, the legal position of the Roma and 'Gens du Voyage', the metaphoric and official qualification of the supposedly non-sedentary communities, was put at the top of the security policy agenda by the government of the French Republic. From the outset, the right-wing party led by Nicolas Sarkozy took a harsh stance towards the 'Roma' immigrants, who had long been accused of being a major criminal community, illegally occupying camps that were never officially declared to the municipality, and denounced as illegal immigrants.

In an incredible move to generalise the issue, the denunciation also included every 'nomadic camp' existing on French territory, as well as their dwellers, although they had long been legally integrated into the French national community by rules of citizenship. During this 'summer of shame', as it is now called by pro-Roma activist organisations, the 'securitarian turn' ('virage sécuritaire') not only targeted so-called 'illegal immigrants'—who actually happened to be EU citizens, eligible to travel to every Schengen country—but anyone linked to 'Gypsy' communities. Some invoked the dark years of the Vichy regime and the persecutions of the Gypsy people during the Second World War in France and Europe; others denounced 'fascist' methods and reactionary politics. Maybe the most accurate characterisation of these events is even more pessimistic: a glance at history shows that the targeting of 'the Gypsy' and the associated waves of rejection, intolerance and legal exclusion or physical deportation should not be seen of episodic or unexpected turning points in modern French history. Rather, they seem to be the regular product of a long Republican tradition stigmatising the Gypsy community through a complex system of police regulation, administrative statuses, identification and control practices, constant surveillance, and rejection of the so-called 'nomadic' way of life. In other words, the attack on 'the Roma' during the summer of 2010 was in a certain way overdetermined by the administrative history of France's treatment of its Gypsies (Canut, 2011).

Proper analysis of the genealogy of the 2010 summer crisis involves looking deep into the history of the Republican regime, established at the end of the nineteenth century, in order to understand the ambiguous stance of the French Republic towards the Gypsy community. In 1912, a conjunction of circumstances lead to the creation of a special status for the Gypsies, epitomised by the creation of the 'anthropometric notebook for nomads' ('carnet anthropométrique des nomades'), one of the first biometric and portable identity documents in Europe. This document, which was only abolished in 1969—when it was replaced by the 'Carnet de circulation'—successfully legitimised the discriminating practices this community had been subjected to at all levels of the French public security apparatus, from local to central. The establishment of this document resulted from an interesting dialectic which, although it was common to many other European countries of the time, had specific features as far as the French case was concerned.

An historical overview of the relationship between the French state and the Gypsies throughout the twentieth century will show how the creation of a legal and administrative category locked these individuals into a 'paper trap'. In fact, it seems that the daily requirements of the documents imposed on Gypsies were meant as a system for controlling geographic mobility as well as exerting genealogical surveillance on families and related families through filiation and matrimonial links. In a way, this very peculiar legal apparatus liberated the expression of intolerance and allowed the implementation in the functioning of the state and municipal institutions of the idea that a juridical and practical exclusion was both necessary and urgent. But at the same time, the underclass found itself divided into fractions defined by a degree of weakness. Interconnected families, with strong ties to a given territory or even sedentarised, were better protected than isolated groups or travellers who strayed from traditional routes of circulation. In this hierarchy, 'international Gypsies', understood as those who engaged in transborder migration in caravans, constituted the most targeted sub-category. At the same time, they were excluded from the French state's 'nomadic' category, because of their supposed foreignness, and they could not claim the 'right' to possess a 'carnet anthropométrique' with all its attendant benefits. On the other hand, they were fully considered as Gypsies and were particularly targeted as Gypsies, nomads, foreigners, and illegals.

It is precisely when the Law defines a sub-category of resident non-citizens, on the basis of nationality, ethnic identification or way of life, that the possibility of becoming an outlaw moves from being a risk to part of the normal order of things. In this way, the history of the French legal categorisation of the Gypsy population demonstrates the intense and progressive involvement of the state apparatus and its role in creating an underclass, repeatedly excluded and rejected by authorities.

'La Question Tsigane': The emergence of the 'Gypsy Issue' in the nineteenth century

During the second half of the nineteenth century, French public authorities were willing to regulate more stringently and more accurately the domestic movements of people, with a particular emphasis on the countryside, criss-crossed by many individuals on the fringe of society. In the wake of the industrial revolution, economic and social transformations undermined living conditions in rural areas and triggered previously unheard-of movements of population. As a rural exodus set more and more people on the road, regulating vagrancy gradually became a key policing issue (Chatelain, 1976; Wagniart, 1999). During the Second Empire, the growing influence of the concept of public order in policing practices led the authoritarian regime of Napoléon III to reorganise police forces in the countryside, creating an increasingly dense police network throughout the country (Payne, 1966; Le Clère & Wright, 1973; Caulier, 2008; Cartayrade, 2008). Local regulations were implemented at the *département* level to supervise the movement of street acrobats, pedlars, and vagrants. In this context, the circulation of Gypsies gave rise to more frequent clashes with police forces and sporadic crises, ultimately leading to the implementation of the first regulatory framework destined to increase and generalise special surveillance of such communities.

Caravans approaching cities, entering villages or crossing border *départements* would elicit a rapid and semi-coordinated response from the police, who subsequently sent their hierarchy numerous reports highlighting how difficult it was to meaningfully control caravans as they travelled across municipalities. Information, too, circulated with increasing speed, through the press in particular. Newspaper articles contributed to the impression of Gypsies in the countryside as a form of 'social plague'. This bears witness to a mutation of Gypsy representations in the modern popular imagination, a mixed bag of fascination, ancient fears and repulsion.

The case of a caravan that was spotted near the Belgian border at the end of May 1866 is particularly significant, reflecting both novel surveillance attempts and the undeniable powerlessness of the authorities. A group of Gypsies arrived in the town of Bettignies, located in northern France, a few hundred metres from the Belgian border (Coupain, 2003; Nézer, 2005). Upon its arrival, the caravan was described as a 'band of ragged Bohemians numbering ten families, maybe sixty to eighty persons with twenty-seven horses and just as many wagons'.[3] The massive, spectacular, clattering arrival of this group stunned the locals, and the police tried to stop them from entering the French territory. Questioning by customs officers revealed, however, that some of them had enough money to pay customs taxes, and owned German passports bearing a visa delivered by the French consulate in Berlin. The police commissioner sent from Maubeuge was thus left with no legal means of expelling them and had no choice but to look on as they set up their camp in the very heart of Bettignies. Instructions sent by the prefect of the Nord *département*, however, explicitly ordered that this caravan be prevented from entering France—neglecting to specify only what means should be used.[4]

The next day, a great hustle and bustle awaited the commissioner, who described the scene as follows:

(…) The men started to vociferate while the women and children implored heaven, and the only way to stop that demonstration was to persuade them that mounted gendarmes were about to come and take them to the border. This had a magical effect: horses were harnessed to their wagons, and the band, escorted by a dozen armed men and the commissioner (…), set out for Belgium. No sooner had they passed the border pole than they started shouting and being rude to the commissioner (…), before fleeing as fast as their small Ukraine horses could.[5]

Following this hurried departure, letters were exchanged with the neighbouring towns to try and track the Gypsies, but no practical measures were taken to enable the police to implement efficient surveillance and the caravan simply vanished.

The whole episode is interesting insofar as it highlights the essentially empirical nature of restrictions on the movement of Gypsy groups in late-Second Empire France. The resources available to the local commissioner looked rather flimsy, as evidenced by the imaginary threat of bringing in the *gendarmes*. In response, the Gypsies had built a solid experience that enabled them to dodge detailed questioning. By using several languages or presenting IDs and visas unknown to the authorities, sometimes even simply illegible, they managed to catch the police, very few of whom were professionals, off-guard. Displaying large amounts of money—a way of inspiring respect or, on the other hand, eliciting defiance—was one more element in this cunning strategy built upon subtle stratagems and self-staging to both impress and confuse others. Generally speaking, mobile Gypsies who roamed the countryside in border areas or in the interior benefited from a rather weak regulatory framework: while their movements could appear to have been hindered by the authorities, the porosity of borders and administrative limits, along with their intimate knowledge of the areas they crossed, ultimately granted them a great deal of freedom, as has been demonstrated in many studies about Gypsy mobility in nineteenth century France (Reyniers, 1991, 2006; Robert, 2004; Vaux de Foletier, 1973, 1981).

Indeed, from the very fluidity of Gypsy movement to the powerlessness of authorities and the xenophobic surge directly aimed at Gypsies—now considered as not only allogeneic, but also pathogenic—everything came together to inspire the first regulatory apparatus implemented on a national scale. In 1864, the public safety agency at the Ministry of the Interior ('Direction de la Sûreté publique du ministère de l'Intérieur'), explicitly critical of the fact that no specific legal framework catered for the Gypsy population, drafted a circular that considered extending high police surveillance—usually reserved for big-time criminals—to all individuals 'known as Bohemians', insofar as they could be considered vagrants or dangerous foreigners.[6] The *Sureté publique*, with a particularly fragile position and almost no resources at the time, hoped to encourage Gypsies to settle down by forcing them to have a proper address, as explained below:

By assigning each of them with a distinct and compulsory place of residence, the government will be able to disseminate them, thus breaking apart these criminal conspiracies that indulge in begging under various guises, when not resorting to pilfering or theft.[7]

The lack of meaningful human and material resources to implement such a measure condemned this project from the outset; similarly, the call for reinforced controls at the borders remained theoretical. Several years later, at the end of the Franco-German war, a circular from the Ministry of the Interior drew a pessimistic picture of 'Gypsy measures', conveying the powerlessness of the authorities:

In several places of the country, the presence of Bohemians—whose mischiefs are worrying the populations—has been signalled. Authorities are almost powerless in this respect: they do practise a trade or at least pretend to, and as such cannot be condemned as vagrants; in any case authorities can no longer put them under efficient surveillance as, ever since the 8 December 1851 decree, individuals put under high police surveillance are free to choose their place of residence, which in turn makes it impossible to break gangs apart into various towns; finally, they cannot be expelled, since no foreign government is willing to accept them. It is absolutely vital to prevent all individuals who are unable to justify their name and citizenship to enter the national territory.[8]

Prefects were thus required to reject vigorously all individuals who were not in a position to give proof of these two elements when crossing a border; in practice, the territorial limits were considered a defence against potential migrations of Gypsies inside the country. Such proposals merely showed the general inefficiency of the available legal framework; calling once again for increased border surveillance could only be perceived as yet another admission of powerlessness.

'Nomads': Developing a social category at the beginning of the Third Republic

In the early years of the Third Republic, the Ministry of the Interior published several regulations insisting on strengthening the surveillance of Gypsy populations on a national scale. These bills and circulars recommended implementing preventive surveillance of the borders, called for 'vigilance' from authorities, insisted on the necessary 'rigorousness' that should be enforced toward them, or even tried to ban caravans from stationing in certain municipalities.[9] In many *départements*, prefectural circulars recommended that mayors or policemen actually evicted them and prevented caravans from staying for any length of time. The term 'nomads' ('nomades') soon became the usual appellation of this ethnic group, characterised by its lifestyle and alternatively called 'Bohémiens' ('Bohemians'), 'Romanichels' (from 'Romni') or 'Tziganes'.

The first important measure was implemented in March 1895 and took the form of a national census of all 'nomads, bohemians and vagrants' travelling in France. This step came against a backdrop of violent outbursts towards Gypsies at the end of the nineteenth century, a growing 'administrative intolerance' in the *départements*, and intense pressure exerted by local elected officials on national representatives. The historical context has often been examined from a long-term perspective, but this can be identified as a major transitional leap toward a more stringent control regimen (Filhol, 2006; Asséo, 2007b; Sitou, 2007). The 1895 census operation was perceived at the time as an infallible remedy, as evidenced by an article published in the *Petit Journal*:

On the same day, at the same time, everywhere in France, they have been surrounded by the gendarmerie; they had to tell their name, first name and place of origin, so that from now on, it will be possible to subject them to the laws that govern foreigners in France.[10]

The census was carried out in the space of a single day, 20 March 1895, but remained incomplete, the *gendarmes* and *gardes-champêtres* (village policemen) who were in charge of the operation being unable to span entire *départements*. The registries that were created for the occasion compiled information that enabled authorities to identify and track individuals as well as groups; however, homonymy, identity theft and identity dissimulation remained possibilities. IDs were delivered by city councils especially for the occasion, bearing the name and first name of everyone in each 'band', their 'apparent occupation', nationality, gender and age, place of birth, place where they came from and alleged destination. No centralised recording system, however, was even planned at the time.[11]

The results of the census were examined by a special non-parliamentary committee which produced a report in March 1898, highlighting the size of the nomadic population—numbering an estimated 25,000—and the lack of personnel to implement meaningful surveillance (Rivière, 1898: 498; Challier, 1913: 152). The lack of training, if not the outright incompetence, of *gardes-champêtres* drew the sharpest criticisms; however, what was more generally stigmatised was the weakness of the country police force (Police des campagnes). The Ministry of the Interior subsequently—in June 1898— proposed to establish a 'permanent control process of all country police'.

In the 1900s pressure on nomads—foreign nomads especially—increased, so much so that individual identification of persons gained momentum within the French police forces (About, 2004). Studies covering the period show that several factors combined to encourage the authorities to strengthen the legal apparatus, perceived as inefficient. Insecurity in the countryside was a central issue in this plan. At a time when police forces as a whole, along with the central services of the Ministry of the Interior, were undergoing reform, a new force was created in 1907: the 'Mobile Brigades' ('Brigades mobiles'). This new action force, active on the whole territory and whose officers were recruited and trained for that specific purpose, was endowed with special powers regarding nomad control (Berlière, 2004). The role of these brigades in matters of surveillance and identification was clarified as follows in a ministerial circular:

They shall photograph and identify, whenever legally possible, vagrants, nomads, Gypsies, be they travelling alone or in group, and shall send the photographs and identification reports—established according to the anthropometric method—to the general control department.[12]

From March 1908 to July 1909, 7,790 nomads were recorded and categorised and their individual report cards were specifically filed. On 5 March 1908, a special circular from the Ministry of the Interior, warning the prefectures that nomads might constitute a health hazard and spread contagious diseases, authorised preventive, coercive measures:

When caravans arrive on a fairground, a doctor should automatically visit them and check whether he finds any disease. At the least sign of illness, take stringent measures for isolating and disinfecting them.[13]

The turn taken in 1907 can be explained by several factors: the transformation of the police as an institution, the increasing presence of police forces—a hallmark of modernity—in the countryside, the growing importance of identification in French policing methods, and a deep-rooted animosity towards Gypsies in French society. Gypsy control can be understood as the very purpose of a new form of 'territory policing' embodied by these mobile forces, marking the advent of an allegedly modern form of policing (López, 2008).

Another factor that was instrumental in the emergence of the 'Gypsy issue' was the multiplication of border crises. In the 1900s, the regulation of Gypsy movements within Europe changed radically. Exacerbated xenophobic feelings, combined with an increasingly ethnic understanding of the concept of nation, led commentators to indulge freely in what might be dubbed unrestrained free speech. Anti-Gypsy feelings were vented increasingly openly, as evidenced by a number of articles in the press, riddled with threatening metaphors: 'invasion', 'déferlement' (flood), 'irruption', 'fléau' (plague), such were some of the terms that were used to describe Gypsies in newspapers (About, 2010). These circumstances were marked by a 'contagion of discourses' (Dornel, 2004, p. 255): the rejection of vagrancy and condemnation of wandering coincided with the stigmatisation of poverty and denunciation of foreigners. A new field, 'nomadic science', even appeared, describing the anthropologic traits and criminal pathologies of a group that was considered as both allogeneic from a national and ethnic perspective, and socially maladjusted (Zimmermann, 2007; Uerlings, Patrut, 2008). Caravans were stopped, prevented from moving by police forces from both sides of the border. In such a context, several cases involving border-crossing by caravans that were subsequently immobilised gave rise to repeated crisis situations, at the borders with Belgium, Luxembourg, Germany, Switzerland, and Italy (Arsac, 1933; Fombaron, 1989). Groups of Gypsies were constantly being chased, considered as foreigners in all countries they crossed, which reinforced the idea that they were fundamentally resistant to the very principle of national citizenship. At the international scale, a proposal for globally solving the 'Gypsy issue' was put forward by Switzerland in 1909, but dropped precisely because none of the countries that were approached agreed to recognise Gypsies as members of the national community (Egger, 1982; Asséo, 2007a).

In France, the late 1900s saw a heated parliamentary debate that was meant to put an end to the issue of categorising 'nomads'. This term targeted all so-called 'floating' ('*flottantes*') populations living in the countryside, a topic that raised passionate discussions following complaints relayed, among others, by members of parliament from border *départements* (David, 1907). To MPs, regardless of their political side, the crux of the matter was solving the alleged insecurity issue: all marginal people were targeted, as well as social categories belonging to the rural sub-proletariat; Gypsies, however, were at the core of the bills under discussion (Piazza, 2002). 'Nomads' is a word improperly used to designate communities that have generally 'settled' in a circumscribed area for quite a long time, but still are considered an allogeneic ethnic community, characterised by a way of life that definitely sets them apart from the national community (Delclitte, 1995; Asséo, 2002; Filhol, 2007).

The 16 July 1912 Act regulating 'the practice of itinerant trade movement of nomads' was a consequence both of the stigmatisation which began in the late Second Empire period and of the gradual strengthening of an administrative and policing category based on a particularly restrictive definition (Dupont, 1913). Indeed, the pressure exerted by the representatives of fairground people and pedlars, relayed by MPs at the parliament, was instrumental in enacting this piece of legislation that further isolated 'nomads' from a legal point of view and, crucially, in terms of policing regulations aiming to identify not only individuals, but also families and vehicles, in both time and space.

This ground-breaking Act, which required all Gypsies living in France to carry an anthropometric notebook ('carnet anthropométrique'), inspired by the documents that had been in use since the 1880s to identify released repeat offenders, has to be understood within the wider framework of measures taken in western Europe (Lucassen, 1997; Bonillo, 2001). In France, the rejection of 'nomads', which at the time was considered common ground by politicians—most of whom had rather conservative views—happened concurrently with the adoption of identification and control methods. A corollary of this tightening phase in Gypsy control was the development of homemade bypassing techniques: dilatory strategies to escape police forces, control-avoidance practices (use of multiple languages, deliberate vagueness about one's origins, multiplicity of IDs), identity theft, use of multiple patronyms, first names or nicknames, and destruction of identity documents. However, these forms of resistance only served to gradually increase police pressure and create more opportunities to discuss the legality of their status. Hence, from 1912 onwards, the new regulatory framework brought about a regimen of constant suspicion that led to the systematic rejection of Gypsies, not only to the physical and symbolic fringe of society, but also to the margins of law itself.

The 'Nomads' regimen: Exclusion, administrative instability and arbitrary measures, 1912–1940

It should be noted at once that the anthropometric notebook that was imposed upon French 'nomads' until 1969 was not a mere synthesis of innovative identification techniques, but also the very purpose of an original 'remote control' system. This identity document was heir to the legal identification practices introduced in France during the 1880s, in particular anthropometry as applied to suspects in criminal cases and to convicted criminals. Influenced by policing innovations in identification, it had to include an anthropometric description, fingerprints, and a proper 'mug-shot'. Moreover, this notebook opened a new era in the history of identity documents insofar as it combined the format of passports, 'carnets de saltimbanques' (street acrobat notebooks), and 'livrets ouvriers' (worker notebooks) and integrated the rational distribution of information pre-scribed by the physical description cards used by police forces (About, Denis, 2010). However, the most significant aspect was its theoretical role as a remote control tool for mobility, applying to families methods hitherto reserved for so-called criminal categories.

Indeed, in the early twentieth century, identity documents existed that were at once portable, individual and descriptive. Repeat offenders were supposed to carry one, as were some other categories of the population subject to the colonial authorities, that wanted to monitor their move-ments, and be able to control their status and social position. By extending such practices to other populations either *a priori* considered as dangerous, or exceptionally kept under surveillance as an ethnic minority, or controlled individually, collectively, and mostly as a family—the notebook system was comprised of both individual and family records, thanks to the group note-book—the process of criminalising one specific group within the metro-politan population took a tangible turn (Filhol, 2004). Finally, this note-book, which was to be signed/stamped by the authorities upon arriving and departing from any municipality, came to represent the constant surveil-lance of Gypsies in France, even though the system was only rationalised in practice in the early 1930s. Still, this document was a decisive element in the repressive policies imposed upon Gypsies, enabling authorities to acti-vate a number of arbitrary measures in the mid-1930s. In more than one way, the notebook system enabled and facilitated the compulsory 'station-ing' and internment system implemented against Gypsies in France from September 1939 onwards (Filhol, Hubert, 2009).

Theoretically, the task of running the anthropometric notebook system—maintaining the files, delivering and renewing the notebooks—was entrusted to prefectures, which were in charge of dealing with the 'nomad issue' in France (Arsac, 1933). But in the early years, no less than four enti-ties, whose resources varied considerably, were involved in the registration process: legal identification bureaus located in *préfectures*—initially in Paris, Lyons, and Marseilles, as well as in central police stations—'brigades mobiles' forces, brigades of *gendarmes*, and several prisons equipped with identification services. This organisational juxtaposition made legal dispositions more difficult to implement, as this situation created many loopholes: in 1924, a general review of the functioning of the system showed that many ill-equipped *départements* were in fact not registering nomads at all (Mossé, 1924).

Given the lack of proper standardisation, the Direction de la Sûreté (the Ministry of the Interior's public safety branch) considered that during the interwar period, the main objectives should be to centralise identification operations and standardise processes. Over that period, the police surveillance system underwent frequent modifications, as individual bills were enacted and gradually rectified, improving the whole scheme. In 1920, two circulars specified the conditions governing the issuance of notebooks and stressed the necessity of creating, in each police station, 'loose-leaf registries destined to tighten the surveillance of nomads', in other words the idea was to create a registry of nomads in each municipality; in 1922, another circular clarified how such registries should be maintained and, in 1923, it was deemed necessary to append information about the military status of nomads. In 1926, another harmonisation Act reduced the period of validity of the anthropometric notebook to two years and a ministerial circular was sent to prefects of border *départements* to remind them that foreign nomads should not be allowed to enter France; in 1928, a piece of legislation reaffirmed the compulsory nature of mugshots for nomads—adults and children alike—the cost of which should be borne by the persons concerned, unless indigence could be proved—which was tantamount to raising a special tax on these populations. That same year, in order to simplify administrative procedures, the possibility of extending the validity of the notebooks without going through the process of submitting all supporting documents anew was granted. Finally, in 1930, another circular reinforced the measures regarding the exclusion of foreign nomads from the French territory and attempted to define conditions for potential transit through the national territory, in order to speed up deportations (Vohl, 1937). Incidentally, this bill was put forward just before a tripartite agreement was reached between France, Belgium and Luxembourg to prevent foreign Gypsies crossing their borders.[14]

In 1934, the administrative services of the Ministry of the Interior reviewed again the control system of nomads and established an inspection report, stating that 'ministerial instructions pertaining to the application of the law (…) [are] too often neglected or not applied' and that a general overhaul of the practices in prefectures and subprefectures was necessary (Louvel, 1934). While restating the initial motive of the law—'defending the countryside against incursions from nomads'—and reaffirming how complex the final legislative project was for the three categories concerned— 'pedlars', 'fairground stall keepers or industrialists', and 'French or foreign nomads'—the report once again mentioned the burden of suspicion borne by the last category, comprised of allegedly 'homeless people, wandering aimlessly, and practising indeterminate, ever-changing activities'. This report covered three aspects: the first concerning the administrative management of written records; the second pertaining to the reinforcement of the limits giving access to nomad status, which, ever since 1930, had been restricted to people who were already registered; and the third regarding the tightening of the control and surveillance measures applied to individuals, especially in matters of stationing.

In order to achieve improvements in these areas, the organisation and functioning of the various administrative services was minutely observed. In fact, task distribution within prefectures and subprefectures revealed a complete lack of preparedness. A unique employee was often in charge of peddling regulations, foreigners, naturalisation matters, deportation and return of aliens, and passport delivery, as was the case in the Landes, Lozère, Cher and many other *départements*. The Gironde prefecture, however, had one specialised employee specifically working on nomad matters. The prefectures of Paris, the Rhône, and Bouches-du-Rhône being attached to the state police, nomads were dealt with by trained police officers there. Given the diversity of situations, efficiency varied greatly between *départements*.

In spite of these hurdles, the efforts devoted to improving the notebook system in the 1920s and 1930s bear witness to the commitment of the authorities to improving the efficient administration of the Gypsy carding process, and to tightening regulations and controls. Some major flaws, however, persisted well into the 1930s, such as the use of chronologically filed descriptive cards, the systematic lack of a separate file for each card, the absence of systematic numbering of individuals, or even the existence of pre-signed documents. More striking, however, is the will to ensure literal application of the 1912 Act. As noted by the author of the report:

The economic crisis deprived many individuals from their job and resources, inducing them to resort to expedients. Many of them, forced as they were to seek employment on the road, have attempted to be registered as nomads in order no to be charged for vagrancy. (Louvel, 1934, p. 799).

Just as nomads could obtain fairground stall keeper or pedlar status, outcasts in need of identification documents granting them freedom of movement might seek refuge in the 'nomad' category. As the report read:

(...) the number of nomads is growing; all of them, incidentally, being nationals. Many unemployed workers request an anthropometric notebook, so as to try their luck outside without being suspected of vagrancy. (Louvel, 1934, p. 799).

Hence, the notebook system, apparently extended to new categories, seems to have regrouped an increasing number of outcasts in the early 1930s, and uncovered a little-known aspect, drawing a border around a socially and economically marginalised group characterised by a paper-made object.

The most important point in the inspection report relates to the identification measurements used for delivering the notebooks, and the conditions in which these measurements were taken. Reservations made in the previous report (in 1924) seemed just as relevant as ever: a great many players were involved in the process (mobile brigades, prisons, local civil servants), and the various operations (photography, fingerprinting, anthropometric measurements) were not carried out simultaneously. A 1926 circular made provision for nomads to be regrouped at a given date in order to carry out all operations collectively, but application was rather patchy. Police forces often seemed to react quite harshly to this situation, carrying out identification control operations of their own to compensate for the structural flaws of the system.

In the mid-1930s, multiple crises erupted sporadically here and there, generally leading to the removal of camps or eviction of caravans. In the autumn of 1934 in Lyons, the Rhône prefecture explained for instance that a group of 'romnichals who were stationing illegally on the city's territory necessitated several interventions from police forces'.[15] In 1935, quite unusually, a circular from the general control department of the criminal police section of the General Bureau of National Public Safety (Contrôle général des services de police criminelle de la direction générale de la Sûreté nationale) unambiguously mentioned 'certain families of the Demestre nomad family'. This circular featured an introduction and a general presentation of a fifty-seven-strong group who allegedly had been roaming several *départements*, Orne in particular, where the Gendarmerie was said to have 'dislocated' the group shortly before March 1935:

(...) in order to prevent these families from reuniting, zones of circulation have been imposed upon them, with group and anthropometric notebooks bearing mention thereof.[16]

Eight lists were appended to the circular, each of which, under the name of the head of family, listed all its members, all modifications to be made to the group notebooks, and the authorised *départements*. The purpose of this circular, which was sent to all prefects in France, was quite clear: excluding these groups from certain cities and exerting particularly stringent control of their situation.

In 1936, after the corpse of a child had been discovered along a road somewhere in suburban Paris, investigators turned their attention to 'nomads', launching what the press was to call a 'dragnet' ('rafle') throughout the whole French territory (Arqué, 1936). Within a couple of days, a general review of the notebook system was carried out. The Gendarmerie-led operations were described as 'mathematical', seizing the opportunity to pitch the rigorousness of the law against the assumed savagery of Gypsies:

The control? (…) It was merciless, insensitive as the law should be to so much savage poetry, haloing in fierce romanticism the harsh 'emancipation' of nomadic races. (Arqué, 1936)

In the Paris area, certain families were targeted in particular—the *Petit Parisien* newspaper story listed names (Demestre, Winterstein, Lagrenée, Valentin, Consantien…) with alleged connections to criminal cases, minor offences, or brawls. Hence, this extended control operation was justified by linking Gypsies, violence and crime.

What happened during the 1930s was in more than one way preparing the ground for internment decisions later to be made by the Vichy regime and carried out by French police forces (Peschanski, 1994; Filhol, Hubert, 2009). Hence, a system implemented during the Third Republic, based on designing a legal category that ran contrary to the principle of equality as well as on discriminatory policing and administrative practices, durably established a class of individuals who were subsequently ostracised from society. French Gypsies, subject as they were to constant and random controls, were put in a state of legal exception that only served to reinforce the prejudiced views of officials and non-nomad sections of the population. This regulatory framework, duly inscribed in French Law, only fostered the negative representations associated with the many 'difficulties' that seemed to mark their presence on the national territory.

A discriminatory regimen that persisted after 1945

Despite the persecutions that French Gypsies suffered during the Second World War, their status did not change after 1945 and the anthropometric notebook system persisted for more than two decades. Archived material reveals a worrying continuity indeed in registration and naming practices, seen in a set of registries from the Bouches-du-Rhône *département*, which were continuously updated from 1942 to 1967.[17] On 14 November 1969, immediately after the repeal of the Act of 16 July 1912 regarding the registration of Gypsy 'nomads', a question was submitted to then Minister of the Interior Raymond Marcellin, asking him to clarify the French government's position about a recommendation from the European Council regarding 'the situation of Gypsies and other nomads in Europe'. The French Minister's reply, in his willingness to both display some attachment to humanist values and pose as the protector of public order, restated the fundamental ambiguity of French authorities toward these populations (*Journal Officiel*, 1970). The repeal of the discriminations established in 1912 was hailed by the Minister, however the 3 January 1969 Act 'regulating peddling and stall keeping, as well as the regimen applicable to travellers in France who do not have a fixed home or residence' was presented as both an answer to alleged aspirations from the affected populations themselves and, crucially, as a measure catering for 'the necessity of a much-needed piece of regulation'.

This new, special regulatory framework had explicit objectives: 'fostering either integration into society or sedentarisation, which more and more Gypsies long for nowadays'. Such allusions did cast some doubt on the actual 'insertion' of Gypsies into the national community, implying—in accordance with a long tradition based on deep-rooted prejudices—their essentially allogeneic character. Moreover, regulations were presented as a means of 'fostering' the rejection of non-sedentary life, as was—so we were told—the wish of those concerned, who apparently understood the error of their ways. By alluding to professional training courses that would enable them to 'practise an activity and secure an income that their traditional trade no longer guarantee[d]', the minister assumed that their 'trade' did not really qualify as a professional activity, thus hinting at the probably illegal nature of their economic status. In another development, the issue of stationing was defined as a key 'problem', a complex and disturbing one: 'it remains all the more worrying as solving it almost conditions the effectiveness of the socio-educational action that has been undertaken'. To put it plainly, authorities recognised that they were unable to find land to set up caravan sites, admitting the 'persistent animosity' of surrounding populations, with the excuse that similar reactions could be observed in other

European countries, which ultimately justified regulatory 'supervision'. Finally, the answer given by the Minister of the Interior suggested that two categories could be distinguished: on the one hand, the 13,000 Gypsies living in the Paris area, whose situation was considered 'difficult in spite of unrelenting efforts to improve it'; on the other, sedentarised communities to be found in several municipalities, such as Laval (La Jaunaie) or Le-Plan-de-Grasse ('hameau tzigane'), where 'encouraging results' had been observed, 'proving these populations' real capacity to adapt'. In other words, the 'good Gypsies' are those who manage to wipe out the most conspicuous characteristic of such communities—the so-called 'nomadic' lifestyle—and decide to conform to the common rules of society, diluting their difference, fitting into society. The wording—'sedentarisation', 'insertion', 'adaptation', 'integration'—clearly appears as euphemistic here, hiding the oft-repeated wish that, as a community, they simply vanished from society. Hence, a modern version of interwar forms of discrimination openly persisted during the 1950s and 1960s (Aubin, 1996, 2000; Reyniers, Williams, 2000).

The 3 January 1969 Act introduced a new system: two 'circulation booklets' ('livrets de circulation') (type A and B) and one 'special circulation notebook' ('carnet spécial de circulation') were implemented, and another legal-administrative category was created, called 'Gens du voyage' (lit. 'Travelling People'). To this very day, these documents enable the authorities to exert permanent control, with the constant risk of having one's situation thoroughly examined by police forces and administrative authorities alike. The very existence of these documents perpetuates a *de facto* situation of discrimination: searching for possible offences, control officers must be able to recognise 'travelling people' even before requesting these documents, necessarily interpreting their physical and sartorial appearance in the light of the prejudices and stereotypes that inform the Gypsy condition in France.[18] On the dark side of policing practice, 'ethnic' electronic files and computer databases were often maintained well into the 1990s, unbeknownst to public opinion. These files, which violate the equality principle, are more than just clues to a discriminatory identification and control system: they actually stem from a long Republican tradition that, ever since the early twentieth century, has attempted to find a practical solution to the issue of defining Gypsies in legal and policing terms.

The crisis that took place during the summer of 2010 certainly pertains to a very specific context. Just as the European space was undergoing a major reconfiguration because of the integration of new eastern Member

States in the Schengen space, movements of Roma migrants from Romania and Bulgaria suddenly reactivated ancient fears. Moreover, loaded topics such as national identity and security opened the floodgates to a wave of direct stigmatisation of Gypsies. In a climate of economic crisis, with weakened European economies, the national-securitarian discourse finds an easy target in such minorities, still widely shrouded in prejudice. This French crisis, however, has the upside of exposing the resilience of old Republican practices toward Gypsies. By wrongly mixing up 'Travellers'—direct heirs to the 1912 Act on 'nomads'—and 'Roma'—people from eastern Europe— the political discourse highlighted the risk inherent to processes aiming to inscribe individuals within administrative categories that eventually trap them into a given status, which is by definition an immobile one. Such confusion is quite telling in terms of the power of the forms of discrimination that have been endured by Gypsies in France, be they French nationals or not. The many prejudices, rooted in a long legal, administrative and policing tradition, suddenly resurface in our modern times, announcing a new era in French-style anti-Gypsyism.

Analyses of the French case have shown how prejudice has been included in the legal apparatus by the creation of an exclusive category. The discarding of social and negative representations concerning Gypsy communities in the making of the law and directly in parliamentary discussion has produced a context, activated by mass media and the escalation of xenophobic discourses, that has led to the categories, designed by the police and administrative regulation system, into which individuals have suddenly been placed. The category of 'Nomads' was in fact the primary result of daily surveillance of families across the country. It must be underlined that this powerful system of control has led not only to individual persons as juridical subjects but to entire families being considered as targets. The discrimination process was cemented by the creation of a mark of shame, which manifested itself in the special identification document, that testifies to concrete exclusion from common civil status. In the long term this system of exclusion has underlined the supposed difference that seems to be the main characteristic of the Gypsy people.

PART 2

FROM LOCAL CONFLICTS TO RESHAPINGS
OF THE SOCIAL IMAGINARY

7

SILENCING AND NAMING THE DIFFERENCE[1]

Kata Horváth

The village where we did our fieldwork is a settlement of about 1,800 persons on the border between the north-eastern Hungarian counties of Borsod and Heves. In this village the distinction between Gypsies and Hungarians rests on a strongly embedded tradition.[2] We first experienced this ten years ago as young students in anthropology when we lived for some months with a family on the Gypsy settlement. During this time it proved practically impossible to develop deeper relationships with the 'village Hungarians' beyond exchanging greetings. This was not only because we were unable to offer any satisfactory explanation as to why we had moved into a 'Gypsy family', but also because our Gypsy 'family' kept track of our attempts at crossing the boundary and viewed these with great mistrust. Since we were outsiders who had joined them, our host family continuously expected us to prove that we belonged to the Gypsies. After a while we gave up trying. We accepted that the relationship between 'the Hungarian' and 'the Gypsy' had some features that made it impossible for anyone to act from within both categories.

We thus discovered a village order in which the Hungarian-Gypsy distinction created a strong and rigid boundary between two groups: everybody knew exactly who was a Gypsy and who was a Hungarian, which were the Gypsy families and which were the non-Gypsy families. (The idea of the 'obviousness' of darker skin colour that operated in this closed village context provided an unambiguous, distinguishing signal and means to allocate people to the Gypsy category.) There were absolutely no kin ties (for example mixed marriages) cross-cutting this boundary and 'mixed friendships' were extremely rare.

The fact that the 'two sides' were clearly defined did not mean that there was no contact between these people, rather that any interaction was fundamentally defined by the Gypsy-Hungarian distinction. In fact, numerous forms of mixed interaction existed. Workplaces, consumption activities, public holidays, school and the public spaces in the village provided frequent points of contact, but in all of them the Gypsy-Hungarian distinction operated, and indeed crucially defined the mode of interaction.

There were two fundamental aspects or principles by which this distinction operated. On the one hand the distinction clearly demarcated the Gypsies' place in relation to Hungarians. The Gypsy had a place in the school but he/she sat in the back row, or attended the remedial class; he/she could be employed as garbage collector at the cleaning company in Eger, or as a cleaning woman in the city hospital; in addition he/she could work as day-labourer for the villagers, or could collect scrap and hand it in for recycling. The Gypsy lived in the village but stayed in a Gypsy settlement, in one of the four settlements the village had. The Gypsies' place was self-evident, the context of contacts was fixed, and routine interactions were best described as those of 'patrons and clients'. This could be seen most clearly in the typical village wedding party where the presence of the Gypsies was taken for granted, but they were placed there in a very peculiar role. They stood in front of the house where the party was taking place, waiting until someone brought them the drinks and cakes to which they were 'entitled'. In this way, the Gypsies too became participants in the event. In short, the Gypsy-Hungarian distinction functioned so that in the village the Gypsy was always allocated a place, but their positions (for example in the remedial school), roles (for example as the 'disabled') or possibilities for action (for example collecting snails) were clearly distinguished and had an inferior status. This was one of the defining features of the situation.

The second aspect was just as essential. This was the unspoken nature of the Gypsy-Hungarian distinction. In any given situation one could only assume that the Gypsy-Hungarian distinction was what was driving an interaction and defining the relationship between the participants. That this was what was really going on was never stated publicly. As long as the

Gypsy remained unnamed, the fundamental forces shaping an interaction and the fate of the people whose lives were shaped by this distinction, operated in a silenced (and repressed) manner.

In summary, in this village, until recently, the Gypsy-Hungarian distinction functioned through being kept unspoken. The hierarchical arrangement through which 'the Gypsy' became subjected came, in this way, to be naturalised and perceived as self-evident. It was no accident that the most important taboo was against uttering the word 'Gypsy' since the whole mechanism of subjection was based on this prohibition and silencing of the real terms of distinction. The main threat to a mechanism of this sort lay either in public acceptance of being Gypsy or openly calling other people Gypsy (*lecigányozás*). And since the mechanism of not naming perfectly suited the Hungarians—the Gypsies had their place at work and so on, including, as we have seen, even at celebratory events like wedding parties, and in those posed no threat—nothing motivated them to question the order, or to start openly naming people as 'Gypsy'.

It is more difficult to explain how this order became domesticated among those who ended up on the Gypsy side of the distinction without them being explicitly named as 'Gypsies'. Our aim here is to explain this, but also to show how this form of coercive distinction also created room for manoeuvre for the people who ended up on the Gypsy side of the distinction. Which strategies were possible and which were impossible under this mechanism of subjection? What did it mean 'to be a [unnamed] Gypsy' in this village under these conditions?

We have to emphasise that these questions refer to the past because recent events have brought a different logic into the Gypsy-Hungarian distinction—a logic which revealed the old system to us. Uttering the word 'Gypsy' openly (both as self-ascription and in calling people Gypsy) has become more natural and this has been related to the dissolution of the earlier order. Two of the Gypsy settlements of the village were dissolved in a resettlement programme (*telepfelszámolás*) and the families who lived there were resettled in houses inside the village. New construction enterprises were created by Gypsy businessmen and Gypsy children became the majority in the local school which thus became 'Gypsyfied' (*elcigányosodott*). These transformations forced locals to question the earlier position of the Gypsy in the settlement, in the remedial school, or in low status jobs. The simple residential relocation of 'the Gypsies' made visible differences previously taken for granted, and this visibility has increasingly forced difference to be named. Relationships based on silence can function no more and talk about such distinctions has undermined the fundamental basis of the previous arrangement.

The example of the school demonstrates this. As the number of Gypsy children increased in the local school, Hungarian parents gradually removed their children and enrolled them in a school in a neighbouring village. As a result, only Gypsy children now attend the local school. In this process, voicing the category 'Gypsy' became inevitable because it was obvious that those who left were the 'Hungarians' and those who stayed behind were the 'Gypsy' children. In this situation, being a Gypsy does not mean the same thing as it did before. Until the category 'Gypsy' was explicitly brought to life through social action, Gypsyness in the school could be mainly experienced as a disadvantage, as a handicapped form of Hungarianness, which brought with itself a pressure to adapt to dominant patterns. But if 'they call us Gypsies' (*lecigányoznak minket*), then efforts to accommodate to the mainstream make no sense. As one mother told us: 'They tell us directly to our face, Kati, that it is because of the Gypsy children that they take the Hungarian ones out of the school'. Now being stigmatised continuously in the school, a feeling which is loaded also with the hurt feelings from the earlier insulting position of being labelled as 'poor', handicapped, uncivilised etc., has created a situation where Gypsyness can be assumed and represented primarily through opposition.

The dissolution of the Gypsy settlements (an EU funded programme) ran parallel with the events in the school. In this case it was less stigmatisation than ways of voicing the Gypsy that became important. The dissolution of the settlement was initiated and carried out by a local Roma NGO acting in its own right after it failed to reach an agreement with the local municipality. In this way resettlement became an explicitly 'Gypsy programme' and was perceived by the Hungarians as a brutal breach of the old order, as a kind of loss of territory (*térvesztés*). In consequence, they tried to prevent it by all means. As a result of this programme the 'Gypsy' category appeared in a totally new form in the village, as a resource which could be mobilised to intervene in the social order of the village. This also meant that in the framework of such a 'Gypsy programme' the families moved into the village 'as Gypsies'. So, just as in the school, the actual transformation of the social order and naming 'the Gypsy' were connected. The Gypsy left his/her customary place, became visible, occupied a new place, and became a synonym of the changes and problems of an increasingly unpredictable world.

As just presented it would appear that changes in the Gypsy-Hungarian relationship stem from mechanisms internal to the village, from changes in the status and social location of those in the Gypsy position, but this is an illusion. Rather, these changes arise from multi-level transformations connecting internal events of a village to processes on the national level. The strategy which placed the Gypsies on the periphery of all kinds of institutions without naming them was based on a tacit consensus which had its roots in the long period of János Kádár's rule (1956–86/9). That regime intended to dissolve ethnic, religious and other differences but failed in this. Instead it simply suppressed their public expression. In 'our' village, which its inhabitants today consider to be attached to a Christian-conservative world-view, this pattern continued after 1990. It was able to do so because nationally, too, the 'Gypsy' continued to remain unnamed. This continuity is all the more striking because, after 1990, the systematic disadvantages suffered by Gypsies and numerous processes of exclusion were now openly analysed and named by social scientists and policy makers began to introduce measures like mandatory school integration programmes and the dissolution of segregated Gypsy settlements. In the end it was these measures, rather than any discursive change, which induced transformations in the local order by making naming the Gypsy unavoidable. Naming the 'Gypsy' became in fact the only discursive possibility, the only speech form accessible to locals when trying to make sense of the changes they have experienced in their personal lives since 1990.

Local experience seeks publicly available discourses with which to interpret the changing social order. And the dominant discourses present in Hungary today construct the Gypsy as a dangerous difference that threatens Hungarians. As a solution to the dangers posed by the Gypsies, these discourses propose their expulsion from the political community. Silence is now presented as a means of deceiving 'the Hungarians'. These discourses leave no space to reflect on the local situation, where for decades it was precisely the silencing of the Gypsy-Hungarian distinction that made the social order function, and 'the Hungarian' was not endangered by the presence of Gypsies because the latter were systematically allocated symbolically inferior positions.

But today, when the previously self-evident distribution of social roles and the old hierarchies of the village are disappearing, when feelings of being 'at home' give way to general uncertainty, locals find themselves naming 'the Gypsy'. The category 'the Gypsy' takes central stage because, after a long period of invisibility, it has the potential to condense and make explicit the experience of insecurity and loss of territory (*térvesztés*). This had a further pernicious consequence. Because 'naming the Gypsies' (*cigányozás*) became a ready-made solution for constructing narratives about post-communist socio-economic transformations, this made it impossible to develop shared narratives which would account for the experience of both the 'Hungarian' and the 'Gypsy' side of the village. Creating a common narrative would have involved reflecting on the predefined trajectories and possibilities inherent in each side's own social position in order to define the social responsibility each carries today. In the present setting we see little chance of this.

Silencing difference: The traditional functioning of the Gypsy-Hungarian distinction

For ten years now I have worked among Gypsies, alongside my colleague Cecilia Kovai, as anthropologists in this north-east Hungarian village. In this chapter I examine how the category 'Gypsy' came to be invested with an extraordinary density of meaning through a continuous negotiation that surrounded this term in the everyday life of the Gypsy settlement. In strong contrast with the situation found in the public sphere of the village, where the appearance of the issue and category was rigorously tabooed, inside the Gypsy settlement open discussions about 'the Gypsy' were a staple of conversation.

As argued in the previous chapter, the distinction between 'Gypsy' and 'Hungarian' was fundamental to village life, but in public everything happened as if social distinctions were not about Gypsyness. Gypsies were variously singled out, in the school, for example, as disabled or disadvantaged, at the workplace as inferiorly qualified, in the village hierarchy as less educated, poorer, less cultured, in everyday situations as someone worth pitying or despising, or earning a paternal smile or benevolent praise. But 'Gypsyness' was not named in a direct manner.

This way of making a social distinction created the illusion on the Gypsy side that the key to their separateness and inferiority was not their Gypsyness but the sort of behavioural characteristics mentioned above: lack of education, poverty, or lack of civilisation (*kulturáltlanság*). This situation also carried a promise that difference might be abolished with effort, with upward mobility, or by acquiring culture. This form of distinction also offered a promise that spoke to the individual person: the 'Gypsy who is not named' can hope to dissolve his difference, in contrast to the Gypsy who is named, whose inferiority cannot be changed. In this logic the category Gypsy itself stands for an unchangeable, permanent, inferior status. Any individual should, therefore, aspire to avoid his 'Gypsyness' being realised or acknowledged in public. Calling somebody 'Gypsy' had only one meaning—it was a form of stigmatisation which, when explicitly and directly uttered, narrowed or even closed down the person's freedom of action (*mozgástér*). Therefore individuals struggled to develop behaviour, relationships, and survival strategies that enabled them to avoid being called a Gypsy.

Individuals felt the necessity to try continuously to hide, disguise or dissolve any difference that did appear in a social situation. Therefore Gypsies lived their lives in a state of continuous adaptation and orientation to the mainstream (*igazodás*). The cunning of this mechanism lay in the fact that it was precisely the illusory promise of dissolving difference that guaranteed and reinforced the existence of difference.

On the Gypsy side of the distinction, the experience of being despised, considered inferior, and of making continuous efforts to adapt to the mainstream, was further burdened by a constant uncertainty if the behaviour of others or one's own status in any given situation was connected with one's Gypsyness or not and, if connected, how so. The only way to have removed this uncertainty would have been by restructuring the meanings associated with 'Gypsyness'. But while public situations in the village produced these experiences of 'Gypsyness' they offered no means of reinterpreting them since Gypsyness was unnamed there. This meant that the only domain for negotiating the meaning of 'the Gypsy' became the family and the neighbourhood. This brings us back to our field experience that life in the Gypsy settlement involved a continuous negotiation about Gypsyness. Whilst this open discussion stood in apparent contrast to the avoidance observed in public spaces, I argue that discussions in the settlement are better interpreted as part of the same phenomenon as the silence in the village. Negotiations about Gypsyness were themselves a means of dealing with and reconstructing the experience of adaptation to and orientation towards the mainstream.

The ambiguity experienced around the 'unnamed' Gypsyness in public situations, the eternal insecurity regarding the interpretation of encounters and their own position in these situations, demanded that Gypsies locate and interpret these common experiences. The constant insecurity, for example regarding the best way to behave in order to avoid being shamed in public (*leszégyenülés*) forced them into continuous negotiation when not on the settlement. Through such negotiation, the experience of subjection received a specific significance and took on a life of its own. In this way, the various forms of adaptation were presented as different forms of enacting Gypsyness: offering a ground on which to construct internal distinctions and separations between the various Gypsy extended families. By reinterpreting and restructuring the experiences of their (social) presence in the village they built an increasingly solid 'Gypsy world' with its own autonomous realm of meaning. Through this work of interpretation the Gypsies surrounded themselves with the insecurities and tensions associated with their presence in the village, trying to replay and resolve them. But they could not communicate these reinterpretations back into the public sphere (because of the rules of public presence), so their experience became their own, a kind of set of 'Gypsy experiences' that reinforced the difference between them and the Hungarians. This became the difference (let's call it Gypsyness) which they tried to conceal in the village. The Gypsy position, and the distinction which brought it to life, continuously reinforced itself.

The urge to hide Gypsyness pushed the interpretation of the experiences of 'being Gypsies' into the domain of family and neighbourhood relations. But it is also obvious that it was only by dealing with these experiences amongst themselves, by transposing them to the sphere of internal relations, that they could work to solve the tensions inherent in the categorisation: only here could the stigmatising meaning of the Gypsy be turned into a room to manoeuvre. But as soon as the category Gypsy offered room to move it increasingly acquired meanings that would need be disguised or hidden in the public space of the village.

Our informants experienced their presence in the village mainly in terms of orienting themselves to the mainstream, covering up, disciplining the self and one's peers. But at the same time, and in parallel to this work of disguise, there was a constant exchange, amongst themselves of hidden glances, winks, and acknowledgement of simulation. We observed a kind of double presence, in which Gypsyness was an object which was covered up but which could, at any times, be revealed to be present by a distanced or external glance on the situation. So, we noticed both huge efforts to meet the expectations of the Hungarian environment and an extremely ironical attitude to the meanings attributed by this environment. But one thing remained certain: Gypsyness did not appear in public as an openly assumed collective experience or as a collective resource.

Home (the Gypsy settlement) was the domain of a continuous rearrange-ment of dense human relationships. These relationships were, in one sense, constantly questioned by the fact that everyone engaged in their public denial when outside of the settlement. In all the efforts to adapt oneself to the mainstream, when in the village, at work, in school and so on, every-body tried to show that he/she was better than the others. This 'better' was created by each individual as he/she tried to get rid of their own 'Gypsyness' and any signal which would have made it recognisable. The logic of the strategy involved proving to outsiders that he/she was not 'that kind of Gypsy', in the sense of 'a Gypsy who behaves like a Gypsy'. As a conse-quence, when anyone returned home, they needed to reiterate their rela-tionships to their family and neighbours. And this was only possible through the creation of a 'common Gypsyness'. The behaviour of other Gypsies in the village was a constant object of criticism—in terms of being 'shameful', or conversely 'putting on an act' or 'toadyism' (*nyaliskodás*)—but this could only be done from the perspective of a 'common Gypsyness'. The insecurity and mistrust which stemmed from the effort to adapt could only be dissolved through the culvitation of this 'common Gypsyness'. This also meant that reinterpretation of family relationships implied the redefinition of Gypsy existence and the relation of the speaker to it. In this way, the closeness of relations with one's relatives, the security and warmth of the family, were experienced as a reinforcement of Gypsyness.

This was not, however, an unambiguous process. In the promise of becoming one with the 'common Gypsy', in the continuous efforts to create something common beyond difference, lay an insidious trap. This trap was rooted in the fact that at the same time as they experienced the distinction which put them on the Gypsy side in the village, differences were being created among themselves. The publicly unnamed, hierarchical differences between 'Gypsy' and 'Hungarian' were pushed onto the Gypsies and they interpreted these as differences in the degree of adaptation, as differences between families. And this, in turn, led to a situation where only those in the Gypsy position were forced to work interpretatively on the social experi-ence produced by the Gypsy-Hungarian distinction. This was a Sisyphean task because what appeared to be internal differences among the Gypsies were, in fact, the product of broader social differences, which created the inferior position of the Gypsies as a whole, as well as their minority status. Dissolving these differences was impossible because they were reproduced in the very process of their negotiation. The continuous negotiation about difference only increased social distance. In addition, the internalisation of Gypsy difference produced a fragmented and divided 'Gypsyness' which could only express itself through its internal differences and was incapable of publicly presenting a 'common Gypsy experience' because that was over-ruled by arguments about the possible strategies of adaptation and rivalries between adherents of different strategies.

It is important to see how all this appeared when looked at through everyday situations and the day to day relationships of the Gypsy settle-ment. This is how we ourselves reached our understanding of the logic of silencing difference.

Minority experiences of the unnamed

Ten years ago, as young students in anthropology, when we moved into one of the Gypsy settlements of the village it was composed of more than ten families living in cave-dwellings (*barlanglakás*). Our most immediate impression of this settlement, which has since been dissolved, was that events which appeared to us as the smallest and most innocent of everyday situations could trigger profoundly felt questions about Gypsyness. There was a continuous fear of being stigmatised as Gypsies and all gestures were hedged with vigilance. At the same time there was also a constant engage-ment with one's 'own Gypsyness'.

Vigilance was maintained in all situations, even those that were not related to one's 'own Gypsyness', so long as they involved speakers from outsider positions ('external to the Gypsies'). Regardless of its content, the speech of outsiders could easily be interpreted as stigmatising (*cigányozás*) and, therefore, as offensive. On one occasion, for example, there was a moment of vivid social life inside the house of our family when nobody was paying attention to the television that was providing background noise, broadcasting some entertaining show. All those present were actively engaged in interaction with each other. Suddenly, one young girl heard something and, interrupting herself mid-sentence, turned around and yelled at the host of the TV show: 'Don't you call us Gypsies!' (*Ne cigán-yozzá'!*). Observing such increased vigilance it became obvious to us that being called Gypsy was a real source of danger. It was clear that the Gypsies must avoid the offence of being labelled Gypsies by the outside with all means at their disposal and counter the implications of that. In so far as they could do this, they enjoyed some freedom to manipulate the meanings of the term 'Gypsy'; if one could play with the meaning of being a Gypsy, being such could not be a real danger. And, indeed, play with the meanings of Gypsyness was continuous.

During the period of our fieldwork there were three extended Gypsy families in the village, which distinguished themselves one from the other. Some of them were living in the cave-dwellings, others in so-called 'standing houses' (*fennálló házak*). Among the individual families there were smaller or bigger differences in their mode of life. They expressed these differences among themselves as different experiences of being Gypsies, of realising Gypsyness. 'Our family' often referred to one of the other families, nicknamed as Sasoj, who were living in cave-dwellings, as 'dirty' (*retkes*); they emphasised their incomer status and their origins from the village of Bogács, and they stigmatised them as 'Vlach Gypsies'. In this way the Sasoj became representatives of an 'exaggerated Gypsyness' which was alien to our family and therefore considered also dangerous. On the neighbouring hillside, a family living in 'standing houses' were considered, from the same perspective, 'fussy' or 'queasy' (*kényes*). Referring to them, members of our family noted sarcastically, that 'those ones already became big Hungarians' or more exactly 'they pretend to be Hungarians' (*teszik magukat magyarnak*). They thus represented another form of Gypsyness to be avoided. Differences between families were, in this way, conceptualised as different forms of Gypsyness. Along these lines, relatively rigid boundaries were drawn between the extended families, boundaries that were similar in strength to those separating local from 'stranger Gypsies' living in other localities, even if these were, in some cases, relatives.

Discussions about 'internal' differences were kept on the agenda not only by reference to other extended families or stranger Gypsies but also regarding one's own family within a single Gypsy settlement. The constant accusations about difference and the efforts to counter these gave a great intensity to settlement life. The central accusation, broadly speaking, concerned the problem of 'belonging'. Accusations sought answers to questions like 'To whom do you give?', 'Whom do you value more?' (*Kit mibe nézel?*) 'Whom do you cling to?' (*Kihez húzódzkodol?*). These questions of belonging to the family were also ways of asking 'How do you live your Gypsyness?' and 'Is your Gypsyness similar to mine?'. A particular form of expressing blame involved teasing. Teasing accusations were voiced at any moment within the close family or within neighbourly relations, and they were denied, or countered, by turning them back on the accuser, which most often dissolved the banter into shared laughter.

Once, for example, we were sitting on the terrace of the village bar. On the main road of the village a group of relatives were approaching and they, who knows why, omitted to greet us. 'Gee, these are not even greeting us! These already became Hungarians!³ What are you pretending?'—a voice said from the terrace. 'Look! Are you too here?'—one of the relatives turned to us. 'You already became so rich that you're already drinking cola early in the morning in the village?' A man approached us: 'You haven't said that you invited me! So should I greet you for nothing, when you fear (*sajnálsz tőlem*) sharing a bit of cola with me!' And the reply came: 'Come on Józsi, damn you (*rohadjámeg*), what you want to drink?'

In another situation, children were teasing each other: some brothers and cousins left the settlement together to go school. On this occasion, a boy was mocked because he was hurrying: 'Look, how Illés is running! Take care nigger, don't be late to school!' 'I go faster',—said the boy, and stopped to wait for the others. 'I do not want to walk with you! You are stupid Gypsies (*bornyú cigányok*), you make me ashamed in the village!'

It seemed as if the negotiations about 'the Gypsy' were motivated by a constant wish to rearrange difference and dissolve it. From the perspective of the participants in these situations this may have been the case. But if we take a step back we see that people created differences and dissolved them just in order to create new differences the next moment. But why did they create these internal differences as they moved from one situation to another? Why was it not enough simply to greet one's relatives instead of accusing them of having 'deserted the Gypsyness', and why did they, in turn, return the accusation by blaming material differences (*úriak vagytok*— 'you're such gentlefolk') and stinginess? Why was Illés warned that he is 'black' when he hurried to school? And why did he appeal to the shame of the Gypsies instead of waiting for the others or leaving them behind? Why did the category Gypsy function through its differences and why were the Gypsies able to, and why did they need to, talk through these differences?

The main accusations concerning difference, as we have seen in the case of differentiation between the families, is that one 'pretends too much' (*teszi magát*) or that one causes others 'shame' (*leszégyenít*).

To be ashamed or to cause somebody else to be ashamed could happen only with respect to the Hungarians. The potential for shame was implied by anything and everything connected to the state of being 'Gypsies': to be ashamed was to become Gypsy. So, it was understood that the 'natural' Gypsy 'from home', the Gypsy who is hidden inside each of us, will surface, will be exposed. Anything which revealed Gypsyness could provoke shame: if small children left the Gypsy settlement without the permission of their parents and entered the village wearing their home clothes or even barefoot; if the dogs from the settlement would not be chased home and followed their masters all over the village; if somebody in a public place (in the bus, the consulting room etc.) was too loud, too unrestrained, or disorganised; if somebody dressed up in clothes that were too rosy; if it was revealed that one lives in a cave-dwelling; if, in the school, they found lice in one's childrens' hair; or if one's skin was 'too dark like a Gypsy'; or, whatever this might mean, one looked like, talked like or behaved like a Gypsy. To be ashamed meant that 'Gypsyness' had surfaced, it had been uncovered, and so appeared in a public situation. The blame of making others ashamed, as a consequence, meant that someone, a person or a family, through behaviour or life strategy turned themselves into 'Gypsy', or 'even more Gypsy' than could be tolerated, and because of his/her proximity to others dragged them down with themselves. A typical example of this involved the Sasoj family I mentioned earlier. The Sasoj family sent their children over to the 'Hungarian woman', barefoot, for bread. This produced a meaning of Gypsyness which seemed shameful for the other families. Similarly, when our family went to collect snails early in the morning and on our way back we asked the driver of the bus to take us to the village with our big sacks and in dirty clothes, the 'obvious' representation of Gypsyness also came to the surface of the interaction. (There are some who prefer not to collect snails because of this; others will carry the sacks themselves on their backs all the way back to the village.)

The immediate consequence of this situation of shame can be seen in the occasion just mentioned when our family, after handing in the snails and pocketing the money, was drinking cola on the terrace of 'Kati's' bar. For the Sasojs by doing this we were 'showing off' (*tesszük magunkat*), but from the perspective of the 'Hungarian like Gypsy family' we represented 'shame' because of our dirty clothes (having just returned from collecting snails) and the loud behavior of our family in the middle of the village.

The accusation of 'showing off' (*teszi magát*) acquired meaning in connection to being ashamed. Because the Gypsy 'as he is at home' could not be represented in public, precisely because Gypsyness is shameful, everybody 'showed off' one way or another when he/she was not at home in the settlement. But this could always be blamed, was always more clearly seen, in each other. To 'show off' meant that you pretended that you were better

129

than the common Gypsy 'from home'. You pretended to be cleaner, richer, more Hungarian, or more to the liking of the Hungarians. But you could pretend as much you wanted—warned the accusations—the signals of your Gypsyness would always be there. The most common remark applied to each other—'he shows off but he is more Gypsy (*cigányabb*) than me!'— expressed this clearly. All the more so if we also consider its variations: 'He shows off, but his mouth is distorted (*félreáll a szája*) because he's so hungry!'; 'He shows off, but dirt is eating into his neck! (*eleszi a retek a nyakát*)'; and 'He shows off, but he is darker than me!'

Adapting to the Hungarians and the problem of belonging

Accusations of 'showing off' and 'making one ashamed' drew the contours of a Gypsyness that experimented with different forms of public presence, and tried to avoid the dangers of being shamed. These accusations also made visible a context, a village milieu in which the Gypsy could be present because s/he was trying to adapt to the expectations of the majority. Because of this, variations in the strategies of adaptation, which involved different forms of enacting the Gypsy in this milieu, all touched on the question of attachment to one's family. But how was a Gypsy's relation to the local Hungarians turned into a question of family attachment?

The condemnatory attitude of the villagers who passed by Kati's bar could be clearly sensed when they saw a group dressed in dirty clothes, wasting time in the middle of the day in the bar. The villagers would never greet such people first; in fact, they would turn their faces away, trying to avoid even being addressed. Those sitting on the terrace, when they saw villagers approaching, started to discipline each other, both trying to adapt to village norms and also claiming to each other that they are trying. Some of them hissed (*lepisszegi*) to those who were talking dirty or too loud, called attention to their dirty clothes, half-seriously chased home those who were not behaving properly in the village ('*itt befele bornyúskodik*'). Then they greeted the Hungarians politely '*Csókolom!*' ('*Baisemain!*') '*Csókolom!*', '*Csókolom, Marika néni (Marika dame)!*' in the *vousvoyer* register. '*Hello!*' (*Szervusztok*)—the Hungarian woman replied hastily, using one of the more informal greetings available in the *tutoyer* register. 'You said *Marika néni*! But she was not *Marika néni*!' 'Look, man! She surely was *Marika néni*! Not the one in the upper-village, the other from down there!

I know for sure, Mom works for her as a day-labour. She is a decent Hungarian woman...'

As the woman passed by the terrace a rather dense social situation unfolded in front of our eyes but, ten years ago, we were quite certain that the word 'Gypsy' would not be uttered. This kind of situation, with all its provocations, with the inherent shame and elements of disdain, was a Gypsy-Hungarian interaction. This would become explicit the next moment when some Gypsy relatives arrived and they received the provocative comment: 'Gee, these ones are not even greeting us! These already became Hungarians! What are you pretending?' Compared to the unnamed mode of the previous situation with the Hungarian woman, here the Gypsy-Hungarian distinction is voiced openly. While the silent situation showed the Hungarian-Gypsy relationship in action, the second situation transposed the Gypsy-Hungarian distinction into the playground of kin relationships.

This playground made it conceivable that the fear of being 'ashamed' might be made to disappear. Teasingly, they re-enacted the 'Hungarian non-greeting' and the hierarchical relation it created. They named, for each other, what could not be named in the previous situation; discarded the shame of the previous scene, replaying the conflict among themselves. In this way they freed the meaning of 'the Gypsy' from its shameful associations, from being despised and filled it, transformed it, with the experience of the closeness of relatives. This playground created familiarity, dissolved the shame inherent in the Gypsy-Hungarian distinction, but also produced strong meanings for the in-group which had their own coercive force. When in this playground the Gypsy-Hungarian distinction was dissolved, the 'common Gypsy' was introduced, which demanded that the experience of Gypsy-Hungarian interactions be handled 'within the Gypsy' space. This led to a world with increasingly autonomous meanings. Let me expand.

From the perspective of this world, the Hungarian was a constant 'outside': s/he did not have a real face; the village was inhabited by 'Hungarian women' and 'Hungarian men' as if in general. The Hungarian environment was a condition perceived as constant, it was the frame into which the Gypsy had to fit, or towards which one had to adapt in order to get by. The real issue, then, was how the Gypsy presence was realised. The differences which can be negotiated were, inevitably, only those between the Gypsies. From an insider's perspective, everything of importance happened 'within the Gypsy'.

The scene within which all this took place was kinship relations, which were structured by questions like, 'To whom do you give?', 'Whom do you stand aside?', 'Whom do you value more?', 'Whom do you cling to?', questions which focused on the issue of belonging and internal differences. These questions contributed to the creation of a closed world which reinforced itself, that is, 'Gypsyness'. But the origins of this world lay outside it, in the hierarchies of the village. The events that unfolded in front of the bar demonstrated this. In spite of not naming the Gypsy explicitly, the position of the Gypsy came into being, and as a denigrated category. People could experience the Gypsy position through being despised (as the reactions of those sitting on the terrace testified: they greeted politely, disciplined each other, and winked to each other at the same time), and through the uncertainty about how Gypsyness was present in any given situation. Those who ended up in the unnamed position of the Gypsy recreated the distinction among themselves as part of an attempt to dissolve the insecurity surrounding their presence in public space. They brought it into the specific 'playground' of talk among their brothers.

This playground was organised by the promise of commonality that made the challenges thrown up by distinction appear 'solvable'. But this promise was the same promise that defined their presence in the village and in the broader social space! Not naming the Gypsy carried the promise of the potential disappearance of the Gypsy-Hungarian distinction, therefore the Gypsies used all means at their disposal to sustain the silence. But it was also precisely the unfulfilled promise of the disappearance of this distinction that led to the situation in which they replayed the ambivalent experiences of adaptation in the context of 'inner' relations. This re-enactment, in turn, created a new promise of commonality beyond difference. This time 'common Gypsyness' was on offer. In fact this was just a variant of enacting the Gypsy; it amounted to another strategy of adaptation. The promise of the public dissolution of the Gypsy-Hungarian distinction produced the 'common Gypsy' and pushed it into the domain of the private sphere, but it also created distinctions within it, organised along lines of social division generated by different strategies of adaptation.

The social promise of the dissolution of the Gypsy-Hungarian distinction that was sustained by not naming the Gypsy was an extremely destructive mechanism. It made the 'differences' of the Gypsies disappear from the public sphere, while reinforcing them elsewhere. This double mechanism, the experience and reproduction of difference and its constant occlusion, could only be bridged by a collective social suppression. This collective suppression redirected the task of dealing with the ambivalent experiences generated by drawing this silent distinction to a subgroup of the people whose whole sense of identity was impacted by the social device of silence. In this way a group was created which reiterates its experiences in its 'own language' again and again while this separated them from their environment by an ever rising threshold. During the suppression of public distinctions, social experiences and practices diverged to an ever greater extent. And later it was the easiest thing in the world to name these divergences as 'Hungarian' and 'Gypsy', considered to represent some kind of fundamental difference. Today, in the moment of naming them, what seems to be the 'Gypsy' is presented as distant and dangerous and beyond obvious explanation but is, in fact, totally understandable if we look at it as the accumulation of the minority experiences produced by the order of the past decades. The majority society knows very little about this experience of the minority—that is the inner coping mechanisms produced from the inferior position of a hierarchical order. These experiences could not be publicly presented and in the process of 'big adaptation' people made huge efforts to hide them.

Returning to our previous example of children leaving the settlement on the way to school; this situation was exactly about the experience of 'leaving home'. The school (up until its eventual 'Gypsyfication') was a scene where the Gypsyness was unnamed and presented as disability. Here Gypsyness could only be experienced as a handicapped Hungarianness and in terms of coping with the shame and disadvantage of that position. These experiences were strongly present in the relationships between the children but, as it was customary in other areas of social life, they were translated into differences between families, and therefore reinterpreted as different forms of enacting 'Gypsyness'. For example, those who attended the remedial school, which itself raised the danger of 'shameful Gypsyness', were assumed to belong to the 'dirty Sasoj family'. Negotiations among the Gypsies about their experience with the school were carried out in the language of family differences. But as one arrived at school these inner negotiations about the 'Gypsy' were not communicable. In school Gypsyness, as we have suggested, could be presented only as disadvantage, as inferiority, so the children could only adapt to this situation and conceal as far as possible meanings of Gypsyness they might have brought from their family context. The school as the institution that taught the order of society to the children showed clearly how minority experiences were produced and at the same time rendered totally unrepresentable in the public sphere.

In this public sphere, the 'Gypsy' was always produced indirectly, through using some other quality, usually a category implying subordination and inferiority. This was based on the self-obvious fact that the 'Gypsy' was, and had to be, something pejorative, something negative, which needed to be silenced, that nobody would like to assume, and that would unavoidably produce a sense of shame when it surfaced. And of course this was a self-reproducing structure. Those people who were turned into the 'Gypsies' of this order (*a rend cigányai*) coped with this pejorative Gypsy-ness through their everyday relationships. Not being named directly as Gypsies but through indirect designations, gave them their room to move. This room was a predictable and safe space for them in the order and hier-archy of the village, where they were not subject to serious abuses or open attacks. If they had responded with confrontation they would have under-mined the safety of their situation. Although from the perspective of the present this mechanism seems extremely dangerous, as we see, the logic of an extremely refined oppression, and the traps this order produced, are also obvious, from the perspective of those who lived by this order it secured a liveable and predictable room to move. And it was the sense of safety in these inhabitable rooms of social life that encouraged the Gypsies to accept the constraining roles linked to permanent subordination that confined them to these rooms.

The old order carried the promise of the possibility of 'exiting' Gypsy-ness, escaping from it, while it simultaneously created those private and family stages where the Gypsy could be assumed and enacted, and the burdensome meanings attached to it dissolved. At the same time it both practically excluded opportunities for mobility and made experiencing or working to create a common Gypsyness impossible. Various discourses about poverty and disadvantaged social positions caused the social role of the Gypsy, with its own actions and political will, to vanish from public life. The Gypsy was turned into a totally passive social position, was invested with potential for activity and the generation of meaning only within his/ her family relations. Being in this social role one could only reinforce the social order and the hierarchy within which there was no valid social posi-tion from which Gypsies could join in the social game. Transforming the village hierarchy from the position of the Gypsy, engendering a dislocation of the social order from that perspective was unimaginable. Yet, in the trans-formations of the past years, which have involved the dissolution of the old safe order and the hierarchy of the village, the Gypsy obtained a key role. While earlier, explicitly naming the 'Gypsy' was absent even in the context of interactions based on the Gypsy-Hungarian distinction, today even the experience of the dissolution of the safe social world of the past can be expressed through 'the Gypsy issue'. This transformation has begun to etch in the lines of a new order of Gypsy distinction and a different social presence which creates new constraints and new spaces to move about in for those who end up on the Gypsy side. But these are strongly determined by the dynamics of the previous order of distinction presented here.

8

ANTI-GYPSYISM AND THE EXTREME-RIGHT IN THE CZECH REPUBLIC 2008–2011

Gwendolyn Albert

Taking accounts in the Czech media as its main source of material, this chapter will review the events surrounding recent elections in the Czech Republic, during which a resurgent extreme-right has specifically played the anti-Gypsy (anti-Roma) card in hope of attracting votes—in the regional and Senate elections of the autumn of 2008, the elections to the European Parliament of 2009, the elections to the Czech lower house of May 2010, and the municipal and Senate elections in the autumn of 2010. This chapter will review whether the global economic crisis is really a factor, analyse voter turnout in the elections, and describe the political impact of the large-scale neo-Nazi riots of November 2008 in the north Bohemian city of Litvínov. Comparisons to the previous heyday of extreme-right political success in the mid-1990s will be drawn and the present-day response of Roma organisations to the violent extremist targeting of their community will be outlined. The paper argues a) that anti-Gypsyism is a cultural habit in the Czech Republic which provides a sense of continuity in the face of societal change; b) that however much people may agree with the extremists' anti-Gypsy message, and however violent they are willing to be with respect to their Roman neighbours, Czech society is still reluctant to consciously, demonstratively embrace right-wing extremism, as that would

137

mean relinquishing 'victim' status; and c) that despite their poor electoral results, the extreme-right parties have pushed the political atmosphere in the Czech Republic toward the right and confirmed the political acceptability of anti-Gypsyism.

In the autumn of 2008 and the spring of 2009, the Czech Republic held elections to regional-level government and the Senate (2008) and to the European Parliament (2009) during which two extreme-right parties, the National Party (Národní strana, hereinafter 'NP') and the Workers' Party (Dělnická strana, hereinafter 'WP'), played a significant role in giving voice to anti-Gypsyism in the country. Not since the 1993 electoral success of the Republican Party (Republikanská strana or SPR-RSČ, hereinafter 'RP') had proponents of extreme-right views achieved such national visibility or influenced debate in Czech society to such an extent. However, by the time elections to the Czech lower house took place in May 2010, those particular incarnations of these extremist parties were essentially defunct. The National Party collapsed of its own accord, while the Workers' Party was banned in February 2010. WP members regrouped as the Workers' Social Justice Party (Dělnická strana sociální spravedlnosti, hereinafter 'WSJP') and fielded candidates in the May 2010 elections to the lower house and again in municipal elections in the autumn. Some WP tactics were adopted in 2010 by the upstart Public Affairs Party (Věci veřejné, hereinafter 'VV'), which is now the junior partner in the centre-right governing coalition.

While the NP, the WP, and the WSJP have never enjoyed national-level electoral success, national electoral results are only one way to measure their significance. The impact of their activity has been to push politics ever-rightward in the Czech Republic from the ground up, in effect mapping to what extent various local populations would tolerate the extremes of anti-Gypsy political action. Centre-right parties such as the Civic Democrats (ODS) have monitored the public's reaction to the extremists' antics and then appropriated those tactics for testing, mostly in the impoverished north of the country. The extremists' overt anti-Gypsyism has been mostly tolerated in the name of free speech, speech to which the centre-right has not much objected, as it understands the extremists are giving voice to beliefs which are held, as opinion polls relentlessly show, by 80 per cent or more of the Czech population. This hatred has had a profoundly negative impact on the Roma minority in the Czech Republic and has resulted in intensified attempts at pogroms against them in the autumn of 2011.

The National Party—a bark worse than its bite

The NP, officially registered in 2002, was founded by the relatively young and photogenic Petra Edelmannová. Despite having very few actual supporters, the party punched above its weight in terms of media impact, staging events and producing material that were specifically anti-Gypsy, including campaigns against removing an industrial pig farm from the site of the former Nazi concentration camp for Roma at Lety in south Bohemia.[1] The most recent and final example of the party's impact was its television advertisement for the June 2009 EP elections, which despite its blatantly anti-Gypsy content was broadcast by public station Czech Television before being pulled;[2] Czech TV was subsequently reported to be filing criminal charges against the party.[3] The ad can still be accessed on YouTube quite easily and is worth describing in detail for what it shows us about Czech anti-Gypsyism.

The video opens with a drawing of a white sheep kicking a black sheep off the Czech flag (an image Czech media commentators said was first used by the Swiss People's Party; the NP claimed to have permission to use the image, but Czech media quoted a Swiss People's Party spokesperson as saying he had no knowledge of such permission having been granted).[4] After this image, we read that 'THE FINAL SOLUTION TO THE GYPSY QUESTION PROPOSED BY THE NATIONAL PARTY IS A BLUEPRINT FOR ALL EUROPEAN STATES'.[5] We next see a photograph of two men, both of whom are missing teeth and are clutching an axe together, who are evidently supposed to be 'Gypsies'; the text 'STOP BLACK RACISM'[6] appears over their faces. The screen after that reads 'NP against integration of inadaptables'.[7] The next image is that of run-down blocks of flats with laundry hanging out to dry on the balconies (a stereotypical Czech image of 'Gypsies'), followed by a photo of a garbage-strewn entrance to a dwelling. The next screen reads 'NO! favouring of Gypsies',[8] followed by an image of four 'Gypsy' adults and a child, and then an image of several 'Gypsy' men at a swimming pool wearing oversized gold jewellery. The next screen reads 'WE DEFEND CZECH NATIONAL INTERESTS',[9] followed by 'STOP! their demanding and thieving mentality',[10] followed by a photo of several 'Gypsies', including children, standing and sitting in close proximity to one another in a living room. The next image is that of several 'Gypsy' women, almost all of them carrying infants, captioned 'YOUR TAXES—THEIR FUTURE!'.[11] This is followed by a screen reading 'We do not want black racists among us'[12] and then video footage of a 'Gypsy' woman gesticulating angrily at the camera (and therefore at the viewer). The next screen reads 'We don't want parasites among us',[13] followed by more images of 'Gypsies' in groups or singly, ending on an image of several 'Gypsy' men standing in a line, one of whom is shouting and gesticulating with a golf club. The next screen reads 'WE PROTECT YOU AND YOUR FAMILY'[14] before the ad ends with a photo of Edelmannová and the exhortation to send 'Petra' to the European Parliament (EP).

Comments were still being posted beneath this one-minute video on YouTube in August 2009, most of them in Czech and in favour of the content. Commentators wrote entries such as 'the Roma are the cancer of the Czech Republic', 'something should be done about [Gypsies]', or 'blondes aren't stupid' (a reference to Edelmannová). One commentator wrote that while he agreed with the video, it was 'probably too harsh' and would lead to the country being 'thrown out of all world organisations except for the "Stop Gypsies Organization"'.

The 'final solution' referred to at the start of the NP ad was the centrepiece of its 2009 EP election campaign, a proposal to deport all Roma from the Czech Republic 'back' to India. In central Bohemia, the NP candidate list even included a police officer, Jaroslav Bernášek, who was not a party member. While the law on police service says officers are not permitted to be members of political parties or movements and are not permitted to 'undertake activities that benefit' parties or movements, the Police Presidium said neither Bernášek's candidacy nor his potential election were necessarily a 'benefit' to the party and that his candidacy was therefore legal in their view.

The Workers' Party—roving watchdog

While the NP had a disproportionately large impact in the virtual world through its official party website and others for which it is responsible,[15] it is the WP that has had a harmful impact on Roma in the real world. This party was registered in 2003 by former members of the RP and is headed by Tomáš Vandas, once secretary to former RP chair Miroslav Sládek.[16] Media report WP membership at around 300; the party scored three municipal seats in 2006. In the 2008 regional elections it seated no one, but reported receiving 29,000 votes; its candidate in the Vysočina region was a prominent neo-Nazi activist, Erik Sedláček, acquitted earlier this year of charges of 'promoting a movement aimed at suppressing human rights', allegedly due to police mishandling of the case against him.[17] During 2008 and 2009, WP election rallies were attended by various neo-Nazi and/or ultra-right groups, such as the Autonomous Nationalists (Autonomní nacionalisté), National Resistance (Národní odpor), or the now-defunct National Corporativism (Národní korporativismus), which recommended that all its former members join the WP when it ended its own activities in April 2008. The WP seemed to have more or less successfully united these disparate groups around an anti-Gypsy platform. While the NP caused a stir with its claim to be establishing a militia called the 'National Guard' (which essentially never materialised), it was the WP that actually sent out what it called its 'protection corps' of uniformly dressed party members to 'monitor' predominantly Roma neighbourhoods, claiming it had to 'address' complaints from 'decent' (i.e., non-Roma) citizens as the police were allegedly failing to do so. This 'monitoring' has resulted in violence, most notoriously in the north Bohemian town of Litvínov in November 2008, as will be explored in more detail below.[18] The 'protection corps' phenomenon prompted the Czech Federation of Jewish Communities and other civil society organisations to demand the government outlaw the WP, a demand which was reiterated by more than 3000 signatories to a petition delivered to the Czech government in August 2009.[19] The story of the effort to ban the party will also be covered below.

In most places the WP's 'monitoring' was resisted by members of the Roma community, by activists who identify as 'anti-fascists', and by other non-Roma of no particular affiliation. Local and state police, including riot units and anti-conflict teams, were repeatedly called into action at WP events during 2008 and 2009. Despite the widely reported violence that accompanied the WP 'protection corps' patrols, election rallies and marches, their blatantly racist rhetoric, and their attempts to schedule gatherings in order to exploit dates of neo-Nazi significance, very few municipal authorities attempted to prevent the party from convening gatherings in their towns, and even fewer have permitted organised counter-gatherings (to say nothing of publicly supporting them). Some of the WP gatherings were even attended by neo-Nazis from other European countries, such as when the WP held a 'Day of Freedom' rally on 15 August 2009, two days prior to the anniversary of the death of Rudolf Hess (deceased 17 August 1987).[20]

Fantasies of victimhood and anti-Gypsyism

While both the NP and WP spent more than five years building their 'brands', it was their recent use of specifically anti-Gypsy rhetoric and their targeting of places associated with Roma (Lety, specific Roma neighbour-hoods) that propelled them to the forefront of media attention more than anything else. Both parties rejected being described as racist or neo-Nazi even as they attempted to foster a general fear of foreigners (and, in the case of the NP, Muslims).[21] The WP also consistently referred to government corruption. However, none of those topics ever generated the response that their targeting of the Roma—their anti-Gypsyism—did. A brief exploration of anti-Gypsyism is therefore appropriate here.

Valeriu Nicolae has argued that anti-Gypsyism is a 'distinct type of racist ideology' in which 'dehumanisation of the Roma appears to be a legitimising myth that serves to justify the majority's abusive behaviour towards this minority'.[22] With respect to the case of the Czech Republic, his observation that 'a tremendous amount of energy is spent in justifying or legitimising political, economic, and cultural exclusion of Roma' rings particularly true, as does his observation that 'anti-Gypsyism has such contempt for reason, facts, and intellectual debate that it requires little effort to justify its often ideological contradictions and changes, a feature that links it strongly with fascism'.[23] In the case of the Czech Republic, even human rights defenders have perpetuated the highly emotional nature of the debate on relations between the 'majority population' and the Roma minority. For example, upon first taking office as Human Rights and Minorities Minister in the Topolánek cabinet, Michael Kocáb, famous as a dissident in communist Czechoslovakia and as a rock musician, made 'I love Roma' one of his first declarations and has been characterised in the mainstream media ever since as basically 'unhinged'.[24] During his time in office, Kocáb made a significant contribution toward highlighting not only positive examples of Czech-Roma co-existence in the country but the fact that members of the Roma minority are the target of various abuses committed in the name of the majority society, some of which will be described below. However, the overall tenor of his efforts has had less to do with rationality (or even legality) than it has with emotional appeals to moral principles. The Nečas cabinet formed in July 2010 no longer includes the post of Human Rights and Minorities Minister; Kocáb was appointed to the lower-profile office of Human Rights Commissioner and then removed from that position in September 2010. The post then remained unfilled for six months thereafter.

As the NP television ad showed, today's perpetrators of anti-Gypsyism in the Czech Republic reject being identified as 'racist', and a key component of their psychology is that they insist they are in fact the 'victims' of racism.

They label the Roma 'racist', and the terms 'black racism' or 'Gypsy racism' are enjoying a vogue. Vehement expressions of dislike of the Roma are socially acceptable in the Czech Republic, where it is not unusual to encounter people who preface anti-Gypsy rhetoric with 'I am not a racist, but…'. This is not limited to the extreme-right; for example, former Christian Democratic party head Jiří Čunek, whose meteoric rise to power in 2006 was largely based on anti-Gypsy rhetoric and deeds, received a great deal of societal approval for his claim that the extended family structures of Roma constitute an inherent violation of the Charter of Fundamental Rights and Freedoms.[25] Such stances are crucial to understanding Czech anti-Gypsy politics: the non-Roma 'majority society', which has the power to exclude the Roma and has done so for generations, views itself as the victims of those it excludes, and attempts to usurp the rhetoric of rights to justify its behaviour. It is as if, on a societal level, the same twisted reasoning that makes it possible for domestic abusers to 'blame the victim' for the abuser's violence is at work in the dynamic between those who predominate in Czech society and those in the numerically insignificant Roma minority.

A more in-depth exploration of Czech anti-Gypsyism requires more space than is available here; the association of Roma ethnicity with social deviance in the former Czechoslovakia, including its gender dimension, has been quite extensively analysed by Sokolová.[26] Historical context is obviously crucial, and it is worth recalling that for the entire twentieth century, Czechoslovak (and later Czech) society essentially underwent large-scale political upheaval once a generation. This is a society that began the twentieth century as part of the Austro-Hungarian Empire, achieved an independent democracy only to become a Nazi protectorate, briefly reconstituted that democracy before becoming a communist dictatorship, was 'fraternally' invaded by the Warsaw Pact even during the course of that dictatorship, and after the neo-Stalinism of the 'normalisation' era, emerged at the end of the twentieth century to be ushered into the EU, globalisation and NATO at lightning speed. It is not surprising that members of this society might feel they are the victims of all kinds of forces beyond their control, many of which challenge their sense of identity. In a desire to commune around a source of their victimhood, they seem to be focusing on one of the few constants in their environment for all these years: the Roma.

My personal experience of the past fifteen years in Czech society is that many non-Roma in the Czech Republic regularly seek validation from others of their status as victims and are averse to narratives that might place them in the role not just of 'perpetrators', but even of persons responsible for their actions. Many people not only desire to be seen as victims of the Roma, they genuinely believe this to be the case. In the absence of direct personal experience, non-Roma relate claims of Romany transgressions to other non-Roma for which they are usually unable to offer proof (even if the claims defy reason) and which they assume will be unquestioningly believed by their interlocutors. These fantasies have transitioned into twenty-first century modes of communication with ease; for example, a recent email spammed to millions of Czech internet users and purporting to be from the Labour and Social Affairs Ministry warned readers that Roma who had never been employed or paid into any pension scheme were nonetheless receiving greater retirement benefits than non-Roma who had worked all their lives and paid in. The ministry had to issue a press release to correct the record.[27]

That these claims of victimhood are often based in fantasy is clear, as lack of contact with Roma is the norm; after all, the Roma population in the Czech Republic accounts for, at most, 2.5 per cent of the entire population. In addition, the Roma are defined by Czech society as essentially 'foreign', as most have their origins and family ties in neighbouring Slovakia. Many non-Roma in the Czech Republic therefore perceive the Roma as a population that is perpetually on the verge of exponential expansion through immigration from 'the east'. Lastly, a dominant tenet of Czech anti-Gypsyism is that reports of Roma being victimised by non-Roma must be automatically rejected as almost categorically impossible. Examples of this will be described below.

Mainstream parties test extremist rhetoric; Extremists test violence

The elections in October 2008 to regional government and to one-third of the Senate seats sent a clear signal to the centre-right coalition, led by the Civic Democrats (ODS), that the electorate was displeased. Voter turnout for the regional elections and for the first round of the Senate elections was 39.52 per cent, the highest turnout ever for a regional race;[28] for the second round of the Senate elections, turnout was 29.85 per cent. Opposition Social Democrats (ČSSD) won all thirteen of the regional races, an astounding mandate, as well as twenty-three of the twenty-seven Senate seats contested. This victory fuelled their efforts to continue to seek no-confidence votes, and they later succeeded in toppling the Topolánek government on the fifth such attempt in early 2009 during the country's first-ever EU presidency, a political move glossed by the centre-right as essentially 'treasonous'.

Neither the NP nor the WP fielded candidates in the 2008 Senate race, but in the 2008 regional elections, the WP ran in all thirteen regions in coalition with the Democratic Social Justice Party under the name 'The Workers' Party for the Abolition of Fees in Health Care', except in the Plzeň region, where it ran under the name 'The Workers' Party—No to the U.S. Radar!',[29] achieving its best results there with 1.47 per cent of the vote (its nationwide total was 0.9 per cent). The NP ran only in the central Bohemian and Moravian-Silesian regions, earning 0.41 per cent of the vote and 0.28 per cent of the vote respectively.[30]

The attention-grabbing antics of the extremist parties during their regional campaigns prompted mainstream parties also to exploit anti-Gypsyism in their campaigns. Dymo Piškula, the mayor of Břeclav and head of the SNK-ED (Association of Independent Candidates—European Democrats) candidate list, in the south Moravian region ran billboards reading 'Do we close our eyes to the Roma problem? NO!' His regional party programme claimed that:

… the Roma problem is starting to prey on a large group of people. In the majority of cases they get away with not respecting the laws… The government cannot continue to make only cosmetic changes. It must also allocate the necessary finances to make it possible for restrictive measures to be taken immediately. We must find a solution and put an end to the privileging of only one particular population group. Let's stop the abuse of the social system; the laws must apply to all.

There, in Moravia, his party received only 1.39 per cent of the vote.[31]

Candidates for the governing ODS party also resorted to anti-Gypsyism during regional elections in northern Bohemia. Incumbent Jiří Šulc (ODS) came in second place with 20.57 per cent of the vote in the Ústí region compared to 32.78 per cent for the Social Democrats.[32] ODS posted election banners in the Most and Ústí districts, reading, 'Gadje, get to work so we can be better off'. Police found nothing illegal about the ads, which Šulc claimed were aimed at drawing attention to 'welfare abuse', a priority issue of the ODS. He rejected criticism of the campaign as racist and claimed the slogan was an actual piece of graffiti he had seen on a block of flats in the predominantly Roma-occupied housing estate of Janov in Litvínov.[33] Later that November, as a result of WP 'patrols', that housing estate would become the site of the largest riots in the country for nine years.

These campaigns took place against a backdrop of rising neo-Nazi activity specifically targeting the Roma. In August 2008 the Interior Ministry's Unit for the Detection of Organised Crime (Útvar pro odhalování organizovaného zločinu—ÚOOZ) released its report for 2007, which said Czech extremists in the 'white power' movement were adopting the tactics of similar groups abroad, including having registered political parties convene events which illegal groups could then attend.[34] Later that month, in Hradec Králové, the WP convened an unannounced demonstration where the speeches included neo-Nazi ideology. Activist Ondřej Cakl, who has been documenting the neo-Nazi movement for more than a decade, was physically attacked by neo-Nazis there, as were journalists, but official police reports said there were 'no incidents'. The Association of Liberated Political Prisoners and their Survivors (Sdružení osvobozených politických vězňů a pozůstalých—SOPVP) issued a statement on the event reporting that police on hand had not intervened.[35]

Starting on 6 September 2008, there was a separate arson attack on a different Roma family elsewhere in the country every weekend, fortunately without serious physical injuries. The first attack was in Moravský Beroun (Moravia), where two Molotov cocktails were thrown into a Roma-occupied home. One week later, someone set fire to a Roma family's caravan in the town of Kozulepy (Bohemia).[36] The third attack took place around 3:00 am the next weekend, when a Molotov cocktail was thrown into the ground-floor flat of a Roma family living in a former military barracks in Bruntál (Silesia), setting the kitchen on fire. Five people were sleeping in the flat; luckily no one was injured. This wave of attacks was similar to those committed against the Roma in 1996–98 and was only the beginning.[37]

October 2008 saw the start of the WP harassment of Roma at the Janov housing estate in Litvínov. This particular location had seen a rise in Romany residents in recent years as a result of real estate developers attempting to gentrify neighbourhoods elsewhere in the country. Indigent and indebted residents, many of them Roma, were persuaded to give up their tenancies of potentially valuable real estate in Prague and other cities in exchange for relief from their debts and relatively low-cost housing at Janov. Unlike the communist regime, during which demographic change was engineered by government, the invisible hand of the market was now determining who lived where, and the non-Romany residents of Janov felt their officials were failing them.

The WP announced it had received numerous complaints from local residents about the behaviour of their 'inadaptable' neighbours and that it would be sending its 'protection corps' to 'monitor' the situation. On 4 October, twelve members of the 'protection corps', dressed all in black with white armbands, met with resistance from seventy Roma residents, some carrying sticks, who came out to prevent their march; police narrowly averted a direct clash between the two groups.[38] One particular verbal exchange between a physically slight female WP activist and a Romany man twice her size was broadcast on national television, with the predictable result of incensing many non-Roma. On 12 October, police were investigating who had spray-painted graffiti threatening the Roma in Litvínov with death on two separate buildings.[39] On 20 October, 500 police officers, including helicopter surveillance, had to be called out to protect the Roma from an attempted pogrom by aggressive neo-Nazis who did not hesitate to engage the police in violence.[40] The clashes claimed four injuries (three police officers and one extremist). Police arrested four radicals who attacked police officers and held another six for questioning over weapons found in their cars; one man was later charged with disorderly conduct.[41] The WP then held a gathering in Prague on 28 October, the national holiday commemorating the founding of Czechoslovakia and a favourite rallying day for Czech nationalists; 200 supporters turned out, and of the thirteen detained ten were carrying blade weapons. Three youths attacked a random passerby, severely injuring his head, in the metro stop nearest the gathering just before it began.[42] Two Romany men were also attacked that day in Hodonín by five neo-Nazis attending a demonstration there; one victim managed to flee but the other one suffered a broken nose.[43] On 8 November, two young Roma men were brutally attacked in Havířov by a group of neo-Nazis, one sustaining serious brain injury and paralysis.[44]

The Litvínov riot

On 17 November, which is now a state holiday in honour of the Velvet Revolution, the biggest event of the decade in terms of racist violence took place immediately following a WP gathering on the main square in Litvínov. Neo-Nazis exchanged tips online prior to the event on how to best arm themselves to do battle with the police. In the end, 1000 riot officers were needed to protect the Janov housing estate in Litvínov from hundreds of neo-Nazis from the Czech Republic and abroad, who tried to march on the Roma there. After two hours fighting extremists, who threw paving stones and Molotov cocktails, set police cars on fire, and destroyed journalists' equipment, the police succeeded in preventing the pogrom, patrolling long into the night to prevent further attacks by individuals. The clashes resulted in seventeen injuries, half of them police, three of them journalists and one a human rights observer. The Roma and their supporters held a peaceful demonstration on the streets of Janov during the riot, but non-Roma residents were captured on video applauding the neo-Nazis, calling for the police to 'let them in', and shouting racist insults at the Roma demonstrators. The event was also covered by international television channels.[45] The operation cost CZK 40 million (USD 2 million). Police later confirmed that the neo-Nazis were armed with materiel only available to members of the armed forces, such as various types of explosives.[46] The dozen or so rioters who were arrested were not kept in custody and prosecutions against any of them have yet to begin.

The Romany residents at Janov were just about the only people subsequently to praise the police intervention. Human rights activists criticised the police for not nipping the march in the bud, while for non-Romany locals the use of state police to specifically protect the Roma served to exacerbate their sense that Prague was distant from and indifferent to their local grievances.

In the aftermath of Litvínov, the Czech government made an historic attempt to request the Supreme Administrative Court dissolve a registered political party (for other than technical reasons). Unlike the successful dissolution of the Communist Youth Union, which will be explored below, the government failed in its attempt. The brief submitted against the WP in February 2009 was so weak as to prompt speculation among civil society observers that the move had essentially been for show.[47]

Anti-Gypsyism as a career-saver: 'Operation Lifesaver'

In the meantime, the anti-Gypsyism card was being played by yet another local-level mainstream politician in Bohemia, Chomutov mayor Ivana Řápková (ODS). Her story is a classic example of a politician scapegoating the Roma in an effort to redirect the public's attention. Řápková's tenure had been marked by scandals surrounding the leasing of publicly-owned real estate to a town councillor, a decision to build a recreation centre on the town outskirts criticised by many as wasteful, and her petulant removal of the director of the local zoo due to his criticism of her decisions. Faced with 6000 signatures on a petition calling for her resignation, Řápková launched 'Operation Lifesaver', a move intended to divide Chomutov voters into two camps; the 'decent' and the 'inadaptable' (understood to be the Roma), and to underscore the governing ODS party's commitment to counteracting 'welfare abuse' (again understood as committed by Roma). Many tenants in municipally-owned flats owed the city back rent, so Řápková staged a well-orchestrated and well-publicised stunt: she arranged for collections agents, accompanied by police officers, to accost welfare recipients as they were receiving their monthly stipends in cash from the town hall, monies intended for food and other necessities which, in theory, cannot legally be subject to collections.[48] In a completely illegal procedure, police officers asked those standing in line to prove their identities; the collections agents who were standing right beside them would just 'happen' to overhear the person's name, look them up on the list, and deprive them of their cash on the spot. The town hall even sent the media advance information that this would be taking place, including specially prepared materials in their press package of unattractive video footage from the local Roma ghetto, and later provided the media with access to the images from the CCTV cameras located above the counter concerned in the town hall (itself a violation of the law on the protection of personal information). In an example par excellence of the lengths to which those committed to anti-Gypsyism will go to establish their view of the Roma as a threat, the faces of the police officers captured in the images were digitally manipulated to render them unidentifiable and protect their identities, while the welfare recipients' faces—those of the 'criminals', in effect—were clearly visible.[49]

Řápková's moves were immediately criticised by the office of the Czech ombudsman and by Human Rights and Minorities Minister Kocáb, national authorities perceived by many as far removed from local concerns in Chomutov. Indeed, the mayor even played on this distinction by challenging the minister to come and live in the Roma ghetto and see how he liked it. Other cabinet members were more oblique in their characterisations of her illegal schemes and Czech President Václav Klaus, the country's most popular politician, even stood by her, calling her a 'rationally behaving' politician and saying he did not have a particularly strong opinion about the confiscation of benefits: 'Madame Mayor, I believe, speaks rationally, reasonably, she makes rather clear arguments—*she is no extremist* [emphasis added]…', the president said, before going on to undercut Minister Kocáb's human rights mandate by characterising him as an isolated official leading a 'nifty non-ministry'—'A real minister has 500 bureaucrats who supply him with thousands of materials, documents, decisions from morning to evening'.[50]

Řápková responded to the criticism by maintaining Operation Lifesaver had been aimed at 'inadaptables', not at Roma. Over the past few years this term has become broadly accepted and used in the media; Czech Green Party chair Ondřej Liška has noted its roots in Nazi terminology.[51] Embodying notions of social class and expectations of social conformity, this de-ethnicised term provides Czech proponents of anti-Gypsyism with a way to refer to the Roma without seeming racist. Be that as it may, residents of Chomutov reported a sharp rise in unabashed anti-Gypsyism following Operation Lifesaver. As commentator Jaroslav Blažek noted: 'Go into the pubs and supermarkets of Chomutov, listen to people on public transit. Statements such as 'I'd shoot all those Gypsies', once considered shameful, have now become socially acceptable to the greater public'.[52]

Locals who work with the Roma community in Chomutov say the town hall had not previously tried to send social workers to the indebted families, had never systematically monitored the situation, and had never asked for the town's legal status as 'special beneficiary' in its capacity as landlord to be acknowledged by the courts. In other words, instead of taking the legal route to collecting debts in a justifiable manner, the whole event was staged in order to provide the mayor with the image of someone who knew how to get the town's money back from the wastrels who had been 'stealing' it.[53] Some of the families whose welfare was collected in this way were left with the equivalent of only €38 for the month; moreover, the collections agents included their own exorbitant fees in the amounts collected. 'Operation Lifesaver' primarily rescued Řápková's career for a time and turned her into something of a national hero; the local petition calling for her resignation was soon dwarfed by an online one with more than 100,000 people writing in to support her tough measures. She has since gone on to become an MP and continues to promote various repressive measures against the 'inadaptables'.

The Vítkov arson attack

Meanwhile, revitalised by its court victory, the WP went on to hold an unprecedented march in the north Bohemian town of Ústí nad Labem on 18 April (a few days prior to Hitler's birthday). The event saw hundreds of neo-Nazis, some of them from Germany, standing on a town square named after the village of Lidice while listening to a speech in German that called for the revival of the Reich. Police intervened only against the few counter-protestors who turned out that day.[54]

That same evening elsewhere in the country, three Molotov cocktails were thrown into the home of a Romany family in the town of Vítkov, resulting in an infant suffering third-degree burns over 80 per cent of her body and the amputation of several fingers. Four suspects were arrested, charged with racially motivated attempted murder, and brought to trial.[55] Their ties to neo-Nazi organizations and the Workers' Party, their participation in the Litvínov riots, and the timing of the attack as a celebration of Hitler were a major part of the prosecution's case.[56] The media reported that WP leader Vandas personally associated with arson suspect Jaromír Lukeš, and that another suspect, David Vaculík, was a long-term sponsor of the party, charges Vandas denied even as he continued to insist that no one in the party is either an extremist or a racist. The defendants were convicted in October 2010 and received extraordinary sentences of either twenty or twenty-two years. The Czech President, Klaus, said he found the sentences 'unexpectedly high'.

The WP exploited the media attention it received as a result of the police investigation into links between the suspects and the neo-Nazi movement, and Vandas used the charges as a forum for reiterating his own critique of the major political parties, referencing mainstream press reports that those parties' sponsors include suspected mafia members.[57] The fact that the police investigation of the Vítkov arson occurred during the run-up to the lower house elections played into Vandas' attempt to portray himself as the 'David' against the 'Goliath' of the system, allowing him and his supporters to revel in that prized status in Czech society, that of the underdog and victim.

In response to the arson, Romany civil society organisations and their allies, including Amnesty International, immediately coordinated simulta-neous protest gatherings in fourteen locations in early May throughout the Czech Republic; solidarity events were also held in Canada and the United Kingdom. In three of the Czech locations, neo-Nazis fearlessly attacked the demonstrators. The worst incident was in Řápková's Chomutov, where members of the WP[58] and illegal neo-Nazi groups threw smoke bombs at peaceful demonstrators while police looked on. Civil rights observers imme-diately wrote a letter of protest to the authorities over this unprecedented police laxity.[59] In her response, following the logic of anti-Gypsyism, Mayor Řápková blamed the Romany demonstrators for the incident, characterising them as essentially equivalent to the neo-Nazis, for which she was subsequently again criticised by Kocáb from distant Prague.

The Vítkov arson attack galvanised the Romany community nationwide to a degree not seen since the Velvet Revolution; the demonstrations to protest the attack were attended by more than 3000 people across the country, the vast majority of them Roma, most of whom signed petitions and contributed almost three-quarters of a million crowns (€30,000) toward relief for the victims, money about which much envy was later verbalised.[60] Involving Romany victims as it did, this attack had to be reframed to fit the tenets of anti-Gypsyism, and so the national discussion offered various theories of the attack to fit that frame: the attackers must have been other Roma, perhaps loan sharks angry that they hadn't been paid; the family was alleged to have hoarded fuel in their home, which explained the total destructiveness of the fire (i.e., they were to blame); the family was even alleged to have performed the arson themselves. The anti-Gypsyism did not stop with mere speculation, but impacted every aspect of the family's treatment by the town of Vítkov. During the six months it took to find them adequate substitute housing, the family was accommodated in a temporary shelter next to the dog pound. Locals refused to have them as neighbours and petitioned the mayor to keep them out of town, and they did eventually end up relocating elsewhere.[61] Child welfare authorities attempted, unsuccessfully, to institutionalise the family's other children. The mayor maligned the family's reputation and said the donations collected on their behalf might even end up confiscated by regional authorities if they could not hurry up and find themselves a place to live.[62] The family's sudden celebrity made them the target of death threats and obsessive neo-Nazi online chatter. However, over time the unquestionable total innocence of the infant victim and the media coverage of her struggle to overcome her injuries have managed to humanise, for the first time, the Romany victims of neo-Nazi violence in the Czech Republic.

Many in the Romany community now felt the situation had become one of life or death, similar to the violence in the mid-1990s that had prompted the first wave of Romany emigration to Canada and resulted in the introduction of visas for all Czech citizens in 1997. Those visas had been lifted in 2007, but both Litvínov and Vítkov prompted new spikes in emigration from the country to Canada. During the Canada-EU summit in May 2009, Canadian officials hinted that visas would be reintroduced for Czech citizens and made good on that hint in July 2009, a move which Amnesty International later criticised.

The Fischer cabinet cracks down

In May 2009 the caretaker cabinet of Jan Fischer was sworn in. There had been speculation that the position of Human Rights and Minorities Minister would not be retained, but in the end Michael Kocáb was the only minister to continue over from the previous cabinet; this may possibly have been due to the country's place in the international spotlight during the Czech EU presidency, the EP elections, and the negative attention Litvínov and Vítkov had drawn. Prime Minister Topolánek had been tone-deaf on social issues in general and the performance of his Interior Ministry with respect to rising neo-Nazi violence was not as robust as many human rights observers would have liked, particularly where the attempt to dissolve the WP was concerned.[63] Extremists were busy during May, with 500 attending the WP May Day rally in Brno (two were arrested for vandalising a police vehicle and six were brought before the courts on charges of 'promoting a movement aimed at suppressing human rights and freedoms'). The party was also looking forward to the June release of the first issue of the newspaper published by its youth group (Workers' Youth—Dělnická mládež), *National Resistance* (also the name of a banned neo-Nazi organisation).[64] Several other WP rallies that month met with significantly more resistance from ordinary citizens than previous ones had, but in Litvínov police persisted in arresting even peaceful counter-demonstrators, moves which were subsequently criticised (quite unusually) by Czech Social Democratic Party leader Jiří Paroubek.[65]

In early June 2009, Czech police conducted an operation they said was the result of a year-and-a-half of planning, raiding the homes of ten prominent neo-Nazis, five of whom were taken into custody. The crackdown has had ominous consequences, with police confirming that the families of Fischer and the Interior Minister, Pecina, were now under protection after threats were made against them by neo-Nazis.[66]

The EP elections

The NP, the WP and a revived RP[67] all fielded candidates in the June 2009 EP elections. Voter turnout was 28.22 per cent. The Civic Democrats won with 31.45 per cent of the vote in all regions except Olomouc, where the Social Democrats were victorious. The campaign was marked by high school and college-aged voters using social networking sites such as Facebook to organise egg-throwing attacks against Czech Social Democratic Party leader Jiří Paroubek.[68]

Unlike some other EU Member States, right-wing extremist parties in the Czech Republic did not win any EP seats. The elections featured two new specifically euro-sceptic parties, Libertas.cz and the Party of Free Citizens (SSO), which did not succeed. The results for the extremist parties are nevertheless instructive as to the relative success of the various brands. The NP received 6263 votes nationwide (0.26 per cent) and the RP received 7492 (0.31 per cent). Two events of significance for the WP had occurred between the polls in October 2008 and June 2009: the Litvínov riots and the Topolánek government's subsequent failed attempt to have the party dissolved. In the end the party received 25,368 votes, or 1.07 per cent of the total. In the greater Most district (where Litvínov is located) the party earned 3.67 per cent, and its result in the town of Litvínov itself, the site of its most intensive activity, was 7.81 per cent of the vote.[69]

Even though the NP's television ad for the EP elections has gone on to live a life of its own on the internet, it backfired for them in the real world. The ad was immediately forcefully condemned by Prime Minister Fischer, as well as the Secretary General of the Council of Europe, who issued a statement saying it fell 'well outside' the limits on the right to freedom of expression established by the European Convention.[70] Of the extreme-right parties, it seems the WP's investment into real-time rallies and 'monitoring' of Roma neighbourhoods paid the most dividends; the government's failed attempt to dissolve the party also gave its leader Vandas the aura of the 'unjustly persecuted'. While the party had finally crossed the 1 per cent threshold, which guaranteed it state support, media reports immediately after the election suggested the WP might not be receiving the funds immediately, as it had submitted a financial report for 2008 to parliament that lacked information on its donors, such as addresses, birth-dates, or even names.[71]

The WP had its own problems with the EP campaign: Czech Radio refused to broadcast two WP ads, including statements such as, 'We reject the government policy of Gypsy racism when the Gypsies are paid from our taxes so they do not have to work and spend their free time harassing decent people'.[72] Unlike Czech television, which in the case of the NP ad claimed to have been unsure which option was more illegal (to broadcast or not), Czech Radio concluded it would be illegal to air the WP ads and also said it would press charges against the WP. For its part the WP filed its own charges against the radio director on 'suspicion of interfering with the course of an election'. The party also convened a demonstration against the decision in Prague in late May; in a rare example of proper procedure in such cases, the gathering of about sixty supporters was dispersed by a city official with the help of police after Vandas veered into illegality during his speech by calling for 'National Socialism'. Protesters then attempted to march on Czech Radio, a plan they had not announced to authorities beforehand, and were arrested after a brief scuffle.[73]

Meanwhile, commentators on the Czech Supreme Administrative Court's decision to reject the Topolánek cabinet's application to have the WP disbanded were satisfied that the outcome could not have been otherwise, as courts in the Czech Republic do not perform their own discovery and the government's case had been very poorly made. Upon issuing its verdict the court said it had repeatedly asked for further evidence to be submitted by both sides and had received none. The Czech political scientist, Jan Charvát, called the Interior Ministry's work 'sloppy';[74] despite being relatively abundant and accessible, evidence of the WP's connection to perpetrators of violence had not been submitted to the court. The Czech Social Democratic Party leader, Paroubek, called for Interior Minister Ivan Langer's resignation after the verdict was announced.[75] Langer's response to the decision was instructive: 'The court for the first time has described the general criteria according to which it decides in cases where it evaluates a proposal to abolish a party for contravening the legal order'.[76]

This response should be viewed in the larger context of efforts to remove the Communist Party of Bohemia and Moravia (KSČM) from political life in the Czech Republic. The KSČM has been a constant presence in the Czech Parliament and at the EP, garnering an average of 15 per cent of voter support during the past twenty years of democratic elections; their results in the 2010 lower house elections were 11.27 per cent, the fourth-greatest result. While they have never been invited into government, like other small parties in any proportional system their votes can be crucial on issues where the margin of support for a particular measure is close. In recent years some right-wing senators have led a campaign to ban the party, arguing it was a mistake not to outlaw it in 1989.

The party's youth wing, the KSM, had been in existence since 1990 as a registered civic association. The government first filed for it to be de-registered in 2005, based on the fact that its programme called for the 'revolutionary overthrow of capitalism' ('*revoluční překonání kapitalismu*'), which the government argued posed a potential violent threat. The ministry dissolved the association in 2006 and an appeals court upheld the decision in

2008. The government's decision does not seem to have particularly affected the KSM; it has continued its activities, including its website, as an unregistered, 'banned' organisation. The government's case against the organisation did not refer to any allegations that it or any of its members had actually participated in any violence or conspiracy.

Dissolving a political party is an order of magnitude more serious than de-registering a civic association, and some commentators have suggested that the 'banning' of the KSM was simply a dress rehearsal for what will eventually be the dissolution of the KSČM. Efforts to dissolve the WP are being viewed in this light as well. The Fischer cabinet repeated the WP effort successfully in February 2010, hiring a private attorney to finish the job the Topolánek government had bungled (intentionally or not). Polls showed the vast majority of those polled agreed with the party's dissolution: 74.6 per cent agreed the WP should be abolished and 80.7 per cent considered its members to be Nazi-promoting extremists. Media coverage of the Vítkov arson and the links between the suspected arsonists and the WP may well be responsible for this acceptance.

The Workers' Party is banned, long live the Workers' Social Justice Party

This societal condemnation of infant-maiming arson, however, did not parlay itself into either greater sympathy for the Romany minority or less support for anti-Gypsyism. The numbers of Roma fleeing the Czech Republic to request asylum in Canada (not a low-cost endeavour) prompted the Canadian government to reinstate visas for the country as a whole. Canadian officials were quoted in the Czech press as saying the Roma were migrating for 'economic reasons' and that 'unscrupulous operators' were involved, claims which have never been substantiated. Czech, and even some Canadian, media coverage of the exodus and the visa reintroduction was rife with anti-Gypsyism, claiming the Roma were simply seeking a better system to scrounge off and ignoring the fact that hundreds of Romany asylum-seekers were being deemed in genuine need of protection by the Canadian refugee system. For the Romany community, reinstatement of the Canadian visas simply underscored the similarities between the current social climate and that of the mid-1990s, so devastating for their community (while Czech society as a whole is not even minimally aware that this has been the Roma experience). The visa reinstatement was, of course, collectively blamed on the Roma; the responsibility of the Czech government, or violent extremists or, indeed, of the larger society was quite unthinkable, as the logic of anti-Gypsyism requires.

The anti-Gypsy violence also persisted into 2010, with Molotov cocktail attacks now being reported primarily from northern Moravia. One incident took place in a district of Ostrava led by Senator Liana Janáčková, once a member of ODS, now a member of the Free Citizens' Party (SSO), who has been notorious for racist and xenophobic remarks stretching back more than a decade, but has never been stripped of her immunity so she could face prosecution. Again following the logic of anti-Gypsyism, Janáčková issued an official press release insinuating the victimised Roma family had staged the attack themselves so they would be able to claim asylum outside the country. She was later forced to publicly apologise; police arrested and charged the family's non-Romany neighbours with committing the crime. A mother and son were sentenced to seven and four years respectively.

Extremists in suits

The May 2010 elections to the lower house saw a 62.6 per cent voter turn-out. The WP had regrouped as the WSJP and improved on its 2008 results, capturing 1.14 per cent of the vote. The surprise of the elections, however, was the 10.88 per cent of the vote captured by the upstart Public Affairs Party (Věcí veřejných—VV), a result which may indeed be the true legacy left by the extreme-right on contemporary Czech politics.[77] For starters, VV chair Radek John, who became Interior Minister, removed two Romany candidates from the party's lists in two different regions at the last minute and was sued by one of them.[78] A well-known television personality, John was a newcomer to the party and has left legal control of it in the hands of Executive Vice-Chair Jaroslav Škárka, a provocative ideologue who rejects the 'extremist' label but whose blog features a column on the topic of 'inadaptables' (sample headline: 'How to Take a Trip to Canada for Free', about the recent Roma exodus). The Green Party (2010 results: 2.44 per cent of the vote) charged Škárka with racism during the campaign. Most insidiously, VV took a page from the WP handbook and sent 'patrols' out in Prague which the Christian Democrats (2010 results: 4.39 per cent of the vote) and the Greens both called unacceptably reminiscent of Nazi and communist practices. Video footage from the patrols was posted to the party website showing young people in reflective 'safety vests' speaking with people in a park whom they labelled 'inadaptables'. They warn them they

157

shouldn't litter, shouldn't be drunk in public, and should stay away from the playground, and then summon police officers after finding injection needles and other paraphernalia nearby. As political scientist Miroslav Mareš told the press: 'VV places an emphasis on order and security, which is classic for this kind of nationalist politics. Their patrols may be aesthetically different from the Workers' Party, but their content is the same'.[79]

'Aesthetically different' is a crucial observation here. While party leader Vandas dresses fairly neutrally, in public he is more or less constantly surrounded by people who dress like who they are—members of the neo-Nazi subculture. In a society that places a premium on conformity and cherishes its 'victimhood', people are unlikely to identify with those dressed for street combat. In contrast, VV has convinced a familiar face from Czech television screens to represent it and has maintained the bland visual style of a mainstream party. This may have been part of the key to their overnight success. As rabidly as many non-Roma claim to feel about the Roma in the Czech Republic, they would like social conformity to be enforced without drawing much attention to itself, or without requiring their conscious attention at all.

The run-up to the municipal and Senate elections in the autumn of 2010 saw mainstream parties in the north of the country exploiting anti-Gypsy rhetoric. The Social Democrats, for example, erected billboards reading: 'Why should I regret being the majority nationality in my homeland?' VV ran a candidate in Chodov (west Bohemia) who had previously been a member of the NP and its (inactive) National Guard paramilitary organisation. In the north Bohemian town of Krupka, municipal elections had to be repeated three times because local parties engaged in vote-buying among impoverished residents, including Roma.

Neo-Nazi agitators expanded their targets in the autumn of 2010 to include more than just Romany people. In September, five neo-Nazis were arrested in the north Bohemian town of Most after physically assaulting those protesting against the extension of coal mining limitations there. In October, a five-member 'civic patrol' of the WSJP tried to provoke a conflict at a drug addiction treatment centre in Prague.

In November 2010, the mayor of Nový Bydžov (north Bohemia) published an anti-Roma declaration on the town's official website in response to reports of the rape of a non-Romany woman allegedly committed by a Romany man. (The perpetrator was subsequently sentenced to ten years in prison.) Neo-Nazis hailed his remarks and the WSJP offered its 'assistance' to him. In February 2011, the mayor convened a meeting of sixty other mayors from around the country who then signed a declaration calling on the Czech government to give them greater powers to address their alleged 'difficulties with Romany people'. Czech MP Ivana Řápková (ODS) was there to suggest legislation for them to support.

In March 2011, the international neo-Nazi organisation, Blood and Honour, and the militant terrorist group, Combat 18, launched a new website in the Czech Republic. The WSJP convened a demonstration in Nový Bydžov which included a march on its Romany neighbourhood; mounted police brutally intervened against peaceful counter-demonstrators who attempted to block the march. Police also failed to prevent neo-Nazis from assaulting three Romany locals after the event was over (one was hospitalised with a concussion).

In April 2011, the WSJP convened a demonstration in Krupka (north Bohemia) including another march on a Romany neighbourhood. Clergy and counter-protesters, including hundreds of Romany people, gathered for religious worship to block the march and were brutally dispersed by police during those religious services.

In May 2011, civil society successfully organised to block a Labour Day march in Brno (Moravia) by the WSJP. The director of the Museum of Romany Culture there received violent hate mail. In Votice (central Bohemia), four locals attacked migrant workers from Romania whom they believed were Romany, verbally abusing them before breaking into their building and brawling with them (police pressed charges).

In June 2011, eleven neo-Nazis marched through Krupka (north Bohemia) dressed in black, carrying flaming torches and wearing masks. The event was organised by a group calling itself the 'Order of the Cogwheel' and linked to the WSJP (whose logo is a cogwheel). Romany residents in Vsetín (Moravia) reported they were subject to verbal assault and to coming home to find their apartment doors kicked in and their mailboxes destroyed. The WSJP also held a rally in Krnov (Silesia) which was counter-protested by Catholic priests without incident.

In July 2011, twenty masked neo-Nazis with the 'Order of the Cogwheel' carried flaming torches as they marched through Most (north Bohemia) and headed to the Romany-occupied housing estate of Chanov. The invitation to the event was posted to Facebook and was clearly intended to provoke Roma. An arson attempt with a flaming torch was then committed against a Romany family in Býchory (central Bohemia) later that month (there were no injuries). Meanwhile, more anti-Gypsy rumours were spreading online, claiming that Romany people were falsely claiming higher electricity costs in order to increase the amount of welfare they received and then cash in on refunds for the unused power.

Inter-ethnic violence dramatically accelerated in August 2011. In the town of Nýrsko (west Bohemia), two men armed with baseball bats attacked a Romany family in their home, who resisted and threw them out; the assailants then sent word to the family that they would be killed sooner or later.

In the town of Nový Bor, Romany juveniles won money at a gaming room, but were refused their winnings by the barmaid. When they verbally assaulted her, other non-Romany customers physically assaulted them and kicked them out. The Romany juveniles then returned with several Romany adults armed with machetes and assaulted the customers, causing severe injury to three people. Police arrested three perpetrators but two remained at large as of October 2011. The ethnic dimensions of the incident were stressed in subsequent media coverage. Local mothers convened a non-violent demonstration in protest at the violence. In Varnsdorf (north Bohemia), a specifically anti-Roma protest, which was of a more raucous nature, was held by locals referencing the machete incident.

A Molotov cocktail attack was committed against a Romany home in Krty (central Bohemia); one man suffered second-degree burns as a result. Local residents there unanimously condemned the incident and said it must have been committed by outsiders.

In Třebíč (Moravia), the leader of the 'Order of the Cogwheel' was arrested after attacking the director of a children's sports match with a knife. He was carrying a total of seven knives and a fake pistol.

In Rumburk (north Bohemia), a group of Romany youths reportedly assaulted a much smaller group of non-Romany youths outside a disco. The ethnic dimensions of this incident were stressed in subsequent media coverage. Seven suspects were immediately charged and some were remanded in custody. Four ethnic Czechs brutally and randomly attacked a Romany man in Rumburk the next day, and a neo-Nazi association called 'Civic Resistance' convened a demonstration there for 26 August in response to the disco attack. The town hall declined permission for that event, but did permit the Social Democrats to convene their own rally at the same time and place. Some 800 locals turned out and the rally deteriorated into a rampage through the town. After singing the national anthem, a lynch mob of roughly 500 people of all ages and both sexes roamed the streets trying to break into Romany dwellings for several hours, shouting 'Gypsies to the gas chambers', throwing pieces of wood and rocks at Romany homes, and trampling down a fence. Police prevented physical clashes but were unable to stop the psychological warfare from being waged.

It was later revealed that a local Romany family had been threatened with murder by their neighbours earlier that day; when they called the authorities for help, they were told either to barricade themselves in their home and call the police if someone tried to break in, or to leave town. They fled on foot, walking fourteen kilometres through the woods to seek safety with relatives in a neighbouring village. The next day, about thirty Romany residents protested the rampage in Rumburk, but were instructed to disperse by police.

September 2011 saw multiple demonstrations organised by locals[80] against Romany people in north Bohemia every weekend. On 2 September, several hundred locals marched through Varnsdorf for two hours, attempting to attack the Romany tenants of a particular residential hotel; police prevented physical clashes. That attempt was repeated on 3 September and on 9 September; none of these marches were ever announced to authorities or stopped. On 10 September the WSJP officially convened a chain of anti-Roma demonstrations, first in Nový Bor, then in Varnsdorf, and then in Rumburk; hard-core neo-Nazis led the marches, which resulted in forty-one detentions and six injuries; police used water cannons to disperse the mob in Varnsdorf and were criticised by locals for protecting the Roma. On 17 September, 400 locals marched through Varnsdorf; police again prevented them from physically accessing the targeted Romany residences. On 24 September, the marchers added the home of the vice-mayor to their itinerary after he spoke out against them. Many more marches were scheduled for October 2011, including ones in major cities.

While government officials have attempted to portray these events as the result of neo-Nazi provocation, it is clear that a shift has occurred in north Bohemia. The locals who are spending their weekends marching against their Romany neighbours may or may not vote for ultra-right parties next year, but one thing is clear: they do not consider their open desire to commit violence or their racist slogans as 'extremist'. They consider them normal and justified by the violent incidents perpetrated by Romany individuals, which have proven to be the last straw.

Affluence no panacea to fears of extinction

As I have argued elsewhere,[81] in the case of the Czech Republic, I believe it is facile to suggest a causal correlation between right-wing extremist violence and the current global economic crisis; indeed, for contemporary examples of this phenomenon, the argument could just as easily be made that such groups are a product of relative affluence, especially where the resource-intensive organisation of political parties (as opposed to ad hoc groups) is concerned. Adherents to far-right ideology are nothing new; as elsewhere in Europe, they have been a part of the Czech political scene since the early twentieth century. Moreover, the Czech economy is relatively stable within the EU, indeed the most stable of all of the former communist states. While we might hypothesise that relative affluence and stability (and therefore more for the perpetrators to lose) explains why the recent spate of anti-Gypsy violence in the Czech Republic has not resulted in fatalities, as it has in Hungary, it is equally likely that the lower fatality rate is simply a product of chance with respect to the Czech arson attacks. There can be no doubt that the intent of these attacks is the same in both countries.

Starting in the early 2000s, the NP and the WP steadily attempted to build up a party base for their own ideological and political reasons, and they did so during a time of relative affluence. Given the historical success of the RP, which actually entered parliament in the early 1990s, as well as the electoral success of similar parties elsewhere in Europe, it was not unreasonable of them to believe the effort would eventually bring them a slice of power. In August 2008, while both parties were hard at work campaigning, the Czech Statistical Office reported that unemployment, as calculated by the International Labour Organisation, had actually fallen during the second quarter of 2008 to 4.3 per cent, the lowest level since 1996.[82] Indeed, in 2008, the Czech crown was performing so strongly against both the dollar and the euro that Czech exporters were even beginning to worry their products might become too expensive. Conservative financial management prior to the current crisis meant Czech banks were never involved in the hedge funds and other financial instruments that wreaked such havoc elsewhere, and the European Commission predicted Czech GDP would shrink by only 2.7 per cent in 2009, one of the mildest forecasts in the EU.[83] General economic conditions, then, are not necessarily the main factor at play in this recent extremist upsurge.

As Karel Čada notes elsewhere in this volume, the Workers' Party has garnered the most support in under-developed parts of northern Bohemia, areas which were some of the most intensively exploited for resources during the twentieth century and which are still being targeted for exploitation today. Coal mining and power production have resulted in large-scale environmental destruction, the destruction or relocation of entire villages (an ongoing practice), and severe harm to human health there. When many communist-era industries were closed in the 1990s, unemployment soared in the region, and the situation has yet to stabilise. However, while these local economic factors might seem to prepare the ground for the temptations of extremism, they do not adequately explain why local Roma—not capitalism, corporations, or politicians—have become the locals' punching bag.

Indeed, while the number of Roma residents in Litvínov, the site of the 2008 riots, had been rising, it is worth noting that conditions in the town did not warrant it for inclusion in the map of 'socially excluded Roma localities' produced by the Czech Labour Ministry in 2006. Moreover, while media reports did their best to make it sound like a hell-hole, the Janov housing estate is indisputably in better shape than many run-down urban areas throughout the country. The 'unsightly ghetto' argument as a cause of anti-Gypsyism really does not fly in this case. Over the course of extensive soul-searching in the town after the riot, it transpired that the residents of Janov who were otherwise so vocal about 'Roma crime' had not even been calling the police to report it. Indeed, a police station was opened at Janov in the aftermath of the riot, only to be closed within a few months for lack of use. The Roma, it would seem, are essentially hated merely for having become an increasingly visible presence on the streets of the town.

As has been amply documented elsewhere by historian David Crowe and others, anti-Gypsy prejudice and violence existed in central Europe long before the capitalist system and its critics ever developed. In this sense it is a cultural touchstone, an article of faith which can be counted on to provide a sense of stability and group cohesion to the society as a whole, not just to extremist subculture. While the Czech Republic has long been criticised internationally for its systemic discrimination against the Roma in access to education, employment and housing, and for serious human rights abuses such as the forced sterilisation of Roma women, the content of such criticism and the background assumptions about human rights upon which it is based are rarely discussed or analysed in detail in the Czech media. Rather, inside the Czech world, such international criticism is interpreted as part of an ongoing narrative in which the Czechs are alone against the world, the perpetually misunderstood victims. The rest of the world is simply not to be trusted, and the historical experience of the twentieth century is called upon as ample proof of this fact. Perhaps the most influential constructor of this narrative has been the Czech President, Václav Klaus, who takes his proudly isolated stances on issues ranging from the Lisbon Treaty to global warming because he knows they will continue to garner him support with the Czech public, many of whom view him affectionately as a kind of rebel cowboy on the world stage.[84]

Given these societal propensities, cyclical outbreaks of extremist violence against the Roma (which seem to be occurring once a decade so far) might be understood as simply the most exaggerated expression of a constant existential anxiety which lies at the heart of the Czech experience, namely, that the Czechs will literally cease to exist as a people. This was recently voiced most famously by Klaus when he warned that the Czechs would dissolve into the EU 'like a sugar cube in a cup of coffee' should the country become a Member State.[85] Many in Czech society today are profoundly cynical about their ability to influence their democracy or to achieve justice through their legal system; it has not helped that many key decisions of the past twenty years, such as the decision to separate from Slovakia and the decision to join NATO, were made without even the appearance of consulting public opinion.

For this reason it is instructive to compare the general societal response in the Czech Republic to the recent extremist violence with the general societal response to an issue which has clearly prompted more civic action than any other in recent times, namely, opposition to the installation of a US radar base in the country as part of an anti-missile defence system. This opposition has consistently been reported to be as high as 75 per cent, spanning both the generational and the political spectrum. Public outcry over the mere possibility of this radar base has resulted in unparalleled civic engagement: dozens of demonstrations nationwide over the last few years, with attendance in the hundreds, even 'chain' hunger strikes. In contrast to the activism spurred by the threat of this system being installed (along with US soldiers), incidents of neo-Nazi violence that have resulted in the actual destruction of property and serious harm to individuals have prompted nowhere near such a societal response.[86] Nor, in fact, have we seen any such organising around the demand for economic opportunity, not even in the beleaguered north, where unemployment ranges seasonally between 12 and 20 per cent.

One of the only other areas in which Czech public opinion is quite as unified as it is in the cases of the US radar base and anti-Gypsyism is that of opposition to annulling the postwar Beneš Decrees, the legal basis for the violent expulsion of ethnic Germans and Hungarians from the reconstituted Czechoslovakia. It is here that we find perhaps the most interesting parallel to the current cases of anti-Gypsy violence. Any acknowledgment that this postwar violence was perhaps disproportionate, or that some people may have been unjustly targeted solely on the basis of their ethnicity— in other words, that instead of being the victims of the overall circumstance, the Czechs (and Slovaks) became, for a time, the perpetrators—remains unacceptable to the vast majority of public opinion. The parallels with the Roma situation are obvious. Unfortunately, the association of Romany people with violent crime has now been revived in the minds of most Czechs by the machete attack of August 2011, which both the Czech Prime Minister and the Czech government Human Rights Commissioner felt the need to declare was somehow 'equivalent' in repulsiveness to the Vítkov arson attack. This incident will be cited as evidence of Czech victimhood at the hands of the Roma for some time to come.

At an estimated 2.5 per cent of the population, the Roma in the Czech Republic are too small a minority to wield any sort of political influence. The irony of their situation is that despite being perpetually maligned as 'inadaptable' outsiders, as a result of the totalitarian past they are, in fact, some of the most culturally and linguistically assimilated Roma in Europe. As long as fear of extinction continues to operate in the Czech psyche and to be exploited by its leaders for political gain, societal sanction for violence against outsiders in general and the Roma in particular will continue as well.

9

SPACES OF HATE, PLACES OF HOPE

THE ROMANIAN ROMA IN BELFAST

Colin Clark and Gareth Rice

Drawing on Bauman's (2006) work on 'liquid fear', alongside Žižek's (2009) more recent work on violence, this chapter investigates the forced departure of Romanian Roma families who were living and working in south Belfast during the summer of 2009. The sustained physical attacks on the Roma by Loyalist youth gangs, prompting this rapid exit from the city, has chilling echoes with Northern Ireland's violent past, but to what extent could these recent racist attacks be regarded as 'the new sectarianism'? We approach this complex question through a separation of 'politics' and 'the political' as encapsulated by the violence and the state's (lack of) reaction to it. In conclusion, we suggest that the immediate Loyalist violence against the Roma was not the 'real' event, as such, but rather how this reality appears to observers around the world. It is the failures of Northern Irish social cohesion which will fester in the minds of other potential immigrants long after the Roma have returned to their central and eastern European homelands.

... the central human right in late capitalist society is *the right not to be harassed*, which is a right to remain at a safe distance from others (Žižek, 2009: 35, *emphasis in original*).

Introduction: changing landscapes

The shifting borders of Europe have told many stories over the years—and these stories have mostly been driven by economics, politics and war. So it was that on 1 January 2007, following the successful accession of several other central and eastern European countries in 2004, Bulgaria and Romania joined the European Union. At that time, the ever-optimistic (and once-suspended) Romanian President, Traian Băsescu, declared that Romanian membership presented an 'enormous chance for future generations' and that the EU was 'the road of our future... the road of our joy' (BBC News, 2007). And so it was that freedom of movement across Europe for the A2 countries became a reality. However, this was not matched by the freedom to work, as many draconian conditions and restrictions on employment were imposed on travelling A2 citizens. Also, as has been witnessed in Italy, Hungary and, most recently, France, it was not matched by the freedom to live your life feeling safe and secure. President Nicolas Sarkozy's anti-Roma campaign has sparked an international outcry, with human rights organisations accusing France of 'collectively expelling a single group' (Hollinger and Bryant, 2010: 3). Certainly, the words of Băsescu would sound hollow and empty to those Roma whose makeshift camp outside Grenoble—one of an estimated 300 in France—was razed to the ground, and equally to the Roma in south Belfast who were forced to flee their homes in the summer of 2009. Not so much the road to joy or Sarkozy's 'voluntary return procedure' (ibid.) as the road to a forced eviction. Doubtless, past events in Italy, Hungary and Northern Ireland gave Sarkozy some political comfort, knowing the Roma are the European neighbours that nobody really wants.

Indeed, in a letter to *The Guardian* on 26 June 2009—some ten days after reports first came in of the Romanian Roma in south Belfast being driven from their houses to seek sanctuary in first a church and then a leisure centre—Dimitrina Petrova of the Equal Rights Trust stated something that resonates vividly when examining closely the events in Northern Ireland during the summer of 2009, as well as France in 2010. Considering the hardening attitudes towards the Roma across Europe and, specifically, the exodus of Roma from south Belfast to Romania in June 2009, she is blunt on the dynamics of East-West relationships and how things are working at a new level. As she puts it, and her incomprehension is clear to all:

… a large group of Roma families are leaving a western city in which they had sought refuge. This is something new. In over 15 years of working with Roma communities across Europe, I have never witnessed a community *willingly return-ing* to Eastern Europe, even in the face of sustained prejudice, violence and discrimination.[1]

As Petrova argues, Northern Ireland has made sustained progress in recent years, via the peace process, in resolving longstanding conflicts between Protestant and Catholic neighbours in the North—although Loy-alist and Republican paramilitaries continue to punish and discipline mem-bers of their own respective communities (see Monaghan and McLaughlin, 2006), to say nothing of the recent attacks by dissident Republicans on so-called 'British targets'. However, there is a general consensus that North-ern Ireland's political climate has become more stable since the Good Friday Agreement was signed in 1998 (Northern Ireland Office, 1998). This is not to suggest that we should romanticise a new form of populism, but rather is an invitation to think more critically about it. The particular form that populism took in Belfast could be interpreted as failed 'integralism' (see Holmes, 2000; see also the introduction to this volume) since the Roma were ousted from Northern Ireland society rather than made to feel included. Following Berezin (2009), the failed 'integralism' was partly due to a failure of the relationship between people and polity—a spectacular breakdown in institutional trust—but also, as we argue below, a separation of the political and politics (Mouffe, 1995). Moreover, as long as Unionists (Protestant) and nationalists (Catholic) struggle to come to terms with their conflicting pasts, commonly known as 'The Troubles', it will difficult to imagine how Northern Ireland might become a successful example of 'inte-gralism'. This raises a more general issue—beyond the scope of this case-study specific chapter—in critically examining Europe's 'commitment' to its own citizens and its pledge to allow free circulation across borders.

To begin, we should review how events transpired. It was in the summer of 2009 when a small community of Romanian Roma in south Belfast, some twenty to thirty extended families in total, were subjected to organ-ised and sustained racist attacks (to both person and property) by local mili-tant Protestants known as Loyalists. These orchestrated actions of violence drove the Roma families from their homes to seek refuge, at first, in a local church and local leisure centre, and then, eventually, to seek a return to their country of origin (funded by the Northern Ireland Office). Given the complex nature of these unsettling events, there are many different avenues of investigation which could be undertaken, such as the response (or lack of it) by the police and local authorities or an examination of the local anti-racist protests in support of the families' right to live and work in the city (Mitchell, 2003; see also Nagle, 2009). Explaining the violence against the Roma is open to a multiplicity of interpretations but, given Northern Ireland's history of sectarianism, we want to pursue one main line of enquiry raised by the BBC's Mark Simpson, amongst many other commentators: namely that 'in some parts of the city, racism is the new sectarianism' (BBC News, 2009). In siding with Brass (1997: 6) we are well aware that 'the 'official' interpretation that finally becomes universally accepted is often, if not usually, very far removed, often unrecognizable, from the original precipitating events'. It is for this reason that we want to further examine, inter alia, the purported existence of a new sectarianism.

The claim that racist attacks against the Belfast Roma reflect 'the new sectarianism' bears chilling echoes of Northern Ireland's troubled past when, up until 1998, Catholics and Protestants were engaged in a bloody and divisive civil war (Shirlow, 2006). But how accurate is this claim and what does it tell us about both racism and sectarianism? Are the two issues, both conceptually and in practice, not fundamentally linked within the Northern Irish (and, by extension, the West of Scotland) context? What is it, exactly, that is 'new' here, if anything? Is it possible that the attacks on the Roma were an extension of violence against a social group who were mistakenly branded as Catholic?[2] As a secondary concern, the chapter will proceed to examine some of the debates that have been aired vis-à-vis the 'rights and responsibilities' of, in particular, Roma migrants arriving in cities in search of new socio-economic beginnings. At a policy and practice level, what have been the means and methods of engaging in, and promoting, intercultural dialogue and social cohesion in Belfast? What strategies of integration have been followed through and what actors have been central to this process: has it been the church and voluntary sector groups, as would be expected? How does this episode in Belfast compare, for example, with earlier events in Italy where Romanian Roma were deported on grounds of alleged criminal conduct and being 'a public threat' (BBC News, 2007)? Focus here, explicitly, has been on the conduct of those being targeted: rather than being perceived as a case of 'blaming the victim', events have been largely interpreted as the Roma being the authors of their own, deserved, misfortune due to alleged examples of anti-social behaviour—such as begging and being rude and aggressive to 'locals' and shopkeepers. It must be asked here: what are the historical and contemporary factors that have allowed such interpretations to be raised, and commonly accepted, and why did this particular event happen in Belfast and not Glasgow, London or Liverpool, where tensions have also been apparent between Roma migrant communities and their local neighbours? What is the 'Northern Irishness' or 'Belfastness' of this example and is it all connected to this suggestion that 'racism is the new sectarianism'?

The chapter is structured around four main sections, all drawing in different ways, upon Bauman's (2006) notion of 'liquid fear' and Žižek's (2009) more recent reading of violence. To begin with, a useful framework relating to the fate of the Roma in Belfast is sketched out. Central to our argument here is the Roma's brush with what Žižek (2009) refers to as 'post-political bio-politics' which in the case of Northern Ireland reflects the failure of direct political solutions to protect the Roma. We use Mouffe's (1995) distinction between 'politics' and 'the political' to account for the roots of this failure. Following this, the next section discusses the case study material in some detail and we pay particular attention to the violence against the Roma, trying to unpack which progressive and reactionary agents had the finger of blame pointed at them and the main consequences and reactions to the attacks. After this, the next section turns to public policy issues related to the case, and the final section traces what happened to the Belfast Roma after the violence. In conclusion, we flag up a larger concern that the real event, in all of this, was not the immediate attacks on the Belfast Roma, but how this reality will continue to fester in the minds of other potential migrant groups to the city. In essence, was this a Loyalist warning shot across the bows to other migrant groups who may now think twice about arriving in Belfast?

Two sides of a similar coin—fear and violence

To try and understand the events in south Belfast during the summer of 2009, two different conceptual approaches are employed. They are, in a sense, two sides of a similar—if not the same—coin. On one hand we have fear. Bauman (2006) has made a habit of identifying the false assumptions of modernity. For example, modernity was supposed to be the period of human history when the fears that pervaded social life in the past could be left behind and human beings could take control and tame the uncontrolled forces of the social and natural worlds. Yet, we look around us, and we can see that fear still holds good in a manner of forms, whether environmental or 'man-made'. Our uncertain times bring out 'the fear'—anxiety takes a hold and can lead to irrational actions and behaviours on various Goffman-like stages. Bauman suggests we have a range of 'liquid modern fears' and he constructs a non-exhaustive list and sets about examining the common sources of such fears in order to analyse the obstacles that emerge that prevent the rendering of such fears as harmless and benign. Security and self-confidence have a lot to play here, and in this chapter are relevant both in relation to the fears of Roma families (their personal safety and 'new lives' in Ireland) as well as the fears of the local Protestant youth (losing their stated 'heritage and traditions' as well as employment). In the latter case, such fears led to displays of violence against those deemed responsible for inducing anxiety—the Roma.

For Bauman (2006), we are all—some more than others—living in liquid times and this stage (or version 2.0) of modernity contrasts with earlier forms where 'solid' modernity could be spoken of. The relative security of these earlier times has long-since evaporated, argues Bauman. Indeed, the shift or movement from solid to liquid states has created challenges for individuals and communities like never before. For Bauman, it is a question of missing or eroded social and institutional frameworks—the rules of the late-capitalist game have changed and no one is quite sure what the new rules actually are (if any even exist) and where democracy and justice fit into the neo-liberal models that have arisen. That is, such frameworks are not able to solidify as they once did and take a concrete shape, so human planning and actions are now determined by other means. Just like 'flexible' labour markets, human life has become fragmented and more about short-term endeavours and episodes—'projects' that often fail to weave together to offer anything like a 'career' or 'progress' that was once such a strong feature of modernity, for the contented majority at least, as Galbraith (1993) might put it. Indeed, although Bauman (2004) might suggest that the Roma are a part of an 'outcast' group who have been rendered as having 'wasteful lives' by the extremes of modernity, it might also be suggested that the opposite is true. That is, in this context, Bauman's work on liquid life and fear can be usefully applied to the actions of the Roma: the families that travelled to south Belfast in 2009 illustrated many of the features of liquid modernity, such as acting and planning in conditions of uncertainty, estimating both the gains and losses of both leaving Romania and arriving in Belfast. There was evidence in their actions—their fluidity—of being ready and willing to change tactics at very short notice and abandoning commitments and loyalties in order to seek out new economic and social opportunities.

On the other hand, we also have violence. According to Brass (1997: 5) 'if one starts with the premise that violence in which innocent persons are harmed and killed is an evil, such a rhetorical strategy provides a poor vantage point and one must, therefore, take a stand rather in relation to the whole process of construction and contextualization'. In view of this premise, how might we interpret the Loyalist attacks on the Belfast Roma? Some commentators suggested that the Roma were 'blamed' by Loyalists for stealing scarce housing in a desirable location and what few jobs were available. Given Belfast's history of segregation, Loyalists may have also been concerned about a loss of 'their' territory through a visible 'Romanisation' of south Belfast (although this is one of the more religiously mixed areas in the city). What both these explanations have in common is what Žižek (2009:38) refers to as 'the proximity of the Neighbour'. In other words, no matter how far away the Roma could have been from the Loyalists in Belfast, they would always be 'too close'. As Žižek (2009: 50) explains:

Since a neighbour is, as Freud suspected long ago, a traumatic intruder, someone whose different way of life (or, rather, way of *jouissance* materialised in its social practices and rituals) disturbs us, throws the balance of our way of life off the rails, when it comes too close, this can also give rise to an aggressive reaction aimed at getting rid of this disturbing intruder.

For Žižek (2009), the proximity of the Neighbour is nested within what he calls a 'post-political bio-politics'. The term post-political refers to a politics completely drained of all its content and ability or willingness to be used as an agent of change in social or economic policy, and in a more general sense, its full integrations into the world of American popular, consumer and entertainment culture (see Bageant, 2008). The 'post-political' is thus, 'a politics which claims to leave behind old ideological struggles, and instead, focus on expert management and administration...' (Žižek, 2009: 34). 'Bio-politics' is most associated with Michel Foucault and Jacques Rancière, whose work seeks to elucidate the consequences of political power on all aspects of human life. In Italy 'post-political bio-politics' took a turn for the worst when in 2009 the Senate approved a new emergency decree known as the 'security package'; a series of discriminatory and persecutory measures that will affect the Roma people, immigrants and the homeless. The new legislation calls for ethnic profiling under the guise of the registration of all people with no fixed address, encourages doctors to report 'illegal' immigrants and allows for civilian 'anti-foreigner security' patrols (i.e. officially sanctioned vigilantes) to work alongside the police.[3] For Žižek (2009:

34), bio-politics (in the post-political sense) is 'ultimately a politics of fear' focusing on 'defence from potential victimisation or harassment'. If we follow this argument then the case of the Belfast Roma highlights the presence of a weak 'post-political bio-politics', one that failed to protect its victims from their Loyalist attackers.

For the purposes of further accounting for the 'Belfastness' of this case study, a further distinction needs to be made between the political and politics. The difference is explained by Mouffe (1995: 262–63):

By 'the political', I refer to the dimension of antagonism that is inherent in all human society, antagonism that... can take many different forms and can emerge in diverse social relations. 'Politics' refers to the ensemble of practices, discourses, and institutions which seek to establish a certain order and to organize human coexistence in conditions which are always potentially conflictual because they are affected by the dimension of 'the political'.

Therefore, 'the political' cannot be restricted to forms of institutionalised practices, even if such practices may formally form the sphere of 'politics'. The point here is that 'the political' (Loyalism) is an extreme variation of Unionism ('politics' in form of an elected Assembly) which often fails to maintain social cohesion.

Belfast's Romanian Roma in Loyalist crosshairs

The timeline, as much as the political and economic context and background, is vital to appreciate and 'get right' here. Events transpired roughly as follows, according to various news reports:

On 11 June 2009, the police received reports—the first they said—of an attack on the home of a Roma family on the Lisburn Road. Over that weekend, from 12 to 14 June, the police receive more phone calls from families living in properties on two streets in south Belfast. The police respond and investigate. On Monday 15, an anti-racism rally was held in the area by members of the community who support their Roma neighbours. This rally was subjected to verbal abuse and bottle throwing from a small group of young people who were intent on disturbing proceedings. On Tuesday 16, matters escalate and gangs of youths gathered in two streets that have Roma family houses on them, shouting abuse, leaving graffiti and throwing rocks and bottles through windows. The scenes were reminiscent of intensifying violence against the Roma, including attacks with petrol bombs, hand grenades and rifles in Hungary, Italy and other countries across Europe. As a result, a number of Roma families—numbering over 100 people—left their properties and met outside one house to try and feel some degree of 'safety in numbers'. It is from here that the families were transported to a church hall (the City Church, on University Avenue) where they spent the evening. The next day, on the Wednesday, the families were moved to the Ozone leisure centre, on Ormeau Embankment, in the city.

However, these events did not just begin in June 2009. In March 2009 premeditated violence against Eastern Europeans in Belfast erupted at the Northern Ireland vs. Poland football game. While the rioting was not linked to the far-right, local reportage suggested there was a hard-core of Polish nationals who came to the game without tickets but with a very clear intent to cause trouble and disruption (*Belfast Telegraph*, 2009). As a result of that trouble, over forty people were forced to leave an area ('put out') of Belfast due to intimidation (something similar to what was seen later with regards to the Roma). It was reported that Polish supporters from Scotland travelled to the match and unfurled an Irish Tricolour with 'IRA' on it, in support of Celtic's goalkeeper Artur Boruc (Collins, 2009).

The role of faith and the church is important here, as a place of refuge to those fleeing persecution. It was the City Church, a non-denominational grouping, which took in more than 100 Roma people—men, women and children—at very short notice when the attacks intensified. Pastor Malcolm Morgan of the church was reported as saying:

A number of volunteers were cleaning outside the church when the phone call came. I just said to them: 'Guys, we've got a new job to do', and they responded magnificently. I made a couple of phone calls to a Christian agency which helps people in need, and they turned up within an hour with food. The city council arrived, the lord mayor arrived, The Red Cross came. A local landlord came, had a look and turned up an hour later with 15 mattresses... it was great to see—that was the best of Belfast, the acts of kindness (Popham and McKittrick, 2009).

From the church, due to issues of space and available facilities, families were moved to the Ozone leisure centre on the 17 June. As Scraton (2009) has noted, the images on TV of these events reminded us of Hurricane Katrina, an event that also influenced Bauman's work on 'liquid fear'. As Scraton suggested, poignantly, sports halls are not always a place of fun, energy and exhilaration, and they do not always free and liberate our minds, exhausting our bodies. Sports halls can be the places desperate people flee to, becoming makeshift dormitories for survivors where possessions in black polythene bags are scattered across the indoor tennis courts. In the sports hall, it was evident that those who had worn their racism and sectarianism as badges of honour had seemingly won.

The worry for locals, especially with regards to Poles, is the catholicising of local Protestant schools in south Belfast. There appears to be a strong belief that Poles, and other groups from CEE, hold Republican sympathies. After speaking with Jackie McDonald, an alleged brigadier of the south Belfast Ulster Defence Association (and also 'community worker'), (Collins, 2009: 7) stated: 'Eastern Europeans bear the main brunt of Protestant anger. They're accused of "Romanising" the empty streets in south Belfast, as well as taking the few remaining jobs'. Indeed, Alan Skey, who spent sixteen years in jail as a Loyalist militant, is full of praise for the Good Friday Agreement and the apparent ceasing of outright sectarian struggles, but now speaks out against 'foreign bodies' in the city. These 'bodies', he argues, take away employment opportunities from local Protestant youth. As Skey put it, 'I took up the struggle to keep that British flag flying. Now loyalists and republicans are oppressed in their own country due to foreign bodies' (Gergely, 2009).

Why did the Roma leave Belfast?

Why did the Roma leave rather than seek protection from the police and authorities? Was it concerns over safety or hard economics? The context is important here. Unemployment in Northern Ireland stood at 6.7 per cent in April/June, 2009—a little below levels in the UK and the European Union. However, at 51,000 people, the number of those claiming unemployment benefit in July had almost doubled compared with a year ago (and this masking an artificially inflated state sector, as Northern Ireland has the highest proportion of public sector workers in the UK, some 30 per cent of all employees in 2005 versus 20 per cent or fewer across the south of England). Unfortunately, there are no reliable statistics for Roma employment because the Roma are often fearful of identifying themselves in official census returns (Fox, 2009). However, as is common across the European Union, the Romanian Roma in Belfast were to be found typically working in low-paid jobs—such as selling newspapers (*Belfast Telegraph*) and flowers from traffic islands and washing cars, not to mention begging (McDonald, 2009). These are public and visible occupations and as such it can attract unwelcome attention and comments from those who feel, in some way, hard done by, and the reported words of Derek Orr go some way to reflect this sense of annoyance and anger:

You can't walk into a bank or shop on this road without a Romanian woman shoving a copy of the Big Issue under your nose or begging you for money. I don't mind the Poles and the Slovakians who come here. They work hard, harder than indigenous people from here, but all you see now are these Romanians begging and mooching about. We'd all be better off—them and us—if they went back to Romania or somewhere else in Europe (McDonald, 2009).

The *Irish Times* (10 July 2009) journalist, Dan Keenan, reported that Michael Graham, the principal officer in charge of housing and regeneration in Belfast, had suggested that whilst fears over safety was an issue, the decision to leave was more to do with being unable to claim welfare benefits. He said: 'Racism was certainly the catalyst by which the people finally determined that they wanted to go home, but I still believe that had these people been entitled to public funds, which unfortunately they were not, their decision may have been different'. However, being able to claim public funds is hardly comforting when being subjected to sustained attacks. As Anti-Racism Network spokeswoman Barbara Muldoon said, Mr Graham's comments were irresponsible:

One of the myths that has stoked up racism and racist attacks on migrants has been the fallacy that they are in a country to claim state benefits. This myth has been exposed time and time again, and for anyone in a senior public position to raise this myth when attention needs to be focused on racism itself is irresponsible.

Similarly, Jolena Flett, of the Northern Ireland Council for Ethnic Minorities, suggested that the main reason Roma had left was out of fear for their lives and the safety of their children (BBC News, 9 July 2009).

Rather than provide more permanent living arrangements for the Roma, the Northern Ireland Housing Executive were left with little choice other than to supervise the return of approximately 100 Roma men, women and children. The costs of the Roma leaving were estimated to be some 37,000 euros and public officials have admitted that lessons were to be learnt from the events of summer 2009. Indeed, Director of Housing, Colm McCaughey, said:

It is important… to review and learn lessons from their [the Roma's] dreadful experience. Hard questions must be asked about how so many people came to be living in so few homes. What were the circumstances by which they came to be living here? And how did our community respond to them?

The Housing Executive stated clearly that the Roma were not regarded as 'benefits tourists' (Keenan, 2009).

On pointing a finger—who is to blame?

Is it so-called right-wing factions and disgruntled Loyalists that are to blame for driving the Roma out of south Belfast? Certainly, this was an age-old message of hate and fear that the Roma have been used to for centuries but, in summer 2009, it was delivered via suitably twenty-first century means. Texts and emails were sent across Northern Ireland in mid-June with a rather poorly constructed rhyming 'hate message' telling the 'gypsies' to get out of Belfast:

Romanian gypsies beware beware / Loyalist C18 are coming to beat you like a baiting bear / Stay out of South Belfast and stay out of sight / And then youse will be alright / Get the boat and don't come back / There is no black in the Union Jack / Loyalist C18 'whatever it takes'. (McDonald, 2009).

There have been arguments questioning exactly who was engaged in the attacks. Jimmy Spratt, of the Democratic Unionist Party and a member of the Northern Ireland policing board, pondered why the attacks on a church, which provided shelter for Roma being attacked, could be presented as a 'Loyalist attack'. He argued, further, that the attacks were not 'racist' at all. Indeed, Spratt was not alone and Sinn Fein board member Alex Maskey also queried the motivations of the attacks and suggested things merely 'got out of hand' and it was 'media assumptions' that tagged the incidents as racist (Moriarty, 2009). Responding to the complaints, Alistair Finlay, Assistant Chief Constable of the PSNI, stated that the church authorities had called the incidents in as being racially motivated but they soon became reinterpreted as acts of 'criminal damage'. Reasons for this re-classification are unknown but, to speculate a little, it may have something to do with the relative youth of the attackers involved—a sense of 'youthful pranks' that went 'a bit too far'.

Another theme to be identified in the media reporting of the events was the notion that there is now a general mood of 'acceptable everyday racism' in Ireland and this has, to some extent, replaced sectarianism. Is a climate of racial hatred to blame? In a 'special investigation' for *The Daily Mail*, of all newspapers, Andrew Malone (2009) asked the question on everyone's lips: who was to blame for these attacks? Speaking to a group of young people aged fourteen to twenty, gathering materials for the July bonfires (to remember the Battle of the Boyne), he was told that the Roma 'had it coming'. They were involved, the young people said, in the bottle and rock throwing, the taunting and the jeering that caused windows to be broken and Roma families to flee their homes, because this area of south Belfast was 'their place'. As Malone reports, these sentiments are felt elsewhere. Across the Village there are signs of hatred—racist graffiti and overheard voices talking about special treatment and the 'slyness' of the Roma. Everyone seems to have had washing stolen from their lines by the Roma—or a bike from the back lane. There are feelings of being under siege, and of being unable to speak out in case the accusation of 'racist' is thrown at you. Malone speaks to thirty-nine-year-old Belfast delivery driver Anton Bremner who told him, in a rather exasperated tone:

In 1969, people were chased out of their homes because of religion. Now it's because of race. The last thing anyone needs here is more division and conflict. For God's sake, after all the bloodshed over the years, can't we all just live peacefully alongside our neighbours, whatever religion or race? (Malone, 2009).

Interestingly, anti-racists were also accused, by some, of being a cause (not a solution) to the anti-Roma sentiments. Derek Hanway, of the An Munia Tubar Travellers Support Group, went on the record as suggesting that certain sections of the anti-racist lobby were partly responsible for Roma being forced to leave Belfast in the first place. In the magazine 'Fortnight', Hanway argues that Socialist Workers Party (SWP) activists' presence outside Roma homes attracted unwelcome attention and was not asked for. He claimed that many were acting like 'pumped up vigilantes' and were drinking carry-outs in the garden of one house which had previously been attacked. As he put it: 'This response strengthened the Roma families' sense of fear and attracted more unwelcome attention to their homes'. This chimes with similar cases elsewhere when 'outsiders' get involved in 'local' issues (see Gheorghe and Pulay, 2009). Hanway also criticised the police, suggesting they should have realised that the presence of the activists was having a detrimental impact on relations. As he said:

The PSNI should have mitigated the need for these 'protection people', reassuring families of their protection, along with sending a confident message to all that they were now in control. This would, I believe, have provided enough confidence for families to remain in their homes and avoided the need to 'evacuate' the families to City Church, escalating the problem and the problem of what to do next. (BBC News, 16 July 2009.)

However, one of the activists accused by Hanway, Gary Mulcahy (from the Socialist Party), responded by saying that when nine separate attacks on three different houses on the same road happen, local people who are against racism have a duty to act. He also argued that the Roma families were extremely supportive of the stance taken by anti-racist groups and they received hospitality from the families affected. Given the outcome of the case Mulcahy's response to the accusations from Hanway seem somewhat bombastic:

Racist attacks need to be combated in the communities where they are taking place. By mobilising the local community, racists can be isolated and the ability of the far-right to gain a foothold can be cut across. There is no doubt that the residents' action has succeeded in isolating the handful of thugs responsible for carrying out the attacks. The trade union movement together with young people and genuine community groups must also respond quickly to confront racists carrying out attacks in communities, by organising local protests and campaigning against racism (Mulcahy, 2009).

Consequences and reactions to the attacks

There are no excuses, and no arguments that can justify what happened. Immigrants are welcome here, they bring a wealth of culture to Northern Ireland and they bring their ability to contribute to our society. They are not separate from it but part of it. (Barbara Muldoon, Anti-Racism Network, cited in Moriarty, 2009).

One of the positive consequences of the events in Northern Ireland was the degree of inter-ethnic cooperation and support that came from within Ireland and also from over the water. Responding to events in Northern Ireland, Hindu statesman Rajan Zed and Rabbi Jonathan B. Freirich issued statements from Nevada, California demanding a public apology from Northern Ireland's First Minister, Rt Hon Peter Robinson, over the treatment the Roma had endured. They also called on Jose Manuel Barroso, current President of the European Commission, to visit Romania and meet with those families who had fled Northern Ireland and apologise, offering resettlement opportunities in NI. Interestingly, Zed appreciated and spoke openly about the religious dimensions to the events and called on religious establishments and leaders to show open support for all minorities being targeted in the way the Roma had been, noting that in previous months other minorities, not just from CEE, had been abused in Ireland (eNewsWire, 2009).

Another positive consequence, however, was the mobilisation of opposition to the attacks. A demonstration of this solidarity came in the form of a 'love music, hate racism' benefit concert on 4 July. Taking place at the Oh Yeah Music Centre in Belfast, the concert featured local act The Vals who noted the show was a good opportunity to show contempt for racism, but also a way of welcoming 'migrant friends and neighbours living and working in Northern Ireland' (Cross Rhythms, 2009).

It is worth noting that the attacks also caused diplomatic tensions. The First and Deputy Ministers met with the Romanian ambassador, Dr Ion Jinga, at Stormont in June to discuss what could be done to calm the situation and what support could be given to the victims of the attacks. Similarly, the Romanian Consul General, Mihai Delcea, met with the Social Development Minister, Margaret Ritchie, to discuss the attacks and also to meet the families living in emergency accommodation that had been forced out of their homes (BBC News, 2009).

However, it was not just the attacks themselves that shocked people around the world. It was also some of the information that came to light following the attacks. For example, Anna Morvern (2009), an immigration lawyer in Belfast and writing for the Institute of Race Relations, noted that as well as the attacks, at least two other issues had shocked her just as much. One such issue was the actions of the police in moving the Roma away from their initial shelter in the City Church to other parts of Belfast. She argues this decision gave rise to more separatism and isolation for the families involved and sent out the wrong messages to those behind the attacks— it legitimated a kind of racially motivated 'protective custody'. Also, Morvern notes that after the attacks the living conditions that Roma families were living in became better known—overcrowding on a level that was simply not acceptable in Northern Ireland, such as eighteen people living in one terraced house.

For Amnesty International (2009), Nicola Duckworth, the Europe and Central Asia Programme Director, reminded the authorities they had a job to do and that the safety and protection of minorities was a key duty:

Racist attacks are unacceptable and illegal. The Roma have every right to reside in Belfast and be treated with respect and dignity like any other citizen of the city. The Northern Ireland authorities have an obligation to ensure that the Roma and Romanian population in Belfast are given the protection they require in order to enjoy a safe and durable future there. (Amnesty International, 2009.)

It is worth noting that it was not just the Roma who were attacked and received threats. For example, Patrick Yu, from the Northern Ireland Council for Ethnic Minorities, reported incidents of people from central and eastern Europe being 'put out' (that is, forced to leave the city). Also, Yu himself was threatened, via letter, from the UDA (Ulster Defence Association) youth-wing—they demanded he leave Ulster or be 'blown up'. In the letter, which was later released by the police, it was made quite clear what the consequences of staying in Belfast would be: 'No sympathy for foreigners, get out of our Queen's country before our bonfire night (11 July) and parade day (12 July). Other than that your building will be blown up. Keep Northern Ireland white. Northern Ireland is only for white British'. Yu suggests that this was simply a 'scare tactic' and trying to reignite racial tensions, pointing out that when violence occurred warnings were not usually given.

Although the police disputed the contention that the violent episodes were planned or organised by Loyalist groups, Yu is less than convinced and thinks that families were targeted by far-right and Loyalist groups on the basis of country of origin and their location in the city of Belfast. Religion was a factor as well and, in thinking such things, Yu is not alone. Martin McGuinness, Northern Ireland's Sinn Féin Deputy First Minister, told Irish radio that: 'There is no doubt that the people responsible for this emanate from the loyalist community'. (Murray Brown, 2009.) Going further, Garavelli (2009) argued that:

The police continue to insist there is no evidence to suggest the racist violence has been orchestrated, but everyone knows there is a history of link-ups between Loyalist paramilitaries and far-right groups such as the BNP, Combat 18 and The White Nationalists. If the UDA or the UVF were not actively behind this violence, then they at least turned a blind eye.

Policing and legal sanctions

The Northern Ireland Secretary, Shaun Woodward, admitted that when the attacks occurred the police 'did not know enough' about the Roma community in its areas. In the Commons, he was asked by Conservative Philip Hollobone (MP for Kettering) why the PSNI had not been more aware of what he called 'simmering tensions' between Roma and local Protestant youths. Woodward commented that these 'incidents' had been 'relatively isolated'. However, admitting that 'lessons had to be learned', Assistant Chief Constable Alastair Finlay did note that much work had to be done in offering support to Roma in the city:

'We didn't, probably, know enough about the Romanian community. We didn't have the ability to, perhaps, reach in and understand what was going on in their lives and what their fears and apprehensions were, and perhaps we came to that slightly late. What we are seeing now is increased dialogue with the Romanian community. There is no support network for Romanians in Belfast and that is something everybody is keen to see supported'. (BBC News, 2009.)

His superior, Sir Hugh Orde, took a much firmer line to begin with, however, and rejected claims that response times to dealing with incidents involving the Roma were slow—ranging as they did from one to ten minutes (Keenan, 2009). He stated that the force had taken seven calls in four-and-a-half days and the situation had been 'difficult'. Accounts vary, however, as MLA Anna Lo said that some responses had come hours after events and some even went unanswered. Similarly, Barbara Muldoon of Anti-Racism Network said while she welcomed the comments, last week's attacks were a repeat of similar incidents dating back six years. As she said:

I think the police were incredibly slow to act over the last week, didn't do what they ought to do, now they say that they've learned lessons. But we've been here before, we've heard this before, when are these lessons going to be learned? When are we going to have a situation where people don't return home because they have no confidence that the police can protect them? (BBC News, 2009).

However, what is not in doubt is the extent and severity of the violence on offer. As reported by Henry McDonald for *The Observer*, homemade pipe bombs—of the type used in sectarian incidents—were discovered in the Village area of south Belfast. Shotguns were also discovered in the area as well—by Ulsterville Drive. There appeared to be some evidence to suggest that these pipe bombs and guns were, rather than being from any Loyalist weapons cache, from Combat 18/neo-Nazi groups in England and had travelled over the water.

In terms of legal sanctions, in late July, it was reported that twenty-one-year-old Shane Murphy of Donegall Road was subjected to an exclusion zone order, preventing him from returning to the area (Lisburn Road, Belfast—BT9 postcode) where abuse occurred outside houses where Roma were living (*Belfast Telegraph*, 25 July 2009). He is accused of being involved and was refused bail at the High Court as it was felt he would harass witnesses in the case. He faces charges of threatening and menacing Roma families living in a property on Belgravia Avenue, as well as making racist comments at an anti-racist demonstration held to support the Roma. Similar charges were also brought against an unnamed fifteen-year-old and a sixteen-year-old (BBC News, 21 July 2009). In total, over the period, it was reported by Chief Constable Sir Hugh Orde, that six people were arrested over the events—three being charged and released on bail and three being released on bail pending further investigation (Moriarty, 2009).

Public policy and public relations

Consequences were sharp and felt after the attacks happened, both in terms of economy and reputation. In terms of public policy in Northern Ireland, reaction to events has been swift, with different Stormont departments examining how policy can change to address issues relating to migration, racism and sectarianism. The Social Development Department, as well as the Office of the First Minister and Deputy Minister, are looking at initiatives to prevent racist incidents in the north from 'rocketing', as the Assembly has been warned. A new 'Cohesion, Sharing and Integration' programme is being planned that will, according to First Minister Peter Robinson, offer 'a framework for us, moving forward into a new society based on tolerance and respect for cultural diversity'. He went on to suggest that the plans would tackle racism in a 'substantive and holistic way' (Keenan, 2009). Of note, here, is the fact that in these discussions the First Minister specifically stated that racism and sectarianism were 'inextricably linked'. From the City Council's perspective, the lord mayor of Belfast, Naomi Long, conceded that the council had faced difficulties in engaging with Roma in the city:

It has been difficult for us to get connections, particularly with the Roma community in Belfast. The council has tried to engage with them but because of their experiences of discrimination in other parts of Europe, it has been difficult. It has been an extremely damaging time for our international reputation and one of the challenges moving forward is how we try and engage these people who are involved in these attacks. (BBC News, 2009).

One thing that can be said is that since the signing of the Good Friday Agreement over a decade ago, Northern Ireland has changed in many ways. For one thing, relevant to the focus of this chapter, it has witnessed an increase in inward migration—especially following enlargement of the EU in 2004. As in Scotland, it has mainly been Poles seeking work in the north but also numbers from India, the Philippines and other parts of the globe. For a small country that has been, historically, largely white and English-speaking, these are not insignificant changes although, to be sure, the impact of migration has been mostly positive. To be sure though, the context of increasing resentment—directed towards minority ethnic communities in Ireland—cannot be under-estimated. Smyth (2009) reports that during 2007, according to the annual report of the EU Fundamental Rights Agency, racist crime in Ireland recorded the third highest increase across the

EU (from 173 crimes in 2006 to 224 in 2007). Over the period 2000 to 2007, reported racist crimes in Ireland increased by over 30 per cent. Even so, there are still widespread concerns of under-reporting of such crimes and the worry that the recent global economic meltdown will see another 'spike' in figures.

Likewise, in June 2009, a report was published from the Equality Commission of Northern Ireland which demonstrated that prejudicial attitudes in the north were becoming more transparent, especially in relation to minority ethnic groups and sexual orientation. Over half (51 per cent) of those surveyed (1,071 people) said they would be bothered or concerned if their neighbour was a Traveller. Similar findings were expressed in relation to sexual orientation and migrants. Indeed, 20 per cent of those surveyed confessed to holding negative views about east European migrants. Interestingly, figures appeared to indicate that in terms of religion attitudes are changing—only 6 per cent said they would mind living next door to a follower of a different religion (Equality Commission for Northern Ireland, 2009).

Of course, it is not just a question of policy. It is also PR. Moriarty (2009) notes that Belfast, of late, has been an easier sell to the tourists and business sectors. The peace process gave a new confidence to the city and investments, like visitors, started to flow in. However, the reputational damage these events might cost is, for the moment, still to be calculated.

Roma on the move: From Northern Ireland to Romania and back

In response to the attacks, it was notable that some Roma chose to stay and not return to Romania. They were the exception, however, and were, literally, just a couple of families. The men had work and knew that a return to Romania would not improve their lot, even with the spotlight shining on them in south Belfast and threats and intimidation being a daily experience. The Northern Ireland authorities had initially attempted to persuade the families to stay, recognising the worldwide attention and 'shaming' the issue was quickly gathering. This did not have much success and reassurances from the police and politicians fell on deaf ears. Peter Popham and David McKittrick, from *The Independent on Sunday*, spoke to one of the (anonymous) men who stayed in Belfast and, as he put it, 'there is nowhere for us to live and no work for us to do in Romania, so we have no intention of going back' (Popham and McKittrick, 2009). Indeed, speaking to

The Observer, Fernando Teglas, one of the Romanians boarding a flight to Budapest from Dublin on 27 June 2009, said he was sad to be leaving well-paid work but felt he had no choice but to return with his wife and children. After checking in at the airport, Teglas said, 'I had a really good job selling the *Belfast Telegraph* around the city but it's too dangerous to stay now'. Teglas's home on Wellesley Avenue, close to the university district of south Belfast, was one of two properties under repeated attack from racists in June. When asked about his prospects and those of the other families, he said, 'I'm coming back to no job and no home. The Roma are the last people to be hired back in Romania and the first to be fired' (McDonald, 2009).

Most of the Roma families flew back to Romania on 27 June, over seventy people in total. Flights left from Dublin airport and arrived at Budapest, with families crossing the border into the Bihor region in north-west Romania via coaches. Some twenty-five people had already left prior to this departure date and only two dozen were indicating they were remaining. Speaking of the exodus, Anna Lo MLA (Member of the Legislative Assembly) referred to it as being a 'sad day'. She went on to say that:

I can understand why they have chosen to leave but I am saddened that it has come to this. I was, however, encouraged by the support and solidarity shown by many here for the Romanian people, and I hope that this positive action can be seen as a true reflection of Northern Ireland. These tragic events should be a wake up call for the Stormont Executive to ensure there is a strong strategy in place to address prejudice and create a genuinely shared society. (Newsletter, 2009).

Amnesty International (2009), noting the fact that most of the Romanian Roma in Belfast were flying home, were quick to issue a statement suggesting that for those families returning life would not improve. The organisation reminded us that a series of murderous attacks in the 1990s, alongside rampant human rights violations and discrimination, had left the position of the Roma in Romania as insecure at best in relation to most social policy provisions, as well as negative relationships with the police and other authorities. The Director of the Northern Ireland programme for Amnesty, Patrick Corrigan—more used to speaking on religious persecution and discrimination—was quoted as saying:

Given the scale of discrimination faced by Roma people in Romania, that these families are now leaving Northern Ireland to return home, reveals the extent of the trauma they have suffered here. The Northern Ireland authorities, especially the police, need to be much more vigilant in protecting the rights of these and other

SPACES OF HATE, PLACES OF HOPE

minorities living here. The Romanian authorities should take note that the eyes of
Europe are on them and their treatment of these returnees and the wider Roma
community. (Amnesty International, 2009).

Some journalists were sent by their UK-based publications to Romania,
to track down some of those families who had returned to see what had
happened to them. Aida Edemariam, for *The Guardian*, visited the village
of Tileagd which is close to the Hungarian border, beside Oradea. Here she
encountered various reactions to those Roma who were bussed back from
Budapest, after the flight from Dublin to the Hungarian capital. Local
policemen were hesitant to comment whilst concerned Romanians across
the country wrote letters to newspapers to disassociate themselves from the
newly returned. Edemariam also heard the familiar tales: accusations of
stealing and anti-social behaviours as well as the claims of Roma who were
discriminated against in education, housing, employment and access to
public services and bars and clubs. She also spoke with Tara Bedard of the
European Roma Rights Centre who tries to track the movements of those
Roma forced to return to Romania from different European countries, with
little luck. Most tellingly, Edemariam asked one anonymous twenty-five-
year-old man she met at the village of Vadul Crisului why he thinks Belfast
is so bad, when compared to Italy or Spain? He replied that 'Maybe it's the
spirit there. Maybe people are more violent. I don't know I'm guessing. But
surely they could find a way to solve it peacefully, not like this'.

The BBC reporter, Nick Thorpe, travelled to Batar in Romania—also
near the border with Hungary—where he met with Ioan Fechete (thirty-six)
who had travelled to Belfast with the intention to find work and save
money in order to rebuild his collapsing house in the village. In two months
he had saved over 600 pounds, but then the attacks started to occur and the
'common decision' was made that people should go home. Thorpe also met
with Iosif Fechete, who was also in Belfast and witnessed the attacks first
hand—having a petrol bomb thrown through the window of the house he
was living in on Lisburn Road (BBC News, 9 July 2009).

Finally, writing for the BBC, reporter Petru Clej (2009) surveyed the
Romanian press agencies and outlets, noting that the returning Roma were
treated with a degree of sympathy. For one thing, the 100 or so returning
Roma were referred to as 'Romanians', not 'Roma' or 'Gypsies'. This alone
was rather unusual. One newspaper, *Evenimentul Zilei*, published a report
entitled 'The Extremists' Neighbourhood' in which local youths were interviewed, on Belfast housing estates, indicating that more abuse and intimi-

dation was forthcoming. However, as is common when the internet is concerned, online features saw much more hostile and negative comments. One such comment read 'The Irish have won a battle—the Romanians have lost. Congratulations, they did the cleaning' (Clej, 2009).

After a little time the story disappeared from the front pages but then took on another twist. In early August 2009, just six weeks after most left the city, it was reported that some of the Roma who had fled Belfast in June had returned to the city. About a dozen men came back, with work secured, and their families were to follow (with children, in time for the new school term). The return trip was self-funded and, as Derek Hanway stated, it was simply people returning to work, as EU citizens (BBC News, 6 August 2009). Naomi Long, mayor of Belfast, reacted positively to the news that some families had opted to return. She felt it was a 'vote of confidence' in the city and the people. As she said:

I think it's hugely encouraging that after being able to go home and reassure their families about the situation here that they feel confident enough to be able to return to Belfast, pick up and build a new life for themselves that they had already started here. Most importantly, good neighbours can be a part of that process of just making people feel valued and welcome (BBC News, 6 August 2009).

However, the return was not welcomed by all and, in a televised interview, the Finance Minister, Sammy Wilson, stated that aspects of the return left him 'disturbed':

The allegations the last time were that they were brought here by their own people, to be exploited, put in totally unsatisfactory housing conditions and probably made to work for less than the minimum wage. I am not so sure that we want to encourage that kind of thing, because it brings not only problems for the people who come back but problems for the society into which they come.

Paddy Meehan, an anti-racism campaigner who received a death threat for the role he played in organising anti-racist protests at the attacks in June, also welcomed the return and said that: 'I've been speaking to a few of the Romanians that have moved back... they don't want to raise a huge amount of attention to themselves, they just want to get on with their jobs and their lives' (*Belfast Telegraph*, 12 August 2009).

Discussion and conclusion: Towards a more tolerant Belfast?

Belfast's lord mayor, Naomi Long, who took on a very visible and supportive role during the events in 2009, often referred to the attacks against the Roma as a 'stain of shame' on the city. That is, they had left an imprint, a mark that would not easily go away. These attacks, she reflected, would be bad news for the economy of Northern Ireland and its reputation, in these peace process years. The idea of Belfast as a diverse and tolerant city after years of sectarian violence had been dealt a serious blow. This would be a 'stain' that would merge with others that were starting to fade, both the racial and sectarian spillages of earlier times. But what is to be done about Ireland? It is something of a paradox—a country that is, on one hand, famous for the 'craic',[4] whilst on the other hand also well known for the violent religious hatred that has kept communities apart for generations. The peace process hops and skips along, guided by former 'terrorists' and/ or 'freedom fighters' whilst the Celtic Tiger, built up via inward and outward economic migration, has now turned on those who come searching for a better life. The notion of a tolerant and diverse Northern Ireland, getting over its 'historical issues' with sectarianism and racism, has now been blown apart. Indeed, one theme in the reporting of the attacks on Roma in south Belfast—that 'racism is the new sectarianism'—has been a recurrent byline in Northern Irish politics since, at least, the signing of the Good Friday Agreement in 1998. Whether espoused by politicians or anti-racist groups, this idea has taken hold. It is suggested that young Loyalists are now turning to the BNP and Combat 18 to further racist ends, in place of playing with sectarian politics. But how true is all this? Has sectarianism transformed into open racism? Just how different are they in form, appearance and practice anyway?

So, is racism the new sectarianism? Fionola Meredith (2009), writing for *The Irish Times*, suggests it is much more complex than this simple equation. The mood, she feels, has changed. Judging from the public response there are people who feel there is a level of justification for the attacks. There are the usual slogans being applied—they should return to their own country, they are taking housing and jobs, they do not belong. But is Northern Ireland the race-hate capital of Europe? The sociologist Chris Gilligan (2009) is wary of making such judgements. Rather than applying simplistic—not to mention hysterical—labels, he argues that we should instead 'examine… the interplay of tough immigration controls, the British state's treatment of Romania as a second-class European country and dilapidated housing'. For Gilligan, the wider context is more important and he also suggests it is important to remember that it was a very small minority of people who were actively involved in taking action against Roma families.

What seems to have occurred, one avenue of enquiry, is that the trade of learning sectarianism has 'prepared' people for learning and practising racism. But why are the attacks largely coming from the Loyalist community? Is this about a defence of 'Britishness'? It could be, as there is a feeling that the influx of eastern Europeans is bringing about a 'Romanisation' of once Protestant areas. On this issue, Anna Lo (from Hong Kong, the only member of the Northern Ireland Assembly from an ethnic minority, who represents the Belfast South constituency) had this to say: 'Really sectarianism and racism are very similar, twin evils of prejudice and intolerance'.

The ensuing violence, however, was not simply about achieving 'the abolition of the dimension of the Neighbour' (Žižek, 2009:36) but, also, a more general attack on dominant western cultural constructions of Romania as a second class European country (Gilligan, 2009). It is within this context that we might begin to understand the reasons behind the attacks, which included a purported Roma-Irish Republican connection and the economic threat of foreign bodies stealing jobs from Protestant and Loyalist youth (Gergly, 2009). If 'The Troubles' are anything to go by, then attacks on Irish Republicans and Catholics are nothing new, but what is interesting about the case of the Romanian Roma is that it raises the following question: is racism the new sectarianism? We are wary of making such judgments and as this chapter has shown the situation is far too complex for such crude interrogation. There is, however, a larger concern that the real event was not the immediate attacks on the Belfast Roma, but in how this reality appeared to observers around the world. The reality of the viciousness that went on in Belfast belongs to the temporal dimension of empirical history; the media reportage that focused on the failure of social cohesion belongs to eternity. Addressing this failure should be a central plank of Northern Ireland's new 'Cohesion, Sharing and Integration' programme.

10

SEGREGATION AND ETHNIC CONFLICTS IN ROMANIA

GETTING BEYOND THE MODEL OF 'THE LAST DROP'

Stefánia Toma

On May 31st, 2009, approximately 400 Hungarians from the village of Sanmartin gathered together and went to 40 houses belonging to Roma in the area. Against a background of increased tensions, connected to stealing (from the Hungarians' crop-fields and houses), the Hungarians damaged Roma houses, breaking windows, destroying the doors and roofs of houses, TV sets and aerials. Several cars were also damaged and several dogs in the yards of the Roma were killed. On June 3rd, 2009, a Roma house was set on fire. That same day, the Roma left their homes and spent the night in the woods or in the fields, under the open sky.

For approximately a month, ethnic Hungarian citizens have gathered almost daily, in groups of 200 persons, going to Roma houses and threatening their inhabitants. In the last two weeks, the Hungarians agreed to gather every Monday evening in order to 'monitor' the Roma as well as the implementation of a 'protocol' agreed, with the mediation of the City hall, on June 8th, 2009 by both sides (Roma and Hungarians). Each time, although the Police were present, Hungarian groups threatened the Roma, perpetuating the permanent state of tension among the Roma who have since returned to the village.[1]

At the beginning of the 1990s, Romania was the scene of a number of violent conflicts that involved Roma and local majority populations, both

191

Romanian and Hungarian. One of the first documented cases was in Mihail Kogălniceanu (Constanţa county), in October 1990, when the Roma and Romanian population were involved in a serious violent conflict that resulted in the destruction of homes belonging to Roma families (Preda, 1993). But, without any doubt, the conflict which gained the largest attention in media and public discourse was in Hădăreni (Mureş county) in 1993 (Haller, nd.). During the conflict between the Romanian majority and Roma minority inhabitants, four people lost their lives and fourteen Roma houses were burnt down. While the number of such conflicts decreased to some extent after 1995, Roma-related tensions did not; though their nature did alter, owing to a double dynamic—the authorities gave considerably more attention to these situations (Vintileanu—Ádám, 2003), and changes in the macro-social-economic situation during the period of restructuring generally offered new opportunities to the different groups for economic accommodation. So, while the number of violent conflicts decreased, new Roma-related tensions appeared: for instance, conflicts were no longer between local populations, but between the Roma and police forces (and other authorities).

After a relatively peaceful period (between the years 1995 and 2000), we have, more recently, experienced a re-emergence of so-called ethnic tensions. In Transylvania, two incidents were recorded near Braşov (in 2007 and 2008) and, more recently, during the summer of 2009, there was violence in Harghita county. These conflicts followed a very similar scenario to that seen in the earlier disputes: property belonging to Roma families was threatened and destroyed by the local majority. However, the context conflict and the methods of resolution had changed. These more recent cases received intense media coverage and immediately entered public debate. The media presentation of the conflicts allowed for a broad variety of interpretations. In labelling these events as 'ethnic conflicts', however, it constrained alternative understandings, as well as post-conflict strategies.

The present article argues that in order to understand these conflicts we first need to explore the social patterns behind these events. I argue that these are not unique or particular events, the character of which is encapsulated in conditions in a specific locality, region or timeframe, but can instead be interpreted as socially embedded processes that are framed by larger social, economic, cultural and political factors. I argue that the so-called ethnic conflicts should be seen as processes with demographic, social-economic, legislative/institutional, symbolic-attitude and conflict-management aspects that shape their development. To do so, I first address the way these events were understood and interpreted by different actors. Secondly, I look at ways that the perception of the causes of the conflict determined intervention strategies and affected local post-conflict events. I show how the interpretation of the disputes as 'ethnic conflicts' resulted in ad-hoc intervention strategies which could have been avoided if the actors had better knowledge of the background to each case. In order to do this, I first present a typology of the public discourses around the events in Harghita county, followed by a short discussion of recent research on Romanian Roma, which I relate to the broader conflict studies literature.

I use three main types of data. The first is a survey that targeted social workers in 1900 rural communities in Romania and aimed to investigate institutional relationships between local authorities and Roma and the ways these relationships influenced the perception of the conflicts between Roma and the local majority population.[2] Local authorities are institutional actors with direct experience of most of the projects and development programmes targeting the Roma in Romania. Moreover, these institutions mediate between national and local levels. Through this sociological survey we tried to understand the relationship between ethnic discrimination and residential/educational segregation, on the one hand, and local conflicts between Roma and the local majorities on the other. The second source of data is a report based on fieldwork carried out in two rural communities where conflicts occurred in 2009, as well as one community with a similar socio-demographic profile where no such conflict occurred.[3] The third type of data I draw on is a database of a mass-media monitoring programme which, among other topics, also focused on 'ethnic conflicts in Romania' in which the Roma population was involved.[4]

Narratives and understandings: 'What happened in fact?'

Recent events in Harghita county opened a space for the circulation of diverse discourses on behalf of different public actors: journalists, politicians, state bodies and various civil society actors. These different interpretations and the lack of a coherent, shared understanding of the events rendered an efficient approach to conflict-resolution rather difficult.

A number of reports were published relating to various conflicts and situations of intense tension. In addition to the dominant perspective focusing on human rights and minority protection, some of these reports also offered an analysis of the socio-economic problems which Romanian Roma face. Another issue that emerged in the media discourse was that most of the conflicts, and the violence in such cases, are to be understood as a form of collective punishment[5] provoked by various delicts committed by the Roma and their general delinquency—all of which remains unprosecuted by the authorities. Such reports also reinforced the practice of labelling violence between different ethnic groups as ethnic conflicts rooted in ethnic hatreds. In some cases, they suggested that Roma victims of such violence should be declared internally displaced persons (IDPs).[6] These reports focus on the problems Roma face in Romania: racism, discrimination and social exclusion, a low level of education, a high percentage of unemployment, a precarious health situation and bad living conditions. References to the cultural and lifestyle differences between Roma and the majority population abounded, with many comments on the Roma's willingness to maintain traditional customs and ways of life, as well as on the intolerance of the majority population towards difference, all of which are seen as significantly contributing to outbreaks of conflict (just as in the earlier cases of Hădăreni and Mihail Kogâlniceanu).[7]

A common conclusion is that a legislative approach is not enough to understand nor to manage conflicts where the ethnic aspect is important, because the law guarantees a resolution only to the issue of violence, but does not offer remedies for post-conflict tension and for situations in which the risk of reappearance of conflict has increased.

The mass-media also emphasise another aspect of the conflicts: 'Roma delinquency' and the responsibility of the authorities in not dealing with this. Through monitoring the mass-media—predominantly national and local newspapers—we have noticed that little attention is paid to the relationship between local Roma and the majority population.[8] In the aftermath of a conflict, the number of articles discussing events that took place on the margins of the conflict grew considerably. Two features deserve particular attention. One is the way the role of the Roma community in the conflict is presented. The second is the issue of responsibility for the trouble. In both cases media discourse reflects the locally asymmetric power-relations between the majority and minority. In most articles, the Roma community is presented as problematic, living outside the law, irresponsible and threatening, while the local majority population is usually presented as being in a vulnerable position. This vulnerability stems from two different causes: on one hand, the threatening Roma; on the other hand, the lack of a protective presence by the authorities. Local or regional authorities are presented intervening with short-term solutions to managing conflicts, hoping to defuse tensions but lacking a coherent, long-term programme for solving local problems.

Another set of discourses arose from national, civil-society representatives. Their interpretation and recommended intervention programmes can be divided broadly into two comparatively coherent groups of discourses. One is represented by Romani CRISS, a Roma human rights organisation, which clearly stated that the individual and collective rights of the local Roma population were violated in these cases:

On May 31st, 2009, against a background of increased tensions, an inter-ethnic conflict broke out in the Sanmartin locality, Harghita County... The conflict developed in a classic pattern—with a community that is numerically and socially dominant at regional level. There had been an accumulation of tensions in relation to the co-habiting minority and no engagement by the local authorities. In this context the majority applied the principles of collective justice. This constitutes further proof of the lack of responsiveness of the national and local authorities and their inability to act to either prevent or solve this kind of large-scale problematic situation. The authorities' attitude is even more worthy of condemnation given that messages indicating the imminence of conflict are systematically transmitted through various channels, including those of Roma NGOs'.[9]

They went on to argue that 'this situation constitutes an act of internal displacement of persons and violates fundamental human rights and the internationally assumed obligations of the Romanian state.[10]

The second perspective was represented by a group of Roma and non-Roma human rights activists, civil society representatives and intellectuals who underlined the importance of shared responsibility, incorporating the roles of various actors, including the local communities, local and national authorities, the mass-media and civil society organisations. They argued that the 'economic crisis, a confusion of values, hatred and distrust of "everything that is different", an inefficient state and justice system in Romania and Hungary increasingly manifest themselves, on a local level, in violence against Roma. Poverty and lack of life-perspectives generate fears about economic survival among the vulnerable, marginalized, excluded groups which in some cases leads to violations of property. The lack of democratic conflict mediation and lack of experience in management of tension tends to reinforce current conflicts and encourages extremist political forces using racist ideologies... Our discussions have revealed a need to assume shared responsibilities for shared risks'.[11]

In conclusion, approaches to these conflicts can be grouped under four main categories that are not necessarily exclusive: elements of one can be found in the other, there are certain overlapping ideas, but the core idea is different.

The first involves a discourse around 'Roma delinquency'. This is a 'blame the victim' approach, and far from a new phenomenon in Romania as regards the Roma. Surveys show that anti-Roma feelings are strong in Romania and that stereotypes about Roma show no sign of declining (ISPMN—CCRIT, 2008; Fleck-Rughiniş, 2008).

The second, 'minority rights' discourse places the accent on the victim status of Roma and focuses on the crisis of Roma political and civil representation, which is aggravated by a parallel increase in nationalism and the emergence of racist movements across Europe. This approach countenances the possibility that the conflicts in Harghita county were influenced or even deliberately initiated on the model of extremist initiatives in Hungary (Gheorghe, Pulay, 2009: 4–6). This interpretation appeared in various ways, blaming the influence of the Hungarian mass-media or the direct involvement of Hungarian extremist groups. This last suggestion was linked to recent, local political initiatives in Harghita county that aimed at establishing (territorial) 'autonomy' for the Hungarian minority in the region, a concept strongly associated with a form of territorial separation.

The third, 'economic deprivation' discourse offers a macro-economic interpretation of the conflicts, leaving a reduced space for the ethnic aspect of the conflicts. In such writings, the major causes of the conflicts are unresolved challenges of the post-socialist transition and the inefficiency of the development projects targeted at some regions in Romania, including Harghita county.

Last, but not least, there is the discourse of 'shared responsibilities'. A group of Roma activists together with non-Roma social scientists formulated a statement about shared responsibilities. According to Nicolae Gheorghe, one of the Roma activists involved, he and his colleagues aimed '… to take the first steps towards a statement of shared responsibilities integrat[ing] the tasks and challenges of the different actors within the local communities, the local and national authorities, the media, and NGOs at the same time. It is important to note here that shared responsibilities are not limited to either the "Roma" or the "non-Roma", the "Hungarians" or the "Romanians" but they bear implications for each and every actor'.[12]

The first three approaches offer different explanations of the conflicts. Although they share some common elements, each puts the explanatory accent in a different place. The fourth, 'shared responsibility' discourse tries to avoid not only the trap of an exclusionary approach but also the finger-pointing method of attributing a cause of the conflict. It focuses instead on potential ways to create a common base for discussion between different actors.

Theoretical background

The striking thing missing from these interpretations is a social scientific discourse, which would include in-depth analysis of the causes and consequences of these conflicts. Without such an analysis no proper intervention programme, no post-conflict strategy for removing social tensions and no conflict-management strategy is likely to be developed.

In Romania there have been, relatively speaking, a large number of conflicts between the local majority population and Roma communities. Despite this, in comparison with neighbouring countries, there is little sociological or anthropological research in this area. Articles published usually fail to go beyond narrative descriptions and accounts of the actors involved and the physical damage suffered by each side. An exception to this approach is the early work of Marian Preda on the 1993 Mihail Kogăl-niceanu conflict. Here, Preda rejects an overly rapid attribution of the label 'ethnic conflict' and argues for a deeper social and economic contextualisation of events (see also Kiss et al., 2009, although they do not deal explicitly with situations of conflict). There are also some surveys of public opinion but these mostly focus on the perceptions of conflict among the Romanian population (ISPMN—CCRIT, 2008; ISPMN, 2009; Fleck, Rughinis, 2008). Taking into consideration the frequency of violent conflict and the unstable political and economical climate in Romania, it is clear that this analytical gap needs to be closed—perhaps through the kind of triangulation of different research methods (survey, community study and mass-media analysis) that a recent report used to identify structural factors leading to local tensions (Magyari, Fosztó, Koreck, Toma, 2010).

The international literature on conflict-analysis offers a useful basis for a new approach: though it offers a broad palette of divergent insights, ranging from primordialist theories (Kaplan, 2005) through arguments about cultural pluralism (Furnivall, 1948; Smith, 1992), to approaches highlighting the importance of modernisation processes in ethnic mobilisation (Deutsch, 1966; Gellner, 1983). All these approaches have been heavily criticised for

197

overestimating the importance of inter-ethnic difference in generating conflict, forgetting that, in most cases, ethnic tensions fail to turn into open ethnic conflict. More recent work has tried to identify those factors that maintain tension at a given level below that at which ethnic conflict breaks out (Fearon and Laitin, 1996; Brass, 1997; Kaufman, 2001; Forbes, 1997). These authors have pointed to the importance and role of informal social institutions in the prevention of conflict.

The most comprehensive interpretation of ethnic conflict is offered by Anthony Oberschall, whose strength and weakness is the combination of diverse theories in one model. Oberschall's starting point is that in analysing conflict we can never derive causes from a single factor. As an example, he mentions the notion of ancient ethnic hatreds (which appear in collective myths) which can indeed be reinforced thanks to the interests of manipulative elites, but also through tendentious identity politics. But, besides these factors, one must also introduce a consideration of the level of security a population feels in a certain political and economical context and which can lead to a spiral of insecurity (Oberschall, 2007). In the same analytical style, Bartos and Wehr stress the importance of differentiating between the causes and consequences of a certain conflict. They demonstrate how earlier analyses were compromised by confusing causes and effects such that a consequence of a conflict, increased tension, for example, is considered as its cause, thereby misleading the intervention and conflict-management strategies.

A further consideration is that while sociological approaches tend to offer macro-analyses, looking at civil wars like those in the Balkans (Gass 1994, 1997),[13] anthropological inquiries remain at the micro-social level, offering a completely different definition of ethnic conflict which ranges from inter-personal disputes to civil war. We want to combine these approaches as macro-structural changes, along with trends in the mass-media, have an impact on local structures.

In our analysis, we follow Mabel Berezin, who argues that 'events are important for *what* they force us to imagine—and these imaginings may generate hope as well fear, comfort as well as threat—rather than *how* they determine choice. Events are sociologically and politically important because they permit us to see relations and interconnections that speak to broader macro and micro level social processes' (Berezin, 2009: 15). Hence we were not interested in a linear interpretation of how the causes of a conflict lead to certain interventions. Rather, by stepping behind the conflict event, and attempting to explore its broader socio-economic context, we hope to account for those factors that contribute to the outburst and escalation of conflicts.

The indefinable last drop—stereotypes, attitudes, tensions

While, in the literature, a situation of increased tension, or the aggressive intervention of the police force, is sometimes referred to as conflict, in this article we have limited our attention to violent confrontation between two ethnically distinguished groups of people. To understand what lies behind these conflicts, we attempted to produce a typology of the phenomenon.

The image shows us the types and the frequency of reported conflicts identified during the large scale survey we conducted among social workers. The base of the pyramid represents situations of low-level tension. By localised conflicts we understand mostly interpersonal conflicts, for example incidents (e.g., exclusion of Roma from bars and clubs or fights there), disputes between neighbours—that is, conflicts involving only a few people. Of course, these may entail some kind of institutional involvement. Intra-community conflicts appear between different extended families or a similar range of persons. The inter-community conflicts are rarest but more intense—whole communities can be involved. The involvement of public institutions is likely in these cases, due to the threat of the conflict spreading.

This distribution of types led us to ask about the local authorities' perceptions of their Roma communities and of the conflicts that arose between them and the majority. A large survey of local authorities thus aimed to identify the factors that singly, or in combination, contribute to a saturation of tensions in a community and then lead to conflict breaking out. We suspected that in localities where we could identify a number of factors contributing to conflict, these factors would, at a certain point, add up to a critical mass. Then, when what we called the 'penultimate drop' fell, this critical mass transformed into what we called a 'conflictual cloud', at which point local actors perceived a latent conflict between different persons or groups. From that point on, the 'conflictual cloud' needs only the 'last drop' to move to the brink of an open conflict or tip over into such. In the event that such a 'cloud' could be recognised in time, a conflict (risk) management strategy would be conceivable. When open conflict already exists, then conflict management would be called for but, in the Harghita county cases we discuss below, we will see how tricky it is to take effective measures. Of course, we must not forget the individual character of the actors in any given situation, whose actions may contribute to the escalation or management of conflict.

The basic elements of a conflict that need to be assessed include its history, as well as the immediate socio-economic context. The actors of the conflict need to be identified and, in this sense, we can differentiate between primary actors (all those who directly participated in the conflict), secondary actors (those who were indirectly involved in the conflict) and tertiary actors (mass-media, mediators, civil society and so on). The third and most important step is to distinguish causes and consequences—always a challenging step and one that brings a degree of subjective evaluation. But here, the following step—separating the goals and interests of the actors—can offer a helping hand. Subsequently, this analytical move can be used in the process of conflict-mediation, because through determining the actors' aims, the conflicts of interest can be recomposed and transformed. Subsequent steps involve understanding the dynamics of conflict and exploring its positive function so as to discover grounds on which reconciliation can take place (Bartos, Wehr: 67).

A survey on the mechanisms of conflict

In 2008, we posted questionnaires to 1900 social workers in the office of all the rural communities in which, on the basis of the 2002 National Census, we identified individual Roma or Roma communities. The decision to use the National Census might, of course, raise problematic questions about representativeness (the Census being based on self-declaration of ethnicity with only one identification allowed). But we did not need to build a representative sample since we wanted to probe the range of mechanisms leading to ethnic tension and conflict. We also suspect that the number of localities where Roma persons or communities live, none of whom declared 'Roma' as their ethnicity during the Census (and so who did not enter our sample), was not significant from the point of view of our survey.[14] We addressed our questionnaire to the social workers because we suspect that they have a better overview of local data concerning different communities in a village than other employees in the municipalities. Social workers have regular contact with members of the local Roma community and a better insight into the socio-economic situation of that community than other employees.[15]

We were, for this reason, less able to determine the actual situation of the Roma population, in the targeted localities, than the perception of officials. In answer to the question, 'Have you observed changes in the size of the Roma population who live in [ethnically] compact communities, due to migration?', we found that 52.8 per cent had observed some change, of which number 79.3 per cent had observed an increase of Roma persons in ethnically 'dense' areas of the village. 48.4 per cent declared that they had noticed a change in the number of the Roma living dispersed in their locality—87.5 per cent of these recording an increase. These were subjective evaluations. It may often be the case that no significant growth in the absolute number of the Roma had taken place, since our question measured, in effect, the increasing visibility of Roma. This might have been the result of sudden changes in the socio-economic status of co-habiting groups and an increased social distance between them.

A clear majority, 71.1 per cent, characterised Roma living conditions as more precarious than those of the majority, while 20.9 per cent considered that the living conditions are approximately the same. Only 10.8 per cent reported that the majority of local Roma had official employment, while 39.4 per cent declared that the majority of Roma were unemployed and 25.2 per cent said that a majority practised some forms of a traditional profession or were small entrepreneurs.[16]

As regards the perception of tensions between different ethnic groups, only 8 per cent claimed to have observed signs of tension during the year 2007. This result is similar to that of a previous survey (See, Fleck et al., 2008) and may indicate that the respondents use a different framework in observing and interpreting tension than we tend to, or that they were adopting a kind of politically correct approach—denying difference and difficulty. The role of such differences in perception can be clearly seen if we look at the number of situations of tension or conflict in which social workers reported they were asked to intervene in some way—which is much higher than the former 8 per cent (see chart 1).

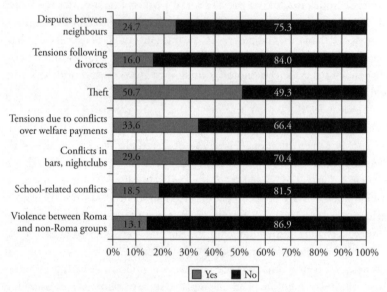

Chart 1: During the last two years, were you contacted in the case of a conflict between Roma and non-Roma persons?

When asked about the causes of conflict, most respondents pointed, in rank order, to the low educational and professional skills level of the Roma, the poverty of the Roma, differences of lifestyle, and the Roma people's lack of interest in integrating into mainstream society (see chart 2).

We can easily see how respondents lay responsibility at the door of the Roma for various conflicts, as in the 'blame the victim' type of discourses presented above. A double discourse appeared in answers to the following question: 'In your opinion, what measures should be taken to reduce the number of conflicts in your locality?' (see chart 3). Respondents were asked to register on a scale from 1 to 5 their agreement or disagreement with a number of statements. A split attitude appears in the high score that the following two statements received: 'Roma should try harder to integrate'

SEGREGATION AND ETHNIC CONFLICTS IN ROMANIA

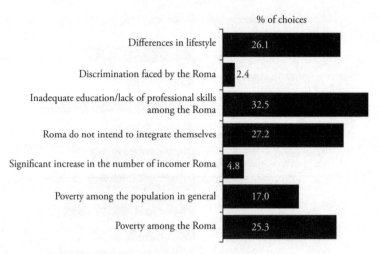

Chart 2: In your opinion, what were the causes of conflict between the Roma and non-Roma population in your locality? Please choose no more than TWO answers that you consider the most important.

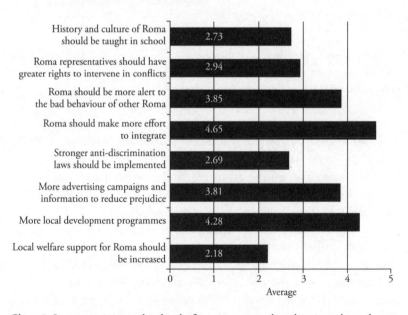

Chart 3. In your opinion, what kind of measures must be taken in order to lessen the number of such conflicts in your locality?

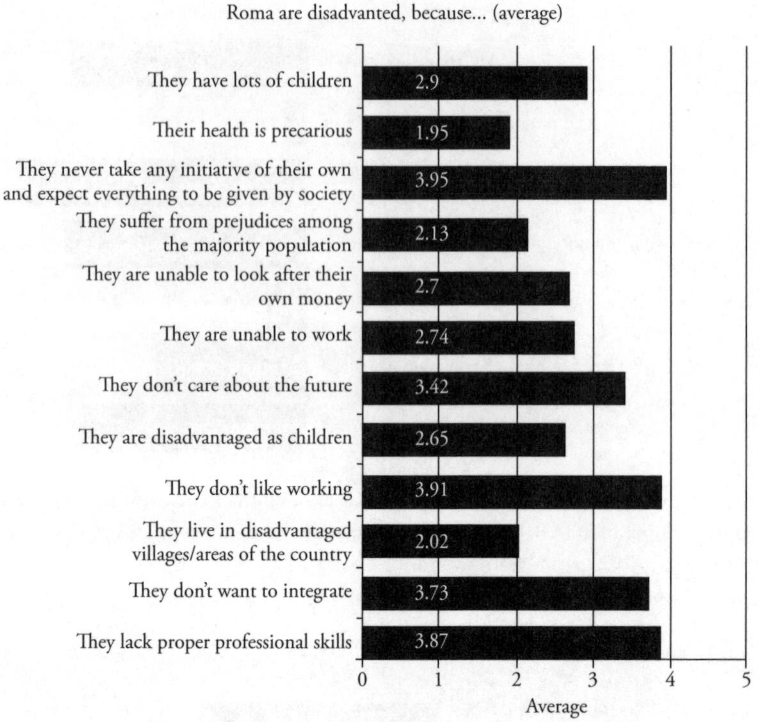

Roma are disadvanted, because... (average)

Statement	Average
They have lots of children	2.9
Their health is precarious	1.95
They never take any initiative of their own and expect everything to be given by society	3.95
They suffer from prejudices among the majority population	2.13
They are unable to look after their own money	2.7
They are unable to work	2.74
They don't care about the future	3.42
They are disadvantaged as children	2.65
They don't like working	3.91
They live in disadvantaged villages/areas of the country	2.02
They don't want to integrate	3.73
They lack proper professional skills	3.87

Average

Chart 4. Recently there have been disputes about the disadvantaged situation of the Roma population in Romania. On a scale of 1 (strongly disagree) to 5 (strongly agree), please indicate your agreement with the following statements.

(average—4.65) and 'local development programmes' (average—4.28)—reflecting, on the one hand, official discourse that stresses macro-structural considerations and, on the other, the kind of general attitudes towards Roma which appeared in the national level survey on Social Cohesion (ISPMN—CCRIT 2008) and in mass-media discourse.

The next two questions (see tables 4 and 5) asked about general causes of the disadvantaged situation of the Roma and measures that should be taken to improve their situation. Here the accusatory attitude can be clearly seen: the statement 'because they have never taken any initiative of their own, they expect everything from society' received an average of 3.95.

The same happened in answers to the next question: 'In your opinion what is needed to ameliorate the situation of the Roma in Romania?' (see

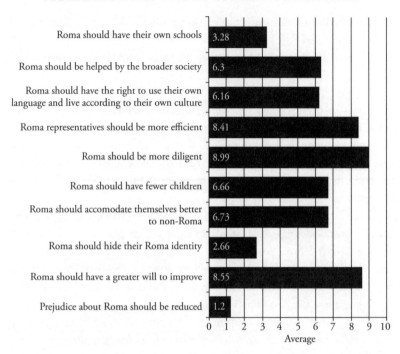

Chart 5. In your opinion, what is needed to ameliorate the situation of the Roma population in Romania?

chart 5). In this case the highest level of agreement was with 'the Roma should be more diligent', 'improve the will of the Roma' and 'Roma representatives should be more efficient'.

The attitudes of the social workers working in the municipal offices express exactly the ideas circulated in mass-media, namely that the Roma themselves carry the responsibility for their precarious situation, lack willingness to integrate, but also suffer from the lack of coherent local development programmes from which they might benefit.

Another set of questions referred to the frequency and types of collaboration the social worker and, generally, the municipality has with other institutions in the locality and various representatives of the Roma community. The most frequent collaborations in both cases are with the local police stations and schools. In localities where the percentage of the Roma population is between 20 and 50 per cent, the frequency of contact with schools and other educational institutions rises significantly (at least daily). Contacts through 'field' or family visits were less frequent.

We were also interested in whether the social workers have regular contact with different representatives of their local Roma communities. Approximately half the respondents declared that there are no such representatives in their locality.[17] Where there were mediators or local Roma councillors, contact was less frequent than with other institutions. An overall comparison of the localities where the percentage of the Roma population is beneath 20 per cent and is between 20–50 per cent shows significant variation in frequency of contacts: the larger the percentage of the Roma, the more frequent the contact with their representatives.

What can we infer from these results? The questionnaire was sent to social workers in municipal offices in rural settlements with a significant (self-declared) Roma community. We started out thinking that since another survey using the same data-set reported that the majority of Roma depend for a regular income on one or more forms of social benefit, and managing these benefits is part of the social workers' tasks, in theory there should be greater contact between the local authorities and Roma in these places and hence a greater exchange of information between different ethnic groups living in the locality. In fact, the data showed that where the Roma communities are not institutionally represented in one way or another, the number of contacts—and we can also assume, the type of contacts—is lower, and the stereotyping attitude is stronger than in localities where the Roma community are formally represented either by 'mediators' employed by the municipality or by elected Roma councillors.

This points to institutional factors, as well as the role of local or regional development programmes, in preventing ethnic conflicts. We were interested in whether the presence of representative institutions plays a role in preventing tensions from transforming into conflicts. It is difficult to say whether there is a direct influence or not, but we can identify a correlation between the regularity of collaboration between such institutions and the emergence of conflicts. (The institutions were: mayor's office, police office, school, church, Roma representatives.) The same tendency can be seen with local and regional development programmes and/or Roma-targeted programmes. In localities without such programmes, and where these localities were economically disadvantaged regions—such as Harghita and Covasna county, or some regions in Moldova region and the southern part of Romania—conflicts were more frequent. This is, however, never the sole factor behind conflict, which always needs the 'last drop' to spill over. This 'last drop' can be more or less anything and it only can be identified through local case-studies.

Beyond the 'last drop'—the full glass

The 'last drop' that tips existent tensions into open conflict can even include seemingly irrelevant events, raising the question why a minor incident provoked such over-reactions. Presumably, in such cases, the glass was already 'full' beyond the brink. The way this 'last drop' is perceived—implicitly, how conflicts are interpreted and represented by local or national actors—plays a fundamental role in the evolution of these situations. The idea of the last drop is itself a matter of perception—it is not the cause of a conflict but, itself, a part of the representation of the conflict.

This brings us back to the third—and most important—step in the assessment of a conflict: the disassociation of causes and consequences of the conflict. This step represents the basis for further interpretations and conflict-management strategies. When tension spills over into open conflict, cause and consequence tend to become blurred. As Bartos and Wehr have noted, 'hostility may be a consequence of one phase of a conflict and a cause of the next' (Bartos, Wehr, 2002: 68).

In the conflicts in Harghita county, the 'last drops' involved a quarrel between a Hungarian and a Roma person in a local bar, in one case, and, in another, a Roma person was caught stealing agricultural goods from a local Hungarian in a neighbouring village. Neither of these situations are rare or so spectacular as to merit a community level conflict. In fact, such events happen regularly in these very localities without having the same consequence. But in both cases, these 'last drop' events appeared as proper occasions to recall old and new grievances about the Roma.

After these conflicts, a number of secondary and tertiary actors intervened: firemen, local and regional police forces, local authorities, NGO representatives and the mass-media. The main lines of their interventions and their narratives about the conflicts were determined by the way each of them perceived the 'last drop'. Even if, in some cases, the interpretation of some of the actors who intervened went beyond the frame of a 'last drop' account by trying to explain the causes of the conflict in a broader social context, their focus was still determined by the memory of similar events in the locality. In this way, these recalled events started to form a 'red line', determining the logic of the interventions, and legitimising them. For example, the local Hungarians remembered similar actions in their villages, as if to underline the innate delinquency of the Roma. The authorities positioned themselves, during subsequent negotiations, as the hegemonic authority with overall responsibility for maintaining order. The human and minority rights activists' initiatives framed their narratives in terms of a highly oppressive majority, the grave injuries suffered by Roma during the conflicts and the long-lasting discrimination they have suffered.

Post-conflict interventions also developed along the lines of these narratives. Local and county authorities formulated a protocol describing desirable power-relations in the localities.[18] The minority rights organisations set up protest marches, but these were not welcomed by the local, Hungarian-speaking Roma, who declared that the interpretation and involvement of outsiders could do more harm than good to local norms of co-existence (Gheorghe, Pulay, 2010: 11–12).

This raises two questions. After carefully separating the causes from the consequences of the conflict, how can one develop a proper equity-based intervention strategy in order to begin a proper local process of communal negotiation? The lack of information and weakness in the background knowledge of the context can lead to misunderstandings, as happened in Harghita county. So, what constitutes such basic knowledge about context and what do we call contributing factors?

During our research we identified five such groups of factors: demographic factors; socio-economic factors; legislative-institutional factors, symbolic-attitude factors; and, finally, conflict-management traditions. It emerges that separating causes and consequences of conflict is easier if these factors are understood.

The demographic factors include the percentage of the Roma population in the locality (both factual and perceived), and a sudden change (mostly an increase) of the number of Roma due to in-migration (which usually means a group of 'newcomers' entering the old structure of the locality). In itself, a certain percentage of Roma or a sudden change in their number is not enough to provoke the anger of the majority. In both villages in Harghita county where the conflicts occurred, the percentage of the Roma population did not exceed 10 per cent, while in a neighbouring, non-conflictual village the percentage of the Roma was over 30 per cent and, moreover, there were there some unregistered families who had recently moved in, fleeing other villages with active conflicts.[19]

The socio-economic context includes housing conditions, unemployment rates, level of education, the type of the Roma community (whether it is compact or dispersed, segregated or integrated, traditional or assimilated), the geographical position of the Roma community, the level of local infrastructure, economic relations between different communities and so on. In both Harghita communities the socio-economic status of the Roma is low. In the terms of Dumitru Sandu's model, they constituted Roma communities with severe problems (Sandu, 2005).[20] But again, these characteristics alone do not allow us to conclude that the highly precarious socio-economic situation itself led to the open conflict between cohabiting communities.

Taking a closer look, we can identify some local structures; social institutions that did have some control over the situation, and the mere existence of which could sometimes ameliorate tensions. These institutions include formal, as well as informal, relations between local ethnic groups. Thus, the presence of community mediators, and Roma health- and school mediators, allows for some form of communication between local authorities and Roma communities. We saw from our survey that in most rural communities such institutions do not exist. And we could further infer that even low levels of communication can positively affect the way local authorities perceive the problems of the Roma. In the three Harghita county villages, the formal representation of the Roma was weak. An elected Roma councillor had served, but only for a short period of time, in two of the villages, and in the third village there had been a young non-Roma community mediator employed since 2007, who had not been replaced when she went on maternity leave. In one of the villages, the lack of formal representation of the Roma was, in a certain fashion, compensated for by a stronger informal network between Hungarians and Roma. In this non-conflictual village, beginning in the late 1970s, Roma families who were hired on the formal job-market (in neighbouring industrial centres and cooperative farms) took loans and managed to buy the houses of old Hungarians, providing for stronger neighbourly relations between the Hungarian and Roma families. This type of informal connection varies from village to village depending on local traditions of managing inter-group relations. In some villages, the institution of godfatherhood, or simply well-structured patron-client relations, can substitute for these such neighbourhood relations (see Toma, 2009). Such informal local social structures actually function as a substitute for formal institutions, such as political representation, education or shared church attendance.

Beyond these groups of factors, we also need to look at inter-ethnic relations in the locality, focusing on the type of stereotypes circulating about the Roma and how these stereotypes are reflected in everyday attitudes and interactions. In his discussion of theories of ethnic conflict, Oberschall (2007: 9–12) argues that the politics of 'identity' and 'ancient hatreds' are embedded in local cultures and forms of socialisation that enable them to 'become activated for aggression at the outset of ethnic conflicts, and resonate with ordinary folk'.

The second question raised is strongly connected to the identified factors, but much more to the way the perception of the conflict's causes change the design of its intervention and outcome.

As for conflict-management traditions, this group of factors decisively shapes the design of interventions and their outcomes. In both localities where tensions turned into open conflicts and immediate, outside intervention was called for, there was a strong tendency to fall back on in-group preferences in the decision-making process (Oberschall, 2007: 5). The resulting protocols of understanding were formulated as a formal result of negotiations between the two ethnic groups but, within them, the point of view of the majority clearly prevailed and was imposed on the minority—clearly expressing the hegemonic character of the exchange relationship.[21] By 'hegemonic exchange' we understand, following Donald Rothschild, a political exchange where leaders make certain resources available to ethnic groups in exchange for local support (1986: 70).

The negotiation process revealed that instead of seeking cooperation, the actors involved were participating in a zero-sum game. On the one hand, the authorities—that is, the representatives of the majority—needed to 'solve the problem' without making bigger waves around the events, but were unwilling to offer more power or resources to the minority. On the other hand, the Roma communities, lacking local representation, had to rely on the representatives of national Roma organisations who, in turn, without knowledge of the local context of cohabitation, merely reproduced their own in-group preferences. Thus the local conflict of interest remained implicit as the parties involved failed to agree what was to be negotiated. According to Bartos and Wehr, 'conflict can originate either in goal incompatibility or in hostility (or in both)…' (Bartos, Wehr, 2002: 29). Incompatible goals can originate in contested resources (wealth, power, and prestige), incompatible roles, and incompatible values (materialised in the separation of groups). According to the model developed by Bartos and

Wehr, if we can identify incompatible goals among two conflictual groups, step by step we can move towards reducing incompatibility. The roots of such incompatible goals overlap with the factors discussed above and their joint analysis can provide the basis for a sustained process of reducing tension instead of ad hoc and short-term interventions.

We follow Oberschall in suggesting that there are five criteria for a genuine process of intervention. First of all, the adversaries should negotiate in good faith without preconditions and without insisting upon non-negotiable demands. The outcomes of the negotiations in Harghita county were published in a protocol which—as we discussed—represented a demonstration of hegemonic power. It was criticised by a Human Rights organisation as follows:

The 'Protocol' designed by the authorities to represent the base for future inter-ethnic relations in the locality provides obligations only for the Roma community and not at all for the Hungarians or the local authorities, representing an additional proof that the precondition for a Roma presence in the locality is the mercy of the majority. Moreover, the Romanian authorities replied to the protest letter submitted by the NGOs reaffirming the protocol and indicating that most mayors from Harghita county had asked for a resolution of the situation with illegal settlements of Roma in this region. Note that both ethnic Hungarians and Romanians have built houses without authorization from the authorities, and yet the mayors request this problem be solved only for Roma. This is another proof of how Roma are not wanted in that area.[22]

The second criterion would be that the key-actors are included in the process. The precondition of this would be for a guaranteed, balanced representation. In Harghita county that was difficult to achieve because of the simple fact that the Roma communities lacked formal representation, and so only informal leaders participated in the negotiations. From the point of view of the authorities, the legitimacy of such informal representation is dubious. The third criterion is that the central issues—the background and goals of actors in the conflict—need to be addressed. Instead of that, in this case, only secondary issues and ad hoc or partial measures were discussed, which simply reinforced the status quo ante: the only question asked was, 'what does the Roma community need to do in future in order to ensure peaceful cohabitation?' The fourth and fifth criteria point to future forms of cooperation which demand a commitment to a sustained process of renegotiation. In this respect, the political composition of the local authority can have a profound effect and completely change the outcome of the negotiations. In one of our villages, the majority of the representatives were members of a moderate Hungarian party. Their engagement in solving the tensions was clearer than in the case of the other locality, where the more nationalist orientation of the administration defined a strategy best described as a demonstration of force against the Roma community. Thus the local balance of power between actors defines the direction of the negotiations.[23]

The problem of interpretation—are these ethnic conflicts or not?

This article leaves the question formulated in the title of this section—whether such conflicts are ethnic conflicts or not—unanswered. The aim was not to offer arguments either way, but to underline that in such cases ethnic labelling is a plausible strategy. Apparently insignificant affrays—like a quarrel in a bar, a fight in a club, verbal aggression—between members of different ethnic groups can invoke concordant memories in the wider communities, and thus lead towards open conflict which effects irreversible changes in the nature of the local society. Old grievances come to be burdened with new ones.

In this article we presented how these 'insignificant affrays' are the 'last drop' in the complex of local grievances that evolve into deeper tensions and open conflicts. We have argued that that the perception of the 'last drop event' determines the overall process of conflict interpretation, conflict-management and post-conflict restructuring. The interpretation of these conflicts in public discourse appears in four main types: a 'Roma delinquency discourse', a 'minority rights discourse', an 'economic deprivation discourse' and last, but not least, a 'discourse of shared responsibilities'. Sometimes the explanatory structures of these discourses overlap, but their explanatory emphases continue to differentiate them. These narratives were circulated directly by tertiary actors to the conflict (the mass-media, NGO representatives) and indirectly by secondary actors in the conflicts (the local administration). The local administration took a direct role only in the phase of conflict-management and post-conflict interventions. But all these direct and indirect interventions were shaped mainly by the way the 'last drop' event was perceived. The 'last drop' event was perceived as the cause of the conflict but, as we argued, it is rather a part of the representation of the conflict and one of the factors of an already existing tension in the community. Mixing up the causes of the conflict with its consequences derives from poor knowledge of the local socio-economic context and the dominance of certain stereotypes operating there. Background knowledge of the local context should involve, above all, an appreciation of the factors that contribute to conflict escalation: socio-economic factors, legislative-institutional factors, symbolic-attitude factors and conflict-management traditions. It is also important to define the specific aims and interests of the local communities if we wish to develop sustainable conflict mediation strategies, since it is through framing these that conflicts of interest can be broken down into manageable elements, and thus be transformed.

PART 3

COMBATING EXTREMISM

11

CUCUMBERS FIGHTING MIGRATIONS

THE CONTRIBUTION OF NGOS TO THE PERCEPTION OF TEMPORARY ROMANY MIGRATIONS FROM MEDOVCE-METETE/SLOVAKIA

Stefan Benedik, Wolfgang Göderle and Barbara Tiefenbacher[1]

On a Sunday in September 2009, there is a small sales booth at a flea market in Vienna, brimming with jars of pickled cucumbers. They have been produced by Romany families in the small Slovak village of Medovce-Metete[2] under the supervision of a Viennese NGO. The income from an improvised stall like this one should support Romany families in Slovakia and thus—implicitly—prevent them from migrating/having to migrate to Austria to make their living. Interestingly, the representatives of the NGO behind this campaign started to become engaged in these issues as a reaction to a documentary broadcast by the Austrian Federal Broadcasting Corporation. This documentary portrayed and discussed the living conditions and needs of the Romany people who were migrating to Graz to beg.

During the past fifteen years, the increasing presence of beggars in this town in the south of Austria turned out to be crucial not only for the public perception of Roma and Romnija (female Roma) in Austria, but especially for the engagement of various humanitarian associations in Romany issues. Whilst large debates in the media and in the public sphere

217

discussed mainly how to dispose of this 'nuisance', it became clear that temporary migration, ascription of Romany identity, poverty and a whole series of images of 'the East' made for a hard to swallow cocktail for a medium-sized town in Austria.

In this contribution, we show how, in this case, public perceptions and the activities of NGOs have been interlinked until 2010, and discuss their mutual dependence. There is a noteworthy transfer of images as well as a prolongation of asymmetric, stereotypical representations which promote an imaginary of the poor 'eastern people' with backward 'culture'. Therefore, we aim to highlight the circumstances and contexts of the emergence of certain opinions and activities. In doing so, we will discuss the often unintentional contributions of NGOs to these narratives, as well as the counter-productive effects of such engagement. We first briefly sum up some of the evidence about the changing reactions to the migrations of Roma/Romnija here. Second, we will turn to some facets of public discourse about these migrations and, finally, we will critically reflect on the activities of two major NGOs partaking in these debates, one secular and one Catholic.

The results of these migrations are structures of exchange that are now complex and well-grounded, allowing and fostering the exchange of money, people and knowledge. These are not unidirectional flows, limited to the movement of Roma/Romnija (back and forth) and the flow of donations in the other direction. Rather, we observe a network that is formed by 'development programmes', media coverage as well as political debates in both countries (Austria and Slovakia), street music and the transfer of goods like the jars of pickled cucumbers mentioned above. Calling this inter-regional connection a means of exchange and a network of communication does not necessarily mean that the routes of exchange are used only beneficially: they have also provided a space for openly hostile and actively harmful interaction. Yet one should not forget that the majority of contributions to the network in question here may result in both advantages and disadvantages for the concerned Roma and Romnija. Besides that, these exchanges are not taking place from positions of equality. In fact, they are shaped by striking economic dissimilarities and are commonly talked of in terms of a pejorative assumption of a 'beggar problem', thus suggesting that migration (particularly immigration from the 'East') is, in general, negative. Approaches like these are based on simplified knowledge, such as the reference to Medovce-Metete (from the Graz p.o.v.) as a Roma/Romnija-only-settlement, one that is even represented by a Romany mayor. Consequently, all the protagonists discussed here treat the Romany identity associated with this place as a synonym for difference, as representing a 'foreign culture'.[3] Voices from inside the Romany communities involved in this exchange have not had and still do not have much active influence on the strategies, narratives and actions that are being invented here. Nevertheless, the latter have exerted significant influence within political, legal and cultural contexts in both regions.

Since the end of 2010, and especially in 2011, the introduction of a general ban on begging in the whole province of Styria changed both the actual migration and the corresponding media discussions. However, these latest developments could not be included in this chapter.

The migration of Hungarian-Slovakian Roma and Romnija to Graz

Recently, scholars have increasingly connected Romany and Migration Studies.[4] Before that, the two disciplines hardly ever exchanged knowledge, neither theoretical nor methodological: Migration Studies, despite immense efforts to change this, have mainly been shaped by teleological and homogenising assumptions and subject to general and broad models (e.g. push/pull, sending/receiving).[5] Applying 'classical' as well as more recent theories of migration, the movement of Romany people is marginalised because of the enduring romantic and romanticised idea of nomadism as a kind of (historical or recent) 'placelessness'[6] that in turn suggests, albeit falsely, that Romany people simply do not 'fit' into the nation state paradigm which dominates much of the migration literature.[7]

For this and other reasons, most of the existing academic work on the migration of Romany people in central Europe has been approached from within Romany Studies. We can group this literature into three main categories: firstly, the analysis of legal and political questions such as the treatment of asylum-seeking Roma;[8] secondly, one finds a relatively high number of academic papers describing the causes for and features of movements within the push/pull model.[9] The third category, examining reactions to migration (by 'receiving societies') is as an area of study surprisingly under-represented in quantitative terms.[10] Besides that, historical treatment of Romany migrations is still rare,[11] and Roma and Romnija are still generally neglected as part of 'mainstream-migrations'.[12]

Discussions on the legitimacy of migration and the background of migrants are nothing unusual in countries which define themselves as 'receiving societies'.[13] Among the core questions of such debates is the public negotiation of legal questions, as well as the definition of the character of the migration (most recently: economic or 'genuine' exile) and the public presentation of (diverse, contradictory) knowledge on the origin and living condition of the migrants in their 'sending-countries'. These processes highlight an (insurmountable) degree of 'cultural difference'.[14] In doing so, they draw on essentialist understandings that facilitate substituting terms such as 'race' and 'ethnicity' with 'culture' and, thereby, produce highly exotic and 'different' 'cultures',[15] including categories of gender and sexuality. Specifically, 'ethnicity' is always defined according to patriarchal and heterosexist norms,[16] with evident effects on the perception of Romany and other migrations.[17]

These 'differences' are often identified by the Hungarian speaking Roma and Romnija from the south Slovak Rimavská Sobota district and the population of the Austrian town of Graz, to which they were and are migrating on a temporary basis. Around the fall of the Iron Curtain, the discussion of beggars (who were evidently Austrian) formed a watershed between the times in which begging was *de facto* unknown in Austria and the following two decades when begging has been a permanent subject of public debate.[18] Between 1993 and 1996, beggars (commuting not only from Slovakia but, above all, from war-shaken former Yugoslavia) undoubtedly became part of everyday life in Graz, where they were simply perceived as foreigners.[19] As such they aroused sympathy as well as irritation and incomprehension. Again and again, they became a target of local media campaigns and individual attacks. Whilst mayors and town councillors were trying to contain mendicancy by new and increasingly creative anti-begging acts, which were enthusiastically acclaimed by business people and shopkeepers in the town centre, some organisations emerged in order to support some of these people. In 1995, and particularly in 1996, efforts were made by local relief organisations to differentiate among the beggars by regional provenance. At first several such regions were defined (Bosnia, Croatia and Slovakia) and there was no exclusive Romany-focus in the discourse in 1995 or until very late 1996.[20] In the following years, much of the help provided by these organisations was aimed exclusively at Roma and Romnija from the village of Medovce-Metete (which was turning into a paradigmatic ghetto and the subject of much media coverage in Austrian newspapers and magazines in the years to come).

Before proceeding further, we should emphasise that all this took place at a time when Romany men and women had already been migrating to

Austria for several decades, either as part of state organised labour migrations (especially in the third quarter of the century from then Yugoslavia), or migrations of refugees fleeing war (especially at the beginning of the 1990s).[21] Yet, it was only in 1996 in Austria that these migrants became visible as Roma and were thus specifically 'ethnicised' for the very first time.

The explosion of the beggar menace: Radicalisation of local political attitudes towards Roma/Romnija

Although the presence of 'foreign' beggars in the town of Graz was discussed in the local media from 1993,[22] the issue of begging only gained significant local attention after the summer of 1996. Then the focus of the discourse was children, their mothers and their alleged 'aggression'. At this point, this discussion became the central political issue within a few weeks and the town council passed a by-law on begging on 5 December 1996.[23] This explicitly prohibited 'intrusive begging' and 'begging by children'. Its effect was the immediate departure of Romany women, supposedly hailing from Croatia or Bosnia (there are disagreements on the question of whether it was an expulsion or not).[24] Another result was the subsequent organisation and structuration of the discourse on the remaining beggars and a bureaucratisation of the treatment of these people, their stay and activities in Graz (by a Catholic NGO that specialised in this issue). Afterwards, there was hardly a single complaint leading to enforcement of the anti-begging law. In fact, for a period of time, it was not clear how the law should be put into practice and beggars were still sentenced for offences against other laws. But the symbolic consequences of the 'begging-ban' were enormous. For instance, the political debates did not cool down after the law was passed but, on the contrary, intensified. Thus, extreme right-wing parties easily demanded more rigorous legal measures which would either ban 'organised mendicancy'[25] (1997) or 'fight' against 'Indian conditions' in the city and for a 'beggar-free'[26] Graz (1999). In 2006, one of these parties even declared begging to be an 'excrescence of crime and human trafficking' which would be 'intolerable in a free state under the rule of law'.[27]

The notable shift of the political and legal discussion can be demonstrated by the fact that, just four years later, even the Social Democratic Party (SPÖ) of Styria decided (in the run up to elections) to demand the establishment of a total 'sectoral' ban on begging in Graz.[28] This commitment was remarkable since it followed directly on a proposal initially brought up by extreme-right parties earlier in 2010.[29] This fits into the suggestion that there is a Europe-wide general radicalisation in political attitudes towards Romany migrants. Further, it suggests that these narratives and fictions are very enduring. For instance, from 1997 to 2010, the number of headlines of the sort 'Roma in Graz are not organised beggars'[30] or 'Beggar study: "Now I do see them with other eyes"'[31] was quite remarkable. Nonetheless, the main argument for the demand of a 'sectoral' begging ban in 2010 was, once again, the alleged 'organised mendicancy'.

It seems promising to ask why these narratives became so enormously widespread and gained such traction. The basic motif behind all these images is the assumption of a specific danger or a hazard threatening the town of Graz and its inhabitants. The practical results of the legal framework created in Graz in 1996 leave no doubt that this menace is related to 'difference' and 'ethnicity'. Although 'race' and 'ethnicity' were never explicitly applied as categories or even mentioned as terms in the legal negotiations (nor in the final law), it is obvious from the context that the targets of the regulations were begging Roma and Romnija.[32] This is not the only paradox: although gender was not referred to in the act, the main targets were Romnija only. On the other hand, begging by children was again and again reported and discussed, even long after the law had been passed.

It is an interesting fact that the main contributors to the discourse surrounding these narratives have always been 'committed' citizens without professional interests in the topic. The second most influential group involved representatives of NGOs, among them a priest, whose engagement we will discuss later, became the symbolic figure of the issue. Besides them, professional politicians and journalists took a prominent part in the debate, but did not shape the discourse as much as the first two. These discourses took shape in a wide range of different media, including the classic mass-media (newspapers, magazines and audiovisual media), but also less widespread means of communication (bulk-mail, flyers, posters and graffiti).

Below we concentrate on mass-media but, as far as the legal discourse was concerned, the adoption of all anti-begging laws passed in Graz so far took place on questionable legal grounds: the key terms, 'aggressiveness', 'intrusiveness' and 'organised mendicancy' could not be defined with sufficient precision, although this had no legal consequences whatsoever and none of the laws has so far been repealed as unlawful by a higher legal authority such as the constitutional court.[33] In fact, as we shall see in the media discourse, politicians from all political parties had problems in defining what was particularly actionable in begging. Statements like the one mentioned above which talked of 'harming the cultural feelings of the population of Graz' are indeed indicative that many of the anti-begging measures have, at least partially, a discriminatory and racist character.[34]

Public reactions to the migrations: Images of beggars in the media

Talking about stereotypes, one might suppose that prejudices and negative images are generally caused by scanty knowledge, which creates a space for the emergence of vague suppositions. To the contrary, the Graz evidence shows that detailed knowledge may also be the basis for the spreading of new, but possibly even more harmful, stereotypes. The perception of beggars in Graz has increased over times in specificity, and seemingly draws on more and more thorough information. But 'new' and supposedly more 'accurate' images produced by these extensions of knowledge remained discriminatory.

In the initial phase of the intensive discussions about beggars in Graz (1989–96) many basic questions were not answered: for example, it remained totally unclear who the people begging were and where they came from.[35] In those days they had neither been defined as Roma nor as members of any other 'ethnic' group. The basic problem seemed to be that the people sitting on the street in the pedestrian areas and the pavements of the city did not quite fit into existing categories. Thus, one of the primary tasks of the media discussion was to create categories which would make sense to local people and create terms that would allow generally comprehensible debates and arguments. These processes of definition and categorisation started with a differentiation: at the beginning the discussion of 'unpleasant incidents' on the streets in the first district of Graz did not distinguish between 'beggars', 'dossers' and other 'troublemakers'.[36] Consequently, 'punks' and 'vagrants', as well as 'youths' or 'social cases', generally featured on the list of people endangering the security and proper condition of the old town.[37] The stereotypes and threatening images in play here were very vague and formed around diffuse and highly generalised assumptions.[38] Only once did a journalist mention a 'beggar-, dosser- and Gypsy-problem'.[39] This reference proves that these narratives were already at least partly 'ethnicised', but lacking firm categorisation or terminology.

Understandably, the first step towards a more complex discussion was to differentiate between the groups involved: the category 'beggar' was invented and linked to certain features. Accordingly, it was made clear that 'beggar' automatically referred to a 'foreigner' and led to talking about 'beggars from abroad'.[40] Although the term 'abroad' (*'Ausland'*) was never explicitly defined, it implicitly denoted 'poor' countries and particularly the European 'East'. From then on, various countries were mentioned as possible homelands. The important aspect of this lack of precision is that it did not make any difference whether one talked about Romanians, Czechs or even people from neighbouring Slovenia or Hungary.[41] Thus, already, the first differentiation opened the way not only to a search for more concrete information but also for more concrete stereotypes. As a consequence, attacks came to be based on common nationalistic images.

NGO-Interventions: The 'ethnicisation' of the beggar-issue

In late November 1996, a parish priest and head of a Catholic NGO, was the first to define the beggars in Graz publicly as Roma: '[t]hey were the well-known, begging Roma'.[42] What he intended with this 'ethnicisation' is revealed by his next sentence. There, the priest compared the planned begging-ban with 'unfortunate times', i.e. National Socialist governance. The emphasis of the suffering of this people and the direct reference to the example of the Nazi genocide of Roma/Romnija is multi-layered: it implicitly connected the issue to a bomb-attack on a Romany settlement in eastern Austria only one year earlier. This attack on Roma and Romnija, which claimed four lives, aroused broad public awareness of the Romany minority and the issue of its 'integration'.[43] The subsequent discussions formed a wide-ranging debate on the minority's plight and, for a while, the authorities monitored right-wing activities rather more intensively than usual. Hence the 'ethnicisation' fostered by the NGO could be seen as an attempt to gain support and stop the strict new policies. Giving the beggars this specific name was intended better to illustrate their problems and to integrate narratives of suffering into the discussion, ergo turn the beggars into victims.

Although the identification of beggars as Roma was successful in terms of giving poverty a face, a fate and an explanation, it also turned out to be harmful. This more exact terminology made it possible for more precise, in this case racist, stereotypes to emerge, and integrated older and newer subtexts of racist images. Additionally, the populist tabloid press welcomed this wording as it allowed them to (re)turn to using the previously, commonly rejected word '*Zigeuner*'.[44] Although these newspapers are known for their provocative, ignorant and insensitive approach to language-use, they could only use this term for a very short period of time, due to its racist reference in the National Socialist period. However, this brief timeframe before switching (via the transitory double terms 'Zigeuner-Roma', 'Zigeuner (Roma)' or others) to the term 'Roma' was long enough to guarantee that subtexts and connotations could be transferred from the old (Zigeuner) to the new wording (Roma).[45]

Despite this, if we look carefully at the short period of time around the end of 1996 we see that the labelling of begging migrants in Austria as Roma was not immediately successful. Theories of homelands became more and more important at the same time and the identification as Roma and Romnija obviously did not answer this question in a satisfactory way. At the same time, two main begging groups became clearly identified and separated. The first one was seen to be formed by silent beggars—mostly men— from Slovakia, the second by Romnija and their children, supposedly migrating from ex-Yugoslavia.[46] There was also an attempt to identify the first group as part of the Hungarian minority in Slovakia.[47] However, the labelling of the migrants as Slovakian[48] was a lot more successful, even if it only survived in the long run in combination with the 'ethnic' term: from then on the word 'beggars' became a synonym for 'Slovakian Roma'.

An NGO creating a 'beggar-village': Medovce-Metete and stereotypes of 'the East'

The second important step towards more thorough knowledge of the beggars in Graz was a localisation of their alleged hometown. The objectification of beggars as a special kind of social 'group' by the media, responsible politicians and the public had taken place from the very beginning of their presence in town, but it is striking to see the extent to which narratives and information diffused by NGO-activists could replace journalist enquiry, fact-finding or simple dialogue with the people concerned.

Once again it was the aforementioned Catholic priest, as head of the Catholic NGO who was the prime mover, when he claimed the beggars of Graz were inhabitants of only one Slovakian village, which we will now call Medovce-Metete.[49] From the NGO-point of view and for the journalists who were interested this represented a crucial breakthrough. From then on it was possible to get an overview of the situation in the 'genuine' village of origin and thus prove the 'authenticity' of poverty (with media coverage, pictures, videos, etc.). On the other hand, this turned out to be a rather weak argument as the power of localisation appeared in certain respects to be rather limited. While the beggars remained generally silent in the streets or limited to a few German words, we think it is astounding that not a single attempt was made by an employee of the mass-media to find out which languages the beggars actually spoke and/or understood. Writing about beggars, therefore, did not inevitably imply journalistic enquiry into who these people were, where they came from, and what circumstances they were living under. Mainstream media coverage of the village did not discuss the fact that the Romany inhabitants of this Slovakian village spoke Hungarian. Thus, 'Medovce' became a synonym for the 'East' in the mainstream perception and did not therefore constitute a concrete localisation, rather pointing to a symbolic area with overwhelmingly negative connotations. This resulted in paradoxical arguments, including frequent attacks on the Czech Republic, eight years after its separation from Slovakia: 'If members of the Eastern Bloc (!) such as the 'Tschechei' [a pejorative term for the Czech part of former Czecho-Slovakia, used particularly by the National Socialist administration during the Second World War] have enough money to join the NATO, then they should take care of their own people'.[50]

In recapitulating these processes, it is apparent that the denomination 'Roma from Medovce', became the central term in these narratives.[51] The definition was applied to all beggars, regardless of their actual national provenance and their 'ethnic' self-affiliation, using the term not only to mark but also to discriminate. It proved effective, irrespective of circumstances: even men who are legally Austrian citizens but are found begging are constantly labelled Roma.[52] How strong this connection has been, and still is, may be illustrated by a statement made by the official representative of the 'autochthonous' Romany minority in Austria, in which he was not emphasising that Roma and Romnija were not just or only beggars. On the contrary, he felt urged to point out that 'not only Roma are begging'.[53]

It was not merely this ethnicised categorisation that made it easier to talk about beggars. At the turn of the millennium it became possible to use the mere word 'Medovce' in newspaper headlines to refer to people begging in Graz.[54] Of course, this should not be read as a euphemism as if it was more complicated to attack Roma and Romnija, beggars or Romany migrants and so a local term was being substituted. As an illustration of how old prejudices and stereotypes easily adopt to new wordings and discursive structures, take the following account (published in a high quality newspaper): next to an image of the only village from which all Graz beggars supposedly came, one read a summary of reasons for the migration: 'The Roma are taken for work-shy by the Slovakian Majority'.[55] Hence not only did more, specific knowledge support a differentiation in public debates, but also the invention of more concrete (and effective) stereotypes.

Excursus: Perception in Slovak coverage

Although the people who are originally from Medovce-Metete featured significantly more often in the headlines of Austrian newspapers than in Slovak ones, there are also a number of articles in their home country dealing with the Graz-Medovce-Metete connection. Interestingly, none of them refers to the activities of the Viennese NGO. The Roma newspaper (*Romano Lil*) and mainstream tabloids (e.g. *Sme*) informed about the engagement of the aforementioned Austrian clergyman who was decorated with epithets like 'longstanding friends of the inhabitants of Medovce',[56] 'priest of the poor' and 'priest of the homeless'.[57]

The dichotomy of 'rich' Austria and 'poor' Slovakia created in the Austrian discourse was also to be found in the Slovak one. Moreover, we even encountered parallel arguments: Medovce-Metete is described as a village in eastern Slovakia[58]—geographically it is located in the middle of the southern part of Slovakia. 'Eastern Slovakia' is also in Slovak discourse a synonym for Romany settlement, backwardness and poverty and the connotations of this term are quite similar to those in Austria.[59] Furthermore, the other part of the dichotomy, which is the 'rich/golden West', was a prominent feature. The town of Graz, represented by the priest, is willing to financially support the deprived village of Medovce-Metete. The clergyman is described as the Messiah,[60] who is able to improve the living conditions of the people and who has the necessary financial resources at his disposal. His engagement is highly praised and his activities to improve the life of the locals by giving them work are seen as encouraging.[61] Even a governmental report on the construction of social housing for the inhabitants of Medovce-Metete mentions that the furniture was financed by donations from Graz/Austria.[62] This emphasises the impact the activities of the Catholic NGO—and recently also of the secular NGO—have had on this village.

The foundation of a pasta production factory by the Catholic NGO, which employs fourteen Romnija, is noted as a positive example of how to improve the local living conditions. Furthermore, it is emphasised that this

227

breaks the widespread stereotype and prejudice that Roma and Romnija are work-shy.[63]

But how and why the connection between Medovce-Metete and Graz was actually established (through Slovak citizens going to beg there) is only mentioned in the Romany newspaper, which is only distributed within a small circle. Naturally, putting these financially precious contacts into the context of Slovak citizens begging on the streets of Graz would demolish the otherwise positive image of them.

However, we note that the coverage in Romany newspapers, as well as in mainstream tabloids, is rather positive and praises the activities of the Austrian priest. This is even more interesting as, in Slovakia, anti-Gypsyism is quite common. Many members of the majority population do not appreciate the organisation of activities for the Romany Community at all.[64] Although only the Romany newspapers gave the full story,[65] we perceive it as very positive and progressive that this was not used against the Romany Community in the local tabloid press—as happened in other countries.[66] Nevertheless, some comments posted by readers of the articles are very negative and contain racist remarks about the activities in Medovce-Metete. For instance, a rather harsh comment concerning the pasta produced by Romnija is also projected onto the Austrians involved: 'Let's hope, that this Austrian takes the pasta with him. If not, I stop eating pasta'.[67]

Although the Slovak coverage is not as extensive as the Austrian, we can say that the activities of the Catholic NGO in Medovce-Metete, which focus on and are carried out on a local level, are reasonably fully and well perceived by a broader Romany and non-Romany public.

The culturalisation of Romany migration: Why is gender relevant?

In sketching analytical approaches to the case of Romany migrants in Graz, we believe that the systematic neglect of gender in mainstream Migration Studies as well as in mainstream Romany Studies[68] does not so much ignore some isolated components of research, but in fact renders existing analyses inadequate and misleading.[69] The 1996 'Act on intrusive begging and begging with children' passed by the city of Graz defined which forms of begging were acceptable and which were not. As we have said, the result of this measure was that while begging performed by Roma (i.e. men) was deemed 'appropriate', that is, legal, the same activity, when performed by Romnija (i.e. women) and their children was defined as 'intrusive' by police and other local authorities and, consequently, these women left the town.[70] It could be argued that this distinction relied on widespread cultural, and necessarily gendered, subtexts that are assumed to constitute an 'own' ('Austrian'/'Styrian') identity. For example, the collective presence of female Romany migrants was defined by local conservative politicians as 'violating the cultural feelings'[71] of the local population. On the other hand, male beggars were allowed to stay in the streets and, eventually, they even gained support from the local Catholic NGO.

In order to appreciate the full significance of the role played by gender in such circumstances, we need first to acknowledge that gender works as a symbolic category. In this case, the male beggars, who were allowed to continue begging in the street even once the new law had been passed, were treated in a paradoxical way: on one hand they were feminised,[72] most evidently in the 'begging posture' which was one of the effects of the begging act's implementation: in order to beg legally, individuals were effectively forced to kneel down when performing this act. On the other hand, it is also possible to read an element of the masculine in the beggars' presence generally, if we consider that the masculinity of the group of beggars has publically (e.g. in letters to the editor) been over-emphasised in fantasies about the collective male body of Romany beggars attacking the immaculate (female) body of the town (or the nation): the serious threat towards the helpless and pure town derives from active, 'well-fed young men':[73] 'Graz, the town of beggars. The multitude of beggars, present especially in the old-town, […] is increasingly responsible for much discontent. It simply mars the streetscape. In hardly any other town or city can one find so many beggars so close to each other'.[74] Thus, according to press and political debates, it was the male in the Romany migrant that was deemed a menace in that their presence contributed to a 'disgusting picture'[75] or the 'defacing' of an otherwise 'tidy' town.[76]

Aggressive women as the main source of racist scenarios of menace

There were a number of other extensively used images in media coverage of Romany migrants in Austria. One important one was the idea of women or mothers that act aggressively. Especially before the bill was passed, newspapers often appealed to readers by featuring Romany women abusing their children or attacking/betraying pedestrians: in the Graz press in summer and autumn 1996, for example, Romany women were often described as if they were the ones sending their own children out into the street, forcing them to either beg or perform music.[77] This fantasy in which parental power/care turns (or, is perverted) into aggression while control/guidance is transformed into abuse was expressed frequently in press coverage and had a huge impact on the public's perception and especially on the legal/political treatment of the 'begging problem'. According to the press and politicians, the list of what aggressive women were capable of was rather impressive. Particularly in letters to the editor, but also in the official discussions in the town council, these women were described as having attacked pedestrians, even spitting on them, refusing donated food, robbing people and acting in aggressive ways towards passers-by. This stereotype of the Romany woman as an aggressive virago was also reflected outside the mass-media, in novels, for example. Here one could read about men who were beaten up 'mercilessly'[78] by their wives and forced to hand over power to them.[79]

To sum up, the majority of articles in the press dealing with begging Romnija indicates that the reference to this specific 'type' is predominantly used to illustrate seemingly 'problematic aspects' of 'Romany culture'. Consequently, it is worth taking a closer look at the subtext implied by the press depiction of the committed/aggressive woman. The idea of a woman—especially a migrant, who must, after all, as a result of where she comes from, have backward ideas[80]—being active in public, challenges what are otherwise accepted as basic social/cultural regulations. A mother who claims power over her own life and who is capable of managing her surroundings independently is perceived as violating the gendered division of labour in particular and the gender order in general.[81] On the whole, active women, in refusing to be passive and by appearing in public, are deemed 'intrusive' and pose an alleged threat to normatively gendered spheres and duties.

Enabling and preventing migration: The Catholic pro-Romany NGO of Graz

As already noted, a clergyman was among the first to provide help and support for foreign beggars in Graz. It is crucial to understand that apart from help to the local poor he targeted his resources only at Romany people, fostering projects that explicitly supported the Roma and Romnija from Medovce-Metete. After 1997, a huge infrastructure project (involving housing, official bureaucracy and even a factory) demonstrated this strong, though unequal connection between 'rich' Graz and 'poor' Medovce-

Metete. Since then, a large number of institutions has been installed under the auspices of a brand name.[82] Meanwhile the priest himself has become a local celebrity in this context. Newspapers call him a 'rebel for charity', which became the title of his autobiography as well. Several times he came into conflict with his church superiors, when his ideas of charity did not fit with theirs.[83] Since 1973 he has been a local priest in Eggenberg, a working class district of Graz. His commitment to those in need, particularly homeless men, intensified in the early 1990s when, not only the first Romany beggars, but also thousands of refugees from war-torn Yugoslavia came to Austria. Today, his NGO's network encompasses more than a dozen different projects, ranging from a kind of mobile soup-kitchen, providing homeless people with food and beverages in the centre of Graz every evening, to several shelters for the homeless.[84] Our focus here is the facilities targeting Romany people temporarily migrating to Graz, taking into account that these facilities exclusively provide their services to Slovak, Hungarian speaking Romany men from the area surrounding Medovce.[85]

The heart of the pro-Romany action of this NGO is a homeless shelter which emerged from an initiative in 1992 when the NGO erected a large tent camp for several hundred refugees. The tent camp later moved into a former factory building, which was substantially restored in 1999. The shelter officially provides 'emergency-overnight-accommodation' solely for foreign men and is used almost exclusively by Romany beggars. In practice, people from Medovce (and sometimes other places as well) are accommodated there for two or three weeks. During the time spent in Graz, they beg, an activity that is made possible thanks to the infrastructure and backing of the NGO's facilities. The shelter provides them not only with washing machines and some services to fulfil their basic needs, it is also a kind of central authority, providing them with all the information and assistance to use all the other local services they might require. Up to ninety men can be accommodated there, where they are supplied with a warm meal per day. Due to the long years of its existence, it is well-known in Graz and very often referred to as a model for similar projects.

One element in the broader infrastructure are the ID-cards handed out by the NGO, established in spring 1997.[86] These are cards, issued in the shelter, featuring a photograph of the card owner, his name and a simple phrase that this particular NGO is aware of the conditions the respective person is living under. The NGO issued these cards as a reaction to media reports claiming that mendicancy in Graz was mainly organised and executed by gangs.[87] The ID-card 'legalises' migrating Romany beggars, and guarantees that the neediness and poverty of the respective person is proven and authenticated by a Catholic NGO.[88] In fact, these ID-cards were given almost exclusively to Romany people from Medovce, mainly for two reasons: first, people participating in the network of Roma from Medovce have privileged access to information about these services; second, the NGO established the network with people from this particular region of Slovakia, quite conscious of the fact that the priest saw them fulfilling certain criteria of neediness.[89] The Medovce Roma in Graz therefore often have to display poverty in a Christian sense or, as Pucher puts it in newspaper interviews, 'rich societies have to bear the face of poverty'.[90]

In 2006 a homeless shelter exclusively for foreign women was founded to cover the need for accommodation of female migrants. Similar to the existing shelter for men, it is primarily used by Romany beggars, who can spend as many nights as they like at the facility. They are provided with one warm meal per day. In fact, the this facility is far less well-known than the one only meant for men. This might indicate that migrant begging activities are predominantly perceived as a male activity. That would fit well into the general structure of aid provided by the NGO, which follows a pattern of a traditional Catholic family model, favouring men at work outside the house and women at home with the children and the elderly.

Pasta production is one of the most recent projects of the NGO. Pasta is manufactured directly in Medovce in Slovakia by Romany women and sold by selected retailers in Graz. The pasta features a number of characteristics similar to those of fair trade products, and it is sold at a comparable price. Students of a Graz High School produced a video clip to advertise the pasta on the internet, stressing that those women employed at the pasta factory not only have a fixed income for the first time in their lives, but also get the opportunity to stay at home with their children, and thus do not have to migrate abroad for work anymore. This pasta production is the only successful project out of a large number which have aimed to remove beggars from the streets of Graz. Interestingly, the migration of people is symbolically substituted by the migration of goods. The pasta project not only stresses once more the archetype of the traditional family (women at home with the children), but it also keeps poverty out of the eyes of the citizens of Graz.

Shaping discourse: Romany migration as presented by the Catholic NGO

During the past twenty years, the aforementioned priest has not only become a well-known and respected advocate for Romany people's basic rights in Graz, but he has also become a main target of racist/xenophobic 'flaming' (internet insults) and even death threats. His personal archive comprises some 8000 documents, featuring every single newspaper article which has ever been written about the work of the his NGO, copies of all agreements ever contracted between the NGO and other groups on behalf of the Romany migrants in Graz and each letter of complaint, support and hate that he has ever received for his commitment. Most of these letters were written after the spring of 1999, when a joint project between the town of Graz and the Catholic NGO failed: the controversial plan had intended to support Romany beggars migrating to Graz with approximately 3500 schilling (approximately 250€ or £220) per month, as long as they would stay in pastoral care instead of begging.[91] Once this plan was made public at the beginning of July 1999, the town of Graz pulled out.[92] The media response was harsh and the reactions the priest received were even harsher.[93] Most letters belonged in the hate mail category (though there were also a considerable number of supportive letters).[94] The homogeneity of anti-'Gypsy' discourse is striking, although this has slightly changed over the years according to the state of local debates.[95] 'Work-shy Gypsy vermin' are contrasted to an industrious local population.[96] Foreigners are classified according to their country of origin, and their 'Gypsyness' or Romany-identity is not of central interest in these approaches.[97] Discrimination and racism are mainly directed at people from eastern neighbouring countries.[98] Foreign beggars endanger the touristic image of the town and, according to the letters, many people feel obliged to assure 'visitors' that those sitting in the streets begging do not belong to the local population. As opposed to western Europeans in the classical sense, eastern Europeans are frequently described as 'work-shy criminals' and 'defrauders'. Interestingly, the communist past of the eastern European countries still plays a role in these pejorative attributions. Very often scoffing references are made to the 'communist paradise'.[99] The style and orthography of the communications indicate all levels of educational backgrounds, though the number of writers with educational deficits appears to be relatively high. Many letters were written by retirees. What had once been the 'Stadt der Volkserhebung' ('The

Town of the People's Uprising', an honorary title given to Graz during the time of the NS-regime, referring to the fact that the city was already ruled by Nazis before the arrival of German troops) has now become a peaceful place of respectable citizens (or at least that is what it would be like, were it not for the Romany beggars). Interestingly, the wrath, anger and hate in such letters focus on the person of the clergyman, 'his' Roma and the town of Graz, which has not yet been successful in establishing a legally effective paragraph prohibiting 'Gypsy' mendicancy. But very few attack the NGO itself, which suggests that approval of humanitarian activities is strongly bound to the question of who benefits from it: thus it makes an important difference whether it is a young Austrian mother of three children or a young Slovak mother of three children who receives assistance.

Managing poverty

Taking a closer look at the NGO's activities, it has to be said that the Catholic organisation has not only done much to improve the conditions under which begging Romany migrants stay temporarily in Graz, but it has also shaped the discussion around this. The NGO has not only established a local network of relief agencies, but is also powerful means of administration and regulation. The issuing of the ID-cards legalises mendicancy in Graz to a certain extent. Although the card is nothing more than a piece of paper, its distribution by this Catholic NGO offers effective protection against certain inconveniences, e.g. police controls. Due to the great demand for the card, its issue was formally regulated shortly after it was first distributed at the end of March 1997. Foreigners from anywhere but Medovce-Metete usually encounter obstacles when they try to obtain the card. In this way, a gap was opened between 'legal' and 'illegal' mendicancy, and the question was also raised as to who deserves pity and who does not. The perceptions of poverty and neediness operate around a loosely conceived notion of guilt and are best seen against the background of a biblical understanding of mercy. The priest's domination of the local discourse becomes evident when one examines how it developed: it was the clergyman who introduced an ethnicisation of the foreign beggars by introducing the term 'Roma'. Following this, he established clear distinctions between: male, native, homeless alcoholics; male, native, temporary homeless people; native, temporarily homeless women with or without children; male, foreign temporary migrant beggars and, finally; female, foreign, temporary migrant beggars. Each of these groups was provided with a specific form of help from an agreed aid organisation.

This and other Catholic relief agencies (Caritas) have repeatedly criticised the mayor and the town council for the restrictions they tried to impose on mendicancy. This puts the role of Catholicism in contemporary Austrian society in general and that of Christian charity in the context of the beggar debate in an interesting situation: a more or less private initiative has taken over a specific part of the welfare state in providing food and accommodation for a group no one else feels responsible for. It is interesting that the NGO claims a labelling power in return. The cards serve as a good example of this, establishing an 'ethnic' border distinguishing ordinary beggars from Romany beggars, the latter representing an archetype of poverty in a Christian Catholic sense, and therefore deserving the sympathy and charity of the citizen.

Helping to help actions of a Vienna-based secular NGO

There is another organisation that was established as a reaction to media reports on the work done by the Catholic NGO from Graz: a Viennese based secular NGO. It started as a private initiative organised by an Austrian non-Romany couple after they saw Austrian TV coverage of the Slovak-Hungarian village of Medovce-Metete and some of its Romany inhabitants supported by the Catholic NGO. Using their infrastructure and networks, including the shop in Medovce run by the Catholic NGO the Viennese organisation has been active for almost three years. Indeed, the pre-existence of this network is the main reason for this NGO to operate in Medovce.[100]

The NGO consists of about ten active members, who are non-Romany Austrians, coming from different (professional, social etc.) backgrounds. All are volunteer workers. Their motivations vary, but the main reason given is a wish to help the poor Romany people in Slovakia, although none of them has experience with working with the Romany community or development aid. Furthermore, none of them is able to communicate in Slovak or Hungarian (Romany is not spoken by any of the inhabitants of Medovce-Metete). All their communication and correspondence relies on a Hungarian/Slovakian-German interpreter who is paid for her work.

Although it is the aim of the NGO to improve the living conditions of the Romany Community in Medovce by stressing the importance of self-help and local initiative, the bulk of assistance is material—people are given

235

goods or money (for food, electricity bills or fire wood).[101] For the NGO, help is organised through a transfer of hard goods irrespective of need among, and possible use by, the beneficiaries.

And, in contrast to the Catholic NGO, the fields of action of the secular organisation are geographically strictly divided. While in Austria goods and money are collected, distributing them happens in Slovakia; this means that while the Catholic NGO works in Austria and in Slovakia with the Romany Community, the Viennese organisation works in Austria for the community and in Slovakia with it. Goods like clothes, toys and dishes etc. are taken by the Catholic NGO's shop in Medovce-Metete, which is run as a second-hand-shop, where the items are sold for a symbolic price.[102] Furniture is mostly given away for free to Romany families, who are chosen by the mayor or his son who are Roma themselves. The latter is working as a social worker.

We approach these practices considering their (post)-colonial aspects: aid is granted by (rich) Austria to (poor) Slovakia.

Cucumbers fighting poverty—the agricultural project of the Viennese NGO

The so-called 'Pickled Cucumbers Project' is the main project of the NGO and can be seen as a seasonal equivalent of the Catholic NGO's 'Pasta Project'. Both projects address women in the first instance in order to give them the opportunity to raise the family income level.

The idea of bringing Romany women into an agricultural project was born in spring 2008. Three women were chosen by the local mayor and given a field to plant cucumbers. The women were in charge of planting, taking care of and harvesting the vegetable. Afterwards they pickled them in their own kitchens. Altogether 2300 jars of pickled cucumbers were produced and exported to Austria, where they were 'sold' for a minimum donation and 20 per cent of it was given to the women. The NGO absorbed the costs of production. This project was also advertised by the ORF (the Austrian national broadcaster) in its coverage of Medovce.[103] As a result, all the jars of pickled cucumbers were swiftly sold. In 2009 the project was expanded. More women—again chosen by the mayor—participated and, altogether, 11,000 jars were produced. In 2010 it was extended to another village and, besides cucumbers, cabbage was also planted and preserved.

The 'Pickled Cucumbers Project' aims to provide work for the unemployed. Members of the NGO believe it will have a lasting effect on the living conditions of the Romany Community. However, they ignore the fact that, first, it provides only seasonal labour and, second, it represents an 'artificially created' occupation. There is no true demand for these pickled cucumbers, since the market where they are sold is artificially created by the NGO as well.[104]

Due to very strict food legislation in Austria (the hygienic standards are not met in Medovce) it is not possible to sell them in mainstream supermarkets and, additionally, the price can never compete with that of commercial pickled cucumbers.

There is thus no sustainability built in to the project. If we assume that—for whatever reason—the NGO crashes, the women in Medovce would not have acquired the required capital to produce pickled cucumbers and would lose their access to the market for their products. This can be interpreted as a clear and strong (post)-colonial relationship.

Counter-productive effects of the NGO's projects

Considered from a short-term perspective, the NGO's help has had a significant positive impact by providing goods that improve peoples' immediate living conditions. However, from a longer-term perspective it may have several counter-productive effects on the Community:

1. Encouraging dependence: supporting families with goods, money for food and paying their electricity bills causes a strong dependence on the NGO. Families who used to survive with a little income are now getting used to a monthly care package from Austria. This guarantees short-term survival but does not encourage the people to become active themselves.

2. Making people helpless: the NGO takes all the responsibility from the families as well as the possibility and freedom to act. People are reduced to objects of the Viennese NGO's actions which control significant aspects of their lives. As the NGO is run by volunteers, who invest all their free time and energy in these projects, the risk that it crashes—if only through exhaustion and natural attrition—is always present. The loss of the NGO's aid would have an immense negative impact and worsen the whole situation of the Romany community, as the people have become used to the aid from Austria.

3. Promoting internal conflicts: the NGO is operating in Medovce with the help of the mayor and the social worker who are Roma themselves. Fami-

lies, who are granted aid, are chosen by them. The choice of families and the way they are chosen appears to be neither transparent nor fair.

4. Promotion and exoticisation of poverty: on its website, the NGO offers people interested in participating, a trip to the Romany settlement.[105] Through this rather unorthodox approach they want to create more awareness of the Romany community. As the NGO sees it, Austrians need to see the living conditions to be touched emotionally and convinced to help. Nevertheless, this 'offer' to the interested Austrian public also has a very negative connotation as, in Austria, Romany settlements are regarded, at least since a book was published by the journalist Karl-Markus Gauß,[106] as exotic locations of poverty, covered in dirt and inhabited by primitive people. This perception of Romany people attracts the attention of Austrians, who are curious and excited to visit such a place. There seems to be a parallel between such sensation-seeking trips and visits to a reservation or a theme park—during them the Roma and Romnija are not seen as equal and they are not truly met 'eye to eye'.

Conclusion: The heterogeneous reactions to Romany migration

This contribution has dealt with temporary Romany migrations from Medovce-Metete in Slovakia to the town of Graz. We have tried to characterise their effects neutrally, talking of reactions to these movements. Hence, we have tried to demonstrate the links between activities that claim to help and those that claim to counter the Roma and Romnija. In a case like this, where we deliberately step outside the dichotomous structure of 'anti-Gypsism' vs. NGO-activities, a complex network of interdependent relations can be identified, revealing broader contexts and consequences. One area of particular interest is the effects of NGO-type institutions which here can be described as counter-productive in their own terms.

Although sustainability is the declared aim of all the NGO initiatives, it is questionable how far this goal is reached. There is no question that it has been both the beggars and the NGOs which have established networks of economic and cultural exchange between the Slovakian and the Austrian site—and these have often been strong and enduring. This has gone far beyond classical ideas of charitable work on migration, including establishing a factory, facilities for housing and new local forms of bureaucracy. These projects are not only driven by a simple interest in helping people though, they are also by a goal of stopping migration or limiting it to certain groups (e.g. men). We also encountered activities that remind us of old-fashioned techniques of development aid, shaped by what appears to be a strongly (post)-colonial perception of the problem: providing families with goods and food randomly according to immediate need has no lasting effect and produces many counter-productive effects. At the same time, in Slovakia it is clear that the projects mirror the expectations and ideologies of the NGOs: the poor who receive help have to fit into certain categories ('healthy' families, sanctified by the mayor) and especially have to obey certain rules (no intrusiveness, modesty etc.). In all these ways, it is not clear how much the Roma and Romnija in Medovce-Metete are truly 'helped'.

It is also striking that such an enormous field of projects and public discussions is characterised by a systematic amateurism—dominated by people who are not familiar with Romany issues, social work or development aid. Some of the NGO activists involved do have experience in a similar field, but none of them is a professional in the narrow sense of the word. This has caused various kinds of clumsiness or displays a lack of awareness that intervention raises certain hopes and expectations. At the same time, we see that Slovaks sometimes refer to Medovce-Metete as a kind of Austrian playground, where substantial, even capital (housing), inputs are made without genuine mandates or a long-term vision. A Czech mayor, in whose municipality many Roma and Romnija live, explained his similar experience as follows: 'NGOs come and go—as they like. But we have to cope and get along with each other for the rest of our lives'.

Finally, this story shows how NGO activities do not simply combat racism or prejudice, even if this is their honest intention. The discussion of threats caused by Romany beggars in Graz illustrates the complexity of interactions in the production of knowledge about a minority. In this case, the 'ethnicisation' of the begging people as Roma or Romnija involved a clear attempt to point to experiences of suffering as a people with an unambiguous reference to specific Austrian racist crimes under National Socialism and the bomb attack in the 1990s. Nevertheless, this form of 'saving' the Roma and Romnija through victimisation turned out to be problematic. It allowed the updating and reconstruction of old racist stereotypes and images.

Most generally, what we have demonstrated, through a discussion of the heterogeneity of discussions and activities in this field of Romany migrations, is that far from there being one policy or attitude towards Roma and Romnija among the public, officials or NGOs, the diversity of (re)actions to new events and this specific minority is the source of seemingly inexplicable developments in these and similar cases.

12

POSSIBLE RESPONSES TO THE SWEEP
OF RIGHT-WING FORCES AND ANTI-GYPSYISM
IN HUNGARY

Lídia Balogh

The context of the tensions between the Roma and non-Roma in Hungary[1]

In Hungary the Roma constitute the largest minority (the estimated number of the Roma population is at least 400–600,000,[2] which is approximately 4–6 per cent of Hungary's total population, and is also one of the largest Romany populations in central-eastern Europe), and practically the Roma are the only 'visible' minority (given the small proportion of migrants in the population).[3] Concerning the Roma as a minority group, one of the most relevant elements of the Hungarian legal framework is the Law on the Rights of Ethnic and National Minorities, passed in 1993.[4] As regards the background—and adequacy for the Roma—of the Minority Act, it is important to note that the Hungarian approach to ethnic and national minority rights has always been defined by a more or less subliminal reference to ethnic Hungarians' Diaspora-rights (in the neighbouring states), and the legal and political consequences of this stance are debated.[5] (The features of the law are to be considered as initiatives by the Hungarian state, intended to show benevolence, and to provide good practice on the international level, by guarding the cultural heritages of the—mostly over-assimilated, except the Roma—national or ethnic minorities of Hungary.)

The Roma population is significantly younger in comparison to the overall Hungarian population, due to lower life expectancy, as well as fertility rates of Roma[6] being higher than those of the general population in Hungary.[7] Compared to the current 4–6 per cent ratio of the Roma population in general, the proportion of Roma children is significantly higher: according to reliable estimates, in 2002, the share of Roma among all newborns in Hungary was 15 per cent.[8]

Prejudices against Roma are pervasive in the mainstream Hungarian society.[9] One widespread stereotype is the close linking of criminality to Roma ethnicity: according to a survey in 2006, almost two thirds (62 per cent) of the adult population of Hungary agreed fully or to some degree with the following statement: 'The tendency to commit crime is in the blood of the Roma'.[10]

The term 'gypsy criminality'—recurrent in contemporary right-wing political rhetorics in Hungary—originates in the socialist era: between 1971 and 1988, there were official data on ethnicity collected and kept by the police and by the prosecution offices, but this practice was judged later as unacceptable in a democratic state. (In 2009, the Chief of Police claimed that the ethnicisation of criminality is unreasonable, because 'crime does not have a colour'.) However, in April 2009, the Parliamentary Commissioner for Civil Rights, Máté Szabó, said in an interview that Hungarian society needs to be warned about 'Gypsy crimes', which are a special type of 'livelihood delinquency', carried out by Roma, who still live in a 'collectivist, nearly tribal society, which stands in sharp contrast with the Hungarian society's individualist approach'. Numerous human rights NGOs and Roma NGOs protested—and also the other ombudsmen (including the Parliamentary Commissioner for Ethnic and National Minorities)—against the statement, and demanded the ombudsman's resignation.[11] Even President László Sólyom expressed concern over the incident, but Szabó did not (or did not have to) resign.[12]

'Gypsy criminality' is often mentioned in connection with specific cases. During the past few years, several serious criminal acts, associated with Roma offenders, stoked up further hatred against the Roma, and not just at local levels. The first tragic incident happened in October 2006, when in the village of Olaszliszka a non-Roma man—a teacher from a nearby city—was lynched by local Roma before the eyes of his young daughters. (The man hit a Roma child who wanted to run through the road with his car, the child left the scene of the accident with minor injuries.) Threatening acts and violent offences against Roma as 'retorsive' acts were carried out after the case in the village of Olaszliszka, which included the burning down of a house inhabited by Roma, another Roma-owned building being shot at with firearms, and the windows of several Roma family homes being broken by stones. The defendants (altogether eight persons, including two minors) were sentenced to a severe penalty on first instance in May 2009.[13] The trial attracted significant public attendance, especially in the political right-wing sphere, as in that context, the deceased victim (Lajos Szögi, the 'Hungarian' teacher and father) become a symbolic figure.

In November 2008, in Kiskunlacháza, a fourteen-year-old non-Roma girl (called Nóra Horák) was raped and killed, and many of the locals connect the case to the members of the Roma community, which has influenced public opinion at the national level as well. While the identity of the perpetrator of the rape and murder was still unknown, another case happened in the same village in April 2009: a twelve-year-old 'white' girl (whose first name was also Nóra) was robbed and assaulted by a group of Roma youngsters. Orbán Kolompár, leader of the EP-candidate MCF Roma Alliance Party—immediately after the case, without knowing the details of the incident—claimed that the incident was most likely just a 'children's mischief', which triggered protests from right-wing politicians, including the major opposition party, Fidesz (the mayor of Kiskunlacháza is delegated by the Fidesz party).[14] Later the police investigation proved that the case was actually much more than mischief, and the perpetrators were older than the victim (sixteen-year-old teenagers). The mayor of the village declared that this case was to be connected to the 'phenomena of under-age Gypsy-criminality'—in reference to the tragic case of 2008. Soon after the European Parliamentary (EP)-elections, the police arrested the suspected perpetrator of the first case (rape and murder), who were—against all presupposition—not of Roma origin. However, the mayor refused to apologise or withdraw his prejudiced statements.[15]

In February 2009, a criminal case which generated a public outcry (even at the international level, as it involved a victim of foreign—Romanian—nationality) was the killing of Marian Cozma, an athlete in the handball team of Veszprém, Hungary. While the details of the case are as of yet far from clarified, the suspects are of Roma origin, which raised again the issue of the 'inherent criminality' of the Roma, and some voices in the discourse also implicated the 'common responsibility' of the Roma. As a reaction to this, Lívia Járóka, Hungarian MEP[16] of Roma origin, commented on the homicide in Veszprém in a press release ('We have to plan our future together'): 'Being a Hungarian, being a Gypsy and being a mother, I was shocked by the news about the tragedy, and for me, it makes this more painful, that the ruthless offenders are Gypsies. Marian Cozma was killed by Gypsies, but not by "the" Gypsies'.[17]

Election campaigns of political parties and the 'Roma-issues'

The opinion leaders of Hungary's current leading extreme right-wing party, Jobbik (a relatively new participant in Hungarian politics), found that anti-Gypsyism is a timely issue by which to gain popularity and power by putting it on the agenda: during its ten-year-long existence, Jobbik re-introduced and reconfirmed the term 'gypsy-criminality' in the political discourse. As for Jobbik's platform, the representatives of the party stand up (verbally) for the rights of Hungarian minorities in the neighbouring countries, and claim to be ready to use 'law and order' in order to crack down on crime. However, without a clearly shaped political programme, Jobbik still remains on the level of emotional rhetoric, using also frequent references to Christianity. Encouraging and utilising anti-Gypsyism has proved to be an effective political strategy. The target groups of Jobbik's supporters are in the Hungarian middle, lower middle and working classes, while the typical Jobbik-voter is male, aged between twenty and forty, employed or a student. As described by an investigative journalist, who conducted a series of inter-views among them, the Jobbik-supporters' political awareness is much higher than the average level of young people in Hungary, they tend to be especially interested in history, they can be mobilised by issues related to the Hungarian minorities living in the neighbouring countries, and they profess anti-Gypsy—and partly anti-Semitic—views. The young people who join the party are primarily attracted by the political intactness, the mythical nationalism and the explicit rhetoric of Jobbik, as well as the sense of com-munity provided by the party.[18]

Jobbik has a strong camp of supporters, not just in rural areas of Hun-gary (for example, in Borsod-Abaúj-Zemplén County—a stronghold of the Jobbik party—where a significant proportion of the population is Roma), but also in the capital city. In the 2009 EP-elections Jobbik gained almost 15 per cent of the votes,[19] and secured three seats in the European Parliament.[20] Jobbik has been running its European parliamentary campaign and general political programme on racist (and anti-semitic propaganda), using, for example, 'anti-Gypsy crime' slogans. Due to Jobbik's campaign and extremists' demonstrations and violent attacks on the Roma in the past years, the 'Roma-issue' had been present as a dominating factor in Hungarian politics around (and even before) the European parliamentary elections. To varying degrees, all political parties and media actors were involved in the debate. For example, the National Election Commission held that the Jobbik party slogan 'Hungary belongs to Hungarians' is unconstitutional. As a result of the 2010 general elections, Jobbik gained forty-seven representatives in the parliament (gaining more than 12 per cent of the votes).

As for the actual number of Roma voters in Hungary, one of the leaders of MCF Roma Alliance Party[21] gave an estimation of about 250–300,000 voters in 2009. According to his calculations, the number of Hungarian citizens with Roma origin is above 1 million, and he takes into account the demographic characteristics of the Roma population (the high percentage of minors), and the proportion of (especially male) adults who are in prison, or who are not entitled to vote as part of judicial penalty. During the 2009 EP-elections, the MCF gained the less of the votes: 0.46 per cent (and no seats in the European Parliament), with 13,431 votes altogether. The campaign of the MCF Party was organised in the 'last minute': it was only in January 2009, during the congress of the party (with the participation of numerous Roma NGOs as well), when the leaders of MCF decided to participate in the 2009 EP-elections. Lacking sufficient sources, their campaign was almost invisible in the media (some video spots were available via YouTube, and the leaders and candidates were invited on several TV-programmes), and their campaign-posters were not displayed earlier than approximately a week before the day of the election. However, the activists of the party conducted intense direct campaign in Roma-populated villages, using desperate slogans, like 'we shall defend the future of our children even at the price of sacrificing our lives'. The MCF campaign was based on the argument[22] that Roma voters had to try and outnumber the Jobbik-voters, because the sweep of right-wing forces will transform Hungary into a 'country, where Roma won't have a place to live anymore'. The other party which is organised on Roma ethnic bases, Lungo Drom, only took one candidate[23] to parliament, in coalition with the centre-right Fidesz Party, and secured a seat in the EP this way in 2009. In 2010, the MCF Party was not even among the applicant parties for the general elections, while the Lungo Drom gained a seat in the Hungarian National Assembly, through its coalition with Fidesz.

Hungarian Guard[24]

The Jobbik Party is considered to be a direct antecedent of the proto-fascist, paramilitary organisation of the Hungarian Guard. After its establishment in June 2007, intimidating marches of the uniform wearing 'Guardists' started to follow various kinds of rural inter-ethnic conflicts and incidents, including more minor incidents of jealousy between Roma and non-Roma men, or cases of thievery with Roma suspects. The Guard was registered as a cultural organisation, aimed at *preparing the youth spiritually and physically for extraordinary situations when it might be necessary to mobilise the people*. Marches were organised in settlements as demonstrations of strength. These were presented as responses to calls for help from the local (non-Roma) inhabitants who addressed the Hungarian Guard.[25] According to Gábor Vona, the leader of the Jobbik Party, the occurrence of the Hungarian Guard is an indicator of the impotence of a municipality, as 'there are settlements where the inhabitants consider their lives unlivable, and they send out a call for help'.[26]

In 2008, the National Prosecution Service asked the Court to disband the association behind the paramilitary rightist radical formation, as it was irreconcilable with the rule of law and violated Roma rights. Several organisations, among them the Alliance of the Jewish Communities of Hungary,[27] and the National Gypsy Council[28] participated in the trial as litigating parties, with the World Federation of Hungarians[29] and the Jobbik Party (and other organisations). The Municipal Court of Budapest ordered the dismantling of the Hungarian Guard in December 2008—in a first instance, non-binding decision—for racial discrimination against the Roma minority, holding that the Hungarian Guard Tradition Protection and Cultural Association, 'aims to create a climate of fear, while its activities—the marching of its members in Roma-populated settlements and the speeches of its leaders—constitute a breach of the rights of other citizens'. However, the Association appealed the decision, and claimed at the same time that the Hungarian Guard Tradition Protection and Cultural Association is not the same as the Hungarian Guard Movement[30]—which is a legally non-existent entity—the actual paramilitary formation, which was thereby considered to be unaffected by the decision (and remained active).

Meanwhile, partly as a reaction to the Hungarian Guard phenomenon, the Ministry of Justice and Law Enforcement proposed a series of amendments to several public order and public safety laws. (According to the bills, group gatherings in public places with an intimidating impact—through speech acts or uniforms worn, etc.—would amount to a petty offence sanctionable with a fine.) Eventually, in December 2008, an amendment to the Criminal Code was passed by the parliament which broadened the scope of the provisions regarding violence against members of certain communities, and defined as disorderly to conduct those forms of otherwise peaceful assemblies which might 'cause fear' among the members of certain communities, or intimidate other people. (It is to be noted that there is an ongoing debate whether law amendment or law enforcement is needed, since, according to some voices, even the current legal framework could be applied in a much more effective and narrow way in different cases, involving [supposed] racist motivation.)

However, the Guard continued to recruit new members in 2009, including youngsters and children. The declared number of the (uniform-wearing) full-members of the Hungarian Guard was 1300 in July 2008, while (according to internal estimations) the number of the active supporters was approximately 5–6000—it is presumed that these numbers are significantly higher now. Remarkably, the professed recruitment policy of the Hungarian Guard was not exclusionary against the Roma: everyone can join, theoretically, whatever her/his origin, whether or not she/he is 'of Hungarian identity'. According to the rhetoric, the Hungarian Guard is not aimed at opposing the Roma, but tackling crime and disorder. (Supposedly, without reliable data, the volume of the accession of Roma individuals to the Guard was a sporadic phenomenon, if it happened at all.)

The impact of the media coverage about the activities of the Hungarian Guard cannot be under-estimated. The quick spread of Hungarian Guard appearances throughout the country (not always in the form of power demonstrating marches, but also by organising recruiting events or other gatherings, connected, for example, to public assemblies of Jobbik) meant that the Hungarian Guard managed to reach practically the whole country, in more or less intimidating forms, and at least in virtual terms. The EP-elections significantly catalysed this process, as the Jobbik party's campaign was apparently built on the popularity—or at least, attractiveness—of the Hungarian Guard among the members of its prospective voters, therefore a lot of Jobbik campaign events involved some kind of Hungarian Guard presence.

A Budapest court of appeal issued a legally binding ruling banning[31] the Hungarian Guard, after the EU Parliament elections (2 July 2009), on the grounds that it 'generated ethnic tension and threatened public order'. The court of appeal upheld a former decision of December 2007, shortly after the Guard's first in a series of anti-Roma marches in Tatárszentgyörgy (the above mentioned village in Pest County, which later became known for the murder of a young Roma man and his child in February 2009). Orbán Kolompár, chair of the National Gypsy Minority Self-Government, welcomed the court's decision with the following words: 'The sober mind has won, and so has democracy, the Roma and the whole country'.[32] After the court decision, 12 July 2009, in Budapest and other places across Hungary, members of the banned Hungarian Guard re-launched as the 'Hungarian Guard Movement': almost 3000 supporters attended rallies in Budapest, and some hundreds at several smaller Guard-meetings throughout the country. The attendants—holding flags resembling those of the murderous wartime Arrow Cross—arrived in civilian clothes, but many of them later changed into uniforms: among them were Prof. Kirsztina Morvai (newly elected MEP, a former member of the UN CEDAW[33] Commission), Gábor Vona (President of the Jobbik Party), Lajos Für (former Defence Minister), and Reverend Lóránt Hegedüs and Levente Murányi (1956 freedom fighter).

The consideration of some organised response to the Hungarian Guard (which is referred to as 'Prikezsia Garda' in public by Roma leaders—the Romany word '*prikezsia*' means 'evil') was a recurrent element on the (rhetorical) agenda of the MCF Roma Alliance Party.[34] (In fact, an organised, yet peaceful counter-action has already taken place in Szikszó in July 2008, when approximately 1000 Roma gathered together for a peaceful demonstration against the Hungarian Guard.) In a press release in August 2008, which caused widespread outcry, MCF leader—and leader of the National Gypsy Minority Self-Government—Orbán Kolompár claimed, in the context of news about violent attacks against the Roma throughout Hungary, that the Roma should join forces: 'I call on Roma society to forget about party politics and other affiliations, and join together for the interests of the Roma in Hungary, and contribute to the establishment of a self-defence movement. Let's demonstrate that we are powerful, and that we are able to defend ourselves if the situation is such!'[35]After the banning of the Hungarian Guard, the organisation of a 'Roma Guard' (as a paramilitarial force, similar to the Hungarian Guard) is apparently not an issue on the Roma political agenda. The debate about this issue resulted in a division between supporters and opposers of this possible radical solution among Roma political leaders—and eventually, the argument of the opposers (who claimed that paramilitarial organisations are not to be reconciliated with the rule of law) proved to be stronger. However, there are still grassroots attempts to form a kind of 'Roma Guard'. (According to the same source, in the village of Örkény, Pest county, militant Roma activists have already designed uniforms for themselves, following the example of the Hungarian Guard.)

Violent incidents involving Roma victims

Some level of 'ethnic tension' has been perceivable during the last two decades in Hungary, and the deterioration of the relationship between Roma and the majority population was observed by the mid-nineties by international minority-protection monitors. Although there have been cases of ethnic conflicts—widely covered by the media[36]—resulting in the abuse of the Roma already around the beginning of the 2000s, in 2008–09, an unprecedented sweep of violence against the Roma community took place in Hungary. Besides 'sporadic' incidents, with alleged/possible anti-Roma motivation in the background, a series of nine attacks, committed by handguns and fire-bombs ('Molotov-cocktails') took place in 2008 and 2009:[37]

– On 21 July 2008, the first attack in the series of nine took place in Galgagyörk,[38] a village near Budapest where, shortly after midnight, ten to fifteen shots were fired at three houses owned by Roma. No one was injured.
– On 8 August 2008, the second attack was committed in Piricse,[39] where Molotov cocktails were thrown at two houses owned by Roma. A woman was shot in the leg when she stepped out of one of the houses.
– On 5 September 2008, the third attack was perpetrated in Nyíradony,[40] where gunshots were targeted at a house inhabited by Roma. No one was injured.
– On 29 September 2008, the fourth attack took place in Tarnabod,[41] where Molotov cocktails were thrown and gunshots fired at three homes in a neighbourhood with a significant Roma population. No one was injured.
– On 3 November 2008, the fifth attack was committed in Nagycsécs, where a forty-three-year-old Roma man and a forty-year-old Roma

woman were shot dead in their home in Nagycsécs. According to the official investigation, petrol bombs ('Molotov-cocktails') were thrown into the house, before the perpetrators used firearms to kill the members of the family.[42]

– On 15 December 2008, the sixth attack took place in Alsózsolca, where several shots were fired at a nineteen-year-old Roma man and his partner in front of their home in Alsózsolca. The young man suffered life-threatening injuries.[43]

– On 23 February 2009, the seventh attack was committed in Tatárszentgyörgy: a twenty-seven-year-old Roma father and his five-year-old son were shot dead as they ran out of their burning home in Tatárszentgyörgy. The man's wife and the couple's two other children were also seriously injured in the attack and had to be treated for severe burns. Despite remnants of the bomb and claims by neighbours, the police originally declared that the cause of the deaths was smoke-poisoning caused by an electric fire.[44]

– On 22 April 2009, the eighth attack was committed in Tiszalök, when a fifty-four-year-old Roma man was shot in the chest outside his home. The police indicated racial motivation behind the crime.[45]

– On 3 August 2009, the ninth—and final—crime took place in Kisléta, where a forty-five-year-old Roma woman was shot dead, and her thirteen-year-old daughter seriously injured in an attack against their home in Kisléta. The girl, suffering life-threatening injuries, remained in hospital for several weeks.[46]

Eventually, the police arrested four men on 21 August 2009, in relation with the serial murders of Roma that left six dead and at least five injured. (DNA analysis revealed that the DNA of the four men was similar to the DNA traces found at several of the murder sites.) What we know about them, for the time being, is that they are between the ages of twenty-eight and forty-two, all four worked part-time as security guards, and one of them (a former professional soldier) maintained a close friendship with his brother-in-law, an active member of the Hungarian police. In August 2010, the police finished the investigation, and proposed a recommendation to the Prosecution Service for filing a charge.[47]

Volunteer civil guards and 'neighbourhood watch' units

Civil guard units are organised typically by the 'mainstream' (non-Roma) communities, often with the explicit aim to protect the non-Roma from local 'Gypsy-criminality', especially in the case of settlements, where the presence of the police is not sufficient or not effective. Therefore, civil guard units might be potential opponents of local Roma communities. However, in some cases, civil guard units seem to be welcoming towards Roma prospective members, but there are not many Roma civil guards countrywide. The reason for the absence of Roma from this formation might be (according to a Roma political leader)[48] that 'there are hardly any adult Roma men, who do not have a bad record'—which is, according to the law, a condition that prevents one from joining a civil guard unit.

In 2009, as a part of a ten-point legislative and policy package of the government called 'Order and Security', announced by the Prime Minister,[49] a village guard programme was launched, aimed at easing ethnic tensions between Roma and non-Roma communities, preventing anti-Roma hate crimes and addressing petty offences. Village guard teams will be organised in affiliation with local municipalities. The municipalities were provided with incentives to recruit unemployed (among them Roma) people into the programme. From 1 January 2010, the per capita wage support is 73,000 Ft + 27 per cent taxes (approx. 37€). During the first three months of the programme (October-December 2009), 1,000 village guards started to work. The last announcement on successful applications by settlements was launched in May 2010. At the time of writing, within the new governmental structure, the coordination of and the financial sources for the programme from 2011 had not yet been secured.[50]

Local inter-ethnic incidents—local solutions?

For the examination of inter-ethnic incidents and the context and morphology of tensions between Roma and non-Roma in communities, I chose two villages in Pest County: Nagybörzsöny and Verőce. The reason behind these choices was that in 2008–2009 both municipalities participated in the Social Crime Prevention Programme of the Hungarian Ministry of Justice and Law Enforcement (coordinated by the National Crime Prevention Committee),[51] by implementing projects in the category of 'Settlement Mediation'.[52] In terms of the comparability of the two settlements, both Nagybörzsöny and Verőce listed inter-ethnic issues as the number-one leading concern in the short presentations about the projects (in the case of Verőce, the reference was to 'ethnic tensions', and, in the case of Nagybörzsöny, to 'conflicts concerning cohabitation of Roma and non-Roma').

Through the field research[53] I conducted in Verőce and Nagybörzsöny, I was intrigued to grasp the local context of the tensions, the interpretations of the incidents by local people, and their views on the prospects of the communities. As a preparation for the planned empirical research, I consulted with the leaders and coordinators of the crime prevention projects: not just the preliminary overview, but also their insight, proved to be beneficial for my work.

Behind the scenes: The case of a village and the inviting of the Hungarian Guard

Nagybörzsöny is a 'dead-end village' in the northern part of Pest County, only a few kilometres from the Slovak border. The nearest city is Esztergom, which used to serve as the regional centre for Nagybörzsöny and other nearby villages. However, because of the curves of the Hungarian-Slovakian border, currently there are no direct logistical connections with it. The local centre, Vác, is accessible by public transportation only through Szob (it takes almost forty minutes to get to Szob by bus, and an hour from Szob to reach the capital city, Budapest). The village lies beside the Duna-Ipoly National Park, surrounded by hiking pathways. The main attraction for tourists is a narrow gauge railway. According to the mayor of the village, the number of inhabitants of the village is almost eight hundred.[54] The second piece of information regarding population is that, based on estimations (or 'common perception'), the proportion of Roma is almost 20 per cent, which is significantly higher than the average in Hungary (ca. 6 per cent). Furthermore—again, according to the mayor of the village—mixed marriages are quite common, and 'those non-Roma who are married to—or live together with—Roma, and who are not dissociable from the Roma regarding their lifestyle, are perceived as Roma, too'.

As for the socio-economic situation of the village, the main factor is the scarcity of local job opportunities. The main public employers in the area are a care centre for the disabled in Ipolydamasd and the prison of Márianosztra. Non-Roma locals hope that an upsurge of rural tourism will improve the economic situation and job opportunities in the village but, as far as they (the non-Roma) can see, the main obstacle to this is the unruliness and untidiness of the village, caused by the Roma. The overwhelming majority of the Roma are unemployed, with the exception of the members of two or three families. The others live on welfare and child care assistance, while many adults of the younger generations have never had a job. Early child-bearing—starting at the age of fourteen or fifteen—is not unusual among Roma (as well as among mixed Roma/non-Roma couples).

As an insightful observer summarises, Nagybörzsöny is an excellent example for the centuries-long cohabitation of people who belong to different nationalities and speak different languages. While their life together was not always peaceful, it was usually not their fault: foreign conquerors, greater politics and untalented, power-tripping local leaders often interfered in their lives by way of wars, religious intolerance and evictions, and these brought to the surface, and strengthened, the human weaknesses, misunderstandings and intolerance towards 'otherness'.[55]

According to a new inhabitant of the village,[56] there are increasingly more and sharper clashes among the members of the population of Nagybörzsöny 'than is usual for an average village'. Actually, some of the frequently mentioned clashes are those between 'newcomers' and 'natives', although they are considered to be not too significant, and manifest mostly as mocking. The enumeration of the existing clashes continues with the historical antagonism between Catholics and Lutherans (indicated by the phenomenon that, when the two church-run schools were merged into one state-run educational institution in 1948, the pupils, belonging to different religions, did not want to sit next to each other).[57] The original majority of the village (before the Second World War) was German speaking—however, they did not share a common ancestor: a part of the village originated from Saxon immigrants (professing the Lutheran religion), while the ancestors of others came from the territory of Slovakia (belonging to the Roman Catholic Church). However, as the importance of religion is decreasing, this angatonism seems to be fading away, but it has been reported that local parents disapproved mixed romances between Lutheran and Catholic youngsters even in the 1970s. Another historical clash—still recounted among elderly people in the village—lies between 'removed' and 'replaced' families, as after the Second World War—according to the principle of collective guilt—about seventy families were exiled from the village, and replaced with families coming from the territory of Slovakia; then, later some of the exiled ones returned.

In the 1960s, the population of the settlement—which used to be about 2000—started to decrease, since many young people chose to move away, given the scarcity of local job opportunities and the poor living conditions. Some of the old dwelling houses and press houses were sold as weekend houses, which created yet another chasm between the local citizens and the 'weekenders'. During the last decades, new immigrants came from Romania who are actually ethnic Hungarians, but are still often referred to as 'Romanians' (which is somewhat stigmatising in this context) by the other inhabitants. Finally, the most noticeable demographic change—which relates to the most significant clash—is the increasing Roma population in the village. However, the Gypsies have also had their own clashes for a very long time, especially between two large families, and although exogamy is not rare, the antagonism frequently manifests as fights and threats.

During the last decade—along with demographical changes and the phenomenon of enduring unemployment—the village experienced a dramatic increase in crime rates which, in some areas of crime, reached a four times higher level than the regional average.[58] Among the main types of criminal acts, burglaries are common—especially targeting weekend houses—followed by receiving goods, blackmailing, and various attacks against local elderly people (and the property of elderly). A significant proportion of the committed crimes are ascribed to the Roma, except the cases of receiving goods. The (suspected) offenders, especially certain members of a large local Roma family, are perceived to be 'leading a criminal lifestyle'. Besides criminal offences—associated mainly with the Roma—local non-Roma are irritated by noisy Roma family reunions, involving dozens of guests, loud music and alcohol consumption. (As it was described, one of the main reasons behind the establishment of the civil police guard was that the police were not helpful in breach of the peace cases.) Besides nocturnal clamour, the main concern of the non-Roma in Nagybörzsöny—many of them interested, somehow, in the income generated by tourism—is the 'usual' and 'disturbing' phenomenon of drunken and noisy Roma individuals (fighting mostly with each other) in the main square of the village, before the eyes of the 'other' inhabitants and the tourists.

Although the atmosphere concerning the relationship between the Roma and non-Roma is perceived as 'very tense' by many of the inhabitants, the community has not yet experienced direct inter-ethnic violent cases (involving Roma and non-Roma individuals and resulting in personal injury or property loss). However, tensions have already led to almost-violent, face-to-face scenes a couple of times, in the period directly preceding the crime prevention programme. According to eyewitnesses, in the last case, external support (friends from neighbouring villages, arriving in cars) was also invited by non-Roma participants of a clash, which is described to have been a direct result of a quarrel in a pub between a Roma and a non-Roma man. Axes, sticks and other weapon-like tools were displayed, but ultimately the incident remained at the level of (reportedly, more or less mutual) threats.

As the proposal of the crime prevention programme indicates, the primary problems to be addressed in the village of Nagybörzsöny are the 'cohabitation-conflicts' of the Roma and non-Roma inhabitants, and the high criminality rates, as these phenomena risk the demographic and economic sustainability of the settlement (keeping in mind, for example, the prospects of the local school and the success of rural tourism). The mediation project (organised within the framework of the crime prevention programme of the National Crime Prevention Committee) was planned to be implemented by a consortium of numerous actors, including the Municipality of Nagybörzsöny, the local Gypsy Minority Self-Government and German Minority Self-Government, the educational institutes of the village, the local civil police guard association, and NGOs.[59] The aim of the project—which was actually a pilot programme—was the elaboration and implementation of a model of effective and adoptable, non-violent conflict-management methods at the local level. In the preparatory phase, a comprehensive survey was conducted, aimed at diagnosing the situation and identifying the problems, clashes, demands and needs—and the possible key actors and institutions, as well. The programme itself consisted of training for volunteers (prospective facilitators of mediation processes), conflict management initiatives, community building activities and various awareness raising programmes. For example, as a part of the project, a Tolerance Day was held in the village—organised by one of the leading minority protection NGOs in Hungary, the Legal Defence Bureau for National and Ethnic Minorities[60]—with awareness raising activities related to the issues of stereotypes, prejudices, intolerance and racism.

Among the key actors of the programme (active participants of the training and other activities) was the mayor of the village, the chief of the civil police guard, and a number of inhabitants who joined as volunteers (for example, for the tasks of organising playgroups for Roma and non-Roma children, or a club for young mothers). However, not everybody was willing to participate. One of them was a representative of the local municipality, who rejected every attempt aimed at involving him in the project. According to his wife, he claims himself to be a 'Nazi', he hates the 'Browns' (i.e. Gypsies), and he can not, and does not want to, forgive 'them' for all the sins and crimes they have committed, and he does not want to bother with their problems, to help them, or to improve his relationship with them— 'he just does not want to sacrifice even ten minutes of his life for dealing with the Gypsies'. The key Roma actors in the village (for example, the representatives of the local Gypsy self-government) were also unresponsive towards the programme, usually for unexplained reasons, but some of them gave hints that their participation in the training and other activities of the programme—together with mainly non-Roma people—would not be supported by the Roma community. In general, only a very few Roma individuals became involved in the various activities, except in the playgroup events, which became very popular among Roma children (and appreciated by their parents, as well).

The effective dialogue aimed at managing a fierce conflict between a local youth gang and the municipality is considered to be one of the success stories of the crime prevention programme. Before the mediation (or rather, the dialogue), the vandalism in the village (breaking flowers, destroying benches on the main square) was ascribed to 'the Gypsies', although the inhabitants of the village were more or less aware of the composition of the gang; the suspected vandalisers of the common property of the village. Actually, when the members of the gang were identified, it became clear that the youngsters were non-Roma (except for one boy, who was half-Roma, coming from a socially integrated family).

As the coordinators of the mediation project concluded, their major disappointment, and maybe the biggest failure of the programme, was that the planned mediation between the municipality and the Gypsy self-government did not work effectively. The planned aim of the mediation was to elaborate an agreement concerning financial issues, since the Roma representatives claimed their involvement in decisions related to the funding of the maintenance and activities of the minority self-government, with a special focus on planned children and youth programmes. (The direct conflict behind the planned conflict managing dialogue was a discordance regarding the pre-finance of a programme for Roma children, when the representatives of the Gypsy Minority Self-Government were suspected by the local municipality of 'giving the money to themselves, never for the children'.) Regarding the failure—i. e. that the dialogue broke down at the very beginning and no agreement was reached by the parties—interpretations of the behaviour of the Roma and non-Roma parties diverge significantly. According to the non-Roma, the 'Roma are not ready to get involved into a dialogue as partners', as the 'Roma are non-cooperative' and 'do not have the communication skills and abilities' needed for participation in a mediation process. On the other side, some members of the local Roma community mentioned cautiously that they did not feel safe, therefore they did not want to 'complain', because 'it might cause trouble later'.

Surprisingly, one of the Roma representatives who spoke about her experiences regarding the project did not mention a real failure: as she perceives it, the situation has already changed a lot, in a positive way, towards a relationship based on mutual trust between the municipality of the village and the Gypsy Minority Self-Government (for example, the mayor has already allowed some payments for the Gypsy Minority Self-Government in advance, for the purpose of a Roma youth programme).

However, just around the end of the crime prevention programme, at the beginning of May 2009, the idea of inviting the Hungarian Guard occurred, and the proposed date for the Guard's visit to the village was the weekend of the annual gastronomic festival of Nagybörzsöny, which is basically a tourist attraction, and a weekend when events related to the mediation project were also held. Ultimately, the Hungarian Guard did not come to the village that weekend. However, the opinions and considerations of the interviewees, regarding both the idea of inviting the Hungarian Guard to the village, and on the phenomenon of the Hungarian Guard in general, gave some meaningful insight into the dynamics of the local community. Supposedly, the idea was not fully elaborated or thought-through, as the divergence of the accounts might indicate: different interviewees remember different dates (regarding the first, three-day-long weekend of May, including a national holiday), chosen for the Hungarian Guard's visit. Apparently, not every one of the interviewees was aware of the plan in detail—or was willing to volunteer information about it. Most of the local non-Roma reported that he/she 'heard that something was planned' concerning the Hungarian Guard, and after all, he/she feels that it was a good decision not to invite them, anyway. However, the representative of the Gypsy self-government rejected the idea that she would have been aware of the plan, and emphasised by repeating her opinion again and again, that 'there is nothing wrong here, we live in peace here with each other, nothing went wrong, nothing needs to be improved regarding the cohabitation of the Roma and non-Roma'.

In addition to the fragmented accounts concerning the Hungarian Guard, and the possible consequences of their visit, including arguments about the possible harmful effects on the cohabitation of Roma and non-Roma (especially the threat of retorsion from the side of the Roma); professed preferences regarding the peaceful, internal conflict management methods (learnt at the mediation training, for example); but also disapproving hints on the dissension in the local non-Roma community (i.e. there was no consensus on the Hungarian Guard issue); a most articulate argument was provided by the chief of the civil police guard, who explained (besides the above-mentioned factors) a crucial aspect: that the media attention, which is usually accompanied with the Hungarian Guard presence, is an undesired feature, as the community—hoping that the flourishment of rural tourism would save the future of the village—intends to develop a peaceful and attractive image of Nagybörzsöny.

Soon after the finish of the crime prevention pilot project—on the eve of the 2009 EP elections—a murder took place in Nagybörzsöny, involving a non-Roma forester and an allegedly Roma perpetrator. This crime case did not gain much attention from the mainstream media—only the official communications of the National News Agency and Pest County Police Headquarters[61] were published by newspapers or news portals, and these sources did not mention anything about the ethnic background of the parties. Only a tabloid provided some details about the crime case, focusing on the fact that, after the killing, the perpetrator stole some low-value personal items from the victim.[62] However, rightist webpages immediately informed the public about the (Roma) ethnicity of the suspect, by referring to the perpetrators as 'The Gypsies'[63]—although there were no signs indicating that there was more than one perpetrator, so the use of the plural was not appropriate.

Using personal power and the threat of vigilance in conflict situations: The case of Verőce

Verőce is considered to be in an advantageous situation, not just for its location (beside the Danube, surrounded by natural beauties, but still very easily accessible from the capital city; the train trip takes only thirty-five minutes from Verőce to Budapest), but also because of various socio-economic aspects. The current number of inhabitants is 3260,[64] and the population is growing (which is not usual in cases of rural settlements in Hungary), due to the continuous inflow of newcomers—among them, wealthy families moving there from the capital city. According to a newcomer in the village—coming from Budapest—Verőce is not a typical Hungarian village anymore, as it is rather 'urbanised'.

According to the mayor's description of the demographic tendencies of the village, the proportion of the Roma is not increasing (which is again unusual for a Hungarian rural settlement), since 'during the last decade there weren't any Gypsies among the newcomers'. However, regarding the actual proportion of the Roma in Verőce, the estimates diverge significantly. According to the mayor's estimations, Roma constitute approximately 6–7 per cent of the inhabitants—which is about the average on the national level, and which would translate to about 200 Gypsies in Verőce, as he notes.

A strong first impression of the village of Verőce includes not just the visible prosperity of the settlement, but a sort of Hungarian nationalist—or ethnocentric—spirit in the atmosphere as well. In 2005, a statue of Albert Wass[65] (the Hungarian nationalist novelist) was erected in the village, which has become a pilgrimage destination for the worshippers of the writer, and there are a series of other new monuments, related somehow to the 'glorious' Hungarian past. The main square of the village, which was rebuilt with EU funding,[66] is decorated with a statue, representing ancient Hungarian fertility symbols. Not just the public, but some semi-public spaces in the village are also charged with Hungarian national feeling: the displayed items on the walls of the office of the mayor are easy to associate with nostalgic irredentism (for example, a huge copy of the lyrics of the 'Anthem of the Szeklers' or a historical map of 'Greater Hungary'). Besides the display of ethno-nationalist symbols, the cultural and public life of the village is also permeated with a similar spirit: for instance, Verőce is the venue of the annual 'Hungarian Island' summer festival, which is a Hungarian/nationalist alternative to the multicultural/mainstream 'Island' annual festival in Budapest. (Almost every year, members of the local Roma community report abuses committed festival by visitors against Roma inhabitants of the village. These cases remain unconfirmed.)

In December 2008, in Verőce, a quarrel in a pub escalated into fierce fighting and physical violence between Roma and non-Roma men, involving baseball bats and other weapon-like tools (the incident became a law enforcement issue, which is reportedly still not resolved). Based on the available accounts, the timeline of the events might be drafted as such: a couple of Roma men, living in the 'upper' part of the village (beyond the railway tracks) went to a pub which is located in the 'lower' part of the village (close to the river). The conflict began when some guests at the pub started to play 'skinhead' music, singing along to the explicit anti-Gypsy lyrics. The fighting soon escalated, and—according to the account of a Roma—a rightist motor bike gang appeared on the scene, after they were called from the neighbouring villages by youngsters among the non-Roma party of the conflict. Under still-unclarified circumstances, the incident resulted in serious personal injuries.

It should be noted that, during night-time, there was no police watch or patrol in Verőce, therefore immediate police intervention was not expected. However, on the very same night—according to the account of a Roma politician who became involved in the conflict management process after the incident—commandos raided the home of the Roma family whose members were involved in the conflict (searching for guns and, reportedly, causing significant property loss during the action). According to local sources, the key person in the affected Roma family, who is associated by the villagers with a series of crimes and disturbances and who participated on the side of the Roma in the conflict, is a non-Roma himself, married to a female member of the Roma family.

On the day following the violent incident, a village assembly was organised by the mayor of Verőce, aimed at listening to both parties before the inhabitants of the village. As a Roma leader from the county remembers, Roma politicians were also involved in the initiation of this meeting and, what is more, both the President of the National Gypsy Government and the Parliamentary Commissioner for Ethnic and National Minorities intended to participate in the meeting (however, eventually they did not attend). According to the minutes of the village assembly[67]—in addition to the mayor, the representatives of the municipality and the chief of the police—both parties of the incident were represented at the meeting. Reportedly, more than 200 people attended the meeting, Roma and non-Roma, including the lawyers of the affected Roma. The meeting—commonly considered as effective or, at least, useful—was led and moderated by the mayor, who said that he wanted, 'Some guarantee, concerning the future, that no one will get into any kind of atrocity', and professed that '… it is not an excuse, if you don't like the music played in the pub. If you don't like the music, then you have to turn away, and leave the place!' He added, 'Of course, lyrics like "every Gypsy must die" are not allowed to be sung in the pub'. In his concluding sentences, the mayor claimed that he wanted to see progress towards not perceiving differences between 'Gypsies and Whites' any more, as there are only two relevant categories: 'righteous people and non-righteous people'.

However, as a Roma political leader of Pest county reports, the story did not end on the day of the village assembly, as the issue of the fierce commando raid (and the reported maltreatment of the Roma by the raid police) was not dealt with at the meeting, therefore the members of the affected family called on external support to protect their interests. According to the Roma leader, who arrived to support the local Roma of Verőce, a closed meeting was conducted with the participation of the mayor (the chief of the police was also invited, but eventually he did not attend), which concluded with a reassuring agreement; the mayor—who was reportedly unaware of the commando raid case—promised to show a protective attitude towards the Roma. As the regional Roma leader professed, in cases like Verőce, where the Roma community is relatively small and defenceless, some external support might be needed from the broader Roma community—for example, by threatening local authorities with the prospect of a Roma power demonstration march.

The mayor of Verőce related yet another development, supposedly related to the violent incident: a couple of days after the village assembly, strangers arrived in the village—in cars with tinted windows—and verbally threatened the Roma family which had been involved in the conflict. When the case was reported to the mayor by someone from the neighbourhood—not by the affected individuals themselves—the mayor visited the family personally, and while asking them to report such cases immediately ('they have my cell phone number, as everyone else does in the village'), he promised protection for the Roma from any kind of external danger. According to the mayor, his visit was highly appreciated by the family and, since that day, 'everything is fine—nothing has happened'.

Conclusions

One of the lessons learned is that the adjective 'inter-ethnic' when used to characterise a relationship or a conflict, might be challengeable at the very local level. As Paul R. Brass phrases the problem, 'inter-ethnic relations have become such a pervasive concern that the interpretation of virtually any act of violence between persons identified as belonging to different ethnic groups itself becomes a political act'.[68] The interviewees in the two local settlements of Hungary seemed to be aware, in a natural way, of this conceptual problem, as became clear from their accounts on community relationships, conflicts, incidents, etc. For instance, an indicator of people's politically untouched consciousness that not every conflict which involves individuals of different ethnicity is necessarily ethnic conflict, was an example given by a non-Roma inhabitant of Nagybörzsöny about his noisy Gypsy neighbours, who 'are not problematic because they are Gypsies, but because they are noisy'.

A community's local investment into peaceful internal conflict management might be perceived as a kind of (temporary) preventive factor when it comes to the involvement of external political forces, like the Hungarian Guard, as the case of Nagybörzsöny indicates. Eventually, it still does not seem to be an absolute guarantee, as far from all of the inhabitants participated in the mediation training programme, and the invitation of the Hungarian Guard was still an option which was considered by the community, after the municipality's participation in the crime prevention programme. (And eventually, after the murder case, this option was actually chosen by the community.)

Additionally, it seems to be correct to raise criticism against some methods, namely mediation, applied by the crime prevention programme, aimed at alleviating tension between local Roma and non-Roma. While mediation is recommended by some relevant OSCE-documents and guidelines[69] (on policing in multi-ethnic communities), and even by the conclusive recommendations of the thematic report by OSCE-ODIHR on anti-Roma hate crimes in Hungary[70] among 'targeted crime prevention programmes and initiatives to combat hate crimes', the case of Nagybörzsöny illustrates that this method is only effective if some important conditions are present. According to the publicly available evaluation report[71] of the Nagybörzsöny project:

Some [non Roma locals] argued that the method of mediation is not compatible with the Roma community. Similar opinion was expressed by the Roma themselves, too: however, according to their narrative, the method of mediation makes the Roma vulnerable, because they might 'get in trouble if they complain'. A very important piece of feedback that mediation implies eligible parties for the negotiations—and the grounds for that might be set by the methods of community development or social work—and not by the methods of mediation itself. A very important conclusion is that if there are significant differences between the positions of the parties, and if on the weaker part there is no effective interest-articulation and well-functioning mechanism of representation... then it is important to get the parties prepared for mediation.

In the other—Verőce—case, apparently, the external threat, coming from an (allegedly) unidentified source, proved to be a key element concerning the emergence of a more trustful relationship between a populous Roma family and the municipality—at least according to the account of the mayor, who tried to demonstrate, by the gesture of offering protection to the threatened Roma family, that he feels personally responsible for the security of all inhabitants of the settlement, including the Roma. And it seems these patronising measures resulted in the easing of tensions in the settlement, at least temporarily.

13

STRATEGIES FOR COMBATING RIGHT-WING POPULISM AND RACISM

STEPS TOWARDS A PLURALIST AND HUMANE EUROPE

Britta Schellenberg

The manifestations of the radical right have changed, but not their exclusionary ideological core. Some segments of European societies feel more attracted to the radical right and conventional (repressive) counter-measures lose their appeal. Against this background and on the ground of comprehensive studies—eleven country reports and various expertises of the Bertelsmann Foundation and CAP—promising strategies for combating right-wing populism and racism are discussed.[1] The analysis focuses on trends within radical right ideology and its organisational structures; it scrutinises the conventional handling of the radical right and offers a set of strategy approaches for both politics and (working) praxis. Advancing a pluralist and humane Europe seems to make a cocktail of measures, a set of strategies, necessary.

Basic elements for promising counter-strategies are marked in the first part of the analyses: such as, a broad approach on the radical right, targeting its different organisational and ideological manifestations. Proper data collection and reporting are highlighted as important preconditions for successful work, as well as quality standards and sustainability of the work. Emanating from the contemporary handling of right-wing radicalism (e.g. cordon sanitaire) problems are identified and possible solutions outlined (e.g. ways to an open and pro-active debate and choice of specific focal points).

In the second part, specific action recommendations are introduced. Basic strategy approaches are reconsidered and specific measures, as well as good praxis examples from European countries, are discussed.

Introduction: The radical right is dead! Long live the radical right!

The classical extreme right is dead: today rarely any European identifies himself/herself with fascist or Nazi organisations of classical layout.[2] Yet the ideological heritage of the classical extreme right does not cease to exist: it is easily detected in the sub-cultural spectre and at movement organisations. On this level, there are openly worn connections to fascism and national-socialism (e.g. symbolism, clothing, celebration of certain events). Hardly recognisable by its appearance in contrast is the part of the radical right, which today is quite successful in the area of politics. We see in different European countries that right-wing radical parties can be successful when their rhetoric has become soft but they nevertheless speak strongly against the democratic elites.[3] However, the old core is visible, first of all as group focused hostility (currently, especially against Muslims, Roma and Jews). Further, those parties have at least anti-democratic, anti-pluralistic and authoritarian tendencies and do, in many cases, still show an affinity with fascism and national-socialism (e.g. the French Front National or the Belgian Vlaams Belang). The right-wing populist and xenophobic parties differ from the old right-wing extremists as they have adjusted to the democratic framework of their home societies. It is against this background that there have been shifts in the language of the radical right: for instance, they rarely use explicitly biologistic concepts of race, but instead talk of 'ethnopluralism'. However, 'ethnopluralism' means a (clear) division of different ethnic groups. Thus racial segregation and 'ethnopluralism' are tied to the same ideological concept. It is the 'wrapping', which seems more acceptable—the old discredited words of Nazi or fascist past are extinguished, but the meaning is all the same.

It is by their more decent manner (no violence and mostly distancing themselves from violent supporters in public) and by their softer rhetoric, including coded speech (e.g. 'US east coast' as synonym for Jewish influence) that the new radical right seems to be more acceptable for broader segments of society. Another consequence of the new outlook of the radical right is that conventional (repressive) counter-measures lose their grip.[4]

However, it is not only right-wing radical parties who are in a process of change. There are also new impulses from sub-cultural organisations of the radical right. They target young people particularly (e.g. by offering protest oriented music or stylish clothing). Even if there is a more obvious orientation towards fascism and national-socialism among such groups the diagnosis is similar: repressive measures may stress the hegemony of the state and might signal shelter to potential victim groups, repressive counter-measures appear to be insufficient and less able to affect the radical right. After prohibitions, organisations just start up again under another name and some groups (like comradeships and autonomous nationalists) or members of the common youth cult surrender not their political ideas but their organisational structures—and thus continue to exist.[5]

These shortly outlined characteristics of the present situation of the radical right are especially important when discussing adequate counter-strategies. As the setting of the radical right has changed and, therefore, the present repressive approach ceases to be effective, sustainable strategies must be discussed in a new light.

Strategies for combating right-wing populism and racism

General recommendations as a fundament of counter-strategies

There is no single strategy for combating right-wing populism and racism, which is universal and guarantees success. Indeed, a strategy can only be successful when tied to a specific political and social context and when many actors engage (from politics, judiciary, media, educational institutions and civil society). However, there are proven measures and good practice examples that can be used as tools in a specific context. First, before proceeding to a discussion of specific measures, I address general requirements, which build the fundament of successful strategies. The general requirements include:

Analyse and inform

Recognise different manifestations of the radical right: A competent monitoring of the radical right is the fundament for any promising strategy development. To successfully combat the radical right it is necessary to look at their present manifestations. For instance, plainly, focusing on political parties is not enough. The country reports describe different manifestations of the radical right, of which political parties are only one. The country reports show that, paradoxically, with stronger pressure on political parties the popularity of social movement organisations and the sub-cultural milieu grows. This finding documents how important it is to monitor the diverse manifestations of the radical right, to elementarily oppose them and to prevent them gaining influence in society.

Record and report: We have a similar finding when looking at reporting. The analyses show that 'hard data', such as membership lists of right-wing radical parties, are weighted disproportionately high for the assessment of the radical right. On the contrary, the results of surveys on attitudes (for instance on hostility towards Roma) and sub-cultural manifestations of the radical right (such as music and extremist youth cults as an offer of identity) are still too little accounted for in national data recording and too little recognised when developing counter-strategies. However, the recording of up-to-date data, monitoring and continuous reporting are necessary for a solid development of strategies. In order to draw an accurate picture of the situation, it is most promising to consult actors of the state along with those from civil society.

Inform and campaign: The public, as well as relevant people and institutions (relevant for implementing counter-strategies), must be informed about the radical right in order to counter-act broadly. Information should also be provided about particular counter-strategies. To reach a broader public, specific measures (e.g. certain projects) need to be campaigned for. In doing so, it is most convincing when one's own values and concepts (like pluralism, democracy, individualism, equality, freedom, etc.) are put forward in a well-grounded and convincing way.

Don't cooperate, but meet challenges head-on

Don't cooperate: the question of how to interact politically with the radical right can't be easily answered. The range of possible dealing with the radical right reaches from ignoring or deliberately excluding them from political arrangements—thus erecting a cordon sanitaire (for instance, in Belgium and France)—to fractional cooperation (in Denmark, the right-wing radical Danish People's Party tolerates the government and demands concessions in return), and, finally, to full cooperation (in Austria, the FPÖ was part of the government; in Italy, Berlusconi integrated right-wing radical parties into government, respectively into his party). None of these options has led to an automatic decline of the radical right. On the contrary: cooperation has resulted in further gains for the radical right (Denmark) or it has, at least, not hindered a comeback of the radical right (Austria). The political collaboration with the radical right has resulted, so far, typically in decreasing or eradicating the financial and legislative measures for combating racism and promoting human rights. In Denmark, for instance, the National Institute for Human Rights was closed down and projects against racism were suspended.[6] In many countries, it is argued that the radical right would sooner or later stumble over its own feet. But even if those parties might temporarily drop out of politics because of internal quarrels or other incompetence, they leave an imprint on socio-political discourses and on national legislation (e.g. immigration)—and they might come back even stronger (e.g. Austria). One can conclude that it doesn't work to just disenchant the radical right by taking them into political responsibility. On the contrary, this strategy results in concessions to those parties and their ideologies.[7]

Show political responsibility: It is of little help when political decision-makers of the centre ground believe they can control the agenda of the radical right by placing themselves ahead of it (for instance, propagating stricter measures on immigration). In fact, it is likely that the attitudes of the radical right will become a bit more acceptable in mainstream society—without seriously tackling societal problems. The democratic elites should accept the political costs they have to pay in order to fight the radical right. They shouldn't be seduced by short-term gains which, for instance, xenophobic election campaigns or building majorities with those parties might promise. Democratic parties have to limit the degree to which the radical right can bring their xenophobic and hostile demands into the pluralistic system. The aim of the radical right is the 'slow erosion' of pluralistic conduct. It is necessary to disclose such aims, to openly condemn them and pro-actively stand up for pluralism and against 'group focused enmity' (Heitmeyer).

Discuss and argue but don't ignore: It is possible that the politics of cordon sanitaire one day might not work any more. This is the case when right-wing radical parties can't be ignored any longer because of the current majority situation. At present, this danger does exist in Belgium: the consequence of the electoral successes of Vlaams Belang and the Liste Dedecker (LDD) may be that, in some communities, it won't be possible any longer

to constitute a governing majority without LDD or Vlams Belang participating. In this case there is no alternative: the cordon sanitaire must fall and
the democratic parties are forced to work together with parties from the
radical right.[8] The example shows that just ignoring the radical right and its
arguments can strengthen the movement, as much as cooperating with
them or adopting elements of their ideology can. The exhausting but most
promising route open to the democratic parties is that of an open and pro-
active debate with the radical right and its ideology. Pro-actively arguing
against the radical right also helps to hinder them from acting as if they are
the only genuine representation of the man in the street or the honest voice
of the people, which other parties exclude for indecent reasons. Of course,
it can be helpful to point our discrepancies between the lifestyle of politicians of the radical right and their ideological demands or to reveal cases of
corruption. The main focus of counter-strategies, however, should be an
open and pro-active debate (German: *Auseinandersetzung*), which discloses
the demands of the radical right and takes them *per se* ad absurdum.

Focus on (institutional) discrimination, diversity and strong civil rights
movements

Focus on (institutional) discrimination: The common basis of the radical
right is 'group focused enmity'. In the ideology of right-wing radicals, only
a homogenous ethnic group (which, in reality, of course, does not exist) is
able to build a 'healthy nation' or to form an 'intact body of a people'. Their
ethnically defined '(We-)group' constitutes by separating itself from a 'for-
eign/other group'. The alleged 'others' are to be excluded—violently if
necessary.[9] For counter-strategies, it is necessary to start from here and
actively counter discrimination. On this note, widening and strengthening
the awareness on discrimination, e.g. by training staff (for instance, at the
administration and executive branch), is a helpful measure.

Focus on diversity: According to the radical right's world view, heterogeneity,
especially ethnic and religious diversity, is taken as the main culprit for
societal and individual problems. The more important, then, it seems to
promote diversity and to count on learning abilities such as accountability
and participation (in the sense of learning the role and feasibilities of the
individual in democratic societies). Here strengthening (political) education
plays an important role: for instance, it is important to explain to pupils
that our immigrant-societies are built on plurality. It is necessary for a good

life in democratic societies to accept individual needs and to strengthen the individual abilities (Hartmut von Hentig)[10]—thus education/learning is an important vehicle in making heterogeneity as an individual and societal fact understandable.

A strong civil society and civil involvement: These are essential partners in combating the radical right. Often civic engagement is based on grassroots-activities, on anti-fascist or liberal-democratic groups. They watch the right-wing radical scene locally, organise protests, often in form of demonstrations and concerts, or they support victims. These actors have a strong influence on the mobilisation of the population. The civic protest 'on the street' not only helps to mobilise the population and to form opinions, but is also of great help when it comes down to pushing back right-wing radicals, e.g. to fight no-go-areas, and to signal that right-wing radicals and their thoughts are not welcome (e.g. in a certain community).

Improve quality and sustainability

Tasks and competences are to be set and (financial) support allocated: Whether it is a small project, work within a community, a supra-regional initiative or a national strategy—planning and coordination are indispensable. Competences and tasks are to be negotiated and set. Thus it is necessary to think about the common financial problems of civil actors and to find ways to cope with them—especially organisations which act in deprived areas.

Anchor quality and sustainability: Developing quality criteria for the work against right-wing radicalism and formulating goals helps to do good and efficient work. The decision to provide financial support to certain projects should be based on clear criteria. Sustainability can only be reached if actors and projects work long-term. Thus it makes sense to integrate good praxis into the standard practice and curricula of civic and state institutions. Learning and advancing projects should, however, be possible. Continuous evaluation, e.g. 'participative evaluation' (Ulrich and Wenzel, 2003), may open up opportunities to improve common practice as well as to develop quality criteria.

Initiate cooperation: Essential for successful work are exchange, opportunities to learn and room for implementation of new impulses. Cooperation and networking is relevant for integrating different perspectives on the topic itself and on approaches to counter right-wing radicalism. Herein it is crucial to bring civil and state actors together to implement joint strategies.

Specific measures against right-wing populism and racism

The general requirements of the strategy for combating right-wing populism and racism, discussed above, are a necessary precondition without which specific measures would hardly work. In the following section, specific strategy approaches and concrete measures are integrated into this framework—and fill the strategies with life. The following strategy approaches, introduced below, show possible ways of dealing with right-wing radicalism: interpretation—repression—prevention (inclusively measures of de-radicalisation). Related to those three approaches, concrete measures are suggested. They draw from the different strategy-levels (law/law enforcement, politics, civil society, education/learning and media) of the analyses described above. The following considerations and good praxis examples (from our European country-sample) intend to encourage integrated strategy development:

Interpretation

The interpretation of the current situation of society is crucial for the spreading of right-wing radicalism. The outcomes of social change and especially their interpretation can generate right-wing radical orientations. Thus political debates are central for considerations about counter-strategies.

Raise and place topics, debate in a differentiating way and stand up against simple accusations: Parties, lobbies and media, but also people who are quite present in the public eye, have a greater responsibility when debating about the problems of a society and must do so in a differentiating way, standing up against simple accusations. A climate of fear against immigrants, for instance, helps the radical right, damages the kit of societies and destroys inter-cultural relations. The goal should be to have unagitated discussions that integrate different perspectives. Therefore it can be helpful to emphasise good examples of immigration and diversity, instead of over-proportionally stressing problematic attempts at integration.[11] *Good practice:* an example is the specific training of members of the Roma-minority in journalism. The initiator, the Centre for Independent Journalism in Budapest, expects from this measure to be better able to voice the problems of Roma and to raise public awareness for them.[12]

Show what the radical right is truly standing for: One must be alerted when members of the radical right demand 'freedom (of speech)'. Such topics are especially popular with the intellectual 'New Right'. They aim to build a bridge between conservatism and the radical right, but they put forward the same ideas as the radical right. Examples are the call for freedom of speech, when racist attitudes are uttered, or the fulminations against 'political correctness', when hostile paroles against minority groups are displayed (e.g. in Germany the newspaper *Junge Freiheit* or the blog 'Politically Incorrect' are actors of the 'New Right'). Such demands should not be confused with democratic concerns, but need to be identified as group focused enmity and the attempt to popularise such radical right ideologies. *Good practice:* scientists and pedagogues in Germany have dealt with the arguments and lies of the radical right and have put together tools and facts to rebut them to the point. Such argumentative training material is used by lecturers of political education, by pedagogues, and also by some German offices for the protection of the constitution (*Verfassungsschutzämter der Länder*).[13]

Identify decision-makers and opinion leaders and strengthen them: To effectively push back right-wing radical ideologies, the public and relevant groups—such as journalists, lawyers and politicians—must be sensitised to the topic. Through the ability to reflect one's own position, awareness-raising can be strengthened. *Good practice*: In Germany, for instance, the German public broadcaster, Norddeutsche Rundfunk (NDR), runs a workshop on 'The challenge of discussing "right-wing extremism" for journalists' for its staff.

A broad mobilisation against right-wing radicalism: It is easier to attract people and civil society organisations when positive goals are put forward and politicians of the mainstream (e.g. the mayor of a city), top athletes or pop stars can be won for activities. *Good practice*: The anti-fascist civil society organisation Searchlight in Britain today attracts a broader public because its campaigns (like 'Hope not Hate') integrate public figures and name positive goals. Also newspapers—*The Guardian* in Britain, for example—can help to put the topic on the agenda by continually reporting on it.[14] The Amadeu Antonio Stiftung in Berlin is another example of successful non-governmental work against right-wing radicalism that counts on the mobilisation of a greater public.[15]

Advertise for democracy and diversity: Rejection of right-wing radicalism and the fight against it is incomprehensible if it is reduced to slogans and sweeping condemnations. It must become clear why the radical right is not acceptable. Thus arguing against the ideology as regards to content is elemental. It is just as important to know one's own values and norms (e.g. freedom, equity, human rights) and to agitate for them.

Repression

Combating the radical right is, in our country sample, very much characterised by repressive measures. Repressive legislation can indeed give a framework for combating the radical right. It can't, however, overcome it causatively.

Make clear limits of the acceptable and stress the hegemony of the state: Repressive legislation can point out the limits of the acceptable. It can also prevent (some) right-wing radicals from committing criminal offences. Repressive measures are, above all, appropriate for stressing the hegemony of the state. However, repression can't abolish any reasons of right-wing radical behaviour nor can it help to cultivate tolerant, pluralistic and democratic attitudes. Therefore repression shouldn't be misconceived as a cure-all. Repressive measures can only curtail certain ways of behaviour because the threat of punishment might be dissuasive.

Protect potential victims: However, repressive measures against the radical right send another important signal: every human being has the right to physical and psychological integrity. To stress this human right and to defend it officially can be an important sign for potential victims (e.g. to strengthen the individual sense of security, acceptance).

Modest punishment of the young perpetrator, support ability to learn/change: All-too severe punishment can be counter-productive for the socialisation of the adolescent culprit, especially the first offender. Severe legislative repression can also produce cases in which punishment is completely renounced—because the consequences for the biography of the culprit are seen as too problematic. Combinations of punishment and additional requirements for social work and pedagogic measures have proven more effective.[16]

Essential repressive measures from European countries of our sample are listed up in the following:

– Anti-racism laws (in B, CH, DK, F, GB, I, S) and laws on anti-discrimination (implemented in the EU)
– Increase in penalty when racist background of the offence (e.g. UK)

- Prohibition of denying the Holocaust (e.g. D, F)
- Withdrawal of state financing of political parties possible (B, discussed in D) and deprivation of non-profit character of an organisation (D)
- Ban from profession and company-induced exemption of right-wing extremists and racists (possible e.g. in NL, partly in UK)
- Activities against criminality in the internet (cf. 'Additional Protocol to the Convention on cybercrime, concerning the criminalisation of acts of a racist and xenophobic nature committed through computer systems', signed by many countries)
- Anti-terrorist laws (so far rarely implemented regarding right-wing radicalism, exemption: some cases in UK)
- Possibility to prohibit organisations (e.g. A, CH, D, F, S) and political parties (A, D, F)
- Prohibition of publications and certain symbols (e.g. D: NS-Symbols)

Use additional measures: Repressive legislation can provide a frame for combating the radical right but has to be filled with further measures to enfold effectiveness. If the state only reacts with draconic punishment some actors would radicalise even further, or the patterns of the manifestations of the radical right would change whereas the ideology would stay the same. The changing of its manifestations does not make the radical right less dangerous.[17] Thus repression can't do without additional preventive, and de-radicalising, measures.

Measures of de-radicalisation

Measures of de-radicalisation are less applicable to right-wing populism than to extremism, and aim at offering support and alternatives for right-wing extremists, enabling them to reintegrate into democratic society.

Target group perpetrators: Measures of de-radicalisation aim at offering support and alternatives for right-wing extremists and enabling them to reintegrate into democratic society. These measures have to be adapted to the individual case in question. The starting point of support programmes is the goal of helping right-wing extremists: the idea is that if their individual deficits and problems (at work, in their social environment, flat hunting) are addressed, the grip of right-wing extremism may be broken successfully. This intervention targets a certain dimension of right-wing extremism: the actions of perpetrators (aggressiveness and violence) but, in contrast, right-wing ideology is rarely being tackled. *Good Practice*: In Sweden, initiatives for dealing with potential violent criminals have been successful: a 'Dialogue Police Officer' has been introduced in order to foster a dialogue with potential violent criminals and prevent violence in the first place. Policemen are getting in touch with violent criminals or violent groups in order to de-escalate tense situations.[18] Exit initiatives support and supervise the leaving of right-wing extremists from the scene, especially criminals. These initiatives are operative in Norway, Sweden and Germany and have been tested recently in the Netherlands.[19] Similarly, the 'Violence Prevention Network' in Germany offers right-wing criminals a conducted, supervised exit. An additional approach is the advice offered to parents of right-wing extremist children by different institutions, such as the *Verfassungsschutz* (office of the protection of the constitution) and civil society initiatives in Germany.[20]

Local community as location for de-radicalisation: In the majority of cases, conflicts emerge in local communities without knowledge of society as a whole. Local communities are central locations for the dissemination of right-wing sub-culture and the escalation of right-wing violence. It is in this environment that right-wing parties have remarkable electoral success. If local communities cover up problems in this regard, it can be assumed that they will intensify. Therefore cities and municipalities have to answer with target-oriented measures. In this context, it is most important to achieve cooperation and coordination between various actors. *Good practice*: Important steps to solve this problem are the conception of positive models (for pluralism, against racism) and an action plan with concrete steps.[21] An excellent model in this field is the Alliance against Right-wing Extremism in the Metropolitan Region of Nuremberg.[22] In addition, the integration of targeted offers (for potential perpetrators) contributes to de-radicalisation (as described above).[23]

Support measures for victims

Effective strategies must not focus exclusively on (potential) perpetrators, but have to address the victims of right-wing radicals as well—victims of physical violence, as well as victims of discrimination. On the one hand, victim support should offer practical assistance and, on the other hand, it should give victims a voice.

Good practice: Examples of good practice are local and regional anti-discrimination organisations in the Netherlands. The main task of these organisations is support for victims of racism and right-wing aggression. They were founded and developed as grassroots organisations in Amsterdam, Rotterdam and The Hague. An example is Radar Rotterdam-Rijnmont,[24] whose work is currently being supported with public money. These organisations have cultivated an excellent communication between themselves.[25] Another example is the victim support office in Potsdam (Germany).[26] In addition, Switzerland has efficient and innovative projects for victim support, especially the development of an online handbook and a legal guide for victims.[27]

Prevention

Preventive and pro-active measures are especially important for combating right-wing populism, because they tackle its roots. In addition to legal steps[28] and political debates, which welcome cultural, religious and ethnic pluralism, de-radicalisation and educational programmes are at the heart of preventing the radical right ideology and activities.

Educational measures

Develop the ability to criticise and to debate on substance: In prevention work, it is most important to establish contact with (potentially) right-wing youth (called 'Longsdale Youth' in the Netherlands)[29] and young voters in general. This age group is strongly attracted to the (sub-cultural) activities of right-wing radicals and is currently over-represented among right-wing voters. Offering workshops (e.g. on xenophobic and right-wing music) can help to stem the rise of right-wing youth culture and its ideology.

Start early and continue with promotion: Important target groups (children, youth, young adults) can be gained, if measures against right-wing populism and racism—i.e. measures for democracy and pluralism—are integrated in the work of kindergartens, schools and youth centres. It makes sense to start promoting awareness early and continue over time.[30] The structural integration of these measures in curricula is welcome. *Good practice*: In France, topics like racism and anti-semitism were integrated in the education of policemen and secondary school teachers.[31] School projects and initiatives like School without Racism—With Courage (a project from Belgium) may help to develop civil engagement against right-wing populism and racism. The German project, Learning and Living Democracy, provides first-hand experience with democracy in schools.[32]

Promote competencies and enable self-reflection (within society): Efficient educational programmes against right-wing orientations are training programmes in democracy and human rights, tolerance, holocaust education, civil society, anti-racism, acceptance of pluralism and diversity, as well as conflict prevention, anti-aggression and mediation approaches.[33] These programmes promote debate with right-wing extremism, its aggressiveness and its orientations. Educational programmes should be geared towards fostering cognitive, emotional and social capabilities. They should pay attention to the needs of the relevant target group.[34]

Implement vocational and further training measures in aspects of the complex field: Valuable work against right-wing populism and for pluralist democracy can be contributed by personnel who are well trained, familiar with right-wing extremist codes and sensitive to right-wing slogans, as well as used to dealing with religious and ethnic diversity. The training of personnel in vocational and further training is, therefore, very important. The target group is employees of public institutions (administration, judicial system, executive, educational institutions), personnel of civil society organisations, and politicians. *Good practice*: The National Courts Administration in Sweden, for example, has developed a training programme for judges, which is focused on hate crimes. Similar programmes have been developed by agencies, which cooperate with the judicial system.[35]

Supportive measures targeting (structural) discrimination

Combating internal right-wing populism and racism: The efficient and credible fight against right-wing radicalism requires a debate on its ideology (like racism) within the public institutions. To enable such a critical debate it is necessary to discuss this topic internally or with external supervisors. *Good practice*: Human rights groups and NGOs like Observatoire des Violence Policiers and Observatoire des Libértés Publiques in France can stimulate such processes. They create initiatives which observe human rights violations through the police.[36] Worth mentioning, also, is the similar critical work done on racism and human rights violations by Amnesty International in Germany.[37]

Employ officials with a migration background and from minority groups: The composition of personnel defines the identity of an institution and can help to establish a sensitive approach towards these topics. It is useful to employ people with a migration background in order to foster a pluralist perspective and achieve a special sensitivity regarding discrimination (measures in this regard have been implemented in Britain and Sweden, for example). *Good practice*: In Britain, creative campaigns have been initiated within the police, e.g. advertising to attract migrants to the service.

Conclusion

The discussion of measures against right-wing populism and racism has proven that a mixture of long-term strategies is the key for advancing a pluralist and humane Europe. There is no single or short-term measure that can neutralise the political and social threat of the radical right. Milestones of a suitable grand strategy are: exchange and cooperation between various actors; consistent denunciation of discriminatory 'othering'; prevention work (including measures of de-radicalisation); emphasis on liberal democracy and its values (like pluralism); expanding public awareness within institutions; and strengthening civil society actors.

The optimal mixture of strategies countering right-wing populism and racism is dependent on the relevant political and social context and on the nature of target groups. The approaches and measures described above offer ideas for the composition of diverse strategies—on the communal, regional, national or European level. They should be interpreted as a set of possible actions, which can be chosen and could ideally inspire the development of innovative measures.

14

HIDDEN POTENTIALS IN 'NAMING THE GYPSY'

THE TRANSFORMATION OF THE GYPSY-HUNGARIAN DISTINCTION

Cecília Kovai

In chapter 6, my colleague, Kata Horvath, has described a shift between two 'social orders' in a Hungarian village where we have carried out field-work during the past ten years: between a world in which 'the Gypsy' was not named but was constantly present under different labels, and the present where 'the Gypsy' acquires a seemingly ever greater prominence. This turn to 'naming the Gypsy' involved not only a set of public events, but also a slow transformation, a reorientation, in discourse, the extent and import of which cannot yet be predicted. New possibilities have been created and the operation of previous strategies has been rendered problematic. In 'naming the Gypsy' an issue has surfaced in everyday speech and public discourse, but also new 'scripts' have been articulated, and new spaces, which are now designated as 'Gypsy', have been created. The recently founded Gypsy organisation and its club-house are examples of this, as well as all those acts which create 'the Gypsy' in other ways than the 'hidden Gypsy' of the past which arose from silencing the Gypsy-Hungarian distinction.

We are able now to see how the social relations that maintained the previous local hierarchy, by silencing this distinction, are shaken and fall apart. But the new directions being opened up are not yet fully defined, so we could do no better than examine the phenomena at a time when the traces of the previous order co-exist with the evidence of its collapse.

The 'Gypsy' that goes together with the family

Although many things have changed in the past ten years, kinship is still, by a long way, the strongest social form through which 'the Gypsy' could appear as if naturally; in which naming the Gypsy goes without saying and does not automatically carry the danger of causing offence. Kinship seems to have a kind of permanent hegemony in this sense. But the close relationship which connects kinship to Gypsyness has a different meaning in a context when expressing the 'Gypsy' could only occur on the scene of the kinship relations, and in a context where people assume their Gypsyness in public and/or the stigmatisation of Gypsies becomes a constant feature of life.

The order that was based on not naming the Gypsy invested kinship relations with enormous power because they became the privileged place for negotiating ideas about Gypsyness. The family, whether in the form of parent-child, sibling—or broader kin relations—became a force that circumvented and transcended the imperatives of this order and the hierarchical positions inherent to it. Kinship terminology (even, for example, terms like the 'disabled') allowed people to talk 'about Gypsies' without actually naming the Gypsy explicitly. This, however, did not disguise, avoid or burden the naming of the Gypsy (since everyone knew that only Gypsies address each other with such nicknames), but filled it with such a strong significance that it presented Gypsyness as an unbreakable bond. Terms like 'brother' or 'my brother' invited people into the most intimate community where differences could not intrude and the experience of Gypsyness could be narrated in terms of family ties. At the same time, as we have seen, kinship created boundaries between different extended families. 'The Gypsy' could thus become the field in which distinctions were made. Because of this practice of forming distinction, one's own extended family became a 'place' which could offer shelter from the dangerous external meanings of Gypsyness but also protected one from the fear that one might lose one's connection with 'the Gypsy'. From the perspective of the Balogh family, the 'Sasoj' family was the one that embodied all the offensive meanings of Gypsyness, they were the 'filthy ones', they were the 'backward ones', while the

Farkas family brought out that accusation—that in any case was levelled at all and every family by someone and lived in everyone as a desire—that in the turmoil of trying to fit in they had become the 'fussy ones', the snobby ones, 'big gentlemen who act like they are Hungarians already'. The safety offered by one's 'own extended family' thus had a high price, because it offered shelter while creating difference. This dynamic made it extremely difficult for 'the Gypsy' to acquire a shared meaning, under which people could gather, overcoming family divisions in order to turn Gypsyness into a broader political call, protecting their interests as a category of people.

While the categorical differences between extended families had a certain stability, it was not at all obvious to which family any individual belonged. Each marriage, past and present, creates multiple ties between extended families. Basically, everyone forms a bridge between at least two kin networks: one from which his father comes and the other where his mother belongs. There is thus no person whose family origins could not be thrown into question and, in consequence, his Gypsyness questioned. Differences between extended families could not become rigid because the dense network of kin relations sometimes created unpredictable ties; when Sasoj girls marry Balogh boys these marriages could revitalise forgotten kin ties.[1] Even if the extended family was not the basis for drawing distinction, there were always other relations which allowed this; some Gypsies 'who are other than us', and so the logic of distinction was always at work one way or another. And this difference was mainly a matter of kinship.

The connection between kinship and Gypsyness seemed to work in two opposing directions. On the one hand, kinship prevented an appeal to a 'common Gypsyness' and, on the other hand, it implied such a commonality because relationships between Gypsies could only be narrated through kinship terms. These apparently opposing tendencies crosscut and pervaded each other. The experiences of family belonging, whether in the context of a wedding party, an economic niche exploited together with the relatives, or just an afternoon spent together in a good mood, are experiences of shared Gypsyness. In the same way, when 'stranger Gypsies' meet each other they seek to find common ground using kinship terms. When a competition of musical talents (*'ki mit tud'*[2]) was organised in the neighbouring village, several family based bands came together from different villages and, by the end of the evening, 'my brother' designations could be often heard, as if the shared Gypsyness of the participants could be created only as ties of kinship.

Kinship and 'Gypsyness' interlocked with each other, investing 'the Gypsy' with such positive meanings as 'motherhood', 'fatherhood', 'brother-hood', and 'love'. Family offered a protection against dangerous meanings of being a Gypsy in this way. This implied, for instance, that the Gypsy could not walk alone, 'others' are always needed—relatives and 'broth-ers'—and, by extension, all the other 'Gypsies' as well. This placed the Gypsy into a community of interdependence. But interdependence meant that one could slip out of it, losing one's relatives and finding oneself alone against the degrading meanings of being a Gypsy, but also the fear that the 'others' might leave one alone by themselves stepping out of this commu-nity. As a result there were constant questions checking on people's 'belong-ing' and these mutual interrogations had a crucial importance because the answers testified to the extent to which a common 'Gypsyness' was shared, or how far the other has departed from it.

Accusations of being different or having departed too far were directed not only at distant relatives or 'stranger Gypsies', but also at family mem-bers, even brothers, and within parent-child relations. Because questions checking on belonging were always directed at kin, the whole issue of Gyp-syness was clarified through family ties. Questioning went like this: 'To whom do you belong?' And the answers were always phrased in family terms: 'husband, wife, son, daughter, brother, cousin of this or that' etc. This question was often asked in everyday situations, but receiving a prompt answer is a matter of urgency in teenage love-affairs. If, for exam-ple, a Balogh daughter falls in love with a 'Sasoj' boy, it is immediately apparent what is at stake. Neither the girl nor the boy could move free from the network of kinship ties; any action either 'drags' her or his imme-diate family with her/him or projects the spectre of losing her/him. Through her choice, the Balogh girl brings 'Sasoj' relatives into her family, a 'Sasoj' son-in-law for her parents, 'Sasoj' brother-in-law for her siblings. The question 'To whom do you belong: to us or to him/her?' asked by the parents or brothers, checks up both on the distance between the daughter or son and her/his parents and siblings and participation in 'common Gyp-syness' shared through family ties.

It may appear to the reader that this local importance attributed to kin-ship, the 'community of interdependence', is somewhat metaphorical but, in Borsod county, with its lack of economic resources, high rate of unem-ployment and strong anti-Gypsy sentiments, it literally provided the basis for survival. The existence of relatives gave the impression that there was someone who could help, even if in reality there wasn't always; it provided a sense of security. The nuclear families that lived in a single household could rely on each other when they needed anything from small items for cooking to the means to explore opportunities to make money. And even if in a given situation they couldn't actually share these resources because they didn't have them, they assured each other that they would have if they could have, and that, meanwhile, they would at least share the lives of the paupers.

In fact, the main issue at stake was ensuring intimacy and proximity. Although the nuclear family was the most important unit and the basis of the household, the family continuously needed to demonstrate its openness to others, as if it were under constant suspicion that it was prone to closure, 'concealing' the resources it commanded. The promise should be kept alive that in this house visitors are welcome, the hosts are willing to share their living space, and they do not deny their presence to anybody. One easily entered other peoples' houses, there was almost no boundary between the outside and inside; people came and went, mainly relatives, but neighbours and friends too. These visitors were not guests in the sense that they did not announce their arrival in advance, and their hosts did not organise anything around them, they simply stepped into the flow of everyday life, then left. If something disturbed this free flow of persons, then questions regarding the Gypsyness of those involved would be raised immediately. Openness was associated with shared Gypsyness, closure was a sign of the loss or denial of Gypsyness, which is the same as displaying Hungarianness. 'You couldn't go in there, they pretend to be Hungarians!'—people said about households that appeared to be closed. Breaking the free flow created the impression of abandoning 'Gypsyness', which also meant removing oneself from the network of kinship. Suspicion floated at all times above every Gypsy that he might like to cut himself off from 'Gypsyness', and 'pretend', as if he were not 'one of us'.

Visitors usually made some kind of request of their hosts: for a little coffee, a small amount of red paprika powder, a cigarette, a couple of onions, flour, small items needed to finalise lunch, or else objects for domestic use, like a bucket with the floor-cloth or a DVD player. All these could be borrowed. And even all these requests could be irritating, the price of denial was too high to refuse. These requests were in fact a way of checking up on the issue of belonging and if someone would not give, then he denied the family bonds and along with that his own 'Gypsyness'. While the flow of requests tested the proximity of the 'other', sharing also reduced one's own possibilities and each household was sucked into: 'Everything I have is dragged away by the Gypsies!' (*Mindenemet széthordják a cigányok!*), as people often indignantly said. These requests had one fundamental feature: they created frustration and a sense of scarcity. Those who give feel they have given too much, those who receive feel they have not got enough. It was always understood in relation to the other party in such exchanges, that there was something that could not be requested or, from the other side, some demand that would never be satisfied, and in this lay precisely the shared Gypsyness of the parties to the exchange, the sense of common frustration, of a common (negatively evaluated) shared Gypsyness, uncorrupted by difference.

The puzzle is where the fear and suspicion that the other would like to leave this community behind, 'deny us', wish himself away from these relationships comes from. The answer lay in the same place that this form of community has its origins: in the Gypsy-Hungarian relation, based on not naming the Gypsy.

Everyone had the experience of 'Gypsyness covered-up', when, following life-strategies based on the order of not naming the Gypsy, he presented himself in the context of a poor as opposed to a well off person, a client vis-à-vis a patron or a 'disabled' member of society as opposed to a 'normal' one, and so on. He did not appear as the Gypsy in a Hungarian-Gypsy relationship. As a result, the main shared experience was the possibility of losing Gypsyness or, put more radically, the potential of denying Gypsyness. The 'common' in these experiences was the recognition in the other of one's own intention, that he too would like to escape the burdens of the Gypsy-Hungarian distinction. Moreover, this happened in a way which pushed the threatening meanings of the Gypsy onto the shoulders of the others by creating distinctions between the Gypsies. Relationships that were based on not naming the Gypsy constantly threatened 'the Gypsy' because all the strategies were based on an avoidance that aimed to maintain the illusion that it was not the Gypsy-Hungarian distinction that determined and guided the nature of encounters and social situations.

The order of not naming the Gypsy was literally the Promised Land: it envisioned a world in which the Gypsy-Hungarian distinction had lost its significance, or at least was not the essential issue. This order offered the tempting promise that if you behaved in a proper way you could leave your Gypsyness behind you, as the source of difference was not rooted in it. The problem with this promise is that it was false. There were several people who put their whole life into the service of 'behaving properly' and in spite of that when, after significant effort, they managed to move from the Gypsy settlement into the village they were received with suspicion by their new neighbours. Everybody was aware that they were 'Gypsies', nobody had forgotten this and the neighbours reacted accordingly. But even if the order had fulfilled expectations and had not been based on an illusion, on a false promise, it insisted that Gypsyness was a condition from which a person should try to escape and that the bright side of life lay somewhere else. So this promise was not only false, but also fixed threatening and offensive meanings of 'the Gypsy' in stone. So, to fulfil the promise required constant self-hatred, continuous self-degradation in an effort to defeat your own Gypsyness. This was extremely painful because you also had to tear apart your kinship ties, the meaning of 'the Gypsy' being almost totally fused with 'relatives and family'. Beyond our own experience in this village, countless life-stories collected by Hungarian sociologists over the past fifty years bear seemingly endless witness to the personal trauma suffered by individuals in this process.

The 'community' of keeping it unnamed

This was an order that ensured a place for 'its Gypsies' by not naming them; it did not exclude them, but assigned to them a 'proper' position. The position of 'the Gypsy' was always to be found on the periphery (in the Gypsy settlement on the edge of a village), in positions of subordination and inferiority (remedial classes, unqualified jobs) and so on. These positions offered the same chances for all Gypsies, creating a kind of equality where everybody followed the same path and acquired similar experiences. Even those few who attended 'normal' (not remedial/educationally sub-normal) classes did not have a very different career from the majority. Soon after finishing school, girls from the 'normal' class gave birth, when they were eighteen just like the others, and all boys went out to earn a living for their family as unskilled or occasional labourers. The order of not naming not only maintained a hierarchical Gypsy-Hungarian relationship but created an apparently egalitarian Gypsy-Gypsy relationship too, a 'common Gypsyness'— which, as we have seen, at the same time generated the possibility of creating certain sorts of difference among the Gypsies. The false promises tempted people to believe they could leave the relationships of interdependence with other Gypsies; suggested that they did not need the others, because Gypsyness was irrelevant. The counterpart of this was that, despite numerous mutual experiences of Gypsyness, because 'Gypsyness' was under permanent assault, there was an ever-present feeling that these shared sentiments needed to be reinforced.

In this threatened condition all and any difference seemed to create a departure from the 'common' and as such demanded equilibration. Whether this involved material or any other difference in positions, or simply an experience that diverged from that of others, difference projected a fatal spectre of departure. In the order of not naming, Gypsyness became a shared experience in the fear of losing the other. This constantly threatened 'common Gypsyness', which was locked into equality, and started to resemble a zero-sum game, where the quantity of 'rewards' could not be increased and only their distribution could be altered. If one had more it meant the other had less. Translated into the logic of kin relations: love and attachment to someone put into question another relationship. For example, if the wife had good connections with her brothers-in-law, her own brothers felt that she was not close to them. As if one could only love by taking away the feeling previously attached to someone else. In a similar way: if someone denied his Gypsy status, he thereby stigmatised others as Gypsies. Anything which belonged to anybody, success, an object, or even a person, appeared as if it would deprive somebody else. If somebody took 'something', by this possessive gesture he left others in their Gypsyness, and became 'stuck-up' (*gizda*), had begun 'showing off', wanting to appear as different or superior.

This milieu, which was so sensitive to difference, could yet tolerate a large scale of 'otherness' if this were reconnected to the experience of common Gypsyness. An openly homosexual male, 'the fag Zsolti', as he was called, lacking family of his own could devote his time to reinforcing ties between his relatives, so he had the reputation of being a 'family man'. His homosexuality, as one can see from his nickname, did not appear as radical difference, only as an individual characteristic that any of us could have.

But any difference could become threatening if the suspicion arose that the person displaying such was motivated by the wish to set himself apart, had given way to the temptations of the 'order of not naming,' believing that he could be different from 'all the Gypsies.'

The will to be different was threatening not only because 'shared Gypsyness' could be destabilised, but also because if somebody claimed they were 'more' it meant that the others were 'less'. If a man bought a car, he immediately provoked jealousy in others without a car, and the wish to acquire a similar one. But note: it was only his 'Gypsyness' that turned him into such an important point of reference; the fact that he had a car was only important when connected to his 'Gypsyness'. 'The Gypsies envy me because I drive a BMW'—says a song by one of the most popular Gypsy singers. What could be more enjoyable in the new BMW than the envy of the 'Gypsies'? is the suggestion. The song is written in the first person singular, so it appears that suspicions related to ownership are well founded: it recognises the temptations which everybody experiences to step out of the relationships of interdependence and to prove that one is different and superior. The phenomenon of usury (the Hungarian term means literally, 'interest bearing money'), which has caught on during the last ten years is a tragic by-product of the same logic, where the enrichment of somebody is in direct proportion to the impoverishment of the others. This practice could only have developed in a period when the force of the old dream of accessing resources outside the Gypsies was fading.

The 'community' of naming it

What happened to 'shared Gypsyness' when the hierarchical Gypsy-Hungarian relations which were based on not naming the Gypsy started to be questioned? 'The Gypsy' began to appear in places where earlier he was not allowed at all or entered only occasionally. He moved into the village, became an employer, changed the ethnic balance in schools, stepping beyond the sphere of kinship he established his 'own' association, and in so doing he left behind the safety of the positions assigned by the order of not naming and exposed himself to the dangers of being named as Gypsy. As a result the 'Gypsy' became visible because he left behind exactly those positions where his presence was covered up. These changes seem to have caused a fundamental disturbance to the mechanisms of social life in the village. And when the Gypsy became visible he was also named. The claim that Gypsyness does not matter slowly lost credit and Gypsy-Hungarian relations were less and less guided by the logic of covering up and adaptation to the mainstream. As a result, the new social conditions also reduced the old option of 'denying'—as well as the dangers of losing—Gypsyness.

The dissolution of the previous order has opened new possibilities for experiencing 'shared Gypsyness' which are no longer necessarily fuelled by the fear of losing it. These possibilities have not appeared out of the blue:

the previous order turned the family and the extended kin-group into resources that could support attempts to question the hierarchy of 'Hungarian-Gypsy' relations. But beyond the naming of the Gypsy, the dissolution of the old social arrangements has induced more radical transformations: 'the Gypsy' is now seen differently and the meaning of 'shared Gypsyness' changes. The question is, what exactly is this difference and what are the dangers and possibilities inherent in it.

To answer this question we need to clarify what we mean by 'naming the Gypsy' in the context of the village. In general public discourse in Hungary, naming the Gypsy has been understood primordially as applying a stigma, committing an offence. This is similar in the village. This seemed to be a necessity, because the meaning of naming derives from the earlier norm that, as we have seen, attached offensive, pejorative meanings to the word 'Gypsy'.

But now naming the Gypsy has new meanings in a village where previously it was only allocated to people in inferior positions. The programme that aimed to dissolve the Gypsy settlement 'named the Gypsy': the call for participation explicitly addressed the Gypsies. The successful application to carry out the program was prepared by the Gypsy association founded a couple of years earlier. As a result, the families who were living on the margins of the village could move into the village but were able to do this only as Gypsies—there was no chance to pretend that their ethnic status did not matter. And future neighbours made no effort to pretend at all: with a few exceptions, most responded with intense protests. As we have seen, the school also turned into a 'Gypsy school' where there is no chance to disguise the fact that most students are Gypsies. Among the public places of the village a club-house appeared which is maintained by the Gypsy organisation, and all the villagers, Hungarians and Gypsies alike, call it the 'Gypsy club house'.

The act of naming therefore brings both new room to manoeuvre within 'the Gypsy issue' and has reinforced offensive and exclusionary stigmatisation. This has involved all those situations in which the distinction of 'the Gypsy' is no longer produced by silencing, disguising or inserting it into other issues (poverty, disability etc.).

The Gypsy issue that has appeared in public discourse during the last few years has reshaped local speech habits too. On the Gypsy settlements everybody became wary of the 'black jeep' driven by the killers who were 'slaying Gypsies' without distinction so long as the victim was Gypsy.[3] Sometimes it was rumoured that the Hungarian Guard was organising a march in the village, and the question as to what 'the Gypsies' should do came up regard-less of their family affiliations or which settlement they lived on (both signs of degrees of assimilation in the old order). The establishment of the local extremist Jobbik organisation and their success among the local Hungarian villagers was an expression of local anti-Gypsyism (*cigány-gyűlölet*) which is not selective as to the target of its hatred—'the Gypsy'. The experience of discrimination, which was present previously but has become increasingly intense—the police constantly check peoples' papers; fine people for no reason; officials became more unfriendly; community work service (deman-ded in exchange for long-term welfare support) humiliates—all these are narrated as experiences of being stigmatised as Gypsies. In these narratives the 'Gypsy' does not appear as something that could be covered up. Here 'the Gypsy' is something carried by all, actual behaviour does not matter; after all—any Gypsy might be the next one to be shot, they are not inter-ested which family you come from, and if you leave the village the police will stop you immediately just because you are a Gypsy. Although it is likely that the outside world never cared very much about the internal distinc-tions within Gypsy communities, the illusion that by relying on such inter-nal differences one might escape the destructive force of being stigmatised as a Gypsy (i.e. become accepted as a Hungarian) was powerfully motivat-ing. Distinctions that mainly existed between extended families, and which previously offered a degree of protection, have now lost their significance in most situations. And even when this strategy is still found it is only as a temporary solution, in the midst of a newly open and generalised stigmati-sation of the Gypsy.

Rudi, if he has a car at a given moment, drives around together with his sons, sons-in-law and brothers-in-law in the neighbouring villages and cit-ies, collecting scrap metal and selling it at the recycling station. He tries to maintain good contacts with the entrepreneurs or private persons who keep larger quantities of such things. One of his clients, the vice-mayor of a small town, sent him the following news: 'Rudikám, when there is the town spring-cleaning[4] Gypsies will not be allowed to enter the town; there have been many burglaries, you know; but tell the police you are coming to me, and they will let you in. I'll keep the things back for you'. Rudi was happy that he was treated preferentially but the exchange also raised the issue of the council's problematic decision: 'How could they know that it was Gyp-sies who had done the burglaries? And what if that burglar band is doing this intentionally during the spring-cleaning just in order to pass the blame to the Gypsies? They are canny! Even if there are a couple of Gypsies who do that, why should they put us all under the same cap?'

The Gypsy issue infiltrates everyday conversation in this way. Ten years ago it would have been difficult to imagine such an openly racist, anti-Gypsy decision and rarely would somebody have assumed the Gypsy stigma when offered an opportunity to draw a distinction between himself and others, and so purge himself of the dangerous meanings of Gypsyness. Rudi could have said that the village Gypsies are different and this kind of suspicion is not valid for them, as he had often done in the past. But now, he did not. In such situations the Gypsy distinction is expressed explicitly; it is talked about openly in relationships between Gypsies and Hungarians. And even if this is not always the case now, people are increasingly entering situations where the Gypsy is named.

As the practice of naming the Gypsy becomes generalised, so relations between Gypsies and Hungarian carry ever fewer connotations of losing or 'denying' Gypsyness. Today, 'common Gypsyness' is not created by fear of losing the other, because everybody is stigmatised in a similar manner. In this way 'shared Gypsyness' has become more permissive of internal differentiation. In the 'Gypsy club-house', which is a milieu created by naming it as Gypsy, Gypsyness is self evident: it is common with no regard to family or social position. The Sasoj children and those from Pirittyó enter the club alike and it is obvious that all the children and the adults who watch over them are Gypsies.

While the order of not naming the Gypsy functioned smoothly, radical difference in positions between Gypsies, such as exist between a boss and an employee, remained unimaginable, because hierarchy was a characteristic of 'Gypsy-Hungarian' relations. Today, many people are employed by a local entrepreneur who uses resources that are, in a sense, inherent in being a Gypsy, in order to run his business. He founded the firm together with his brothers and the workforce is recruited from among his numerous relatives. In an enterprise of this kind Gypsyness couldn't be covered up and, in fact, he is exclusively referred to by villagers as the 'Gypsy entrepreneur'. Furthermore, in contrast with what would have happened in the old order all of them feel part of a shared kind of Gypsyness, despite the difference in position between boss and employee, all of them feel part of a kind of 'shared Gypsyness'.

These new social forms contribute to the transformation of social relations: the Gypsy can become a boss, and as an entrepreneur he can be the social equal of the person who seeks his services. The order of not naming the Gypsy invested kinship (interlocked with Gypsyness) with the power to circumvent hierarchical relations. Stepping out from that hierarchical order, the Gypsy becomes visible and he is named: the entrepreneur can, therefore, only appear as a Gypsy businessman and his employees as Gypsy workers. This has the result that none of them fear that they will lose each other's shared Gypsyness, and this makes the differences between their positions less threatening.

Naming does, however, threaten other kinds of dangers. The word 'Gypsy' cannot be freed of its past, nor of the contexts in which it has come now to be spoken. Naming the Gypsy signals the breaking up of an order, and in these changed circumstances 'the Gypsy' has, at the same time, come to represent all the fears and uncertainties of a new condition. The end of the old order, which dragged on in Hungary for years after the system change, came together with the appearance of Gypsies in all kinds of places from which they had been previously kept out. This change, in and of itself, brought a shift in the meaning of 'Gypsy' in such a way that it remained just as pejorative and abusive a term, but was supplemented now with a sense of threat and 'place-or space-grabber'. For this reason, speaking the Gypsy has never taken place without conjuring up a degree of danger. Although the mechanisms of suppression have stopped functioning and now the differences between relatives constituted under the order of not naming can be resolved—so creating a broader 'common Gypsyness' which can manage differences—this shared Gypsyness is taking shape through confrontation. It seems that naming the Gypsy is dangerous not only to those who are labelled Gypsies, but also to those, who through this act of naming, become 'the non-Gypsies', that is to say are turned into 'Hungarians'. Thus the act of naming was preceded by an increased visibility of the Gypsies, that is their appearance in places and spaces which had been (though in an unspoken manner) 'Hungarian', that had counted as belonging to the majority. Thus the act of naming points to a 'Gypsy' who is a threat to the majority, to the newly named 'Hungarians'. Though the loss of space has not occurred as a result of fundamental and political changes in Gypsy-Hungarian relations, it is experienced as an 'intrusion into the space' of the majority and it is narrated through stigmatising the Gypsies.

Thus the 'Gypsy club-house' only found a place in the village with some difficulty. In spite of the fact that the association and the club-house helps foster a broader 'common Gypsyness' beyond kinship ties, this did not prepare it for confrontation. As we have seen above, the new kind of common Gypsyness, which goes beyond kinship differences, is mainly created against the destructive forces of stigmatisation: the extremist killing-spree targeting Gypsies, the marches of the Hungarian Guard or struggles over school composition. It is no longer fuelled by the fear of losing other Gypsies, but the awareness that we all are under threat because of our Gypsyness.

We cannot know how long this new, shared meaning of Gypsyness, which transcends the differences of kinship and other kinds of distinction and lays a potential basis for representation and a presence in the public sphere, will survive. But it is already clear that the 'common Gypsy', in a way like the new 'shared Hungarian', draws its vitality from a confrontation that excludes cooperation or effortts towards overcoming 'Gypsy-Hungarian' differences. Whichever side of these distinctions we live on, or even if we live outside of them, it is in the interest of all of us that the meanings of 'the Gypsy' should be dominated neither by repression nor confrontation but should acquire a content that could be shared by everyone in some way.

For the time being, however, the sudden appearance of 'the Gypsies' on the village stage, after fifty years of silence and suppression of their voices and, in particular, the appearance for the first time in living memory of 'Gypsies' in a position of social or economic dominance, has upset an entire local cultural order. 'Hungarians' (ie non-Romany Hungarians) who have lived here all their lives are suddenly confronted with the existence of a demographically dominant population, whose existence they had in effect ignored for at least two generations. Other chapters in this volume deal with the political consequences of this shift. I have tried to give shape to and to explain the changes in the habits of everyday life that underpin political change, which political entrepreneurs, inevitably, draw upon as they strive to create and mobilise support in their electoral constituencies.

15

DOGMATISM, HYPOCRISY AND THE INADEQUACY OF LEGAL AND SOCIAL RESPONSES COMBATING HATE CRIMES AND EXTREMISM

THE CEE EXPERIENCE

András L. Pap[1]

This paper was written as a response to an unprecedented series of lethal attacks against Roma in 2008 and 2009 in Hungary.[2] The issues raised in the paper, however, touch on a broader set of questions. The following pages convey the frustration of a central eastern European human rights lawyer facing the misdirection and misinterpretation of the constitutional role of certain human rights principles and arguments, which (i) disarm crucial defence mechanisms that constitutional democracies have and need to mobilise countering anti-democratic extremist movements, and (ii) practically prevent efficient legal action against discrimination and obstruct combating hate crimes in particular. I argue that the lack of readjustment of both the legislative formulation and the practical interpretation of a number of classic human rights (such as free speech, freedom of assembly, protection of informational privacy), which were essential tools and both symbolic as well as practical achievements in the process of the political transition, seriously threaten the functioning of the new and fragile liberal democracies in the CEE region.

Inadequate social responses

In order to understand the phenomena at hand, we need to dwell shortly on the socio-legal developments of the past two decades. Twenty years ago, in the stormy process of the 'refolution', the constitutional revolution that enabled the peaceful transition from communism to constitutional democracy, Hungary—like other, lucky states in the CEE region, which successfully avoided brutal social conflicts or ethnicised civil wars, and where conflicts were diverted to roundtable negotiations with representatives of the retreating regime—was a young champion of human rights and constitutionalism. Even though the textual formulation of constitutional and legislative provisions that concern some of the fundamental rights was, inevitably, rushed and incomplete, this did not cause any disturbance in the process of democratisation, since these provisions were both the guarantees of and practical means for overcoming the communist dictatorship. Free speech meant freely criticising the oppressive regime and campaigning for candidates at the free elections. Freedom of association and assembly meant forming dissident parties and rallies. Constitutional rights equalled democracy and opposing the exercise of these rights (whether or not such opposition was procedurally or textually justified) meant opposing democracy. Those were times to fight for the enforcement of these rights, not for debates on their content, extension and interpretation. Although there was an absence of popular euphoria about all this, there existed a subconscious common understanding about the profound meaning of these core constitutional principles and, in the following years, the socio-legal dynamics in the region were quite promising. An organic development seemed to take place, even if governments were sometimes slow or reluctant in overcoming certain aspects of post-communist institutional legacies by failing to properly reform, say, the judicial system or combat corruption, or respond to maladministration or maltreatment by law enforcement agencies. Activist constitutional courts and ombudsmen, alongside visible and influential human rights NGOs, were formed and were able to shape the process of building a constitutional state.

Despite facing severe economic problems, the fresh air of constitutionalism seemed to permeate the public sphere, which was also inspired by the perspective of joining the ever-appealing club of western political and economic alliances such as the EU and NATO. In the past few years, however, something has dramatically changed: having achieved all of the goals and dreams that people had during 1989–90 (market economy and an unlimited selection of consumer goods, EU and NATO membership, etc.), Hungarian and other CEE societies are unable to digest the stress and frustration that emerged as a social cost of all these changes. Instead of appreciation, or even nationalistic pride over the achievements, there is an unprecedented degree of social, political, and ethnic tension, and pessimism.[3] Along the way, the role and image of the CEE region has also changed in the outside world, torn by the economic crisis. After a miraculous birth and a short and shaky childhood, prematurely, but irreversibly, CEE societies stepped into the age of adulthood. In this world they confront other autonomous and self-interest driven grown-ups, and there is little appreciation for their special status and preciousness, which, until then had been taken for granted and formed an important component in their self-identity. This phenomenon of passing adolescence is also mirrored in how fundamental rights are perceived.

Following the exceptional moment of the transition era, these societies entered the stage of normalcy, where all viable liberal democracies reside: where daily, complex and demanding debates take place concerning the desirable and acceptable interpretation of constitutional rights. Fundamental rights are no longer simple, one-dimensional, black or white substances: democracy is specifically known for the fact that there is room and a crucial need for healthy debates on the daily operation of constitutionalism. Constitutional democracy itself is the interaction of a very intricate web of participants: political parties, the parliament, the head of state, the constitutional court, the ombudsmen, the political press, human rights NGOs, the government, etc.—with each and every member having a separate set and degree of responsibility for spelling out the specific and optimal reading of the constitution. There are no given answers and one-size-fits-all models to follow. Due to historical and socio-political givens, in one fully functional constitutional democracy, there is a need for an elaborate and robust self-protection mechanism, and thus there may be a need to prohibit holocaust denial and to criminalise hate speech; in another, the cornerstone of a stable and well-functioning constitutionalism lies in the very fact of basically unlimited speech, be it political or commercial. In one fully functional constitutional democracy, race and ethnicity are used in official state records; in another, also fully functional constitutional democracy, the prohibition on registering people's race, religion, and sexual orientation is a substantial expectation of the electorate. And so on. Constitutional democracies thrive on free debate concerning the proper recipes for constitutionalism. Hungary, like other countries in the CEE region, in my opinion, is facing severe difficulties in meeting the demands of an adult-democracy in this regard. Many of the aforementioned democratic actors are unprepared to face the new, albeit inevitable and, in a sense, normal phenomena that non-state agents can use constitutional rights in an unconstitutional manner.

In well-functioning constitutional democracies, questions around fundamental rights do not only arise in the context of the state curtailing the people's freedom. Since these rights themselves may very well be in conflict there are often debates about their relative importance. This should, of course, be familiar to young democracies, too, but it seems as though participants in the democratic process sometimes respond inadequately to the necessary task of properly balancing clashing fundamental rights. Sometimes, even human rights advocates fail to understand that imperfections and certain inherent contradictions within the legal system do not reveal the failure of an interpretation that conforms to the constitution and that classic, traditional dogmas (of, say, freedom of assembly, unlimited free speech or personal data protection) are not immediately apparent and omnipresent answers in all situations.

Consider this example: in August 2009, international neo-Nazi organisations were planning a demonstration in Budapest to commemorate the death of Hitler's deputy, Rudolf Hess. Although Article 2 of the 1989 Act on Assembly[4] prohibits demonstrations that would violate criminal provisions (the demonstration would clearly fall under this category, violating several provisions within the Criminal Code), Article 8 only allows for the police to prohibit a demonstration if it will obstruct the functioning of crucial state institutions or severely impede traffic. Thus, the demonstration—which obviously carried a foreseeable risk of violence and intimidation of a great number of people—could not legally be banned, only disbanded in the event of disorder. In this case, however, the Hungarian police decided to ban the demonstration in advance. Clearly, human rights NGOs (among them the one I am a member of) had a well-founded rule of law argument in protesting against this prohibition,[5] especially since a few months earlier the Hungarian police tried to use a textually similarly unfounded argumentation to prevent a Gay Pride March. Nevertheless, as on other occasions, what they thereby did—as the neo-Nazis expected and manipulated them to do—was to create sympathy in the media for, maybe not the cause, but the means. It is quite telling that in the midst of this controversy the police, without hesitation, approved the registration of another, purportedly 'unrelated event', a demonstration initiated by Tamás Polgár, a noted rightist radical blogger (writing under the name Tomcat) and Endre János Domkos,[6] a well-known skin-head leader commemorating Walter Rudolf Hess, a Nobel-prize laureate from physiology in 1949,[7] who was, obviously only a namesake for Rudolf Walter Richard Hess, the Nazi.

The case shows the complexity of the issue: an imperfect, twenty-year-old law and a classic liberal dilemma. This sort of problem is a recurrent, indeed ordinary event in constitutional democracies and ought to be resolved in a routine manner. The answer, however difficult this may seem, is obviously not to approach the law in a selective manner, upholding it when we sympathise with the cause and disregarding it when we do not. We have to acknowledge the complexity of solutions a constitutional democracy may offer. One might say that it should fall under the constitutional role of the police to take responsibility for resolving the contradiction between two clauses of the law on freedom of assembly and come up with an interpretation, tailored to the event in question but in line with the constitution, that favours Article 2. Alternatively, the courts, which have the responsibility of deciding appeals against administrative decisions by the police, might act themselves or they could request a constitutional review by the constitutional court itself. Another possibility would be that the parliamentary legislators could rapidly introduce a bill amending the law. Civil-liberties absolutists may very well decide to argue for the superiority of certain rights, although it is questionable whether there are constitutional super-clauses—like freedom of speech, assembly or data protection—through the lenses of which state actors can afford to and should be obliged unconditionally to see the entire world. This would be particularly dangerous in young, premature democracies like Hungary, because state-actor participants in the constitutional process, who are traditionally conservative and resistant towards the idea of human rights and civil liberties, will most likely use these arguments as an excuse for not protecting other constitutional rights.

Following this long introduction, I turn to a case study of Hungarian law and law enforcement practices because legal issues around extremist movements have been particularly relevant here in the past few years. The Czech Republic has faced similarly unpalatable political forces (see Albert, this volume) but their electoral success is negligible compared to their Hungarian counterparts. And in Bulgaria (see Efremova, this volume) the law has barely come into the matter. I consider first the failure to combat and prosecute hate crimes because of misinterpreted data protection, and second, controversies around the banning of extremist political organisations. This will allow the reader to see how the general arguments discussed above play out in practice. In particular, I will show how the resistance to collecting ethnic data by law enforcement authorities, a resistance that is strongly supported by human rights arguments in Hungary and which seems superficially appealing and constitutionally justified, is in fact neither a constitutional must, nor good policy. Hungary is one of the (many) countries in which extensive legal restrictions on the collection of non-anonymous data concerning ethnic, national or religious identity have prompted law enforcement authorities to simply deny that ethnicity is of significance in their actions—even when these involve the investigation of race crimes. Thus, in the first case study[8] I will argue that surrounded by an omnipresent and legal culture of data protection that claims to trump all other considerations, the authorities refrain from identifying victims' ethnicity. In order to avoid making uncomfortable and—given the prevalent anti-Roma or xenophobic sentiments in these societies—unpopular decisions, law enforcement officials, as well as prosecutors and judges, successfully avoid recognising racial motivation in violent criminal behaviour, even if the existence of racially motivated crimes logically presupposes the notion of membership in a racial or ethno-national community. The outcome is that a narrow and treacherous interpretation of the superficially minority-friendly principles of ethno-racial data protection actually runs contrary to the interests of the victimised groups. The example of race crimes provides a vivid demonstration of the Murphy-law of hate prejudice: notwithstanding the sweetest sounding constitutional and statutory language on equal treatment, free choice of identity and the protection of sensitive data, it is always the discriminatory practice of the majority that actually defines attribution of ethnic affiliation. Thus, when what is at issue is the maltreatment of members of various ethnic groups, no difficulties in definitions arise for the would-be discriminating party, but do arise when state actors are called to defend those discriminated against. In fact, conceptual ambiguities may sometimes worsen the effect of protective measures provided for the victimised group.

The second case study, dealing with the banning of extremist paramilitary organisations, will show that not even the existence of narrowly tailored legislation designed for this sort of case guarantees action if law enforcement operates in a hypocritical and cynical politicised arena.

Inadequate legal responses

In Hungary, as in many places across Europe, there are tragic, historical precedents when censuses and other administrative lists have been used to identify people as enemies of the state and discriminate against them. There is, therefore, an understandable shyness towards practices that include collecting ethnic data without the explicit permission of the concerned persons, or policies that would curtail the free choice of (ethnic) identity. However, such a restrictive approach to ethno-national data classification causes severe constitutional problems.

Hungarian law allows for the handling of data on racial and ethnic origin only with the consent of the person concerned.[9] Articles 2(2) and 3(2) of Act No. 63 of 1992 on the protection of personal data and the use of public data prohibit the handling of sensitive data, such as ethnic origin, without the concerned person's explicit permission. In order to stay on the safe, and less labour-intensive, side of the data protection controversy, officials habitually claim that recording the racial status of victims of racial violence would run against statutory provisions, even though the Criminal Code acknowledges certain racially motivated crimes, such as 'violence against members of a community' or 'incitement against a community', all of which presuppose membership in the given (e.g. racially or ethno-nationally defined) community. In general, as Lilla Farkas points out, with Hungarian law allowing for the handling of data on racial and ethnic origin only with the consent of the person concerned, the effect is to severely impede the prospect of litigation against indirect discrimination or institutional racism.[10] The Hungarian Criminal Code (Act IV of 1978) criminalises four types of behaviour that may fall under the racially motivated category. (Racial motivation is implied in the wording of the law.) These are: genocide (Article 155), apartheid (Article 157), violence against members of a community (Article 174/B),[11] and incitement against a community (Article 269).[12] Nevertheless, it is safe to say that the first two have never, and the latter two have only very rarely occurred in the official record.

Let us look at the statistics:[13] the number for reported and investigated cases are as follows: for 'violence against members of a community' the numbers of reported cases were as follows: 2005: 15, 2006: 13, 2007: 20,

2008: 13, 2009: 23. Out of this only one case was indicated and made it to the court. In regards of 'incitement against a community', the following number of cases were reported: 2005: 27, 2006: 22, 2007: 34, 2008: 24, 2009: 48. This led to only one indictment in the years 2006–2009 and to two in 2005. Concerning perpetrators, the number of indictments were as follows: for 'violence against members of a community'; 2005: 2, 2006: 2, 2007:3, 2008: 11, 2009: 25. For 'incitement against a community' only one indictment reached courts annually.[14]

This should by no means imply that racial crimes and violence are non-existent in Hungary, but rather, as said above, that law enforcement agents, as well as prosecutors and courts, are very reluctant to recognise racial motivation in violent and non-violent crimes committed against Roma and other minority victims. Officers and officials habitually claim that the lack of clear legislative guidelines for the establishment of racial motivation means that most such instances only qualify as nuisance, assault or mischief. On the other hand, many politicians and experts argue that the criminal legislation in force could easily allow for a less narrow, more minority-friendly interpretation. Although it will always be the prosecutor who will decide on what grounds to indict the defendant, she will usually follow the police's determination on the nature of the criminal offence. As for the police, officers claim that in determining whether an offence is racially motivated they take notice of internal guidance issued by the Attorney General that directs prosecutors when considering and qualifying the indictment. This means that the only legal guidance is an internal policy guide, which, needless to say, would not stand up very well against any constitutional challenge.

Another debate, a technical yet important one, concerns the legal status of perceived ethnicity. One could argue that data relating to one's perceived ethnic origin is not explicitly prohibited by the Data Protection Act. Under the aforementioned Article 2 of the Act, sensitive data is defined to include 'personal data revealing racial, national or ethnic origin [...]'.[15] In the approach widely accepted in Hungarian professional literature, the term 'data' must be interpreted extensively to mean any fact, information, or knowledge that can be linked to a person. According to a comprehensive and influential analysis: 'Hungary's information rights regulations do not distinguish between data and information; legal professionals use the two terms interchangeably. Beyond data identifying natural persons, personal data includes everything that can be correlated with a specific person with the help of the identifying data. The information does not necessarily have to be factually true. Indeed, false information could constitute a special case of personal data, as long as it satisfies the rest of the criteria. In this way, data implying Roma origin are regarded as personal data even if the subject in question does not happen to be Roma as well as in cases where he does declare himself to be Roma. Finally, the notion of 'data' also comprises inferences drawn from one or—as is typically the case—several pieces of information. For instance, information must be considered personal (even sensitive) data if it is an inference, whether well-founded or unjustified, from other data (such as a surname more often borne by Roma individuals than by others) that does not in itself necessarily imply minority status'.[16]

Under this approach, absurdly, even the following statements may constitute a violation of data protection laws: 'Nelson Mandela is a black human rights activist'; 'Robert Fico is a Slovak nationalist politician'; 'Ariel Sharon is Jewish'; 'The Pope is Catholic'.

Furthermore, not only inferred data (which is what journalism is built on), but also false data—for example, the statement that 'Stevie Wonder is white'—would be illegal under data protection laws. Hungarian practice, due both to the proper and improper interpretation of the data protection law, is absurd in other areas as well: the media would report that officials found illegal, toxin-laced meat products in a supermarket-chain, but due to data protection concerns, would not disclose the name of the company. Even if a nationally known politician were to be arrested for, say, corruption charges, in line with the guidelines, the police would only use initials of the suspect when issuing a press release. Political bodies, like a parliamentary committee or opposition parties, which are constitutionally intended to assist initiatives revealing data on the conduct of daily business by the state and the government, choose to ignore or even oppose these claims. For example, the Hungarian Civil Liberties Union (HCLU) once had to sue the Constitutional Court for not disclosing a petition sent by a Member of Parliament seeking the constitutional review of a provision of the Criminal Code. The court, in line with the Constitutional Court (the ultimate guarantor of fundamental rights!) was of the opinion that cases initiated by Members of Parliament amount to private data and are to be exempt from disclosure. The case reached the Supreme Court, with the HCLU's requests denied at all instances.[17]

The aversion to transparency, as well as the political and public responsibility induced by such, is also present in a somewhat unexpected realm: the broad practice adopted, most strikingly, by the media. News reports, televised or printed, habitually refrain from publishing the full names of people featured in reports, and use initials or first names at best—even if those mentioned are politicians or other public figures. For example, following the official press release of the police and MTI, the official Hungarian News Agency, media organs used the label 'György H'. to refer to the mayor of District 7 of Budapest, who was arrested for charges of corruption—despite that fact that the identity of the mayor is known to almost everybody in the country.[18] This sort of absurdity is daily practice: a court in a libel case referred to Imre K., a Hungarian Nobel-prize laureate in literature—the only Hungarian ever to receive such a prize. It is also quite telling that the law transposing the EU's racial and other equality directives, Act 125 of 2003 on Equal Treatment, identifies the publication of the names of those found guilty of discrimination as a separate sanction[19] that the Equal Treatment Authority, the equality body established by the law, may (!) apply. And the practice of the newly formed organisation reflects the above attitude: concerning its activities in 2009, the Authority proudly reported that following the 1087 complaints they received, 351 cases were processed by the Authority, which led to forty-eight instances where discrimination was established, of which a mere thirty-three were actually made public.[20]

Banning the Guard

My second example of inadequate response—an intriguing combination of legal, political and social—concerns the case of the Hungarian Guard ('Magyar Gárda'), a paramilitary organisation closely affiliated to a recently emerged right-wing extremist party, the Movement for a Better Hungary ('Jobbik Magyarországért Mozgalom', or 'Jobbik' in common parlance). In this case, the government has clear and undisputed legal tools for action and, according to political statements and declarations, the relevant authorities are instructed to take action against illegal activities. In reality, however, no action is taken by authorities: possibly due to the rather restrained level of protest raised by civil society and opposition political parties—which are aware and conscious of the popularity of anti-Roma political rhetoric. The outcome is the injection of a politico-legal placebo: the introduction of a narrowly tailored, explicitly case-driven piece of legislation to disband the organisation. Despite a binding court order, however, no action is taken to enforce the law and there is no movement to seek a cure for the disease instead of treating the symptoms: seeking to ban the parliamentary and European parliamentary party, Jobbik. This path, of course, could be risky, especially if not done in a 'wholehearted' way, as demonstrated by the Czech case, or if prepared in an unprofessional manner, with, for example, the secret service infiltrating the party, as happened in Germany.

In June 2010, the Office for Democratic Institutions and Human Rights (ODIHR) at the Organisation for Security and Co-operation in European (OSCE) published a special report based on a field study carried out in Hungary on the issue of anti-Roma hate crimes.[21] This is how it presents the facts of the Hungarian case in respect of Jobbik (founded in 2002) and its affiliate, the paramilitary organisation, the Hungarian Guard[22] (founded in 2007, with Jobbik's leader serving as its leader):

A major plank of the party's platform is the need to battle what it refers to as 'Gypsy criminality'.[23] *Jobbik* was able to attract only marginal support in elections prior to those for the European Parliament in June 2009, never having reached 9 per cent support in any electoral district and attracting only 2.2 per cent when running as part of a coalition in the 2006 parliamentary elections. The party then managed to garner 15 per cent of the vote and pick up three seats at the elections to the European Parliament. (…) In the Spring 2010 *Jobbik*, for the first time entered parliament (with skinhead leaders in its grouping), gaining 12.18 per cent of the seats.[24] Generally, *Jobbik* receives its highest level of support in areas where there was a significant Roma minority…

Since fall 2007, their programme has emphasized battling 'Gypsy criminality', and the organization's militant attributes have become more pronounced. The Hungarian Guard has organized and led marches and rallies across the country, particularly in places where inter-ethnic conflicts or attacks have occurred or crimes have been committed in which the perpetrators, alleged or otherwise, were Roma. Events at some locations have apparently been held at the request of local non-Roma residents…. The Hungarian Guard has been joined by a number of other ultra-nationalist formations, including the Goy Bikers (*Gój Motorosok*) and the Nationalist Bikers (*Nemzeti Érzelmű Motorosok*)…

Following anti-Roma speeches made by Hungarian Guard leaders at the 9 December 2007 rally… the Capital Chief Public Prosecutor's Office, in Budapest, filed a motion in the Capital Court calling for the dissolution of the Hungarian Guard Traditional and Cultural Association, arguing that its activities violated the Freedom of Association Act. The motion referred to international human rights norms under the ICCPR, ICERD and ECHR and the jurisprudence of the Hungarian Constitutional Court regarding the right to human dignity. Prosecutors argued that the Guard's activities violate the human dignity and equality of the Hungarian Roma, thus violating their rights and freedoms under the Freedom of Association Act, and that these are sufficient grounds for the group's dissolution under the Act.

Members of the Hungarian Guard demonstrated near the court building during the trial and the proceedings had to be postponed temporarily when a judge's request to be recused after she received threatening anonymous telephone calls was granted by the President of the Court.

In December 2008, the court of first instance, the Municipal Court of Budapest, ordered the dissolution of the Hungarian Guard Association, ruling that the organization's programme is based on discrimination and that it operates as a 'means to create a climate of fear, while its activities—marches by its members in Roma populated settlements and the speeches of its leaders—constitute a breach of the rights of other citizens by violating their right to dignity and equality'.

The Association appealed the decision, arguing that the Hungarian Guard Association for Protecting Tradition and Culture was not the same as the Hungarian Guard Movement—the actual paramilitary formation, which is not a legal entity—and was thereby unaffected by the ruling. The Guard remained active and continued recruiting members, including adolescents and children. On 2 July 2009, the court of second instance upheld the lower court's ruling, referring to Article 5 of the ECHR and Article 4 (b) of the ICERD in its decision. The Guard remained active and, in response, a 14 July Government decree created the statutory offence of 'participating in the activities of a banned social organization', effective 17 July. Based on the statute, anyone who conducts activity that has been declared illegal in a court order banning an organization faces punishment of a fine of up to 100,000 Hungarian forints (about 365 euros). Leading the activities of a banned social organization had already been covered as a misdemeanour under the Hungarian Criminal Code.

The Guard continued holding events and, on 22 August, the town of Szentendre, to the north of Budapest, saw the swearing in of hundreds of new recruits to the 'New Hungarian Guard Movement'. Some participants in the event, including the head of *Jobbik*, took part dressed in the uniform of the banned Guard. The police brought administrative charges against 176 people for 'participating in the activities of a banned social organization'. On 18 November, the Government broadened the range of punishable conduct in connection with a banned social organization, introducing a fine of up to 50,000 forints for anyone who participates in the activities in a banned social organization in any way or who wears the uniform thereof or any uniform resembling that of a banned social organization at a public event.[25]

Despite the fact that the Magyar Gárda has been banned by a binding court decision, lacking government action, its members still hold rallies. The Guard keeps reappearing under new names and with slightly changed uniforms. Jobbik's leader, Gábor Vona, wore a Gárda vest to the inauguration session of the Parliament in 2010.[26] Political parties, and governments, including that of the newly elected right-wing coalition, led by Viktor Orbán, which won a sweeping victory in Spring 2010, are unwilling to take straightforward action against the popular far-right, and engage in an ambivalent Janus-faced politics: sometimes issuing minor fines at isolated Gárda-events, but allowing the party-leader to wear Gárda-uniform in Parliament, and generally showing reluctance to form a uniform front or even to take a firm stance against the anti-democratic Jobbik and its affiliate, the manifestly illegal Guard. What we see instead is the toleration of a proliferating quibbling, where the Guard Movement, a non-legal entity, is free to exist, since it is different from the Guard Cultural Association, or a 'New Guard' ('Új Gárda') is seen as un-touched by the ban on the 'Magyar Gárda', even though its members, leaders, activities and rhetoric is identical, and only its uniform was redesigned slightly.

The way out: Pro-active efforts in line with the constitution

The question is: how to escape from this trap of quibbling, which seems to be particularly deeply embedded in the post-communist societies, and which in fact ridicules rule-of-law constitutionalism and prevents the protection of citizens' fundamental right not to be violated. In the Guard case, the answer seems simple: first and foremost, enforce the law. Thinking back to Murphy's law of prejudice, the solution to the question is, obviously, in the hands of the legislator. However, the very lesson taught by well-functioning constitutional democracies (and this may apply to a broader range of cases too) is that no other participants of the democratic process are relieved from their constitutional responsibilities if the legislators fail to provide adequate solutions. As mentioned above, another accessible route lies in a constitutionally correct interpretation of the existing laws.

To begin with, we should point out that there is a substantial and constitutionally relevant difference between classifying ethno-racial identity for affirmative action, for positive (individual or collective) minority rights, and for providing protection against discrimination and criminal victimisation. When using preferential treatment, members of the minority group have to declare their membership in a minority group as a precondition for being awarded those additional rights. In addition to such a declaration or statement, it may be reasonable to set certain objective eligibility criteria, such as knowledge of the given minority language or participation in a minority organisation. By contrast, a case of discrimination does not involve the affirmation of ethnic identity or making a declaration to that effect, but rather calls for protection against discrimination based on a personality trait assumed by the external world (because of the victim's physical appearance, for example). In this case, instead of attaching additional rights to the optional declaration of identity, the law should offer protection against discrimination based on the prejudices of the majority. The point in anti-discrimination cases is not to prove affiliation with an ethnic group so much as to decide whether the accused committed the discrimination by identify-ing the person as belonging to a group based on stereotypes held by the majority—which, of course, would constitute sensitive data. Even under European and, to stick with our case, Hungarian law, routine blindness of investigative and prosecution authorities to recognise the racial motivation behind crimes, implies a misinterpretation of data protection laws. If the Criminal Code explicitly defines racially motivated crimes, this in itself constitutes a sufficient legal mandate for prosecuting such crimes and for processing the ethnic data deemed necessary for their prosecution. Needless to say, what is to be registered is not the fact that the person is, say, of Roma ethnicity but the fact that the discrimination or the attack has been com-mitted on the assumption that she was Roma.

There are few positive examples that prove that a constitution-friendly interpretation can prevent narrow-minded, dogmatic practices that all refer to data protection issues.

The first good practice example from Hungarian case law came up in a strategic litigation lawsuit brought in 2006, by the Chances for Children Foundation,[27] against the City of Hajdúhadház and two municipal schools on charges of discrimination.[28] In this case, Judge Tamás Endre Tóth appointed an expert to investigate allegations of segregation. Adopting a rather peculiar method, the expert proceeded to ask a committee composed of members of the local Roma government to identify, based on names and home addresses, which of the pupils—all of whom were admittedly person-ally known to the representatives in question—they recognised and consid-ered as Roma. In the next step, the data were rendered anonymous and used to supply a percentage ratio of Roma and non-Roma pupils among the children attending the schools concerned.

In a statement, which the Court admitted for the most part,[29] the coun-sel for the plaintiff insisted that the sensitive data—that stacked up to prove a practice of segregation—had not been processed unlawfully, considering that the appointed expert and the local elected Roma representatives used the latter's official knowledge to define whom they knew/considered/ assumed to be Roma. Moreover, the information was submitted to the court in anonymous form as pure statistical data, and so was unsuited to identify specific natural persons. So, at the stage when the expert report was filed, the ability to identify individuals in a way that could raise concerns over privacy and data protection was out of the question. Beyond any issues raised by the provisions of the Data Protection Act, the counsel also under-lined the importance of considering the implications of the minority law,[30] which assigns to local minority self-governments the essential task of pro-tecting their communities, as well as vesting them with special rights in minority education. She asked how the duty of protecting interests could possibly be fulfilled if the local minority representatives did not know whether the person on whose behalf they took action was Roma or not. The members of the Roma minority self-government of the City of Hajdú-hadház maintained daily contact with the members of the local Roma community, living together with them on or near the settlements and rep-resenting them on a daily basis to the staff and teachers of the accused schools. Years of experience in this small town had taught them not only which members of the community professed themselves to be Roma, but also whom the defendants regarded as belonging to that minority. In other words, the counsel was of the opinion that, pursuant to the anti-discrimi-nation act, it was not the ethnic background professed by the subject her/himself that had to be demonstrated but the defendant's assumption about the ethnic belonging of the subject. In other words, the Data Protection Act does not regulate the processing of data on perceived ethnicity but the data that derives from self-professed ethnic belonging. Finally, the counsel asked the Court, should the defendant claim that its own assumptions about which of the children were Roma diverged from those formed by the minority representatives, that the Court then order the defendant to come out and specifically say which pupils it regarded as Roma and on what grounds. Unsurprisingly the defendants demurred.

A further case in point is a project which was run by the Hungarian Helsinki Committee, in cooperation with the National Police and the Police Academy in the autumn of 2007 and the spring of 2008, which examined traffic stop/ID check practices within the force, specifically searching for signs of discrimination based on ethnicity. Through the six months of the project, police officers performing ID checks in the presence of civilian observers filled in a so-called RK form (a standard form provided for ID checks in the Interior Ministry Decree 3/1995 BM), and were also asked to anonymously complete another form, supplying the details of the action (time, place, reason, result), the sex and age of the stopped individual, and stating whether the acting officer deems the individual to be 'Asian', 'Arab', 'white', 'black', 'Roma/gypsy', or 'other'. The purpose of the survey was to identify the groups most often targeted by ID checks and the most frequently cited reasons for those checks, as well as to gauge the efficiency of these operations in terms of law enforcement and the discovery of crimes. In completing the form, then, officers made a record of the checked individuals' perceived ethnicity—and they did so with the advance permission of the Data Protection Commissioner and the Minority Commissioner, both of who had approved the methodology and mechanism of the survey.[31] As for the results, the survey has revealed that a Roma person is three times as likely as a non-Roma person to be stopped by police for an ID check, and that this discriminatory treatment cannot be justified by citing higher crime rates among the Roma minority, simply because the data do not provide proof for that assumption. In short, on the evidence of the aggregate ethnic data, the researchers found no difference whatsoever in the results brought by respectively checking the IDs of Roma and non-Roma citizens, such as could be used to retroactively justify the police action in terms of a 'reasonable suspicion' or 'objective criteria' underpinning an act of discrimination.

Closing remarks

To sum up the above, constitutional democracy puts a heavy weight on participants of the democratic process: law makers, government officials, law enforcement officers, judges, prosecutors, media workers and human rights organisations alike. Pointing fingers to the others and evading this responsibility is just as harmful as falling victim to sectarianism and monolithic dogmatism. Instead, responsibility, creativity and courage are what constitutional democracies demand and the people deserve.

This paper has taken the legal case history of one country in order to demonstrate some points that are surely generalisable beyond the borders of modern Hungary. Although the nature and history of the extremist movements in the Czech Republic diverge from their Hungarian comrades, it is striking that the Czech authorities have at times got themselves into a similarly difficult situation to the Hungarians. Attempts to ban movements or suppress demonstrations have been half-hearted and it seems that a similar post-communist unease in dealing with conflicts over fundamental rights (free speech versus protection from violation as an individual or as a member of a community) has arisen there. The initial effort in the Czech Republic by the Topolánek cabinet to ban the extremist Workers' Party was so sloppy that many observers suspected it of having been essentially 'for show'. After that government lost a confidence vote, the caretaker Fischer cabinet was appointed and succeeded in making the case to the court that the party should be banned. This second effort was met with general public approval, largely due to media reports linking the party to a particularly gruesome arson attack and to the Litvínov riots. Of course, this has not stopped the individual members involved from exercising their right to association in a new party with an almost identical name. Another loose end, which Czech authorities have yet to tie up, is the fact that those who initiated the Litvínov riots in 2008 have still not been prosecuted.

And the same story can be repeated elsewhere—in other words: the Hungarian case, for all its local absurdity, speaks to a wider European malaise, at least in the new member states and one that—in the light of increasingly aggressive campaigning statements by parties like Jobbik—needs to be addressed urgently.

NOTES

PREFACE

1. Hollande was commenting on Canal+ after a report on the eviction of an illegal settlement of Romanian Rom in the Bouches-du-Rhone department. Widely quoted in the French media, including http://www.lexpress.fr/actualite/politique/polemique-autour-de-hollande-et-son-idee-de-camps-pour-les-roms_1082788.html.

FOREWORD

1. The author would like to acknowledge the extraordinarily thorough and incisive bibliographic research, summaries and discussions provided by Georgia Efremova, without whose contribution this chapter could never have been written. Gwendolyn Albert also provided crucial empirical support at various moments.
2. One reason that it was so unexpected is that the very success of the anti-racist discourse after the Second World War, and more particularly from the 1970s onwards, meant that even the 'racists' have adopted the language of multiculturalism. They could do so because the starting point of such discourse is the same language of pluralism and cultural difference that racism sought to capture in the past. In other words, anti-racism has itself modified the field of racial reference, leading to ideas and practices which may have ambiguous of even straightforwardly racist outcomes (Pitcher, 2009, and see Picker, this volume, for how this has worked in Italy).
3. There is a clear patterning of the violence which merits deeper sociological analysis along the theoretical lines proposed by Natalie Zemon Davies (1973).
4. Impunity for such violence has been ruled on by the European Court of Human Rights. *Šečić v. Croatia* concerned officials' failure to investigate a racist attack perpetrated against a Roma person by private individuals. The Court found both procedural and substantive violations of the Article 3 prohibition on torture and

a violation of the Article 14 prohibition on discrimination taken together with Article 3 under its procedural limb. ECtHR, Šečić v. Croatia, Appl N°. 40116/02, judgment of 31 May 2007.

5. "Romanian Roma Targeted by Extremists in Italy", 20 November 2007, DIVERS Information Bulletin as reported by ERRC, available at: http://www.errc.org/cikk.php?cikk=2893, accessed 15 June 2010.

6. See, for instance, Janos Todor's sobering assessment of the Hungarian government's failures, 2011.

7. See http://www.romea.cz/english/index.php?id=detail&detail=2007_1905. It is hard not to notice the possibly not accidental suggestion that the spin-doctor speaking is Jewish.

8. See also Asseo's internet contribution to *Le Monde* two months earlier, 'Le "nomadisme tsigane": une invention politique', http://www.lemonde.fr/idees/article/2010/07/29/le-nomadisme-tsigane-une-invention-politique_1393596_3232.html. For an official use of the notion of Roma as nomads, listen to the Al Jazeera report from 4 August 2010 with Jacques Myrard, Member of the French National Assembly, www.errc.org/cikk.php?cikk=3616.

9. With the solitary exception of the Austrian Burgenland, where J. Portschy and other national socialists in the late 1930s did present the local Roma as the social problem, over and above that associated with the Jews.

10. See http://hvg.hu/english/20100211_derex_index_extremism.

11. See especially, Chantal Mouffe, 2005: 72–76, for a critique of this kind of approach.

12. To be complete, two other factors have to be added to understand Jobbik's take-off in 2006: i) the painful, some said brutal, economic programme adopted by the re-elected socialist government and ii) the fact that after a speech by the Prime Minister in the former steel town of Ózd it emerged that he had allowed his party to campaign on a pack of 'lies' (his own word). These led Jobbik to join a campaign of street protest against what many saw as an illegitimate government. Jobbik was then able to present this government as the protector of Gypsy criminals (see below, on Olaszliska).

13. Local autonomy in allocative decisions leads, moreover, to an inevitable and systematic transfer of resources towards the middle and away from the poorer sections of society (Szalai, 2008).

14. See Gábor Czene, Visszatéres_a_Cigányozáshoz ('A return to calling Gypsy'), http://nol.hu/belfold/20110204-visszateres_a_ciganyozashoz, Nepszabadsag, 4 February, p. 2.

15. The term that is used in the village and in the article is the abstract Hungarian noun, *a cigányság* with a sense like *Deustschtum* in German—almost untranslateable into English.

16. A vigorous anthropological debate has consequently taken place in the Czech

NOTES pp. [xxxiii–xxxvi]

Republic precisely around the uses of this term (e.g. 2008, Barša, Pavel: 'Konstruktivismus a politika identity. Odpově' Tomáši Hirtovi a Markovi Jakoubkovi' (Constructivism and Identity Politics. Response to Tomáš Hirt and Marek Jakoubek), editoři: Jakoubek, M., Budilová, L.; In: Romové a Cikáni—neznámí a známí. 1. vyd., Plzeň: Leda, 2008: 208–43).

17. Of course, ironically, immigrants and their communities are an important factor in salvaging the welfare state, providing much of the domestic labour that services Europe's aged.

18. And of course just as with 'immigrants' in the west, the untapped pool of Romany labour might provide hope for some kind of internal economic revival and pension rescue in these countries.

19. Mudde suggests that another way people have become more susceptible to populist messages is by becoming more educated and emancipated. Citizens now expect more from politicians, feel better able to judge them, and are less accepting of what elites think of them—Mudde labels this 'cognitive mobilisation'. This would certainly fit eastern Europe and also provides one explanation of why populists profit so much today by breaking taboos and transgressing political correctness. Through the role of the 'emancipated citizen' and his or her contempt for the false-tongued politician, PC speech becomes a contentious issue.

20. And in this way I differ from Mouffe's account of the resurgence of new populist collectivities, which fails to explain why it is the volk-type collectivity which comes to the fore in modern Europe.

21. At the same time there is nothing in the east quite like the problems thrown up particularly in the consociational democracies such as Austria, Belgium, and Switzerland, where the trend towards apolitical or non-ideological politics has been strongest. There, since the late 1960s, there has been a trend towards 'depoliticised democracies' in which administration has replaced politics (governance instead of government). And, perhaps unsurprisingly, it is there that the populist challenge has been greatest; the populist call for a 'repoliticised public realm' space finds greatest acceptance.

22. The defendants (eight persons, including two minors) were heavily sentenced in May 2009. Bódisz, A (2009) Szigorú ítélet az olaszliszkai perben in: Népszabadság, 29 May 2009, http://nol.hu/belfold/szigoru_itelet_az_olaszliszkai_perben.

23. Zsolt Bayer in an article in Magyar Nemzet of 17 October 2006, advised drivers to step on the gas and drive away without stopping if they ran over a Roma child.

24. On 28 February 2009 on Hír TV an interview with the Prime Minister dealing with the scapegoating of Roma was prefaced by three short stories on brutal crimes attributed to Roma, some of which had happened months or years

before. Each story referred to the alleged perpetrators or accused persons as 'Gypsies', although ethnic data is not held by the police.

25. National Security Office, 2008 yearbook.

26. Zsolt Bayer, Cigányliszka, in Magyar Nemzet, 17 October 2006.

27. Berezin's chosen example of this process is the series of significant events which became part of the French public narrative and challenged collective national perceptions surrounding the rise of the National Front between its 1997 party congress and the 2005 constitutional referendum. Apart from following Berezin, I am also drawing on a sociological theory of events that has been the subject of considerable exegesis in recent years (see e.g. Mahoney, 2000 and Sewell, 1996). Berezin refines their approach to suggest that 'events' can be seen as templates of possibility, permitting us to see relations and interconnections that speak to broader macro- and micro-social and cultural processes.

1. POPULISM, ROMA AND THE EUROPEAN POLITICS OF CULTURAL DIFFERENCE

1. This text was originally written in its current format in spring 2010, long before the coming euro crisis had forced its way onto European kitchen tables.

2. The differences, real or imagined, between members of different 'cultural groups of common descent' have of course provided the ground for more than one episode of communal tension in the past few decades in various European states, often glossed as 'racial conflict'. I am suggesting, however, that in our current predicament we are witnessing new and distinctive forms of this fear 'others', and not a reincarnation of 1930s modes of thought.

3. See Fassin, 2011: 519–522.

4. The text of the decree—'Declaration of the state of emergency with regard to settlements of nomad communities in the territories of Campania, Lazio and Lombardia regions'—is, http://www.poslazio.it/opencms/export/sites/default/sociale/social/resourceGalleries/docs/decreti_e_
regolamenti/D.P.C.M._21_05_2008.pdf (January 2010).

5. The text of the ordinance is available at http://www.governo.it/GovernoInforma/Dossier/Campi_nomadi/ordinanza_campania.pdf (January 2010).

6. The European Parliament resolution can be accessed at: http://www.europarl.europa.eu/sides/getDoc.do?pubRef=-//EP//TEXT+TA+P6-TA-2008–0361+0+DOC+XML+V0//EN (January 2010).

7. The text of the Minister's speech is available at http://www.camera.it/_dati/leg16/lavori/stenbic/36/2008/0723/s030.html (January 2010).

8. Data collated from Székelyi et al. (2001).

9. See e.g. http://www.youtube.com/watch?v=yIgDVxBwP1A. Jobbik have been helped by the fact that many of their opponents have tended to bury their heads

in the sand when it comes to the problem of petty criminality in Hungarian villages and small towns.

10. http://euobserver.com/9/29665.

11. http://www.telegraph.co.uk/news/worldnews/europe/bulgaria/4531391/Mayor-of-Sofia-brands-Roma-Turks-and-retirees-bad-human-material.html. The statement flies in the face of the fact that the government is supposedly making progress to tackle problems of Roma integration and discrimination, especially since the start of the Decade for Roma Inclusion in 2005, launched to great fanfare in Sofia.

12. The following excerpt from a TV programme, 'Gypsies: The privileged citizens', run by the leader of the National Guard gives a flavour of this organisation's rhetoric: 'The Bulgarian state is unjust towards its citizens; it privileges one of its minorities at the expense of the rest of the citizens—and this cannot be called integration. And despite of all the care, the majority of Gypsies do not wish to get an education, and despite the existence of special employment programs, they refuse to work as well; the state in turn builds houses for them, which they destroy; such care for the young Bulgarian families does not yet exist. This integration strategy of the government is wrong because it instils a sense of privilege and impunity, which in turn, very logically, implants a sense of resentment in Bulgarians. If this doesn't change, Gypsies will continue to loot, build their houses illegally (including ramshackle constructions on top of gas pipelines), to travel without tickets in city transportations, and to obtain state assistance paid for from the pockets of Bulgarian taxpayers. They will continue to trade with their children abroad, and in Bulgaria become criminals, beggars, and prostitutes. The only ones taking advantage of these programs [i.e. Roma-related state-supported programs] are neither Bulgarians nor Gypsies themselves, but the so-called human rights organizations and the countless scribblers of integration projects. The Bulgarian state must stop this, and provide care only for those who are truly socially engaged and socially productive—because to work is not only a right but an obligation as well, of every good citizen'. Guests in the studio were Krasimir Kanev (chair of the Bulgarian Helsinki committee) and Toma Nikovael, chair of the Gypsy information agency 'De Facto'.

13. As the fighting escalated in the clothing store, the lawyer's daughter also allegedly joined in. All three women were arrested. The controversy was reported in Le Monde of 20 May, but see: http://themoderatevoice.com/73048/fistsfly-in-burqa-ban-feud-in-france/?utm_source=feedburner&utm_medium=feed&utm_campaign=Feed%3A+themoderatevoice+%28The+Moderate+Voice%29.

14. See Le Courier 29–30 May, p. 7, Martigny: des delinquents comme les autres ou des criminals etrangers? But for an example of the kind of ethnographic evidence one could collect more or less anywhere in Europe, see Scott Ward's lovely

film about a south London neighbourhood, available at: http://www.mystreet-films.com/content/two-doors-down. Very similar basic sentiments could be recorded in Slovakia, Czech Republic or Hungary.

15. The institutional framework of which already exists in the Alliance of European National Movements based in the EU parliament, connecting extremist-populist and far right parties.
16. In a survey of anti-immigrant and anti-Muslim populisms, across western Europe, Oesch reached an identical rejection of the old economic-determinist intuition: 'Cultural questions of identity are more important than economic questions of resources' (2008: 370) and issues of national identity nowadays trump anxieties over labour market and welfare competition.
17. I am following Douglas Holmes' dense account of these issues (2000).
18. It is therefore, in its modern form, inextricably linked to the nation state and nationalism (Gellner, 1983).
19. This doctrine combines a very particular balance of activism and conservatism. It is preoccupied with shifting bases of interdependence that involve all groups of society. It supports state interventions oriented towards sustaining the dynamic base of solidarity expressed in reciprocal types of aid and care or stewardship. At the same time it strongly supports the preservation and protection of groups through policies oriented towards preserving their autonomy and 'active agency', thus in effect sustaining diversity and social differentiation/pluralism.
20. For the sake of British readers, I should explain that subsidiarity is here not used in the narrow technical sense common in British discussions of EU law, but referring to a pivotal concept in Catholic social doctrine which 'denotes a means for circumscribing domains of action for public authorities, establishing formulas for allocating governmental powers, and defining norms of social stewardship and the conditions of individual freedom' (Holmes, 2000: 30). See below.
21. Similar to the cultural autonomy within a European framework advocated by some populist politicians in different parts of Europe.
22. The inherent lack of harmony between policies promoting integration—expanding markets, rendering product control transparent and freeing up the movement of goods, capital, people—and those grounded in the specification of 'cultural rights' (maintaining cultural traditions or differential national, religious or ethnic autonomies) has acted as a further institutional break on pluralist fracturing (Holmes, 2000: 34).
23. I am grateful to Georgia Efremova for pointing this out.
24. This chimes nicely with Andre Gingrich's analysis of Haider's politics in Austria where he notes the pull on the educated, professional middle class of the charismatic showman's theatrical assaults on a corrupt and apparently totally unpro-

fessional political class (2006). This is, further, what Efremova found in an earlier study of the young supporters of the National Guard in Bulgaria as well as in a shorter study carried out in the Czech Republic—the disproportionate presence of students and young professionals (personal communication).

25. See also Bale's prophetic comments about extremists in bipolarising party systems: 'They have a significant number of loyal voters; they seem better able to survive institutionalization than was previously assumed; and xenophobia and welfare chauvinism are endemic in every European electorate. There is every chance, then, that such parties will indeed succeed in securing a permanent niche in Western Europe's emerging political market' (2003: 67).

26. In March 1994, Gianfranco Fini's post-fascist NA entered the governing coalition. Then, in March 1998, Le Pen's Front National made a significant showing in the French regional elections, followed in February 2000 with Haider's FPO becoming part of the governing coalition in Austria and then in April 2002 with Le Pen's strong performance on the first round on presidential elections. Of course, not all countries have witnessed the creation of this type of party.

27. See Goodwin for an outstanding discussion of the role of perceived rates of immigration rather than race as a predictor of extremist interest (2011). Those associated with a broadly defined 'old' left often label the populist-integralists as fascists or neo-fascists (see, e.g. Munková, 2008). Sometimes, as in France, this usage derives from local political traditions but, in general, I think it misleading, even if, as a French colleague, Henriette Asseo, suggests we might compromise on 'post-modern fascism'. It is true that parties like Jobbik need to bring on board the traditional (often aged) anti-semitic right with personal or familial links to the historical fascist parties and make use, in part, of some of the symbolism of those parties (e.g. the use by Jobbik of Arrow Cross iconography in Hungary). But this is only part of the story and the less important part. These parties are not, for example, anti-democratic in principle, whereas a fundamental principle of fascism was opposition to the idea of the multiparty, voter driven, democratic, representative polity. Nor are their programmes to homogenise political culture and drive out 'difference' identical to the antiegalitarian leadership cults of the interwar period. In cases, like the British, where the neo-Nazi label can be correctly applied (for example to the British National Party) the constituency of these parties remains insignificant and restricted to traditional 'skin colour racists' (Cutts et al., 2009).

28. See Berezin in particular, but see also Maryon MacDonald (in Gingrich and Banks eds., 2006).

29. Speaking of the European project, Monnet once noted that 'technical aspects at first sight masked its political meaning' (cited in Holmes, 2000: 27).

30. In Britain the popular press keeps up a more or less constant and no doubt eagerly acclaimed commentary on the elimination of British 'standards', nota-

bly imperial weights and measures, beloved of 'autochthonous' street stall traders, and the like. See, for example, the lurid tales of Christopher Booker published each weekend in the Sunday Telegraph: http://www.telegraph.co.uk/comment/columnists/christopherbooker/.

31. A parallel definition of Europeanisation is 'a discursive strategy and a device of power which in particular, through the institutional and administrative capacities of the EU, reorganized group identifications in relation to territory and 'peoplehood" (Bornemann and Fowler, 1997).

32. In fact, the EU really only engages with 'culture' in reference to the 'European culture industry' where 'culture' is reduced to mass culture and understood in commercial terms. As Holmes says, with some justification, 'protectionist directives limiting access to European media markets… have become the core of EU's cultural policy' (2000: 31). Cross national educational harmonisation (Bologna), trans-national degrees and transfer programmes (Erasmus and Marie Curie) are, however, indicators of some broader cultural agenda.

33. The most compelling account of the culture of traditional political allegiance remains Papataxiarchis' doctoral study (1988).

34. Ignazi focuses on the right-wing character of all this—a position I tend to reject, seeing many parallels between right and so-called left-wing radicalism today.

35. As Holmes says, some of these are no doubt marginal, others absolutely essential to understanding the future course and dynamics of European integration.

36. In other words, the roots of today's xenophobia lie precisely in the ethnicised political institutions of modern society and the 'national community of solidarity'. As Wimmer has argued, the constantly shifting balance of power within these institutions leads to an endless renegotiation of the existing 'cultural compromise'—a renegotiation of the major modes of inclusion and exclusion, a reordering of the basic principles of membership and identity (2002).

37. In one country, it seems the issues are even sometimes linked. In the spring 2011 elections for the regional government of Florence the Northern League suggested that if its opponents came to power they would turn the ancient city into a 'Gypsy-Muslim slum' (Nando Sigona, personal communication).

2. ABUSIVE LANGUAGE AND DISCRIMINATORY MEASURES IN HUNGARIAN LOCAL POLICY

1. Hungary's electoral law is among Europe's most complex and combines three systems to elect the 386-member parliament: voting for single candidates from single-mandate district contests (176 seats), voting for party lists in larger territorial districts using proportional rules to award seats (152 seats), and proportionally allocated compensation seats from national compensation lists (58 seats).

2. In Europe there are basically two main models of local municipal systems and

local administration: integrated and fragmented. Administrative rationality is prioritised in the integrated model over the principle that each settlement has the right to elect its own local municipal council and mayor and determine its policy locally, while in the fragmented model these priorities are reversed.

3. Sixty-five per cent of villages were categorised as 'settlements without a purpose' in 1971; these villages were excluded from development resources and their citizens were refused building permits and, therefore, loans from the bank.

4. In 1981, 20 per cent of the active population were employed by agricultural co-operatives and state-owned farms.

5. In 2009 Hungary's employment rate among fifteen to sixty-four-year-olds was the lowest in the region and the second lowest among the twenty-seven EU Member States in 2009, according to data published by Eurostat. Hungary's employment rate in the fifteen-sixty-four age group was 55.4 per cent in 2009. The rate in Slovakia was 60.2 per cent and 65.4 per cent in the Czech Republic. The rate for the EU twenty-seven was 64.6 per cent in 2009.

6. Only 28 per cent of those with an education of only eight grades of elementary schools are employed in contrast to an average of 47 per cent in EU countries.

7. For example, Kaposvár's municipal council reported in 2007 that only 0.02 per cent of their pupils are severely disadvantaged in order to circumvent anti-segregation regulations. Two years later this figure 'increased' to 9.25 per cent due to an application the city decided to submit for funding.

8. Virilism, as a voting system allocating privileged positions to certain social levels, was introduced in Hungary's larger cities in 1870 and in Budapest in 1872. In larger cities the system was abolished in 1920.

9. The interview was conducted in 2002. In the 1990s, the village managed to reopen its elementary school which had been closed fifteen years before. But in the 1998 local elections, the mayor and the majority of councillors were replaced. The new leaders of the village were elected by the influential families of the settlements who had already enrolled their children in schools elsewhere.

10. See the action: http://www.cfcf.hu/miskolc1-keresetlevel_hu.html.

11. See the judgement of the Court of First Instance: http://www.cfcf.hu/miskolc1-elsofoku-itelet_hu.html; and the Foundation's application: http://www.cfcf.hu/miskolc1-fellebbezes_hu.html.

3. INTEGRALIST NARRATIVES AND REDEMPTIVE ANTI-GYPSY POLITICS IN BULGARIA

1. BBT, Balkan Bulgarian Television.

2. This is still a more frequent reference to the ethnic Turkish minority than the Roma. It was the early and successful political mobilisation and representation of the country's largest ethnic group (Turkish minority, through the political

party Movements for Rights and Freedoms) which led to the constant reference to the 'Bulgarian ethnic model' at home and abroad.

3. http://www.telegraph.co.uk/news/worldnews/europe/bulgaria/4531391/Mayor-of-Sofia-brands-Roma-Turks-and-retirees-bad-human-material.html. The statement flies in the face of the fact that the government is supposedly making progress to tackle problems of Romany integration and discrimination, especially since the start of the Decade for Roma inclusion in 2005, which was launched and signed in Sofia. It is also important to note the exaggeration of the number of Roma in Borisov's speech: essentially he reversed the figures, for in actuality the numbers are closer to 700,000 Roma and 1 million ethnic Turks.

4. GERB party (Citizens for the European Development of Bulgaria).

5. Today, as an article in the main Bulgarian weekly publication argues that, the Roma should be led out of ghettos dispersed across Sofia, the continuous existence of which poses a national security issue, and packed off to 'Saturn or to Cambridge', wherever but not here. http://www.capital.bg/politika_i_ikonomika/bulgaria/2010/07/09/930365_na_saturn_ili_v_keimbridj/?sp=1#storystart.

6. Such as giving away tea and sandwiches to pensioners (organised over a two-week course at Christmas time for many years); benefit concerts raising funds for donations of history books to schools, etc.

7. At the time of my first meeting with the group in the spring of 2007 the NG had fifty to sixty constantly active members in Sofia (half of them present at that meeting); and another 200 'more passive' members who could be mobilised for a given activity; and many more 'sympathisers'. These numbers have gone up significantly since. Video from an oath ceremony available at: http://www.youtube.com/watch?v=6iWAAFc_RRc.

8. I have written more extensively about these in my CEU Masters Thesis, June 2008, Department of Nationalism Studies.

9. Drawn from my participation in a commemoration expedition with the Guard, part of ethnographic work completed in December 2008.

10. Wimmer develops the important concept of a 'cultural compromise' as a result of a negotiating process, centred around Anderson's formula of the 'imagined community', which entails redrawing the line between us and them, as a blueprint for the organisation of social inclusion and exclusion and the patterning of the basic principles of identity and belonging. In this context, he has convincingly argued that nationalism is the main cultural compromise of modern society.

11. This is Stamatiov's reworking of the concept of 'public sphere', originally developed by Habermas, as the space in which 'reasoned communication' orients social action, with its idealised version of reasoning and rational argumentation.

12. Titled 'Gypsies: The Privileged Citizens'. Guests in the studio were Krasimir Kanev (chair of the Bulgarian Helsinki committee) and Toma Nikovael, chair of the Gypsy information agency, 'De Facto'.

13. See, for example, Janez Lenarcic in 2008 OSCE report 'Sustainable Policies for Roma and Sinti Integration', p. 38.

14. http://news.plovdiv24.bg/23451.html.

15. Bill proposal to increase imprisonment of up to four years and ten-fold increase in penalty fee (currently up to three years and a fine of 1,000BGN); according to Bulgarian law, a sentence of up to three years is a suspended sentence, but up to four years a prison sentence (necessarily served).

16. NG newspaper, Issue 3, August 2008, 'Gypsies—the Most Authentic Anarchists at home', p. 8.

17. 10 December 2007 'The degradation of youth and its causes', 15 September 2008 'Why is Today's Youth so Banal, Uneducated and Ill-Mannered?'. Not accidentally, the guest in studio for this show was Galin Yordanov, author and director of the publishing house which brought Hitler's *My Struggle* to the market in Bulgarian in 2001, followed by several books by Volen Siderov. Part of the discussion was focused on Yordanov's opinion of Hitler's book as a school tool and a literary work of art.

18. Evident also in NG's aversion to the homosexual community, treated in subsequent shows.

19. Rasate: 'What we witness instead is only called integration. We don't want to integrate Gypsies to Bulgarian society and culture and traditions; instead we want to create a new culture, composed of the remnants of the Bulgarian (which we see in the process of disintegration in the last 18 years) and some fabrications of an incipient/fetal Gypsy culture'—witnessing the Bulgarian ethnos diluting into multiculturalism (an excerpt from the debate 'Integration or Gypsy-isation')', excerpt from a public debate held at the Red House, Sofia. For reference see Efremova, 2008.

20. And it tries to set itself in this light—as opposed to the rest of the 'angry' and 'empty' nationalisms in the country—but tellingly it is Ataka's angry rhetoric which is able to mobilise some disenchanted sections of society but ultimately unable to deliver ('empty platforms capitalising simply on ethnic tensions').

21. 'Kazana duma, hvurlen kamuk'.

22. Ataka's move to delete many of its more extreme statements relating to either Roma, Turks or Jews from their website immediately after elections was widely commented on; the 'softening' of Ataka's discourse was attributed in part to its fear of being identified as anti-constitutional and inspiring hatred. http://www.capital.bg/show.php?storyid=231981.

23. While, as previously mentioned, the opposite is done by the NG, which always advocated religious unity for national salvation.

24. Ataka newspaper, 2 August 2010, http://vestnikataka.bg/show_news.php?id=197498&cat=5.

25. http://www.dnevnik.bg/analizi/2010/08/26/951915_cigani_i_ciganizaciia/.

4. SOCIAL EXCLUSION OF THE ROMA AND CZECH SOCIETY

1. The first survey was entitled 'Ethnic Relations in the Czech Society' (Prague, MENT, Gabal, A & C, 1994), carried out in May 1994 with 985 respondents over eighteen years of age. This survey was representative as regards age, sex, region, house size and education. This survey was organised by Gfk Agency. The second survey mentioned above was organised by the Institute of International Relations and carried out by STEM. It was conducted in 1996 with 1433 respondents (eighteen years and older). This survey was representative as regards age, sex, region, size of home and educational structure. Both surveys used questionnaires and face-to-face interviews. The wording and sequence of questions were identical in both surveys—for details see *Ethnic Minorities in Central Europe* (Gabal et al., 1999). As opposed to both of the above surveys, we changed the wording of several questions in our survey, as the range of problems and their causes have changed in the last ten years. However, the wording of other questions was preserved for comparison purposes. Unlike the above two surveys, our survey was not focused on the climate in relation to foreigners, but solely on attitudes towards the Roma. The last survey, performed using a method for personal interviews between an interviewer and respondent (the 'face-to-face' method) on a representative quota selection of 2616 respondents interviewed in their homes, was carried out by MEDIAN Agency during October and November 2007 (2 October 2007—15 November 2007) throughout the whole Czech Republic. The target group constituted the population of the Czech Republic, aged eighteen—seventy-five years inclusive.

2. After its creation in January 2003, the Workers' Party was profiled as an extreme right-wing nationalist-oriented entity. Aware of its irrelevance in the 2003 to 2006 campaigns, it sought to cooperate with other extreme right-wing political parties, but without success. Its leaders realised that if their party did not remain a marginal entity it would have won the support of neo-Nazis. First the party worked with the extreme right-wing blocs, National Corporatism and, the newly emerging group, Autonomous Nationalists. From the summer of 2007 there were also contacts with representatives of the well-established National Resistance. Some new members of the Workers' Party were recruited from the ranks of these activists.

3. National Resistance (NO) was set up in the Prague branch of Blood and Honor Division Bohemia sometime during the years 1998–99. It was involved in political activities (including public activities on the streets), organising concerts and trafficking of white power music. In the late nineties, National Resistance established itself on the international neo-Nazi scene, developing contacts with German neo-Nazis (Kalibová, 2009: 67).

4. The Autonomous Nationalists were founded in 2007, building on the activities of Nationalist Kladno (*Nacionalisté Kladno*). The concept of autonomous nation-

alism emerged in Germany around 2002 and is represented by a particular person, Christian Worch. Czech Autonomous Nationalists are, in their own words, free and independent, rejecting central control due to its inflexibility, and favour the idea of local groups creating their own political activities and achieving separate representation (Kalibová, 2009: 67).

5. The Roma constitute approximately 2.5 per cent of the Czech population, thus radical parties might be successful only in some regions.

6. Estimation is based on 'Analysis of Socially Excluded Roma Localities and Absorption Capacity of Subjects Involved in This Field' (GAC, 2006).

7. Of this list of problems, most people designated crime as either a serious or moderately serious problem through all the years monitored in the survey. However, this number of people diminished significantly in 2007, compared to the surveys made eleven and thirteen years ago. While almost none of the respondents then considered this problem to be 'marginal' or 'less serious', in 2007 more than 10 per cent said that crime does not represent an urgent problem for them. Crime was designated as being serious or very serious mostly by older respondents. The figures for perception of the economic and political situation and compliance with law and corruption have not changed much in comparison with the surveys from the mid-nineties. The number of people who consider bureaucracy a problem has increased significantly in comparison with 1996. The number of respondents dissatisfied with the state of the environment has remarkably decreased. At the same time, the number of those considering the influx of foreigners as a problem has decreased, together with fears of the rise of racism in Czech society.

8. The CVVM survey 'Relation to Other Nationalities' displayed a similar percentage (published on 8 January 2007—1119 respondents).

9. The answer that foreigners and ethnic groups should adapt themselves as much as possible to our habits was chosen by 75 per cent of respondents in 1994 and by 71 per cent of respondents in 1996. The second variant offered at that time was to let those groups live on their own terms, which was selected by 14 and 22 per cent of respondents, respectively. For the purposes of the new survey, we decided to change the wording of the question and to add a medium option for responses.

10. Gadjo is the Romany word for non-Romany people.

5. LEFT-WING PROGRESS? NEO-NATIONALISM AND THE CASE OF ROMANY MIGRANTS IN ITALY

1. The text of the decree is available at: http://www.poslazio.it/opencms/export/sites/default/sociale/social/resourceGalleries/docs/decreti_e_regolamenti/D.P.C.M._21_05_2008.pdf, accessed January 2010. The excerpt quoted is my translation.

2. The text of the ordinance is available at: http://www.governo.it/GovernoInforma/Dossier/Campi_nomadi/ordinanza_campania.pdf, accessed January 2010. For an overview of the living conditions in the nomad camps, see Brunello, 1996 and ERRC, 2000; about their everyday implications on predicaments concerning legal status and access to citizenship rights, see Sigona and Monasta, 2006.

3. The European Parliament resolution can be accessed at: http://www.europarl. europa.eu/sides/getDoc.do?pubRef=-//EP//TEXT+TA+P6-TA-2008–0361+0+DOC+XML+V0//EN, accessed January 2010.

4. The text of the Minister's speech is available at: http://www.camera.it/_dati/leg16/lavori/stenbic/36/2008/0723/s030.html, accessed January 2010. The excerpt quoted is my translation. On the Minister's reasons for going on collecting data, see also: 'Maroni. Avanti con impronte e censimenti nei campi nomadi', in *La Repubblica*, 16 July 2008, http://www.repubblica.it/2008/07/sezioni/cronaca/sicurezza-politica-11/maroni-piano-nomadi/maroni-piano-nomadi.html, accessed January 2010.

5. For a detailed description of the governmental measures vis-à-vis Roma since 2006, see ERRC et al., 2009. For a legal point of view, see Trucco, 2008.

6. Anti-immigration sentiment, which has spread since the 1990s, is largely rooted in fear of the stranger and fuelled by moral panic around petty crime and insecurity (Dal Lago, 1999; Maneri, 2001; Mingione and Quassoli, 2002; Mura, 1995; Petrillo, 1999). The historic legacy of prejudices against Roma are filled with mythological tropes such as 'the wild nomad' (Piasere, 2006) or 'the kidnapper Gypsy woman' (Tosi Cambini, 2008).

7. Saitta (2010) found a similar pattern in the management of Roma by Sicilian local authorities, describing how policies aimed at criminals, when fuelled by the Berlusconi government's anti-Roma stance, prevented the implementation of long-term measures targeted at social integration (See Saitta, P., 'Immigrant Roma In Sicily: The Role of the Informal Economy In Producing Social Advancement', Romani Studies [in italics please], vol. 1, pp. 17–45). Vitale (2009) has accounted for the demagogy of Italian policy makers in putting forward arguments in favour of the evictions and confinement of Roma by exploiting the already-existing stereotypes on Roma. On the impact of stereotypes in Italy, see Però (1999) who explored the practices of the local municipality in Bologna in confining a group of Roma refugees in a camp close to a dog pound at the very edge of the town, and the rhetoric of tolerance and reception with which the operation was carried out. Piasere (2006) attempted to scrutinise the constitutive elements of the xenophobic discourse vis-à-vis Roma in Italy, examining how in the politically conservative context of Verona in 2005 people were mobilised against Roma settlements. A study of the prejudicial role played by the images of the 'wild nomad Gypsy', so widespread in music (in Bizet's Carmen, for example) and other domains, might be worthwhile.

8. In Bologna (1994–95) Mayor Walter Vitali; in Rome (1997–2000) Mayor Francesco Rutelli; in Florence (1995–97) Mayor Mario Primicerio. In 1993 the first national law for the direct election of mayors by the city population passed; this can provide evidence of the political affiliation of the majority of each urban population at the time.

9. This happened on 3 October 2007 in the periphery of Rome. A man apparently living in a shanty close to the place of the murderer was accused and convicted to life in jail. He was said to be Roma, although he was not so (Bravi, 2009), and—new to Italian post-Second World War history—a violent media and political campaign took place against Romanian Roma throughout the country, which lasted until the end of 2008. This occasion was used by both right and left-wing coalitions to elaborate rhetoric of urban security and the culture of legality. Veltroni's declaration about repatriation is lucidly explained by the collective effervescence which was created around those issues.

10. In Italy the first state-level migration policies begin in 1998 with the so-called Turco-Napolitano law (n. 40/98).

11. In Italy, Roma are not recognised as a national minority. Laws concerning Roma were passed by several regional councils, which promoted the construction of various kinds of camps. These have been established in Veneto (1984); Lazio (1985); the autonomous province of Trento (1985); Sardinia (1988); Friuli Venezia Giulia (1988); Emilia Romagna (1988); Tuscany (1988) and several other regions as well.

12. In 1991 the Italian Communist Party was dissembled as PDS—Partito dei democratici di Sinistra (Party of the Left-wing Democrats) later DS—Democratici di Sinistra (Left-wing Democrats). Other groups were founded such as the Communist Re-foundation (Rifondazione Comunista) and La Rete (The Net).

13. The Italian constitutional assembly drafted the Italian constitution between 1946 and 1948.

14. About this political culture, see S. Tosi and T. Vitale (2009).

15. Text of the law available at http://www.rete.toscana.it/ius/ns-leggi/?MIval=pagina_2&ANNO=1988&TESTO=NIENTE&TITOLO=NIENTE&MATERIA=512&ANNO1=2007&NUMERO=17&YEAR=1988, accessed 13 June 2010.

16. Municipality of Florence, ordinance 2631, issued on 13 October 1987. The excerpt quoted is my translation.

17. See OSCE/ODIHR, 1999, *Report on the Joint OSCE/ODIHR-Council of Europe Field Mission on the Situation of Roma in Kosovo, 27 July-6 August 1999*, Strasburg: Council of Europe.

18. Founded in 1982 by Giovanni Michelucci, a prominent Florentine architect and intellectual, the foundation has always been in the foreground as policy consultant for issues concerning urban planning, with a focus on socially marginalised places such as prisons or, indeed, nomad camps.

19. Concomitant with this reorganisation of perceptions and policy practices, periodical and continuous interfering checks by the police were imposed, with demands for conformity to community standards, including hygienic checks, twenty-four-hour guards, and other such initiatives (Rossa, 1995).
20. Romany culture is described in the document in terms of several typical characteristics, such as a peculiar understanding of time; stealing not being perceived as immoral; and a general flexibility of lifestyle. Accordingly, the research puts forward several settlement solutions (*soluzioni abitative*) as alternatives to the existing nomad camps.
21. See, for instance: 'Oggi la Marcia antinomadi' ('Today the Anti-Nomad Demonstration'), *L'unità di Firenze*, 6 September 1994.
22. Ashkalja is an ethnonym of a Kosovo-Romany grouping
23. According to Perry Anderson 'The Italian left was once the largest and most impressive popular movement for social change in Western Europe' (2009).

6. UNDERCLASS GYPSIES: AN HISTORICAL APPROACH ON CATEGORISATION AND EXCLUSION IN FRANCE IN THE NINETEENTH AND TWENTIETH CENTURIES

1. See the 21 July 2010 joint press release, Association Nationale des Gens du Voyage Catholiques (ANGVC), Union Française des Associations Tsiganes (UFAT), Association Sociale Nationale Internationale Tsiganes (ASNIT) et la Fédération nationale des associations solidaires d'action avec les Tsiganes et les Gens du voyage (FNASAT), http://www.fnasat.asso.fr/positions.htm.
2. 'Circulaire du 5 août 2010 relative aux évacuations des campements illicites' (Circular of 5 August 2010 concerning the eviction of illegal camps), Groupe d'information et de soutien des immigrés—GISTI, http://www.gisti.org/spip.php?article2042.
3. Dossier 'Bohémiens repoussés à la frontière: correspondance, 1866', *Archives départementales du Nord*, hereafter AD Nord, M 204/10.
4. The exact wording was: 'Do not let the band of Gypsies signalled by the Bettignies mayor as stealing, looting and trespassing enter the French territory', written note by the Nord prefect, 'Bohémiens repoussés à la frontière', 30 May 1866, AD Nord, M 204/10.
5. Ibid.
6. Circulaire de la direction générale de la Sûreté publique, 'Au sujet des étrangers connus sous la dénomination de Bohémiens', 19 November 1864, AN CAC 19940494/111, dossier 6270.
7. Ibid.
8. Circulaire de la Sûreté générale, 4 April 1872, AN CAC 19940494/111, dossier 6270.

9. See AN CAC 19940494/111, dossier 6270, 'Professions ambulantes. Nomades, colportage, Ventes sur la voie publique (Mobile occupations. Nomads, peddlars, street salespeople). I. 1802–1921': Circulaire de la Sûreté publique, 26 May 1874; Circulaire de la Sûreté publique, 18 April 1884, 'Professions ambulantes exercées par des personnes de nationalité étrangère' (Mobile occupations purused by foreign nationals); Circulaire de la Sûreté, 7 August 1888, 'Marchands forains et ambulants de toute sorte' (Travelling salesmen and all variety of itinerants); Circulaire de la Sûreté, 29 June 1889.

10. 'Les camps-volants: recensement des Bohémiens en 'rance', *Le Petit Journal*, 5 May 1895.

11. Conservation of census reports varies a lot among *départements*. See for instance the Bouches-du-Rhône file in Archives départementales des Bouches-du-Rhône, 4 M 887, 'États nominatifs des nomades et bohémiens recensés le 20 mars 1895'.

12. Circular of the Ministry of the Interior, 4 April 1908, 'relative aux attributions et au fonctionnement des brigades régionales de police mobile' (concerning the responsibilities and functioning of regional brigades of mobile police).

13. Circular of the Ministry of the Interior, 5 March 1908, 'Nomades. Maladies contagieuses' (Nomads, Contagious diseases), see *Journal des Commissaires de police*, 1908.

14. Circulaire de la Sûreté générale, 'Nomades étrangers', 2 July 1932, AN CAC 19940494/111, dossier 6288.

15. See Archives départementales du Rhône, ADR, 4M 448.

16. Circulaire de la Sûreté nationale, 21 March 1935, Appendices: 'Famille Demestre Voscho', 'Famille Schaenote Paul', 'Famille Demestre Thomas', 'Famille Demestre', 'Famille Demestre Paolo', 'Famille Demestre Démétric', 'Famille Demestre Jean', 'Famille Demestre Joseph Boucolo dit "Mathias"'.

17. Departmental archives, Bouches-du-Rhône, ADBR, 5W3, Registres de transmissions de carnets d'identité de forains et de carnets anthropométriques de nomades au fichier central de Paris, 1942–1969 (Register of salesman's identity books and anthropometric books of nomads in the central files of Paris, 1942–1969).

18. See Fédération nationale des associations solidaires d'action avec les Tsiganes et les Gens du voyage (FNASAT), *Le statut des 'Gens du Voyage' et ses conséquences discriminatoires légales* (The Law concerning 'Travellers' and its discriminatory legal consequences), March 2010, http://www.fnasat.asso.fr/biblio%20virtuelle/Statut%20GV.pdf.

7. SILENCING AND NAMING THE DIFFERENCE

1. This article was originally published in the thematic issue of a non-scientific Hungarian journal (Anblokk). It was followed by three other articles based on the

same research project in this village. Cecilia Kovai's article (see chapter 14) gives an anthropological interpretation of the changing meaning of the "Gypsy family". Balázs Berkovits gives a discoursive analysis of the changing meaning of 'Gypsy work', and especially of the institutional racism of the public labour program (közmunka). Marton Oblath's article analyzes the changing hierarchical order of the village by looking at the history of the last twenty years of the local elementary school.

2. We would emphasise, at the outset, that the distinction between 'Gypsies' and 'Hungarians' is the inhabitants' and not the analysts' view. The analysts aim is to show how this distinction is constructed locally, and how it works in different time periods. Of course, Gypsy people are also Hungarians (Hungarian citizens).

3. We have left the word 'already' in to retain the flavour of the original. *Már*, in Hungarian, is a term much used in the Gypsies idiolect as an emphatic, particularly in mocking or teasing speech, pointing to some abusive excess (translator's note).

8. ANTI-GYPSYISM AND THE EXTREME-RIGHT IN THE CZECH REPUBLIC 2008–2011

1. ROMEA, 'Demagogie na webových stránkách Národní strany', Praha, 24.1 2006, http://www.romea.cz/index.php?id=servis/z2006_0066, accessed 29 August 2009. The party is opposed to the farm being moved because it would acknowledge the Roma as victims and place them on the same level as the 'real victims' of the Nazi occupation, who, in the party's view, were Czech and Czech only. As many as 95 per cent of the Roma indigenous to the Nazi Protectorate of Bohemia and Moravia were exterminated in the Holocaust.

2. The ad is available online at http://www.youtube.com/watch?v=zq-iDgZtfQw, accessed 29 August 2009.

3. ROMEA, 'Národní strana má rasistický předvolební klip, Česká televize podává trestní oznámení', Praha, 20.5.2009, http://www.romea.cz/index.php?id=detail& detail=2007_6180, accessed 29 August 2009.

4. ROMEA, 'Národní strana ukradla hudbu Apocalyptiky i motiv ovcí na svém volebním plakátu', Praha, 21 May 2009, http://www.romea.cz/index.php?id= detail&detail=2007_6190, accessed 29 August 2009. The music behind the advertisement, a piece by the Finnish group Apocalyptica, was definitely used without permission according to Universal Music Publishing, which manages the catalogue rights in the Czech Republic. The media also reported the party had not secured rights to the photos used.

5. 'Konečné Řešení Otázky Cikánské, Které Předložila Národní Strana, Je Návodem Pro Všechny Evropské Státy'.

6. 'STOP černému rasismu'. Note the repeated association in this ad of 'racism' and 'racists' with the 'gypsies' themselves.

7. 'NS je proti integraci nepřizpůsobivých'. The term 'nepřizpůsobivý' (inadaptable) has enjoyed a vogue during the past year in mainstream discourse as politically correct shorthand for the Roma, enabling users to avoid a blatantly ethnic reference.

8. 'Ne! protěžování cikánů'.

9. 'BRÁNÍME ČESKÉ NÁRODNÍ ZÁJMY'.

10. 'STOP! jejich nárokové a kořistné mentalitě'.

11. 'TVOJE DANĚ—JEJICH BUDOUCNOST!'

12. 'Nechceme mezi sebou černé rasisty'.

13. 'Nechceme mezi sebou ty, kteří parazitují'.

14. 'Bráníme Vás A Vaše Rodiny'.

15. In May 2008 the website www.chceteje.cz ('Do you want them?') was publicised by the NP; its content was aimed against immigrants and the Roma. ROMEA, 'O stránky urážející cizince se už zajímá policie', 12 May 2008, http://www.romea.cz/index.php?id=komentare_ukaz&detail=2007_4258, accessed 31 August 2009.

16. Sládek is notorious for having said on the floor of parliament that the 'first crime of the Roma is to be born'.

17. ROMEA, 'Extremist Czech Workers' Party established in 2003', 25 May 2008, Praha, http://www.romea.cz/english/index.php?id=detail&detail=2007_1111, accessed 29 August 2009; Zvědavec, 'Erik Sedláček osvobozen', 17 April 2009, http://www.zvedavec.org/komentare/2009/04/3108-erik-sedlacek-osvobozen.htm, accessed 29 August 2009.

18. ROMEA, 'Extremist Czech Workers' Party established in 2003', 25 May 2008, Praha, http://www.romea.cz/english/index.php?id=detail&detail=2007_1111, accessed 29 August 2009.

19. ROMEA, 'Petice romských sdružení požaduje rozpuštění Dělnické strany', 28 August 2009, Praha, http://www.romea.cz/index.php?id=detail&detail=2007_6677, accessed 29 August 2009. These efforts to establish party militias bring to mind the very successful use made of the Czechoslovak Communist Party's People's Militias (Lidové milice) during the previous regime, an organisation that numbered almost 40,000 members when it was dissolved in 1989.

20. Prague Daily Monitor, 'German, French Extremists Attend Czech Workers' Party Rally', 17 August 2009, Prague/Nový Knín, http://praguemonitor.com/2009/08/17/german-french-extremists-attend-czech-workers-party-rally, source: ČTK 15 August 2009, accessed 29 August 2009. Authorities in Germany, Hungary and Poland banned similar events around that date.

21. The party screened Wilders' film 'Fitna' and has convened demonstrations against a mosque in Brno.

22. Nicolae, Valeriu, 'Anti-Gypsyism—a definition', http://www.ergonetwork.org/antigypsyism.htm, accessed 30 August 2009.

23. ibid.

24. ROMEA 'Kocáb: Romy prostě miluju', Praha, 15 January 2009 http://www. romea.cz/index.php?id=detail&detail=2007_5456 accessed, 31 August 2009.

25. His controversial statement followed both domestic and international criticism of actions he had taken as mayor of the Moravian town of Vsetín, which violated the human rights of Roma tenants there. See the European Network Against Racism Shadow Reports on the Czech Republic for 2006 and 2007.

26. Sokolová, Vera, *Cultural Politics of Ethnicity: Discourses on Roma in Communist Czechoslovakia*, vol. 82 of *Soviet and Post-Soviet Politics and Society*, Umland, Dr. Andreas, ed., ibidem-Verlag, Stuttgart: 2008.

27. 'Výše důchodu závisí na době pojištění a příjmech, nikoliv na barvě pleti', undated, available at http://portal.gov.cz/wps/portal/_th/601/_lpid.698/699/_l/ cs_CZ/_lp. 698/0/_s.155/7226/_s.155/10202?docid=126264, accessed 5 July 2010.

28. ROMEA, 'Krajské volby: ČSSD—ODS 13:0', http://www.romea.cz/index. php?id=detail&detail=2007_5076, accessed 31 August 2009.

29. ROMEA, 'Extremist Czech Workers' Party established in 2003', 25 November 2008, Praha, http://www.romea.cz/english/index.php?id=detail&detail=2007_ 1111, accessed 29 August 2009.

30. ROMEA, 'Neonacisté a extrémisté ve volbách neuspěli', http://www.romea.cz/ index.php?id=detail&detail=2007_5078, accessed 31 August 2009.

31. 'Zavřeme oči před romským problémem? NE!', ROMEA, S romskou kartou neuspěl kandidát na hejtmana Dymo Piškula, Břeclav, 19 October 2008 http:// www.romea.cz/index.php?id=detail&detail=2007_5085, accessed 29 August 2009. My translation from the Czech original: 'romský problém začíná sužovat velkou skupinu lidí. Ve většině případů totiž nerespektují zákony a přesto jim to prochází. (…) Vláda nemůže dál dělat jen kosmetické úpravy. Musí vyčlenit i potřebné finance tak, aby bylo možné provádět okamžitá restriktivní opatření. Musíme hledat řešení, jak zastavit zvýhodňování jen určité skupiny obyvatel. Zastavme zneužívání sociálního systému, zákony musí platit pro všechny'.

32. ROMEA, 'Protiromská kampaň vítězství ústecké ODS nepřinesla', Ústí nad Labem, 19 October 2008, http://www.romea.cz/index.php?id=detail&detail= 2007_5083, accessed 31 August 2009.

33. The term 'gadje' is the plural of 'gadjo', the Romany-language term for non-Roma. It is usually defined as pejorative. The party presumed a striking degree of familiarity with this concept on the part of voters when choosing to use this term in its ads. ROMEA, 'Protiromská kampaň ODS neporušuje žádný zákon', Most, 15 October 2008, http://www.romea.cz/index.php?id=detail&detail= 2007_5054, accessed 31 August 2009.

34. ROMEA, 'ÚOOZ: Pravicoví extremisté čím dál víc prosazují neonacismus', http://www.romea.cz/index.php?id=detail&detail=2007_4807, accessed 10 May 2009.

35. ROMEA, 'Vězni nacismu kritizují policii za skandální nečinnost na srazu extremist', http://www.romea.cz/index.php?id=detail&detail=2007_4789, accessed 10 May 2009.

36. ROMEA, 'Další útok na Romy, podle policie opět nejde o rasismus', http://www.romea.cz/index.php?id=detail&detail=2007_4900, accessed 14 May 2009.

37. ROMEA, 'Další žhářský útok na Romy, tentokrát v Bruntále', http://www.romea.cz/index.php?id=detail&detail=2007_4938, accessed 10 May 2009.

38. ROMEA, 'VIDEO: Romové vyhnali ze sídliště Janov Dělnickou stranu, místopředseda vyhrožuje odvetou', http://www.romea.cz/index.php?id=detail&detail=2007_5009, accessed 10 May 2009, ROMEA, 'Policie obvinila z rasismu muže, který nadával provokujícím neonacistům', http://www.romea.cz/index.php?id=detail&detail=2007_5200, accessed 19 April 2009. Two Roma men who themselves shouted racist remarks while resisting the neo-Nazis were later sentenced to community service.

39. ROMEA, 'Dva nápisy v Litvínově vyhrožují Romům smrtí', http://www.romea.cz/index.php?id=detail&detail=2007_5044, accessed 10 May 2009.

40. ROMEA, 'Neonacistická akce v Janově stála daňové poplatníky 15 miliónů korun', http://www.romea.cz/index.php?id=detail&detail=2007_5139, accessed 9 May 2009.

41. ROMEA, 'Pokus o neonacistický pogrom na janovské Romy', http://www.romea.cz/index.php?id=detail&detail=2007_5074, accessed 9 May 2009.

42. ROMEA, 'Na shromáždění Dělnické strany přišli neonacisté ozbrojeni, policie 13 zadržela', http://www.romea.cz/index.php?id=detail&detail=2007_5128, accessed 9 May 2009.

43. ROMEA, 'Neonacisté útočili v Hodoníně', http://www.romea.cz/index.php?id=detail&detail=2007_5027, accessed 10 May 2009.

44. ROMEA, 'Policie vyšetřuje rasově motivovaný útok v Havířově, část útočníků je ve vazbě', http://www.romea.cz/index.php?id=detail&detail=2007_5388, accessed 31 March 2009.

45. ROMEA, 'Policisté Janov ubránili, neonacisté házeli dlažební kostky a zápalné láhve', http://www.romea.cz/index.php?id=detail&detail=2007_5215, accessed 19 April 2009.

46. ROMEA, 'Romové klidn demonstrovali, neonacisté vyvolali bitku s policií', 17 November 2008, http://www.romea.cz/index.php?id=detail&detail=2007_5213, accessed 5 May 2009.

47. RESPEKT, Opjaková, Kateřina, 'Taková neztracená válka', vol. 20, no. 9, 2009: 21.

48. See Albert, Gwendolyn, 'Hatred is the Cheapest Fuel', *ERRC Roma Rights Journal*, no. 1, 2009: 30.

49. ROMEA, 'On Mayor Řápková's populism', 2 March 2009, http://www.romea.cz/english/index.php?id=detail&detail=2007_1173, accessed 5 May 2009.

50. Právo, 'Klaus—další populista, ktery podpořil Chomutov', 13 March 2009, p. 3.

51. Liška, Ondřej, 'The State is 'Inadaptable', Not the Children', 10 March 2010, ROMEA, available at http://romea.cz/english/index.php?id=detail&detail=2007_1542, accessed 5 July 2010.

52. 'Zajděte do chomutovských hospod, supermarketů, poslouchejte lidi v městské hromadné dopravě. Jindy neslušné hlášky typu já bych ty cikány postří... se te' staly společensky vítanými u široké veřejnosti'. My translation from ROMEA, 'Koho zachránil Záchranný kruh v Chomutově?', 26 March 2009, http://www.romea.cz/index.php?id=detail&detail=2007_5632, accessed 4 August 2010.

53. ROMEA, 'LN: Chomutov šikanuje rodinu, která dluhy platí', 23 March 2009, http://www.romea.cz/index.php?id=detail&detail=2007_5816, accessed 16 June 2009.

54. ROMEA, 'The Neo-Nazi March is Over, Police Took Harsh Action Only Against the Anti-Fascists', 21 April 2009, http://www.romea.cz/english/index.php?id=detail&detail=2007_1191, accessed 5 May 2009. Hundreds of people, including Human Rights Minister Kocáb, protested the march in the days prior to it taking place.

55. ROMEA, 'Tři ze čtyř neonacistů se přiznali v kauze Vítkov, jeden se účastnil i pokusu o pogrom v Janově', 20 August 2009, http://www.romea.cz/index.php?id=detail&detail=2007_6641, accessed 31 August 2009.

56. An English-language documentary about the Vítkov arson, 'Scars of Racism', aired on CNN International in June 2010. See ROMEA, 'Scars of Racism: CNN Documentary Gently Shows the Cost of Indifference to Neo-Nazism', 2 July 2010, http://www.romea.cz/english/index.php?id=detail&detail=2007_1675, accessed 4 August 2010.

57. ROMEA, 'Vandas znal osobně žháře z Vítkova, další obviněný DS sponzoroval', Praha, 24 August 2009 http://www.romea.cz/index.php?id=detail&detail=2007_6653, accessed 31 August 2009.

58. ROMEA, 'Příznivci a členové Dělnické strany v Chomutově zaútočili na shromáždění proti neonacismu dělobuchy', Chomutov, 4 May 2009, http://www.romea.cz/index.php?id=detail&detail=2007_6078, accessed 31 August 2009.

59. ROMEA, 'Open Letter by Non-Profit Organisations Regarding the Neo-Nazi Attack on the Demonstration in Chomutov', Romea.cz, 5 May 2009, http://www.romea.cz/english/index.php?id=detail&detail=2007_1205, accessed 5 May 2009.

60. This turnout was considerably higher than the 600 or so people who attended various demonstrations against the Litvínov riots in December 2008 in Prague.

61. ROMEA, 'Rodina z Vítkova má nové bydlení', 1 September 2009, available at http://www.romea.cz/index.php?id=detail&detail=2007_6702, accessed 15 June 2010.

62. The Prague Post, 'Arson Victims Still Homeless', 24 June 2009, available at http://www.praguepost.com/news/1567-arson-victims-still-homeless.html, accessed 15 June 2010.

63. The Czech authorities were able, however, to deport former Ku Klux Klan leader David Duke from the country in April after determining the book he was coming to promote included Holocaust denial. ROMEA, 'Bývalý vůdce Ku Klux Klanu David Duke musí do půlnoci opustit ČR', Praha, 25 April 2009, http://www.romea.cz/index.php?id=detail&detail=2007_6025, accessed 31 August 2009.

64. ROMEA, 'Jehlička: Evidence Národního odporu neznamená legalizaci hnutí', Praha, 4 May 2009, http://www.romea.cz/index.php?id=detail&detail=2007_6088, accessed 31 August 2009.

65. ROMEA, 'Paroubek zkritizoval policejní zákrok proti odpůrcům Dělnické strany v Litvínově', Praha/Litvínov, 3 May 2009, http://www.romea.cz/index.php?id=detail&detail=2007_6251, accessed 31 August 2009.

66. ROMEA, 'Neo-Nazis a threat to children of the Czech PM and Interior Minister, police are protecting them', 16 June 2009, http://www.romea.cz/english/index.php?id=detail&detail=2007_1246, accessed 16 June 2009.

68. Egg bombardment disrupts Czech leftists, May 27 2009, http://www.reuters.com/article/worldNews/idUSTRE54Q44I20090527?feedType=RSS&feedName=worldNews, accessed 31 August 2009.

69. ROMEA, 'Volby do EP: Zvítězila ODS před ČSSD, KSČM a KDU-ČSL, Dělnická strana těsně nad jedním procentem', Praha, 8 June 2009, 02:04, http://www.romea.cz/index.php?id=detail&detail=2007_6303, accessed 31 August 2009.

70. 'Politicians Condemn Right-Wing Czech TV Election Ad', Deutsche Welle, 22 May 2009, http://www.dw-world.de/dw/article/0,4272743,00.html, accessed 5 July 2010.

71. ROMEA, 'Dělnická strana možná peníze za volby nedostane, měla neúplnou výroční zprávu', Praha, 8 June 2009, http://www.romea.cz/index.php?id=detail&detail=2007_6305, accessed 31 August 2009.

72. ROMEA, 'VIDEO: 42 promoters of the Workers' Party, including Vandas, Kotáb, Štěpánek, Zbela and Šlégrová, arrested in Prague', Prague, 24 May 2009, http://www.romea.cz/english/index.php?id=detail&detail=2007_1228, accessed 31 August 2009.

73. ibid.

74. "Práce vnitra byla šlendrián", říká politolog Jan Charvát z Univerzity Karlovy", iDNES.cz, 'Dělnická strana slaví, soud zamítl návrh vlády na její zrušení', 4 March 2009, http://zpravy.idnes.cz/delnicka-strana-slavi-soud-zamitl-navrh-vlady-na-jeji-zruseni-puo-/domaci.asp?c=A090304_075308_domaci_cen, accessed 31 August 2009.

75. "'Zásadní vina je na straně ministerstva vnitra, které nedodalo ani základní důkazy. Rozhodnutí NSS je tak spíše než o Dělnické straně rozsudkem o neschopnosti ministerstva vnitra, respektive samotného ministra Ivana Langera', uvedl v prohlášení Paroubek". ibid.

76. "'Soud vůbec poprvé popsal obecná kritéria, podle kterých rozhoduje v případě, že posuzuje návrh na zrušení strany pro rozpor s právním řádem', sdělil Langer". ibid.

77. There is not room here to review the effect of this party's choice for Education Minister on the deterioration of inter-ethnic relations in the Czech Republic, but the minister's appointment of an anti-semitic, ultra-conservative (who ran as an NP candidate in 2006) to a high-ranking position at the ministry temporarily paralysed the cabinet in the summer of 2011.

78. ROMEA, 'Věci veřejné stáhly z voleb romského kandidáta, ten je bude žalovat', 26 May 2010, http://www.romea.cz/index.php?id=detail&detail= 2007_8128, accessed 4 August 2010.

79. ROMEA, 'VV patrols are similar to the Protective Corps of the dissolved Workers' Party', 6 May 2010, available at http://www.romea.cz/english/index.php?id=detail&detail=2007_1629, accessed 5 August 2010.

80. The primary instigator of these weekend sprees is a convicted con-artist who was convicted and imprisoned for posing as an assistant to an MP and defrauding the Czech state out of millions of crowns' worth of international travel.

81. Albert, Gwendolyn, 'Hatred is the Cheapest Fuel', in the ERRC Roma Rights Journal, no. 1, 2009.

82. 'Zaměstnanost a nezaměstnanost v ČR podle výsledek VŠPS—časové řady', CSU, 6 May 2009, http://www.czso.cz/csu/redakce.nsf/i/zam_cr, accessed 16 June 2009. 1996 was also the last year in which a series of ideologically motivated racist murders were committed in the country, a spree that lasted about two years.

83. European Commission, Directorate-General for Economic and Financial Affairs, 'Economic Forecast', spring 2009, http://ec.europa.eu/economy_finance/publications/publication15048_en.pdf, accessed 5 May 2009.

84. See Albert, Gwendolyn, 'Is the Czech Republic Still Abstaining on Human Rights?', Heinrich-Boll Stiftung, Prague, http://www.boell.cz/web/52–660.html, accessed 31 August 2009.

85. 'President Grabs Limelight As Czechs Take EU Helm', http://www.rferl.org/content/President_Grabs_Limelight_As_Czechs_Take_EU_Helm/1364700.html, accessed 31 August 2009.

86. The only recent exception was the 2007 attempt by neo-Nazis to march through Prague's Jewish Quarter on the anniversary of Kristallnacht, ostensibly as a protest against Czech involvement in Iraq. Approximately 2000 counter-protesters turned out to prevent them. Roma were not the issue there.

9. SPACES OF HATE, PLACES OF HOPE: THE ROMANIAN ROMA IN BELFAST

1. It should be noted that Petrova's observations are context specific. The idea that Roma migrate west due to persecution is true only in some cases, not all.
2. Although, according to the 2002 Romanian population census, only 4.7 per cent of the population are Roman Catholic with 86.7 per cent claiming affinity with the Romanian Orthodox Church, http://www.recensamant.ro/pagini/rezultate.html.
3. http://nobordersbrighton.blogspot.com/2009/02/officially-sanctioned-racism-and.html.
4. Pronounced kræk/KRAK. This word variously refers to news, gossip, entertaining and enjoyable conversation.

10. SEGREGATION AND ETHNIC CONFLICTS IN ROMANIA: GETTING BEYOND THE MODEL OF 'THE LAST DROP'

1. http://lolodiklo.blogspot.com/2009_08_01_archive.html.
2. Research Report, 'Models of Ethnic Segregation. Rural Ghettos in Romania', prepared by Toma Stefánia, RIRNM, Cluj-Napoca, 2009.
3. Research Report, 'Kettős kisebbségben és konfliktuális helyzetben, a székelyföldi romák', Magyari Nándor László, Fosztó László, Koreck Mária, Toma Stefánia, financed by Open Society Institute (OSI-ZUG—B0092), June 2010.
4. 'Data-Base of Mass-media Monitoring Program: Ethnic Conflicts', developed by RIRNM, Cluj-Napoca, 2008–2010.
5. Besides 'conflict', another central term of our analysis might be 'collective sanctions' but, as we were interested first of all in the perception of certain events, we concentrated on 'conflict' because, in most cases, this was the predominant discursive element. Still, 'collective sanctions' are one constitutive element of the conflicts. See Daryl J. Levinson (2003).
6. Report of Council of Europe—Community and Ethnic Relations in Europe (1992), Building Romanian Democracy: The Police and Ethnic Minorities 1994–1998, Project on Ethnic Relations—Prevention of Violence and Discrimination Against the Roma in Central and Eastern Europe (1997), European Union Support of Roma Communities in Central and Eastern Europe (2000), Conflict interetnic in localitatea Sanmartin, jud. Hargita (Romani CRISS, 2010), p. 15.
7. Prevenirea si Rezolvarea Conflictelor Interetnice, Raport Final, 2002, CRCR, FSD and Dezvoltarea sprijinului local pentru interventii neutre in conflicte interetnice—raport final, 2004, Ambasada Statelor Unite ale Americii, FSD, Bucuresti, Aprilie, 2004, p. 8.
8. During this part of the research we built a mass-media portfolio drawn from

both Romanian and Hungarian sources, containing newspaper articles connected to the conflicts.

9. Shadow Report For the Committee on the Elimination of Racial Discrimination, Bucharest, 27 July 2010, Romani CRISS—Roma Centre for Social Interventions and Studies and Roma Civic Alliance of Romania, pp. 31–2.

10. Romani CRISS—Conflict interetnic in localitatea Sanmartin, jud. Harghita,
June 2010.

11. 'Shared Responsibilities—Common Risks', statement formulated at the working meeting in Targu Mures, 18 August 2009, organised by Divers Association,
Liga Pro Europa.

12. Draft report on Analysing Anti-Roma Violence in Hungary and Romania, prepared by Nicolae Gheorghe and Gergo Pulay, p. 2.

13. In another article, N. Gass (1994) presents a methodology to analyse present
and future crisis and conflict potential using a set of criteria including economic,
social, political and military conditions in a country. According to this study,
Romania showed a higher conflict potential in 1992 than Turkey, Hungary and
Slovakia. Making predictions for the year 1995, the conflict potential class of
Romania grew ahead of that for Estonia, Belarus, Iran and, again, Hungary and
Turkey.

14. A further argument for using the 2002 Census as our starting point was that
this would enable us to build in other variables using other sociological surveys
that draw on the same data. These include the list of Roma communities of
type MIDPROB (Roma communities with middle-level problems) and HIGH-
PROB (Roma communities with high-level problems) as classified in i) Dumitru Sandu's survey 'Roma Communities in Romania—A Map of community
Poverty based on the PROROMI Survey', ii) the LG Survey—Come Closer
and iii) a data-base of documented conflicts between Romanian Roma and
other groups constructed by the Institute for Research into National and Ethnic Minorities (ISPMN). We obtained 1387 valid responses.

15. As defined by Law 705/2001, the responsibilities of the social worker include
social assistance and social services interventions (which, in turn, include determination of family allowances, child, primary services and specialised services).
The results of a recent sociological survey presented in 'Come closer—Inclusion and Exclusion of Roma in the present-day Romanian Society' shows that
the most important income sources for the Roma population are maternity
allowance, child benefit and family allowances (for the 26.1 per cent of the
Roma population). In second place came the Minimum Guaranteed Income
(VMG) for 14.4 per cent of the Roma sample. If we look at the type of localities—urban vs. rural—the data does not change much.

16. We should say that we did not define 'traditional occupation' in the questionnaire so answers here may include day labouring, wood-collection or fruit-
harvesting.

17. In 65.9 per cent of the localities there is no community mediator; in 44.9 per cent of the localities there is no school mediator; in 40.1 per cent of the localities there is no health mediator; in 56.4 per cent of the localities there is no Roma councillor.

18. Minutes of the meeting of the Dialogue Commission in Sinmartin on 8 June 2009.

19. In this case the percentage represents all those who self-registered at the local council as Roma, even though only two persons self-declared as Roma in this community in the National Census of 2002—the majority self-reporting as Hungarian.

20. According to the categorisation model of Sandu, a community can be categorised thus—formally as MIDPROB—if it combines together two out of three indices concerning: accessibility (the geographical position of the community; modernised roads; vicinity of a garbage pit), infrastructure (water, electricity) and income type (guaranteed minimum income and other social benefits).

21. During the one hour meeting, the Hungarian members of the Commission for Dialogue in Sinmartin agreed to ask the following: that the horses of those Roma families who don't have enough agricultural land to supply the necessary food for these animals should be confiscated; the social benefits of those Roma families who own a horse should be ended, as a horse and cart represents an income generating resource; illegally constructed houses and shelters should be demolished; access to agricultural land should be forbidden as trespass, except for the owner, or other agricultural workers in the presence of the owner. In Sincrai the Commission formulated their proposed rules in eleven points. These 'requests' included compulsory education of the Roma children; that the swimming-pool be used only by those with proper hygiene; a demand for permanent 'civilised behaviour' and last, but not least, the Roma were asked to stop any further thefts in the locality. Each point had a built in deadline, though four were deemed to operate permanently.

22. Shadow Report for the Committee on the Elimination of Racial Discrimination, Bucharest, 27 July 2010, by Romani CRISS—Roma Centre for Social Interventions and Studies and Roma Civic Alliance of Romania, pp. 31–2.

23. As Lijphart argued, in plural societies, if one group represents the majority 'its leaders may attempt to dominate rather than cooperate with the rival minority' (1977: 55).

11. CUCUMBERS FIGHTING MIGRATIONS: THE CONTRIBUTION OF NGOS TO THE PERCEPTION OF TEMPORARY ROMANY MIGRATIONS FROM MEDOVCE-METETE/SLOVAKIA

1. This article is partly based on results from a study conducted as part of the research-project 'Contexts and Images of Transnational Romani Migration to Graz' (chaired

pp. [217–219]   NOTES

by Heidrun Zettelbauer) and the 'Research Focus on Migration' project (chaired by Sonja Pöllabauer and Heidrun Zettelbauer), both at the University of Graz and generously funded by the federal-state-foundation, 'Zukunftsfonds Steiermark'. We are very grateful for the huge effort from colleagues and friends; especially, we have to thank Nadine Blumer and Birgit Steinkellner for aiding us in sharpening ideas and reworking this paper. We especially want to thank Wolfgang Pucher, parish priest in Graz Eggenberg and Head of the Vinzigemeinschaft Eggenberg (the most important NGO engaged in Romany issues in Graz) who generously gave us access to his archives. Parts of this article or mentioned findings have already been published in: Stefan Benedik, 'Harming "Cultural Feelings". Images and Categorisation of Temporary Romani Migrants to Graz/Austria', in *Multi-disciplinary Approaches to Romany Studies*, Michael Stewart and Márton Rövid, eds., Budapest, 2010, pp. 71–90 and Stefan Benedik, 'Define the Migrant, Imagine the Menace. Remarks on Narratives of Recent Romani Migrations to Graz', in *Mapping Contemporary History II*, Helmut Konrad and Stefan Benedik, eds., Vienna and Cologne, 2010, pp. 159–176.

2. Medovce is the name of the village in Slovak and is always used in the Austrian media. As the village is located in the south of Slovakia, a significant Hungarian speaking minority lives there and most of the Roma and Romnija begging in Graz speak Hungarian rather than Slovak. Therefore they tend to use the Hungarian name of the village, which is Metete. Some of them do not even know the Slovak term Medovce.

3. For the associated understanding of culture see Benedik, 'Harming "Cultural Feelings"', pp. 81–2.

4. For instance, in the project 'Mapping Contemporary Roma Mobilities in the EU', currently being conducted at the University of Oxford.

5. For critical approaches, see e.g. María do Mar Castro Varela and Nikita Dhawan, 'Queer mobil? Heteronormativität und Migrationsforschung', in *Gender Mobil? Geschlecht und Migration in transnationalen Räumen*, Helma Lutz, ed., Münster, 2009, pp. 102–21; Forschungsgruppe Transit Migration, *Neue Perspektiven auf Migration an den Grenzen Europas*, Turbulent Ränder, ed., Bielefeld, 2007; Andrew Gorman-Murray, 'Rethinking Queer Migration Through the Body', in *Social & Cultural Geography*, vol. 8, no. 1, 2007, pp. 105–21.

6. Cf. Claudia Breger, *Ortlosigkeit des Fremden. 'Zigeunerinnen' und 'Zigeuner' in der deutschsprachigen Literatur um 1800*, (Cologne et al., 1998).

7. See e.g. Thomas Acton, 'Theorising obility. Migration, Nomadism, and the Social Reconstruction of Ethnicity', in *Romani mobilities in Europe. Multidisciplinary Perspectives*, Nando Sigona, ed., Oxford, 2010, pp. 5–10. http://romanimobilities.files.wordpress.com/2010/01/conference-proceedings.pdf, accessed 25 January 2010.

8. See e.g. Claude Cahn and Peter Vermeersch, 'The Group Expulsion of Slovak

340

Roma by the Belgian Government. A Case Study of the Treatment of Romani Refugees in Western Countries', in *Cambridge Review of International Affairs*, vol. 13, no. 2, 2000, pp. 71–82.

9. Central European Romani Migrations has gained interest especially in recent months, e.g. in the conference 'Romani Mobilities in Europe: Multidisciplinary Perspectives' at the University of Oxford. In the last years, while a relatively large number of publications have started to present case studies on central Europe, hardly any discussion on Romany migrations between places within this region has taken place. See e.g. David M. Crowe, 'The International and Historical Dimensions of Romani Migration', in *Nationalities Papers*, vol. 31, no. 1, 2003, pp. 81–94; Will Guy, *Roma migration in Europe. Case Studies*, Hamburg, 2004; Jíři Homoláč, 'Diskurz o migraci Romů na příkladu internetových diskusí', in *Sociologický časopis/Czech Sociological Review*, vol. 42, no. 2, 2006, pp. 329–349; Zdeněk Uherek, 'Roma Migration from Slovakia in the Context of European Migration Trends', in *Sociologický časopis/Czech Sociological Review*, vol. 43, no 4, 2007, pp. 747–74.

10. For an exception, see Nando Sigona, 'Locating "The Gypsy Problem". The Roma in Italy, Stereotyping, Labelling and "Nomad Camps"', in *Journal of Ethnic and Migration Studies*, vol. 31, no. 4, 2005, pp. 741–56.

11. There are, however, some notable exceptions. As a recent example, see Ilsen About, 'An Exclusion Process of Migrants. Control of Gypsies and Border Police in Western Europe, 1907–1914', http://cnrs.academia.edu/documents/0014/8946/About_2009_-_An_Exclusion_Process_of_Migrants.pdf, accessed 18 February 2010.

12. For an example of Roma and Romnija in 'non-ethnic' migrations, see Dieter Halwachs, 'Roma and Romani in Austria', Graz, 2004, http://romani.uni-graz.at/romani/download/files/ling_rom_at_e.pdf, accessed 12 April 2009. The othering of Roma and Romnija as 'ethno-tourists' reinforces this problematic aspect. See Imrich Vašečka and Michal Vašečka, 'Recent Romani Migration from Slovakia to EU Member States: Romani Reaction to Discrimination or Romani Ethno-Tourism?', in *Nationalities Papers*, vol. 31, no. 1, 2003, pp. 29–47.

13. Cf. Ruth Wodak and Theo van Leeuwen, 'Politische, rechtliche und bürokratische Legitimation von Einwanderungskontrolle. Eine diskurs-historische Analyse', in *Gegen-Rassismen, Konstruktionen, Interaktionen, Interventionen*, Brigitte Kossek, ed., Hamburg and Berlin, 1999, pp. 100–129.

14. One of the central features of these debates is that they are controversial, as one can see in the widely-discussed headscarf issue. See *Der Stoff aus dem Konflike sind. Debatten um das Kopftuch in Deutschland, Österreich und der Schweiz*, Sabine Berghahn and Petra Rostock, eds., Bielefeld, 2009.

15. Cf. Angelika Magiros, 'Biologie und Kultur. Foucaults Beitrag zur Analyse des "Rassismus ohne Rassen"', in *Gegen-Rassismen*, Kossek, ed., pp. 292–310.

16. Cf. Anne-Marie Fortier, 'Queer Diaspora', in *Handbook of Lesbian and Gay Studies*, Diane Richardson and Steven Seidman, eds., London and New Delhi, 2002, p. 183.

17. Cf. Benedik, 'Define the Migrant', p. 183.

18. See Habe Hunger, 'Kleine Zeitung', 24 March 1989; Die Bettlerin, 'Kleine Zeitung', 25 March 1989.

19. Cf. Walter Müller, 'Man will die Roma nicht', in *Der Standard*, 10 December 1996, p. 5.

20. See, for instance, Karic Zineta und ihre Kinder, 'Kleine Zeitung', 7 December 1996, p. 26.

21. For the Austrian example, see Halwachs, Roma.

22. See, for instance, Peter R. Swoboda, 'Stadt mit Bettlern', in *Kleine Zeitung*, 24 April 1993; Ute Pinter, 'Gegen die Menschenwürde', in *Kleine Zeitung*, 13 May 1993.

23. Cf. e.g. Helmut Griess, 'Fatales Signal', in *Neue Zeit*, 7 December 1996; Erwin Zankel, 'Maßvoll', in *Kleine Zeitung*, 1 December 1996; Walter Müller, 'Aufdringlichkeit kostet 3000 Schilling', in *Der Standard*, 7/8 December 1996, p. 5.

24. As an example for the expulsion-approach, see Wolfgang Pucher, 'Karic Zineta und ihre Kinder', in *Kleine Zeitung*, 7 December 1996, p. 26.

25. 'Es spricht sich schon herum dass Alfred Stingl. & Co. die Grazer Altstadt mit organisierter Bettelei beleben', advertisment of FPÖ (extreme-right party of the then vice-mayor and second head of the town council), in *Steirerkrone*, 8 November 1997.

26. 'Rossmann [FPÖ-member of town council]… fühlt sich in ihrem Bestreben bestärkt, für ein "bettlerfreies" Graz zu kämpfen… es herrschen "indische Verhältnisse", was die Bettelei betrifft', Dem Bettlerproblem endlich Herr werden, in *Grazer Woche*, 14 April 1999.

27. 'Diese Auswüchse der Kriminalität und des Menschenhandels sind in einem Rechtsstaat nicht duldbar', BZÖ-Grosz: Bleiben bei Bekämpfung der organisierten Bettlerkriminalität in Graz hat. Organisierte Bettlerbanden treiben wieder fröhliche Urstände in Graz, in *APA-OTS*, 13 October 2006.

28. Cf. Steirischer SPÖ Landtagsklub schwenkt auf sektorales Bettelverbot ein, in *Kleine Zeitung Online*, 3 February 2010, http://neu.kleinezeitung.at/steiermark/2283421/steirischer-spoe-landtagsklub-schwenkt-sektorales-bettelverbot-ein.story.

29. Cf. Bettelverbot gefordert, in *Die Woche*, 10 January 2010, p. 4.

30. 'Roma in Graz sind keine organisierten Bettler!', in *Steirerkrone*, 24 May 2006, p. 26.

31. Johanna Bierbaum, Bettlerstudie: 'Ich sehe jetz die Roma mit anderen Augen', in *Kleine Zeitung*, 19 December 2006.

32. This is also indicated by the press reports and comments on the ban, all of them calling the beggars Roma. See, for instance, Roma-Vorsitzender: 'Eine Schande für ganz Österreich', in *Kleine Zeitung*, 11 December 1996; 'Grenzziehung an kultureller Reibungsfläche', *Steirische Wochenpost*, 12 December 1996, p. 15; Bernd Weiss, 'Die Bettlerverordnung von Graz. Ein liberales Vorbild', in *Kleine Zeitung*, 21 December 1996, p. 20.

33. See, for instance, footnote 23. Further 'Grenzziehung an kultureller Reibungsfläche', in *Die Steirische Wochenpost*, 12 December 1996.

34. See 'Diese Bettler-Verordnung muss noch heuer kommen', in *Kleine Zeitung*, 9 November 1996.

35. See e.g. Harald Klöckl, 'Sandler und Bettler in Graz: neuer Vorstoß', in *Die Woche*, June 1996, p. 8; 'Graz: Sandler und Bettler erregen die Politgemüter', in *Kleine Zeitung*, 31 August 1995; Stephan Hilbert, 'Bei Diskussion über Sandler mischten die Betroffenen mit', in *Neue Zeit* 19 October 1995; 'Kein Gesetz gegen Bettler und Sandler', in *Neue Zeit*, 6 November 1996, p. 6.

36. See ibid. '"Sandler-Diskussion": Heftige Reaktionen', in *Neue Zeit*, 20 June 1996.

37. See e.g. Harald Klöckl, 'Sandler und Bettler in Graz: neuer Vorstoß', in *Die Woche*, June 1996, p. 8.

38. See e.g. Harald Klöckl, 'Sandler und Bettler in Graz: neuer Vorstoß', in *Die Woche*, June 1996, p. 8.

39. 'das Bettler- Sandler- und Zigeuner-Problem'. W.M., Sichere Stadt mit 'Hilfe' für die Sandler, Bettler, Zigeuner, in *Steirerkrone*, 18 June 1996.

40. We cite just two examples for this common combination: 'Four beggars from abroad, among them children, sat in Herrengasse-Street, their hands raised'. ('Vier ausländische Bettler, dabei auch Kinder, saßen mit hocherhobenen Händen in der Herrengasse'), Christian Weniger, 'Aktion scharf' vertrieb Bettler aus der Innenstadt, in *Kleine Zeitung*, 19 November 1996, p. 24: 'If I say I want to liberate Herrengasse-Street from beggars from abroad…' ('Wenn ich sage, ich will die Herrengasse von den ausländischen Bettlern befreien…'), Diese Bettler-Verordnung muß noch heuer kommen, in *Kleine Zeitung*, 9 November 1996.

41. All these and other countries of origin arose in discussions about the Romany groups migrating to Graz. See Peter Filzwieser, 'Bettler nächtigten in einer Pension', in *Kleine Zeitung*, 7 December 1996; Peter Gnam, 'Die SPÖ unter Druck: Schwärme von Bettlern suchten Graz heim', in *Neue Kronen Zeitung*, 5 December 1996.

42. Wolfgang Pucher, 'Wir verkraften Bettlerkinder', in *Neue Zeit*, 26 November 1996; Wolfgang Pucher, 'Offener Brief an den Bürgermeister', in *Salzburger Nachrichten*, 28 November 1996.

43. Rieger, Barbara, *Roma und Sinti in Österreich nach 1945. Die Ausgrenzung einer Minderheit als Prozeß*, Frankfurt: 2003.

44. e.g. Peter Gnam. 'Die SPÖ unter Druck: Schwärme von Bettlernsuchten Graz heim', in *Steirerkrone*, 5 December 1996.

45. The renowned tabloid *Neue Kronen Zeitung* played a leading role in coining a synonymic connection between Roma and Romnija and 'Zigeuner'. See ibid. Further, Johannes Kübeck, 'Zwei Wege, damit weniger Roma in der Stadt betteln', in *Kleine Zeitung*, 1 July 1999. This discourse lives on not only among conservative and right-wing intellectuals (see Thomas Chorherr, Merk's Wien: Heut' spielen s'den Romabaron, in *Die Presse*, 12 April 2010) who refused to acknowledge the insulting and racist character of the term 'Zigeuner'.

46. Cf. Susanne Haydvogel, 'Rechtzeitig vor Weihnacht' ein wirklich sauberes Graz', in *Kleine Zeitung*, 5 December 1996, p. 31; Peter Filzwieser, 'Bettler verschwunden', in *Kleine Zeitung*, 7 December 1996.

47. Peter Filzwieser, 'Keine Arbeit', in *Kleine Zeitung*, 10 December 1995.

48. This term hardly ever appeared on its own, but frequently in the form of 'Slovakian Roma'. For an exception, see 'Modell für Slowaken', in *Kleine Zeitung*, 29 April 1998.

49. Gerhard Fetka, 'Gebettelt wird ums Überleben', in *Neue Zeit*, 9 March 1997, pp. 12–13.

50. Miss Jauernig, 'Bettler wollen kein Essen', in *Grazer Woche*, 7 April 1999. In fact, the claim that all beggars must have come from Medovce-Metete was publicly doubted. The critics were mostly as superficial as the generalisation they were attacking, suggesting that none of the beggars actually hailed from Slovakia. Apparently a localisation within the 'East' is no warranty as long as the 'East' is something vague and indefinite. One of the attachés of the Austrian Embassy in Bratislava even suggested that the beggars in Graz might possibly come from Romania. Viktor A. Schneider, 'Die perfekt organisierte Bettelei', in *Die Presse*, 23/24 May 1998.

51. Bernd Hecke, 'Menschen in Hostice im "wunschlosen Unglück"', in *Kleine Zeitung*, 17 July 1999.

52. Graz natives who would pass as 'ethnically white' in other circumstances, were labelled with the ethnicised term 'organised beggars' as soon as they were part of visible mendicancy in Graz. See picture and caption in *Steirerkrone*, 16 December 2006.

53. Rudolf Sarközi quoted in *Roma-Vorsitzender*: 'Eine Schande für ganz Österreich', in *Kleine Zeitung*, 11 December 1996.

54. Bernd Hecke, 'Menschen in Hostice im "wunschlosen Unglück"', in *Kleine Zeitung*, 17 July 1999.

55. Christoph Thanei, 'Die Roma gelten in der Slowakei als arbeitsscheu', in *Die Presse*, 10 July 1999.

56. 'V Hosticiach budú cestoviny vyrábať prevažne rómske ženy', http://www.mecem.sk/rpa/?id=press&lang=slovak&show=8344, 25 March 2008.

57. 'Rakúsko: Farár Pucher pomáha Rómom zo slovenskej obce Hostice', https://www.rnlweb.org/~rnlwebor/modules.php?name=News&file=article&sid=11706, 12 June 2008.

58. 'Štajersko úspešne pomáha Rómom z východoslovenskej obce Hostice', http://2004.rnlweb.org/modules.php?name=News&file=article&sid=1176, 23 July 2004.

59. The most 'infamous' Romany settlements suffering high rates of unemployment, poverty and social exclusion are located in the eastern part of Slovakia.

60. 'Hostice a Graz', http://plus7dni.pluska.sk/plus7dni/vsimli-sme-si/hostice-a-graz.html, 6 April 2007.

61. 'Hostice a Graz', http://plus7dni.pluska.sk/plus7dni/vsimli-sme-si/hostice-a-graz.html, 06 April 2007.

62. http://www.government.gov.sk/15014/splnomocnenkyna-vlady-slovenskej-republiky-pre-romske-komunity-sa-stretla-so-starostami-obci-okresu-rimavska-sobota.php

63. 'Štajersko úspešne pomáha Rómom z východoslovenskej obce Hostice', http://2004.rnlweb.org/modules.php?name=News&file=article&sid=1176, 23 July 2004.

64. This remark is based on the experience of Barbara Tiefenbacher, who was working within an EU-financed programme for one year in a Romany settlment in Slovakia.

65. 'Rakúsko: Farár Pucher pomáha Rómom zo slovenskej obce Hostice', https://www.rnlweb.org/~rnlwebor/modules.php?name=News&file=article&sid=117 06, 12 June 2008.

66. For example, Czech Roma and Romnija who were asking in Canada for asylum (due to racist discrimination in their home country) are made responsible for the re-introduction of visa by the Canadian state for Czech citizens. See f.i.: Fallout from Canadian Visa dispute continues, http://www.praguepost.com/news/1767-fallout-from-canadian-visa-dispute-continues.html, 22 July 2009.

67. Note from 'funkydapp,' http://www.sme.sk/diskusie/1199896/1/5758327/V-Hosticiach-budu-cestoviny-vyrabat-romske-zeny.html#5758327.

68. For particularly notable exceptions, see Paloma Gay y Blasco, *Gypsies in Madrid. Sex, Gender, and the Performance of Identity*, Oxford: 1999; Shannon Woodcock, 'The Ţigan is not a man. The Ţigan Other as catalyst for Romanian ethnonational identity', PhD-thesis, Sydney: 2005.

69. Cf. do Mar Castro Varela and Dhawan, p. 102.

70. Wolfgang Pucher, Karic Zineta und ihre Kinder, in *Kleine Zeitung*, 7 December 1996, p. 26; Müller, Aufdringlichkeit; Walter Müller, 'Man will die Roma nicht', in *Der Standard*, 10 December 1996, p. 5.

71. Werner Miedel, member of the Graz town council at the time, described the situation as follows: 'Because it violates the cultural feelings of the Graz popu-

lation, and also because women and children are being exploited' ('Weil es das kulturelle Gefühl der Grazer verletzt und Frauen und Kinder ausgebeutet werden'), 'Diese Bettler-Verordnung muß noch heuer kommen', in *Kleine Zeitung*, 9 November 1996.

72. Cf. Christina Ho, 'Migration as Feminisation? Chinese Women's Experiences of Work and Family in Australia', in *Journal of Ethnic and Migration Studies*, vol. 32, no. 3, 2006, pp. 497–514.

73. Heide Hoschek, 'Unerträgliche Bettelei', in *Kleine Zeitung*, 13 July 2006.

74. 'Graz, die Stadt der Bettler. Die Vielzahl der vor allem in der Innenstadt [...] sitzenden [...] Bettler sorgt zunehmend für Unmut. Es stört einfach das Straßenbild und in derart geballter Form findet man Bettler kaum in einer anderen Stadt', vojo [i.e. Vojo Radkovic?]: Graz hat ein Bettelverbot, in *Grazer im Bild*, 14 April 2006. See also, Karl Heinz Klammer, 'Bettlerunwesen', in *Steirerkrone*, 22 January 2008.

75. Frau Jauernig, 'Bettler wollen kein Essen', in *Grazer Woche*, 7 April 1999.

76. See e.g. Wolfgang Maget, 'Bettlerjagd. FP blieb mit ihrem Antrag allein', in *Neue Zeit*, 17 April 1998.

77. See e.g. Werner Miedl, 'Das Betteln der Kinder verbieten', in *Kleine Zeitung*, 1 November 1996; Susanne Haydvogel, 'Rechtzeitig vor Weihnacht' ein wirklich sauberes Graz', in *Kleine Zeitung*, 5 December 1996, p. 31; Alfred Stingl, 'Die Antwort', in *Kleine Zeitung*, 3 December 1996; Peter Gnam, 'Die SPÖ unter Druck', in *Steirerkrone*, 5 December 1996.

78. Cf. Ludwig Laher, *Und nehmen was kommt*, Innsbruck: 2007, p. 13.

79. Cf. Karl Markus Gauß, *Die Hundeesser von Svinia*, Munich: 2008, pp. 39–40.

80. Cf. Nora Gresch and Leila Hadj-Abdou, 'Selige Musliminnen oder marginalisierte Migrantinnen? Das österreichische Paradox der geringen Teilhabe von Kopftuchträgerinnen bei "toleranter" Kopftuchpolitik', in *Stoff*, Berghahn and Rostock, eds., pp. 73–100.

81. See for the general model Leonore Davidoff, 'Gender and the "Great Divide". Public and Private in British Gender History', in *Journal of Women's History*, vol. 15, no. 1, 2003, pp. 11–27.

82. 'In Graz gibt's nur noch wirkliche Obdachlose', in *Kleine Zeitung*, November 1996.

83. Walter Müller, 'Man will die Roma nicht', in *Der Standard*, 10 December 1996, p. 5.

84. See www.vinzi.at.

85. Cf. Gerhard Fetka, 'Gebettelt wird ums Überleben', in *Neue Zeit*, 9 March 1997, pp. 12–13.

86. Cf. Graz hat's, 'Jetzt kommt "VIP-Klub" für Bettler', in *der neue Grazer*, 20 March 1997, p. 1.

87. Cf. Walter Müller, 'Keine Anzeichen organisierter Bettelei', in *Der Standard*,

22/23 March 1997. See also, Hilde Böhm, 'Die Bettler: Kriminelle oder Arme?', in *Megaphon*, May 1997, pp. 4–5.

88. Cf. '"VIP_Cards" für City-Bettler', in *der neue Grazer*, 20 March 1997, p. 4.

89. See Johann A. Bauer, 'Stumm auf dem Boden', in *Sonntagsblatt*, 6 April 1996, pp. 8–9.

90. Cf. Gabriele Grössbauer, 'Zum Leserbrief 'Stadt mit Bettlern' vom 24 April 1993', in *Kleine Zeitung*, 1 May 1993. See also, Wolfgang Pucher, 'Auf Kosten der Gestrandeten', in *Kleine Zeitung*, September 1995. 'We have enough money, time and ideas for everything, but for our children. They are not lacking anything in material goods but in a familial feeling of security and in company on their way to a meaningful live' [Für alles haben wir Geld, Zeit und Ideen. Nur nicht für die eigenen Kinder. Es fehlt ihnen nicht an materiellen Gütern, wohl aber an familiärer Geborgenheit und Begleitung in ein sinnerfülltes Leben]. See also, Rainer Seebacher, 'Es ist der Hunger der sie zu uns treibt', in *Kleine Zeitung*, 19 March 1997. 'The beggars are a daily accusation that we are living beyond our means' [Die Bettler sind eine tägliche Anklage, dass wir über unsere Verhältnisse leben].

91. Cf. Elke Jauk, 'Stadt will Bettlerproblem an der Wurzel anpacken', in *Kleine Zeitung*, 21 May 1999.

92. Cf. Sechs Monate, 'Geld für Roma', in *Kleine Zeitung*, 3 July 1999.

93. Cf. Gertrud Strasser, David Pesendorfer, 'Stadt Graz zahlt Bettlern 3.500S Monatsgehalt!', in *täglich Alles*, 4 July 1999. Further Reinhold Tscherne, 'Bei Zuzug weiterer Bettler droht nun die Abschiebung', in *Kleine Zeitung*, 6 July 1999; Elisabeth Holzer, 'Stadt Graz holt bettelnde Menschen von der Straße', in *Kurier*, 6 July 1999; Martin Behr, 'Graz: Disput um Bettler', in *Salzburger Nachrichten*, 7 July 1999; Walter Müller, 'Kein "Gehalt für Bettler"', in *Der Standard*, 7 July 1999; Ernst Sittinger, '"Angst" vor Taschengeld. Bettler flüchteten aus Graz', in *Die Presse*, 7 July 1999.

94. Cf., for instance, letter from Herbert K., Archive Wolfgang Pucher (AWP), 15 July 1999; letter from Anonymous, AWP, 16 July 1999.

95. Cf. Letter from Wolfgang L., AWP, 21 July 1999.

96. Cf. Fax from Anonymous, AWP, 21 July 1999.

97. Cf. Letter Karoline P., AWP, 22 July 1999.

98. Cf. Letter Anonymous (Eine empörte Grazerin), AWP, undated.

99. Cf. Fax from Anonymous, AWP, 21 July 1999.

100. 'Roma sind Europäer', in http://volksgruppen.orf.at/radio1476/stories/72875/, accessed 9 September 2010.

101. See: http://www.direkthilferoma.at/verein/spenden, accessed 9 September 2010.

102. BEHR, A. Dieter, 'Soli-Zwischennutzung' in *Ottakring*, in http://www.uni-vie.ac.at/unique/unique/index.php/schwerpunkt/196–0902/1949-soli-zwischennutzung-in-ottakring, accessed 9 September 2010.

103. 'Thema' 'Gib der Armut das Gurkerl' broadcast on September 28 2009 on ORF 2, see http://programm.orf.at/?story=5712, accessed 9 September 2010.

104. Projekt 'Gurken', in http://www.direkthilferoma.at/projekte and http://www.direkthilferoma.at/verein/gurken, accessed 9 September 2010.

105. Kulturprojekte, in http://www.direkthilferoma.at/projekte, und http://www.direkthilferoma.at/kontakt, accessed 9 September 2010.

106. Gauß, *Hundeesser.*

12. POSSIBLE RESPONSES TO THE SWEEP OF RIGHT-WING FORCES AND ANTI-GYPSYISM IN HUNGARY

1. The paper is based on the following sources: i) field research in two rural communities in Hungary facing tensions between Roma and non-Roma, on the eve of the 2009 EP-elections; ii) media coverage of the politicisation of tensions between Roma and non-Roma in Hungary; iii) interviews with the leaders of the MCF Roma Alliance Party and the National Gypsy Council (Országos Cigány Önkormányzat).

2. EUMAP (2001), *Monitoring the EU Accession Process: Minority Protection, Report 2001*, Budapest: Open Society Institute (OSI).

3. According to the *Központi Statisztikai Hivatal* (KSH) [Central Statistical Office (CSO)], the proportion of foreigners is 1.7 per cent of the whole population living in Hungary, among them a large proportion of ethnic Hungarians, coming from neighbouring countries. For details on the methods of measuring migrant population in Hungary: Hárs, Á (2009) 'A harmadik országokból Magyarországon tartózkodó külföldi állampolgárok a statisztikai adatok tükrében', in *Bevándorlók Magyarországon, Az MTA Etnikai-nemzeti Kisebbségkutató Intézet ICCR Budapest Alapítvány által végzett kutatás zárótanulmányai*, Budapest: MTA-ENKI—ICCR, p. 28.

4. évi LXXVII. törvény a nemzeti és etnikai kisebbségek jogairól, 1993.

5. See András László Pap, 'Minority Rights and Diaspora Claims. Collision, Interdependence and Loss of Orientation', in *Beyond Sovereignty: From Status Law to Transnational Citizenship?*, Slavic Eurasian Studies no. 9, Osamu Ieda et al., eds., pp. 243–54, Sapporo: Hokkaido University—Slavic Research Center, 2006.

6. István Kemény, 'A magyarországi cigány népesség demográfiája' (The Demography of the Roma Population in Hungary), *Demográfia*, no. 3–4, 2004, p. 343.

7. Currently, the Total Fertility Rate (TRF) of Hungarian women is approximately 1.3. Source: Hungarian Central Statistical Office (KSH), http://portal.ksh.hu/pls/ksh/docs/hun/xstadat/xstadat_eves/tabl1_01ia.html.

8. Kemény, István and Béla Janky, 'Roma Population of Hungary, 1971–2003', in *Roma of Hungary*, István Kemény, ed., East European Monographs, no. 702, New York: Columbia University Press, 2005.

NOTES pp. [242–245]

9. MTI (2009), 'Progresszív Intézet: erősen negatív viszony a cigánysághoz', in *Népszabadság*, 3 May 2009, http://www.nol.hu/belfold/progressziv_intezet__erosen_negativ_viszony_a_ciganysaghoz.

10. See http://www.tarki.hu/kozvelemeny/kitekint/20060201.html.

11. 'Ombudsmantársai is bírálják a 'cigánybűnözést' emlegető Szabó Mátét. Hét jogvédő szervezet is tiltakozik, az állampolgári jogok biztosának lemondását követelve', in *Népszabadság*, 3 April 2009, http://www.nol.hu/belfold/a_tobbi_ombudsman_is_biralja_a__ciganybunozest__emlegeto_szabo_matet.

12. 'Sólyom László veszélyt lát az ombudsman nyilatkozataiban', in *Népszabadság*, 8 April 2009, http://www.nol.hu/belfold/solyom_laszlo_veszelyt_lat_az_ombudsman_nyilatkozataiban.

13. Bódisz, A., 'Szigorú ítélet az olaszliszkai perben', in *Népszabadság*, 29 May 2009, http://nol.hu/belfold/szigoru_itelet_az_olaszliszkai_perben.

14. MTI, 'Fidesz: Kolompár kérjen bocsánatot a "gyerekcsíny" miatt', in *Népszabadság*, 5 May 2009, http://www.nol.hu/belfold/fidesz__kolompar_kerjen_bocsanatot_a__gyerekcsiny__miatt.

15. MTI, 'Kiskunlacházi gyilkosság: "Nem kérek bocsánatot!"', in *Heti Válasz*, 26 June 2009, http://hetivalasz.hu/cikk/0906/kiskunlachaza_polgarmester.

16. Lívia Jároka is a delegate of the centre-right Fidesz party, and is member of the European People's Party group of the European Parliament.

17. 'A jövő csak együtt képzelhető el: Magyarként, cigányként és anyaként is megrendüléssel értesültem a tragédiáról és külön fájdalom, hogy a kegyetlen elkövetők cigányok voltak. Marian Cozmát cigányok ölték meg, de nem 'a' cigányok', 12 February 2009, http://jarokalivia.hu/hu/cikk/188/.

18. Szilvia Varró, 'A Jobbik mint harmadik erő. II.—A tiszták' (The 'Jobbik' Party as the Third Power, Part 2—The Clean Ones), *Magyar Narancs*, vol. 21, no. 7, 12 February 2009, p. 10: 'Politikai jártasságuk felülmúlja kortársaikét, különösen érdeklődnek a történelem iránt, megmozgatja őket a határon túli magyarok ügye, cigányellenes és részint antiszemita nézeteket vallanak. A Jobbik-hoz csatlakozó fiatalokat a párt politikai érintetlensége, misztikus nacionalizmusa, szókimondása és a párton belüli közösség vonzza elsősorban'.

19. The national result of Jobbik was 14.77 per cent (with 427,773 valid votes).

20. http://www.europarl.europa.eu/parliament/archive/elections2009/hu/hungary_hu.html.

21. Gyula Rafael, Head of the Pest County Unit of the MCF Roma Alliance Party (he is also an associate member of the National Gypsy Minority Self-Government, responsible for the cooperation with the police).

22. 'MCF: roma szavazatokkal a Jobbik ellen', in *HVG*, 3 June 2009, http://hvg.hu/itthon/20090603_mcf_jobbik_magyar_garda_ifj_bogdan_janos.aspx.

23. Lívia Jároka (mentioned above), who was elected for the second time to the EP in 2009.

24. Magyar Gárda.

25. Ferenc Szlazsánszky, 'A gárda hívásra házhoz megy' (Hungarian Guard for Home Delivery), *Hetek*, vol. 12, no. 30, 25 July 2008, http://epa.oszk.hu/00800/00804/00543/68659.html.

26. Ferenc Szlazsánszky, 'A gárda hívásra házhoz megy' (Hungarian Guard for Home Delivery), *Hetek*, vol. 12, no. 30, 25 July 2008, http://epa.oszk.hu/00800/00804/00543/68659.html: 'Vannak olyan települések, ahol a lakosság nagy része élhetetlennek érzi az életét, és segélykérést ad'.

27. MAZSIHISZ—Magyar Zsidó Hitközségek Szövetsége.

28. OCÖ—Országos Cigány Önkormányzat.

29. Magyarok Világszövetsége.

30. Magyar Gárda Mozgalom.

31. Hungary/Fővárosi Ítélőtábla/5.Pf.20.738/2009/7, 2 July 2009.

32. 'Győzött a józan ész, a demokrácia, a cigányság és az egész ország', see NOL, 'Jogerősen feloszlatták a Magyar Gárda Egyesületet', in *Népszabadság*, 2 July 2009, http://www.nol.hu/belfold/jogerosen_oszolj_a_magyar_garda_egyesuletnek.

33. UN Convention on the Elimination of All Form of Discrimination Against Women.

34. MCF Roma Összefogás Párt.

35. 'Arra szólítom fel a roma társadalmat, hogy tegye félre a pártpolitikai és egyéb kötődését, és fogjon össze a hazai cigányság érdekeiért, és egy önvédelmi mozgalom megszervezésében vegyen részt. Mutassuk meg, hogy erősek vagyunk, és ha úgy adódik, akkor meg tudjuk védeni magunkat!'

36. Vera Messing, 'Egymásnak kiszolgáltatva. Interetnikus konfliktusok és a média' (At the Mercy of Each Other. Interethnic Conflicts and the Media), in *Kisebbségek kisebbsége. A magyarországi cigányok emberi és politikai jogai* (Minority of Minorities. Human Rights and Political Rights of the Roma in Hungary), Mária Neményi and Júlia Szalai, eds., pp. 316–52 (Budapest: Új Mandátum Könyvkiadó, 2005).

37. Zsaru-info (2009), 'Galgagyörktől Debrecenig', *Zsaru Rendőrségi Magazin*, no. 35, pp. 10–13, http://www.zsaru.hu/modules.php?name=News&file=article&sid=2648.

38. Király, A (2009), 'Jól illik a romák elleni támadások gyanúsítottjaira a rendőrségi profil', in *Index*, 25 August 2010, http://index.hu/bulvar/2009/08/25/jol_illik_a_romak_elleni_tamadasok_gyanusitottjaira_a_rendorsegi_profil.

39. EÖKK (2009), *Cigánynak lenni Magyarországon, Jelentés 2008*, Budapest: Európai Összehasonlító Kisebbségkutatások Közalapítvány, p. 218.

40. Ibid, p. 219.

41. Ibid, p. 219.

42. Ibid, p. 221.

43. Ibid, p. 221.

44. Pethő, A., '"A származásunk miatt történt"—riport a tatárszentgyörgyi gyilkosságról', in *Origo*, 23 February 2009, http://www.origo.hu/itthon/20090224-tatarszentgyorgy-gyilkossag-helyszini-riport.html.

45. EÖKK (2009), *Cigánynak lenni Magyarországon, Jelentés 2008*, Budapest: Európai Összehasonlító Kisebbségkutatások Közalapítvány, p. 232.

46. Origo /Független Hírügynökség, 'Petárdának hitték a kislétai lövéseket', in *Origo*, 3 August 2009, http://www.origo.hu/itthon/20090803-beszamolok-a-kisletai-gyilkossagrol.html.

47. Munk, Veronika, 'Kőkemény bizonyítékok a romagyilkosok ellen', *Index*, 9 August 2010, http://index.hu/bulvar/2010/08/09/romagyilkossagok.

48. Gyula Rafael (mentioned above), Head of the Pest County Unit of the MCF Roma Alliance Party (he is also an associate member of the National Gypsy Minority Self-Government, responsible for cooperation with the police).

49. Origo, 'Több kamerát, több rendőrt akar a kormány, in *Origo*, 7 September 2009, http://www.origo.hu/itthon/20090907-rend-es-biztonsag-tizpontos-koz-biztonsagi-intezkedescsomagot-hirdetett-bajnai-gordon.html.

50. V.J., 'Elfelejtett településőrök', *Népszava*, 14 July 2010, http://www.nepszava.hu/articles/article.php?id=323205.

51. OBMB—Országos Bűnmegelőzési Bizottság.

52. See http://www.bunmegelozes.hu/index.html?pid=1555.

53. The actual empirical research was based mainly on semi-structured interviews but, in certain cases, informal conversations served better the purpose of the research. In the case of Verőce, I contacted the following actors: the leader of the crime prevention project (living in Budapest), three local coordinators, the mayor of the village, an officer of the municipality, the vice principal of the local elementary school, a local Roma leader, two Roma political leaders from Pest County, and a relative of one of the non-Roma participants of a violent incident (fighting between Roma and non-Roma). As for the Nagybörzsöny case, I spoke with the leader and coordinators of the project (non-locals), with local volunteers of the project, with the mayor of the village, with the chief of the civil police guard, with a representative of the Gypsy self-government, and with local youngsters.

54. According to the figures provided by the mayor of the village, the population was 795 (19 May 2009).

55. M. Ferenc, Horváth, *Nagybörzsöny* (Nagybörzsöny), Száz magyar falu könyvesháza (Library of Hundred Hungarian Villages), NKÖEOK, 2007, http://www.sulinet.hu/oroksegtar/data/100_falu/Nagyborzsony/index.htm, '... kiváló példája annak, miként éltek Magyarország területén évezredek óta a különféle nemzetiségű és nyelvet beszélő népek egymás mellett. S ha közös életük nem is volt mindig békés, arról legtöbbször nem ők tehettek: idegen hódító

népek, a nagypolitika és a tehetségtelen, felettük hatalmaskodó helyi vezetés sokszor beleszólt az életükbe háborúk, vallási türelmetlenség, kitelepítések formájában, s ezek mindig felszínre hozták, felerősítették az emberi gyengeségeket, a meg nem értést és a mássággal szembeni türelmetlenséget'.

56. 'Gyüttment'.

57. See M. Ferenc, Horváth, *Nagybörzsöny* (Nagybörzsöny), Száz magyar falu könyvesháza (Library of Hundred Hungarian Villages), NKÖEOK, 2007, http://www.sulinet.hu/oroksegtar/data/100_falu/Nagyborzsony/index.htm.

58. Foresee Kutatócsoport Nonprofit Közhasznú Kft, 'Bűnmegelőzés és konfliktuskezelés alternatív utakon—Modellprogram Nagybörzsönyben' (Crime prevention and conflict management on new ways—Pilot programme in Nagybörzsöny), Jogi Fórum, 1 April 2009, http://www.jogiforum.hu/hirek/20280.

59. Nagybörzsöny Község Önkormányzata, Nagybörzsönyi Cigány Kisebbségi Önkormányzat, Nagybörzsönyi Német Kisebbségi Önkormányzat, Nagybörzsönyi Polgárőr Egyesület, Tegyünk Együtt Nagybörzsönyért Egyesület, Börzsönyvidéki Bölcsőde, Óvoda, Általános Iskola, Alapfokú Művészetoktatási és Egységes Gyógypedagógiai és Módszertani Intézmény tagintézménye, Másság Alapítvány, Nemzeti és Etnikai Kisebbségi Jogvédő Iroda, Közösségfejlesztők Egyesülete—Közösségi Kezdeményezéseket Támogató Szakmai hálózat, Prim-Rose Kiadó, Tanácsadó és Kulturális Szolgáltató Kft.

60. NEKI—Nemzeti és Etnikai Kisebbségi Jogvédő Iroda.

61. '*Néhány óra alatt sikerült elfogni a Nagybörzsönyben történt emberölés elkövetőjét. Bravúros gyorsasággal fogták el a zsaruk a tegnap délután, nagybörzsönyi házában holtan talált férfi gyilkosát. 2009. június 8-án saját lánya találta holtan édesapját, K. A. 54 éves nagybörzsönyi lakost. A házból az elkövető készpénzt, egyéb értéktárgyakat tulajdonított el*', (PMRFK).

62. Blikk, 10 June 2009.

63. http://barikad.hu/node/30698 2009.06.08, http://szentkoronaradio.com/belfold/2009_06_09_brutalisan-meggyilkoltak-egy-erdeszt-a-ciganyok.

64. According to the data provided by the mayor of the village on 10 May 2009.

65. Albert Wass (1908–1998), Hungarian novelist, born in Transylvania.

66. László Rab, 'Verőce, a szobrok faluja', (Verőce, the village of statues), *Népszabadság*, 24 January 2006, http://www.nol.hu/archivum/archiv-391722.

67. Jegyzőkönyv Verőce Község Képviselő-Testülete által tartott Falugyűlésről, 3 December 2008, 19:04.

68. Paul R. Brass, *Theft of an Idol. Text and Context in the Representation of Collective Violence*, Princeton Studies in Culture, Power, History, Princeton: Princeton University Press, 1997, p.4.

69. 'Good Practices in Building Police-Public Partnerships by the Senior Police Adviser to the OSCE Secretary General', OSCE, May 2008, http://www.osce.org/spmu/item_11_31851.html; 'Guidebook on Democratic Policing by the

Senior Police Adviser to the OSCE Secretary General', OSCE, 24 January 2007, http://www.osce.org/spmu/item_11_23086.html; 'Police and Roma and Sinti: Good Practices in Building Trust and Understanding', OSCE, April 2010, http://polis.osce.org/library/details?doc_id=3682; 'HCNM Recommendations on Policing in Multi-Ethnic Societies', February 2006, http://www.osce.org/documents/hcnm/2006/02/17982_en.pdf.

70. Organisation for Security and Co-operation in Europe, Office for Democratic Institutions and Human Rights (2010): *Addressing Violence, Promoting Integration. Field Assessment of Violent Incidents against Roma in Hungary: Key Developments, Findings and Recommendations*, June-July 2009, Warsaw: OSCE-ODIHR, 15 June 2010, pp. 32–5, http://www.osce.org/documents/odihr/2010/06/44569_en.pdf.

71. Benedek Gabriella, 'Szakmai beszámoló az Országos Bűnmegelőzési Bizottság által kiírt pályázat keretében megvalósított bűnmegelőzési modellprojektről' (1307/2008/OBMB sz. szerződés), Budapest, 2009. május 29. 11. o. http://foresee.hu/uploads/media/OBMB_Szakmaibeszamolo_Foresee_copy.pdf.

13. STRATEGIES FOR COMBATING RIGHT-WING POPULISM AND RACISM: STEPS TOWARDS A PLURALIST AND HUMANE EUROPE

1. The strategy recommendations are mainly based on the study 'Bertelsmann Stiftung (ed.): Strategies for Combating Right-Wing Extremism in Europe. Gütersloh 2009', and on its predecessor study, 'Bertelsmann Stiftung/Bertelsmann Forschungsgruppe Politik (CAP) (ed.): Strategien gegen Rechtsextremismus, Bd. 1, Gütersloh 2005; Georgi, Viola/Hartmann, Hauke/Schellenberg, Britta/Seberich, Michael (ed.): Strategien gegen Rechtsextremismus, Band 2, Gütersloh 2005'. To provide comparability of the eleven country reports (Austria, Belgium, Denmark, Germany, Hungary, France, Great Britain, Italy, Netherlands, Sweden and Switzerland) the analyses draw upon a detailed guideline. The study is based on the definition of right-wing radicalism by Michael Minkenberg. Cf. Minkenberg, Michael: Die neue radikale Rechte im Vergleich. USA, Frankreich, Deutschland, Opladen/Wiesbaden, 1998.

2. Cf. the eleven country reports of the study, *Strategies for Combating Right-Wing Extremism in Europe*, edited by Bertelsmann Foundation, Gütersloh: 2009, pp. 29–530.

3. A list of the actors of the radical right (political parties, social movement organisations and sub-cultural milieu) of selected European countries can be found in Britta Schellenberg, 'Dispersion and Differentiation: The Structure and Trends of the Radical Right in Europe', pp. 534–536, in *Strategies for Combating Right-Wing Extremism in Europe*, Bertelsmann Stiftung, ed., Gütersloh: 2009, pp. 531–546.

4. For example, in some countries there are anti-racism laws, in others there is legislation against NS-symbolism.

5. Cf. ibid., especially, Damir Skenderovic/Vera Sperisen, *Country Report Switzerland*, pp. 480–87, pp. 463–530.

6. Meret, Susi, *Country Report Denmark, in: Strategies for Combating Right-Wing Extremism*, Gütersloh: 2009, pp. 81–126.

7. Cf. On the danger of the (populist) right and counter-strategies see Orkan Kösemen, 'Strategies against the Radical Right in Europe', pp. 550–52, in *Strategies for Combating Right-Wing Extremism*, Bertelsmann Stiftung, ed., Gütersloh: 2009, pp. 547–58. For detail on the single countries, see Meret, 2009, pp. 81–126, esp.: 82–88 and 99–115; Anton Pelinka: 'Country Report Austria', in ibid., pp. 29–58; Juliane Wetzel: 'Country Report Italy', in ibid., pp. 327–74.

8. Swyngedouw, Marc, 'Country Report Belgium', in *Strategies for Combating Right-Wing Extremism*, Gütersloh: 2009, pp. 59–80, in particular: 69f.

9. On the main topics of the radical right in detail, Schellenberg, Britta, 'Themen, Trends und Gegenstrategien', in Holger Spöhr/Sarah Kolls (Hrsg.), *Rechtsextremismus in Deutschland und Europa*, Frankfurt am Main: 2009 (im Erscheinen).

10. Hartmut von Hentig, *Die Menschen stärken, die Sachen klären*, Stuttgart: 1985.

11. On the media's approach to right-wing populism and racism, deficits and recommendation, see Schellenberg, Britta, 'Rechtsextremismus und Medien', in *Aus Politik und Zeitgeschichte* (APuZ), H.42, 2005, pp. 39–45, http://www.bpb.de/publikationen/6TZNUC.html, 30 December 2008.

12. www.cij.hu (16 December 2008). Cf. Bayer, Jószef: 'Country Report Hungary', in Bertelsmann Stiftung (ed.), *Strategies for Combating Right-Wing Extremism*, Gütersloh: 2009, p. 321f., pp. 285–326.

13. Cf. Wolfgang Benz (ed.), *Legenden, Lügen, Vorurteile. Ein Wörterbuch zur Zeitgeschichte*, München 8, Auflage Januar 1996; Klaus-Peter Hufer, *Argumente am Stammtisch. Erfolgreich gegen Parolen*, Palaver und Populismus, Schwalbach: 2006.

14. http://www.hopenothate.org.uk/, accessed 16 December 2008. Cf. Christopher Husbands, 'Country Report Great Britain', *Strategies for Combating Right-Wing Extremism*, Gütersloh: 2009, w. 275–77, pp. 249–84.

15. Cf. Schellenberg, 2009a, p. 236.

16. Cf. Pelinka, Anton, 'Country Report Austria', in Bertelsmann Stiftung (ed.), *Strategies for Combating Right-Wing Extremism*, Bertelsmann Stiftung, ed., Gütersloh: 2009, p. 43f., pp. 29–58.

17. In more detail, cf. Britta Schellenberg: Strategien gegen Rechtsextremismus in Deutschland. Analyse der Gesetzgebung und Umsetzung des Rechtp. C A P Analyse, München 2008.

18. Lööw, Hélene, 'Country Report Sweden', in Bertelsmann Stiftung (Hrsg.), *Strategies for Combating Right-Wing Extremism*, Gütersloh: 2009, p. 451f., pp. 425–62.

19. Froukje Demant,Willem Wagenaar,Jaap van Donselaar, *Racism & Extremism Monitor. Deradicalisation in Practice*, Anne Frank House: 2009. http://www.annefrank.org/content.asp?PID=909&LID=2 (15 July 2009).

20. Schellenberg, Britta, 'Country Report Germany', p. 208, in Bertelsmann Stiftung (Hrsg.), *Strategies for Combating Right-Wing Extremism*, Gütersloh: 2009a, pp. 179–248.

21. Korgel describes goals and demands for a 'local action plan' in Lorenz Korgel, 'Zivilgesellschaftliche Gegenwehr stärken: Gemeinwesenentwicklung und (Re) Demokratisierung des öffentlichen Raums', p. 255f., in *Handbuch für die kommunale Auseinandersetzung mit dem Rechtsextremismus. Friedrich-Ebert Stiftung*, Molthagen, Dietmar and Korgel Lorenz, eds., Berlin: 2009, pp. 251–67.

22. Cf. http://www.menschenrechte.nuernberg.de/admin/uploads/files/Rex-Handlungsprogramm.pdf, accessed 15 August 2009.

23. Cf. Demant/Wagenaar/Donselaar, 2009.

24. Cf. www.radar.nl/read/rotterdam_rijnmond, accessed 16 December 2008.

25. Schriemer, Rita: The Nationwide Network of Local and Regional Anti-Discrimination Agencies in the Netherlands. Case Study for the European Monitoring Centre on Racism and Xenophobia (EUMC), October 2002; Van Donselaar,Jaap/Wagenaar,Willem: Country Report Netherlands, in *Strategies for Combating Right-Wing Extremism*, Bertelsmann Stiftung, ed., Gütersloh 2009, pp.375–424.

26. www.opferperspektive.de; Cf.Schellenberg, 2009a, p.236.

27. Cf. Damir Skenderovic/Vera Sperisen: Country Report Switzerland, in *Strategies for Combating Right-Wing Extremism in Europe*, Bertelsmann Stiftung, ed., Gütersloh 2009, pp.463–530; http://d102352.u28.netvp.ch/bfr/bfr_index.asp?lang=d, accessed 15 December 2008.

28. A good example is a citizenship law that (also) consists of the *jus soli*, another example is protection of discrimination regulated by law. Cf. in detail for the German situation: Schellenberg, 2008, p. 7f.

29. Cf. In detail, Britta Schellenberg, 'Dispersion and Differentiation: The Structures and Trends of the Radical Right in Europe', p. 542, in *Strategies for Combating Right-Wing Extremism in Europe*, Bertelsmann Stiftung, ed., Gütersloh: 2009, pp. 531–46.

30. Klaus Wahl/Martina Ottinger-Gaßebner/Corinna Kleinert/Susann-Viola Renninger, 'Entwicklungs- und Sozialisationsbedingungen für Toleranz', pp. 106–10, in *Strategien gegen Rechtsextremismus*, Bertelsmann Stiftung/Bertelsmann Forschungsgruppe Politik (CAP), eds., Bd.1, Gütersloh: 2005, pp. 16–179. Cf. Jean-Yves Camus, 'Country Report France', in *Strategies for Combating Right-Wing Extremism*, Bertelsmann Stiftung, ed., Gütersloh: 2009, pp. 157f., pp. 127–78.

31. Cf. Jean-Yves Camus, 'Country Report France', in *Strategies for Combating*

Right-Wing Extremism, Bertelsmann Stiftung, ed., Gütersloh: 2009, p. 157f., pp. 127–78.

32. Cf. Schellenberg, 2009a, p. 221.
33. Cf. Hauke Hartmann/Britta Schellenberg, 'Strategien gegen Rechtsextremismus: Ergebnisse und Handlungsfelder', p. 27f., in *Strategien gegen Rechtsextremismus*, Georgi, Hartmann, Seberich, Schellenberg, eds., Bd. 2, Gütersloh: 2005, pp. 23–31 (16–41). In detail, Albert Scherr/Ulrike Hormel, 'Bildung für die Einwanderungsgesellschaft', in *Strategien gegen Rechtsextremismus*, Bertelsmann Stiftung/Bertelsmann Forschungsgruppe Politik (CAP), eds., Bd.1, Gütersloh: 2005, pp. 80–145.
34. Cf. In detail, Klaus Wahl et al., 2005, p. 64ff.
35. Cf. Lööw, 2009, p. 450.
36. Cf. Camus, 2009, p. 156f.
37. Schellenberg, 2009a, p. 203f.

14. HIDDEN POTENTIALS IN 'NAMING THE GYPSY': THE TRANSFORMATION OF THE GYPSY-HUNGARIAN DISTINCTION

1. The Sasoj and Balogh families are introduced in chapter 7. They are two of the dominant families among the Gypsies in this community.
2. The name of a famous television talent show.
3. Between July 2008 and August 2009, a group of Hungarian extremists, engaged in a systematic racist rampage, killed six Roma in villages in Hungary. At the time of going to press four men are still on trial.
4. This event, known as *lomtalanítás*, is held in all Hungarian municipalities on certain pre-ordained days in the year.

15. DOGMATISM, HYPOCRISY AND THE INADEQUACY OF LEGAL AND SOCIAL RESPONSES COMBATING HATE CRIMES AND EXTREMISM: THE CEE EXPERIENCE

1. Senior Research Fellow, Hungarian Academy of Sciences Institute for Legal Studies, Associate Professor, Eötvös University (ELTE) Faculty of Humanities, Department of Media and Communication, Recurrent Visiting Professor, Central European University Nationalism Studies Program, Member, Hungarian Helsinki Committee, pap@jog.mta.hu. The paper was written under the aegis of the Bolyai Research Scholarship of the Hungarian Academy of Sciences as part of the 68361 OTKA Research Grant.
2. See, for example, http://www.monstersandcritics.com/news/europe/news/article_1494257.php/Sixth-Roma-murder-victim-laid-to-rest, or http://www.time.com/time/world/article/0,8599,1895255,00.html.

3. According to a survey by the pollster institute, Századveg-Forsense, published in March 2009, Hungarians are more pessimistic then ever. The value of the 'comfort index' showed an all-time low (of 18), http://www.szazadveg.hu/kutatas/archivum/kozvelemeny-kutatas-es-partreferencia-elemzes/soha-nem-ereztuk-meg-ennyire-rosszul-magunkat-131.html. Also see *Eurobarometer 63, Public opinion in the European Union*, p. 11, http://ec.europa.eu/public_opinion/archives/eb/eb63/eb63_en.pdf.

4. Act 3 of 1989.

5. See http://helsinki.hu/Friss_anyagok/htmls/614.

6. http://nol.hu/archivum/archiv-100606.

7. http://hvg.hu/itthon/20090903_walter_rudolf_hess_tomcat http://szentkoronaradio.com/belfold/2009_09_03_tomcat-es-domokos-endre-janos-megemlekezese-walter-rudolf-hessrol.

8. For a more elaborate analysis, see András László Pap: 'Human Rights and Ethnic Data Collection in Hungary', *Human Rights Review*, vol. 9, issue 1, March 2008, pp. 109–22.

9. The law, of course, does not prohibit the anonymous collection of census data and the law can, in principle, prescribe other circumstances when ethnic data can be collected.

10. In cases of indirect discrimination not only the ethnicity of the plaintiff(s) but also of the comparator(s) must be established. The latter may prove an insurmountable task. See Lilla Farkas (2004), 'The Monkey That Does Not See', *Roma Rights Quarterly*, 2004.

11. Before 1 February 2009, the name of the offence governed by the Article 174/B of the Criminal Code was 'violence against a member of a national, ethnic, racial or religious group'. As a result of Act No. 79 of 2008 (amending certain acts with a view to protecting order and the operation of justice) Article 174/B of the Criminal Code was extended to cover any group of the population; the name of the offence was also modified to 'violence against a member of a community'.

12. In addition, Article 269 of the Criminal Code involves a sub-paragraph on the ban of using totalitarian symbols (269/B—as a result of the amendment in 1993), and a sub-paragraph (269/C) on the ban of denying, doubting, or trivialising genocide or crimes against humanity committed by totalitarian regimes (269/C). The latter sub-paragraph originally dealt only with holocaust denial (it came into force in February 2010). A few months later, as a result of a legislative initiative of the newly elected Hungarian government, this sub-paragraph was amended: from July 2010—in order to cover the 'EU framework decision on combating racism and xenophobia', 2008/913/JHA—269/C is extended to the crimes of both 'national socialist' and 'communist regimes', and the term 'holocaust' is no longer there in the text.

13. Source: Unified Police and Prosecution Statistical Database.
14. For earlier years, the statistics were as follows: incitement against community cases registered: 1999: 3, 2000: 8, 2001: 12, 2002: 5, and 2003: 11. This meant that the following number of offenders had been identified and indicted: 1999: 9, 2000: 12, 2001: 9, 2002: 5, 2003: 9, and in 2004: eleven identified from which eight indicted. According to official statistics, in 2003 two people were indicted and two convicted under Article 174/B; in 2004, the numbers were eight and six, respectively. In 2007, in cases of 'violence against a member of an ethnic, national etc. group' charges were only filed in six cases, and only nine crimes became known to the public out of the twenty recorded. (In five instances, the complaints were turned down, and in eight cases the investigation was declared closed.) The thirty-four allegations of 'hate crimes' resulted in only one charge being filed, and eight acknowledged felonies being added to the record. (In sixteen cases the complaints were turned down, and the investigation declared closed in another sixteen.) In 2008, 'violence against a member of an ethnic, national etc. group' was reported to the authorities in even fewer, only thirteen, cases of, out of which eight cases resulted in prosecution; twenty-four cases of 'incitement against community' were reported, from which only one prosecution resulted. In 2009, the number of reported cases of 'violence against…' increased to twenty-three, out of which seven cases resulted in prosecution. The number of reported cases of 'incitement against community' doubled to forty-eight in this year compared to the previous year, from the forty-eight cases, three cases were considered as offences, but only one prosecution emerged.
15. The Data Protection Act differentiates the concept of sensitive data within the category of personal data. This sensitive data constitutes a type of personal data referring to an essential trait and thus a vulnerable part of the subject's personal identity, which is therefore given a special degree of protection by law. Of course, not all personal data is sensitive in nature; the notion is restricted to those categories that are expressly listed by the Act. The Act divides sensitive data into two groups depending on the level of special protection accorded to them. On the one hand, we have data pertaining to race, national and ethnic minority background, political opinion or affiliation, religious or other philosophical beliefs, and membership in advocacy organisations; on the other hand, there is data that is related to health, pathological addiction, sexual orientation, and criminal record. Article 2 clause 2.
16. László Majtényi, Iván Székely and Máté Dániel Szabó (2006), *Roma támogatások és jogosultságok egyéni követésének lehetőségei* (Possibilities for tracing individual Roma subsidies and entitlements), Budapest: Eötvös Károly Institute, p. 10.
17. http://tasz.hu/hu/informacioszabadsag/33 (in Hungarian).
18. See, for example http://www.hirszerzo.hu/cikk.hunvald-ugy_ki_verte_at_a_kiraly_utca_15_lakoit.97638.html.

19. Article 16.

20. http://egyenlobanasmod.hu/data/2009tevekenyseg_szamok_tukreben.pdf.

21. Organisation for Security and Co-operation in Europea, Office for Democratic Institutions and Human Rights, *Addressing Violence, Promoting Integration. Field Assessment of Violent Incidents against Roma in Hungary: Key Developments, Findings and Recommendations*, June-July 2009, Warsaw: OSCE-ODIHR, 15 June 2010, pp. 32–5, http://www.osce.org/documents/odihr/2010/06/44569_en. pdf.

22. The full name of the organisation is: Hungarian Guard Association for the Protection of Tradition and Culture ('Magyar Gárda Hagyományőrző és Kulturális Egyesület'). It was registered as a cultural organisation aiming to 'prepare the youth spiritually and physically for extraordinary situations that might require the mobilization of the people'.

23. One example is the statement by Csanád Szegedi, MEP, Jobbik on 21 November 2009: 'The unfortunate and tragic Gypsy terror in Sajóbábony proved that the parties of the parliament have eroded the police and the law-enforcement bodies to such a degree that they are unable to protect the Hungarian population from Gypsy criminality. Contrary to the information provided by the media, the truth is that Gypsy criminals have attacked peaceful Hungarian citizens yet again. The issue today is not only the isolated actions of Gypsy criminals in different settlements but, unfortunately, we have to say, the fact that the Gypsies and the parliamentary parties are terrorizing the Hungarian population in North-Hungary. The Movement for a Better Hungary calls on the national heads of the police to—even if it means using extraordinary measures—stop the Gypsy terror in Sajóbábony too. If the police that have been waiting for taxpayers' money are unable to carry out its job it has the duty to co-operate with the New Hungarian Guard Movement. The gendarmeries of the New Hungarian Guard are ready—with the necessary legal authorization—to restore public order in Hungary'. 'A *Jobbik* fellép a tomboló a cigányterrorral szemben' (Jobbik Steps Up against the Frantic Gypsy Terror), http://zuglo. *Jobbik*.hu/a_ *Jobbik*_fellep_a_tombolo_a_ciganyterrorral_szemben.

24. http://valasztas.hu/hu/parval2010/index.html.

25. Organisation for Security and Co-operation in Europea, Office for Democratic Institutions and Human Rights, *Addressing Violence, Promoting Integration. Field Assessment of Violent Incidents against Roma in Hungary: Key Developments, Findings and Recommendations*, June-July 2009, Warsaw: OSCE-ODIHR, 15 June 2010, pp. 32–5, http://www.osce.org/documents/odihr/2010/06/44569_en. pdf.

26. http://www.economist.com/blogs/easternapproaches/2010/06/hungary_3.

27. 'Esélyt a Hátrányos Helyzetű Gyerekeknek Alapítvány' (CFCF).

28. Judgement No. 6P. 20.341/2006/50.

29. Based on the litigation documents and the kind personal account of Ms. Lilla Farkas, counsel for the plaintiff.

30. Article 5 (2).

31. Ferenc Kőszeg and Lorna Králik, (2008), *Control(led) Group. Final Report on the Strategies for Effective Police Stop and Search (STEPSS) Project*, Budapest: Hungarian Helsinki Committee.

REFERENCES

About, I. (2004), 'Les fondations d'un système national d'identification policière en France (1893–1914). Anthropométrie, signalements et fichiers', *Genèses*, 54, pp. 28–52.

—————— (2010), 'De la libre circulation au contrôle permanent. Les autorités françaises face aux mobilités tsiganes transfrontalières, 1860–1930', *Cultures & Conflits*, 76, pp. 15–37.

About, I., Denis, V. (2010), *Histoire de l'identification des personnes*, Paris, La Découverte.

Amnesty International (2009), 'Attacks against Roma communities are unacceptable and must be stopped', Amnesty International UK Press Release, 17 June, http://www.amnesty.org.uk/news_details.asp?NewsID=18258.

—————— (2009), 'Returning Roma face catalogue of human rights violations at home', Amnesty International UK Press Release, 23 June 2009, http://www.amnesty.org.uk/news_details.asp?NewsID=18273.

André, P. (2010), 'Entretien avec Olivier Legros. Les Roms jouent un rôle de bouc émissaire dans un contexte de crise', *Libération*, 21 July 2010.

Arqué, G. (1936), 'Sur toutes les routes de France les nomades ont reçu hier la visite des gendarmes. *Le Petit Parisien*, 16 January, 1936.

Arsac, H. (1933), *La Loi du 16 juillet 1912 sur l'exercice des professions ambulantes et la réglementation de la circulation des nomades, ses causes, ses précédents, sa portée et son application pratique*, Thèse de droit, Lyon: Bosc frères, M. et L. Riou.

Anderson, Benedict (1993) (1991 2ⁿᵈ edition), *Imagined Communities: Reflections on the Origins and Spread of Nationalism*, London: Verso.

Ashton, E. (2009), 'PSNI "knew little" about Roma community', *The Belfast Telegraph*,9July,http://www.belfasttelegraph.co.uk/news/local-national/psni-lsquoknew-little-about-roma-community-14392932.html.

Asséo, H. (2010), 'Le nomadisme sans frontières est un mythe politique', in *Le Monde* Magazine, 6 September.

—————— (2002), 'La gendarmerie et l'identification des "nomades" (1870–1914)', in J.N. Luc (ed.), *Gendarmerie, État et Société au XIXe siècle*, Paris: Publications de la Sorbonne, pp. 301–11.

——— (2007a), 'L'invention des "nomades" en Europe au XXe siècle et la nationalisation impossible des Tsiganes', in G. Noiriel (ed.), *L'identification des personnes. Genèse d'un travail d'État*, Paris: Belin, pp. 161–80.

——— (2007b), 'Pourquoi tant de haine? L'intolérance administrative à l'égard des Tsiganes de la fin du XIXème siècle à la veille de la deuxième guerre mondiale', *Diasporas. Histoires et sociétés*, 10, pp. 50–67.

Asséo H. (1999). 'La perception des Tsiganes en France et en Allemagne, 1870–1930', in A. Gueslin, D. Kalifa (eds.), Les exclus en Europe, 1830–1930, Paris, Éditions de l'Atelier, 221–33.

——— (1974). 'Le traitement administratif des Bohémiens: marginalité et exclusion', in R. Mandrou (ed.), Problèmes socio-culturels en France au XVIIe siècle, Paris, Klincksieck, 9–87.

Aubin, E. (1996), 'La liberté d'aller et venir des nomades: l'idéologie sécuritaire', *Études tsiganes*, 7, pp. 13–36.

——— (2000), 'L'évolution du droit français applicable aux Tsiganes: les quatre logiques du législateur républicain', *Études tsiganes*, 15, pp. 26–56.

Bagean, J. (2008), 'Life in the Post-Political Age', *Counterpunch*, 24 July, http://www.counterpunch.org/bageant07242008.html.

Bale, Timothy (2003) 'Cinderella and Her Ugly Sisters: The Mainstream and Extreme Right in Europe's Bipolarizing Party Systems', in *West European Politics*, 26 (3), pp. 67–90.

Balogh, Lídia (2009), 'Etnikai adatok kezelése a magyarországi sajtóban' (Ethnic Data Processing in the Hungarian Press), *Föld-Rész*, 2 (3–4), pp. 81–91.

Bateson, Gregory, (1972), *Steps to an Ecology of Mind: Collected Essays in Anthropology, Psychiatry, Evolution, and Epistemology*, Chicago: University of Chicago Press.

Bakalova, Maria (2000), 'Nationalism and Non-Confrontation in Bulgarian Transition Politics', unpublished MA Thesis, Department of Nationalism Studies, Central European University, Budapest.

Bartos, Otomar J., Wehr, Paul. (2002), *Using Conflict Theory*, Cambridge: Cambridge University Press.

Bauman, Z. (2004), *Wasted Lives: Modernity and its Outcasts*, Cambridge: Polity.

——— (2006), *Liquid Fear*, Cambridge: Polity.

BBC News Online (2009), 'Leaders Meet Romanian Ambassador', BBC News Online, 18 June, http://news.bbc.co.uk/1/hi/northern_ireland/8107435.stm.

——— (2009), '"Lessons learned" on Race Attacks', BBC News Online, 24 June, http://news.bbc.co.uk/1/hi/northern_ireland/8116102.stm.

——— (2009), 'Roma's Exit "More Than Racism"', BBC News Online, 9 July, http://news.bbc.co.uk/1/hi/northern_ireland/8141759.stm.

——— (2009), 'Hard Times for Roma Who Fled Belfast', BBC News Online, 9 July, http://news.bbc.co.uk/1/hi/northern_ireland/8143368.stm.

———— (2009), 'Anti-Racists "Fed NI Race Crisis"', BBC News Online, 16 July, http://news.bbc.co.uk/1/hi/northern_ireland/8153386.stm.

———— (2009), 'Youth to Face Race Attack Charges', BBC News Online, 21 July, http://news.bbc.co.uk/1/hi/northern_ireland/8160367.stm.

———— (2009), 'Roma Return After City Attack', BBC News Online, 6 August, http://news.bbc.co.uk/1/hi/northern_ireland/8186496.stm.

Belfast Telegraph, (2009), 'Roma Threat Accused Gets Ban', *The Belfast Telegraph*, 25 July, http://www.belfasttelegraph.co.uk/news/local-national/roma-threat-accused-gets-ban-14430646.html.

———— (2009), 'Roma Return Welcomed', *The Belfast Telegraph*, 12 August, http://www.belfasttelegraph.co.uk/community-telegraph/south-belfast/news/roma-return-welcomed-14450469.html.

Benedek, Gabriella (2009), *Szakmai beszámoló az Országos Bűnmegelőzési Bizottság által kiírt pályázat keretében megvalósított bűnmegelőzési modellprojektről, 1307/2008/OBMB sz. szerződés* (Final Report on the Crime Prevention Model Project, contract no. 1307/2008/OBMB, implemented within the framework of the programme of the Hungarian National Crime Prevention Committee), Budapest, http://foresee.hu/uploads/media/OBMB_Szakmaibeszamolo_Foresee_copy.pdf.

Berezin, Mabel (2009), *Illiberal Politics in Neoliberal Times: Culture, Security, and Populism in the New Europe*, Cambridge: Cambridge University Press.

———— (2009), 'Events as Templates of Possibility: An Analytic Typology of Political Facts', workshop paper, http://www.soc.cornell.edu/faculty/berezin.html.

———— (2009), *Events as Templates of Possibility: An Analytic Typology of Political Facts*, http://www.soc.cornell.edu/faculty/berezin/BerezinEventsasTemplatesFinal.pdf.

Berlière, J.M. (2004), '"Armer les pouvoirs publics contre un fléau social"? La République et les nomades (1880–1914)', *Études tsiganes*, pp. 18–19, pp. 52–64.

Betz, Hans-Georg (1993), 'The New Politics of Resentment: Radical Right-Wing Populist Parties in Western Europe', *Comparative Politics*, 25, pp. 413–27.

BIS (2009), *Annual report 2008*, Prague: BIS (Czech Security Information Service), http://www.bis.cz/n/2009–08–31-vyrocni-zprava-2008.html.

Bonacich, Edna (1973), 'A Theory of Middlemen Minorities', in *American Sociological Review*, 38 (5), October, pp. 583–94.

Bonillo, M. (2001), *'Zigeunerpolitik' im deutschen Kaiserreich, 1871–1918*, Frankfurt am Main: Peter Lang.

Bornemann, John and Fowler, Nick (1997), 'Europeanization', in *Annual Review of Anthropology*, 26, pp. 487–514.

Brah, Avtar (1996), *Cartographies of Diaspora: Contesting identities*, London and New York: Routledge.

Brass, Paul R. (1997), *Theft of an Idol. Text and Context in the Representation of*

Collective Violence, Princeton Studies in Culture, Power, History, Princeton: Princeton University Press.

Bravi, L. (2009), *Tra inclusione ed esclusione. Una storia sociale dell'educazione di rom e sinti*, Milan: Unicopli.

———— and N. Sigona (2007) 'Educazione e rieducazione nei campi nomadi: una storia', *Studi Emigrazione*, 43 (164), pp. 857–74.

Brubaker, Rogers; Laitin, David, D. (1998), 'Ethnic and Nationalist Violence', in *Annual Review of Sociology*, 24, pp. 423–52.

Canut, C. (ed.) (2011), 'L'exemple des Roms / Les Roms, pour l'exemple', *Lignes*, p. 34.

Cartayrade, C. (2008), 'Gouverner la police: Commissaires cantonaux et gendarmes du Puy-de-Dôme au début du Second Empire', in D. Kalifa, P. Karila-Cohen (eds.), *Le commissaire de police au XIXe siècle*, Paris: Publications de la Sorbonne, pp. 123–38.

Čopjaková, Kateřina (2009), *Proč jsou tak úspěšní: Neonacisté ohlásili útok na veřejný prostor* (Why are they so successful: Neo-nazis announced the attack on the public space), Praha: Respekt 18 , 27 April.

Charles, Christophe (2010), 'Peut-on écrire une histoire de la culture européenne à l'époque contemporaine?', in *Annales*, 65 (5), pp. 1207–21.

Challier, F. (1913), *La nouvelle loi sur la circulation des nomades. Loi du 16 juillet 1912*, Paris: Librairie de jurisprudence.

Chatelain, A. (1976), *Les migrants temporaires en France de 1800 à 1914. Histoire économique et sociale des migrants temporaires des campagnes françaises au XIXe siècle et au début du XXe siècle*, Villeneuve-d'Ascq: Université de Lille III.

Caulier, A. (2008), 'S'adapter au temps et à l'espace. Le maillage policier dans le département du Nord sous le Second Empire', in J.-M. Berlière, D. Kalifa, V. Milliot, C. Denys (eds.), *Métiers de police. Être policiers en Europe, XVIIIe-XXe siècle*, Rennes: Presses universitaires de Rennes, pp. 333–44.

Clej, P. (2009), 'NI Romanians Face Uncertain Future', BBC News Online, 24 June, http://news.bbc.co.uk/1/hi/uk/8116063.stm.

Clough Marinaro, I. (2003), 'Integration or marginalization? The Failures of Social Policy for the Roma in Rome', *Modern Italy*, 8(2), pp. 203–18.

Colacicchi, P. (1996), 'Rom a Firenze', in *L'urbanistica del disprezzo. Campi nomadi esocietà italiana*, ed. Piero Brunello, Rome: Manifestolibri (2008), 'Ethnic Profiling and Discrimination against Roma in Italy: New Developments in a Deep-Rooted Tradition', *Roma Rights* 2: 35–44.

Collins, M. (2009), 'An Assault on Us All', *Searchlight*, 410, August, http://www.searchlightmagazine.com/index.php?link=template&story=289.

Consiglio Regionale della Toscana (1987), *Consultazione della IV commissione sulla proposta di legge n. 175: Interventi per la tutela dell'etnia rom.* [Typescript].

Coupain, N. (2003), 'L'expulsion des étrangers en Belgique (1830–1914)', *Revue belge d'histoire contemporaine*, 33, pp. 1–2, pp. 5–48.

REFERENCES

Cross Rhythms (2009), 'The Vals say no to racism with Belfast gig', 1 July 2009, http://www.crossrhythms.co.uk/articles/news/No_To_Racism/36691/p1/.

Cutts, David, Ford, Robert and Goodwin, Mathew. J. (2011), 'Anti-Immigrant, Politically Disaffected or Still Racist After All? Examining the Attitudinal Drivers of Extreme Right Support in Britain in the 2009 European Elections', in *European Journal of Political Research*, 50 (3), pp. 418–40.

Dahrendorf, Ralf (1959), *Class and Class Conflict in Industrial Society*, Stanford CA: Stanford University Press.

David, F. (1907), 'Interpellation sur les mesures que compte prendre M. le Président du Conseil, ministre de l'Intérieur, pour assurer la sécurité dans nos campagnes et mettre fin aux incursions de Romanichels qui infestent notre territoire', *Journal officiel de la République française. Chambre des députés*, 29 October 1907, pp. 1973–74.

Davis, Natalie Zemon (1973), 'The Rites of Violence: Religious Riots in Sixteenth Century France', *Past and Present*, 59 (May), pp. 53–91.

Delclitte, C., (1995), 'La catégorie «nomade» dans la loi de 1912', *Hommes & migrations*, 1188–1189, Juin-Juillet, pp. 23–30.

Deutsch, Karl (1966), *Nationalism and Social Communication. An Inquiry into the Foundation of Nationality*, Cambridge, MA: Technology Press; John Wiley&Sons.

Dornel, L. (2004), *La France hostile. Socio-histoire de la xénophobie (1870–1914)*, Paris: Hachette.

Dupont, P. (1913), 'La loi du 16 juillet 1912 sur les Nomades', *Lois Nouvelles. Revue de législation et de jurisprudence*, pp. 73–128.

Edemariam, A. (2009), 'Unhappy Return: Fear and Loathing Await Fugitives from Belfast Racism', *The Guardian*, 26 June, http://www.guardian.co.uk/world/2009/jun/26/race-attacks-on-belfast-roma.

Efremova, Georgia (2008), 'Noble Nationalism in a Modern Age? The Case of the Bulgarian National Guard', unpublished MA Thesis, Department of Nationalism Studies, Central European University, Budapest.

Egger, F. (1982), 'Der Bundesstaat und die fremden Zigeuner in der Zeit von 1848 bis 1914', *Studien und Quellen*, 8, pp. 49–74.

Ékes, I. (2007), 'The Hungarian Economy and Labour Market', *Ecostat*, http://www.gpn.org/data/hungary/hungary-analysis.pdf.

eNewsWire (2009), 'Hindus and Jews Demand Public Apology from Northern Ireland Government for Attack', eNewsWire, 29 June, http://www.enewswire.co.uk/2009/06/29/hindus-jews-demand-public-apology-northern-ireland-government-racist-attacks/.

EÖKK (2009), *Cigánynak lenni Magyarországo:, Jelentés 2008* (To be Gypsy in Hungary: Jelentés, 2008), Budapest: Európai Összehasonlító Kisebbségkutatások Közalapítvány.

Equality Commission for Northern Ireland (2009), *Equality Awareness Survey,*

REFERENCES

2008, Belfast: Equality Commission for Northern Ireland, http://www.equalityni.org/archive/pdf/ECSurvey2008.pdf.

ERRC (European Roma Rights Centre) (2000), *Campland. Racial segregation of Roma in Italy*. http://www.errc.org/db/00/0F/m0000000F.pdf, accessed August 2009.

EUMAP (2001), *Monitoring the EU Accession Process: Minority Protection, Report 2001*, Budapest: Open Society Institute.

Farkas, Lilla (2004), 'The Monkey That Does Not See', *Roma Rights Quarterly*, 2.

Fassin, Eric (2011), 'National identities and transnational intimacies: sexual democracy and the problem of immigration in Europe', in *Public Culture*, 22 (3), pp. 492–505.

Fearon, James, D. and Laitin, David (1996), 'Explaining Interethnic Cooperation', in *American Political Science Review*, 90 (4) (December), pp. 715–35.

Filhol, E., Hubert M.-C. (2009), *Les Tsiganes en France. Un sort à part, 1939–1946*, Paris: Perrin.

——— (2004), *Un camp de concentration français. Les Tsiganes alsaciens-lorrains à Crest, 1915–1919*, Grenoble: Presses Universitaires de Grenoble.

——— (2006), 'Les Tsiganes en France: du contrôle à la répression (1895–1946)', *Revue trimestrielle des droits de l'Homme*, 17 (68), pp. 989–1008.

——— (2007), 'La loi de 1912 sur la circulation des "nomades" (Tsiganes) en France', *Revue européenne des migrations internationales*, 23 (2), pp. 135–58.

——— (2010), 'La France contre ses Tsiganes', *La Vie des idées*, http://www.laviedesidees.fr/La-France-contre-ses-Tsiganes.html.

Fleck Gábor; Rughiniş, Cosima (eds.) (2008), *Come Closer—Inclusion and Exclusion of Roma in Present-Day Romanian Society*, Bucharest: Human Dynamics.

Fombaron, J.C. (1989), 'Les expulsions de Bohémiens au col de Saales en 1901–1902', *L'Essor*, 144, pp. 2–4.

Forbes, H.D. (1997), *Ethnic Conflict. Commerce, Culture, and the Contact Hypothesis*, New Haven & London: Yale University Press.

Fox, R. (2009), 'The plight of Europe's Roma', *The Guardian*, 22 June 2009, http://www.guardian.co.uk/commentisfree/2009/jun/22/roma-europe-discrimination-attacks.

Furnivall, John Sydenham (1948), *Colonial Policy and Practice*, London: Cambridge University Press.

GAC (2006), *Analysis of Socially Excluded Roma Localities and Absorption Capacity of Subjects Involved in This Field*, Prague: MPSV (The Ministry of Labour and Social Affairs).

Galbraith, J.K. (1993), *The Culture of Contentment* (new edition) London: Penguin.

Gilligan, C. (2009), 'Northern Ireland: The Capital of 'Race Hate'?' *Spiked*, 18 June, http://www.spiked-online.com/index.php/site/article/7043/.

Garavelli, D. (2009), 'Another Way to Hate', *Scotland on Sunday*, 21 June, http://news.scotsman.com/opinion/Dani-Garavelli-Another-way-to.5386376.jp.

Gass, N. (1997), 'An Analytical Model for Conflict Dynamics', in *The Journal of the Operational Research Society*, 48 (10) (October), pp. 978–87.

――――― (1994), 'Conflict Analysis in the Politico-Military Environment of a New World Order', in *The Journal of the Operational Research Society*, 45 (2) (February), pp. 133–42.

Gellner, Ernest (1983), *Nations and Nationalism*, Oxford: Oxford University Press.

Gergely, A. (2009), 'Battle for Jobs Feeds Northern Ireland Xenophobia', *Reuters*, 19 August, http://www.reuters.com/article/latestCrisis/idUSLH77794.

Gheorghe, N. and Pulay, G. (2009), 'Racist Peasants and Discriminated Nomads? Draft Report on Analysing Anti-Roma Violence in Harghita, Romania', Paper presented to the Organization for Security and Co-operation in London.

Gilroy, Paul (1979), *There Ain't No Black in the Union Jack: The Cultural Politics of Race and Nation*, London: Routledge.

Gingrich, Andre (2002), 'A Man for All Seasons: An Anthropological Perspective on Public Representation and Cultural Politics of the Austrian Freedom Party', in Pelinka, Anton and Wodak, Ruth (eds.) (2002), *The Haider Phenomenon in Austria*, New Brunswick, New Jersey: Transaction Publishers, pp. 67–91.

Gingrich, Andre and Banks, Marcus (eds.) (2006), *Neo-nationalism in Europe and Beyond: Perspectives from Social Anthropology*, New York and Oxford: Berghahn Books.

Goodwin, Jeff, James M. Jasper and Francesca Polletta (2001), *Passionate Politics: Emotions and Social Movements*, Chicago: The University of Chicago Press.

Gheorghe, Nicolae; Pulay Gergő (2010), *Racist Peasant and Discriminated Nomads? Draft Report on Analyzing anti-Roma violence in Harghita County*, Romania.

Ghodsee, Kristin (2009), 'Left Wing, Right Wing, Everything: Xenophobia, Neo-Totalitarianism and Populist Politics in Bulgaria', *Problems of Post-Communism*, 55 (3).

Goodwin, Mathew (2011), *Right Response, Understanding and Countering Populist Extremism in Europe*, London: Chatham House, available at www.chathamhouse.org.

Haller, István (nd.), *Conflicte interetnice în România*, draft paper.

Hansen, Thomas Blom (1999), *The Saffron Wave: Democracy and Hindu Nationalism in Modern India*, Princeton: Princeton University Press.

Havas, G., 'Esélyegyenlőség, deszegregáció', in Fazekas, K., Köllő, J., Varga, J. (eds.), *Zöld könyv a Magyar Közoktatás Megújításáért Ecostat*, Budapest, http://www.biztoskezdet.hu/uploads/attachments/ZKTartalom%5B1%5D.pdf.

Hollinger, P. and Bryant, C. (2010), 'Expelled Roma Vow to Return to France', *Financial Times Weekend*, 21/22 August.

Holmes, Douglas R. (2000), *Integral Europe: Fast-Capitalism, Multiculturalism, Neofascism*, Princeton: Princeton University Press.

――――― (2009), 'Experimental Identities (After Maastricht)' in *European Identity*,

REFERENCES

Peter Katzenstein and Jeffery Checkel (eds.), pp. 52–80, Cambridge: Cambridge University Press.

Horowitz, Donald L. (1985), *Ethnic Groups in Conflict*, Berkeley, Los Angeles, London: University of California Press.

Horváth M.T, (ed.) (2000), *Decentralization: Experiments and Reforms*, OSI LGI, http://lgi.osi.hu/publications/books/decentralization/EntireBook.pdf.

——— Ferenc (2007), *Nagybörzsöny*. Száz magyar falu könyvesháza (Nagybörzsöny. Library of Hundred Hungarian Villages), NKÖEOK, available at http://www.sulinet.hu/oroksegtar/data/100_falu/Nagyborzsony/index.htm.

Ignazi, Piero (1992), 'The Silent Counter-Revolution: Hypotheses on the Emergence of Extreme Right-Wing Parties in Europe'.

Ireland Online (2009), 'Loyalists Threaten Ethnic Minorities in the North', *Ireland Online*, 9 July, http://breakingnews.iol.ie/news/ireland/loyalists-threaten-ethnic-minorities-in-north-418065.html.

Iványi, K. (2006), 'Impacts of the New Anti Discrimination Policy', in Kállai, E., Törzsök, E. (eds.), *The Age of Reorganization: A Roma's Life in Hungary*, report between 2002–2006, EÖKIK.

Journal officiel, Chambre des députés (1970), '8577. M. Krieg demande à M. le ministre de l'Intérieur quelle est l'attitude du Gouvernement à l'égard de la recommandation n° 563 relative à la situation des Tziganes et autre nomades en Europe qui a été adoptée par l'assemblée consultative du Conseil de l'Europe le 30 septembre 1969 (question du 14 novembre 1969)',10 January, pp. 62–63.

Judt, Tony (2005), *Postwar: A History of Europe Since 1945*, London: Penguin.

Kalibová, Klára (2009), Rasové násilí a násilí páchané pravicovými extremisty— Situace v ČR po roce 1989, in *Nebezpečné známosti. Pravicový extremismus v malém příhraničním styku (SRN–ČR)*, Dresden: Kulturbüro Sachsen e. V., Heinrich Böll Stiftung, Weiterdenken—Heinrich Böll Stiftung Sachsen, pp. 66–91.

Kaminski, Ignacy-Marek (1983), *The State of Ambiguity: Studies of Gypsy Refugees*, Dept of Anthropology, University of Gothenburg: Sweden.

Kaplan, Robert (2005), *Balkan Ghosts: A Journey through History*, Picador.

Kaufmann, Stuart (2001), *Modern Hatreds: The Symbolic Politics of Ethnic War*, Ithaca, NY: Cornell University Press.

Keenan, D. (2009), 'Orde Defends Force Over Roma Attacks', *The Irish Times*, 19 June, http://www.irishtimes.com/newspaper/ireland/2009/0619/1224249121726.html.

——— (2009), 'North's Racist Incidents Could 'Rocket', *The Irish Times*, 30 June, http://www.irishtimes.com/newspaper/ireland/2009/0630/1224249783915.html.

——— (2009), '"Benefits a Factor" in Roma Exodus', *The Irish Times*, 10 July, http://www.irishtimes.com/newspaper/ireland/2009/0710/1224250387176.html.

REFERENCES

Kemény, István (2004), 'A magyarországi cigány népesség demográfiája' (The Demography of the Roma Population in Hungary), *Demográfia*, 47 (3–4), pp. 335–46.

Kemény, István and Béla Janky (2005), 'Roma Population of Hungary, 1971–2003', in István Kemény (ed.) *Roma of Hungary*, edited by East European Monographs, 702, New York: Columbia University Press.

Kertesi, G. (2005), *A Társadalom Peremén Romák a Munkaerőpiacon és az Iskolában*, Osiris: Budapest.

Kiss, Tamás; Fosztó, László; Fleck, Gábor (eds.) (2009), *Incluziune și Excluziune. Studii de caz asupra comunităților de romi din România*, Cluj-Napoca: Editura ISPMN & Kriterion.

Köllő, J. (2009), *A Pálya Szélén. Iskolázatlan Munkanélküliek a Posztszocialista Gazdaságban*, Osiris: Budapest.

Kőszeg, Ferenc and Lorna Králik (2008), *Control(led) Group. Final Report on the Strategies for Effective Police Stop and Search (STEPSS) Project*, Budapest: Hungarian Helsinki Committee.

Kovalski, Elian (2007), 'Do Not Play with Fire: The End of the Bulgarian Ethnic Model or the Persistence of Interethnic Tensions in Bulgaria?', *Journal of Muslim Minority Affairs*, 27 (1).

Krasteva, Stela (2005), 'Structure, Opportunity, Agency, and Contingency as Conditions for Politicizing Ethnicity: Ataka and 'The Roma' in Bulgaria', unpublished MA Thesis, Department of Sociology, UCLA.

Le Clère, B., Wright, V. (1973), *Les préfets du Second Empire*, Paris: Armand Colin, *Loi du 16 juillet 1912 et décret du 16 février 1913 sur l'exercice des professions ambulantes et la circulation des nomades complétés par les circulaires du Ministre de l'Intérieur des 3 et 22 octobre 1913*, Paris: Henri Charles-Lavauzelle.

Levinson, Daryl, J. (2003), 'Collective Sanctions', in *Stanford Law Review*, 56 (2) (November), pp. 345–428.

Lijphart, Arend (1977), *Democracy in Plural Societies. A Comparative Exploration*, New Haven: Yale University Press.

Liga Pro Europa (2006), *Discriminarea rasială, etnică și lingvistică în județele Alba, Bihor, Brașov, Caraș-Severin și Sălaj*.

Lipset, Seymour Martin and Rokkan, Stein (1967), Cleavage Structures, Party Systems and Voter Alignments: An Introduction, in *Party Systems and Voter Alignments*, Seymour Martin Lipset and Stein Rokkan (eds.), New York: The Free Press, pp. 1–64.

López, L. (2008), 'Les archives contre la statistique officielle? Retour sur les brigades du tigre (Dijon, 1908–1914)', *Genèses*, 71, pp. 106–22.

Louvel, M. (1934), 'Rapport présenté par l'Inspection générale des services administratifs (Exécution de l'article 15 du règlement d'administration publique du 19 janvier 1923), Application de la loi du 16 juillet 1912 relative aux marchands ambulants, aux commerçants ou industriels forains et aux nomades', *Journal officiel de la République française. Annexe administrative*, pp. 795–802.

Lucassen, L. (1997), '"Harmful Tramps". Police Professionalization and Gypsies in Germany, 1700–1945', *Crime, Histoire & Sociétés / Crime, History & Societies*, 1 (1), pp. 29–50.

Magyari, Nándor; Fosztó, László; Koreck, Mária; Toma, Stefánia (2010), *Kettős kisebbségben és konfliktuális helyzetben, a székelyföldi romák*, Research Report, Open Society Institute, June, unpublished.

Mahoney, James (2000), 'Path Dependence in Historical Sociology', *Theory and Society 29*, 29 (4) (August), pp. 507–48.

Majtényi, Balázs (2006/2007), 'What Has Happened to Our Model Child? The Creation and Evolution of the Hungarian Minority Act', in *European Yearbook of Minority Issues*, 7.

Majtényi, Balázs and András László Pap (2009), 'Should ethnic data be standardized? Different situations of processing ethnic data', in Máté Dániel Szabó (ed.), *Privacy protection and Minority Rights*, Budapest: Eötvös Károly Policy Institute, pp. 63–88.

Majtényi, László, Iván Székely and Máté Dániel Szabó (2006), *Roma támogatások és jogosultságok egyéni követésének lehetőségei* (Possibilities for tracing individual Roma subsidies and entitlements), Budapest: Eötvös Károly Institute.

Malone, A. (2009), 'As Hate-Filled Mobs Drive Romanian Gypsies Out of Ulster, We Ask Who's Really to Blame?', *The Daily Mail*, 20 June, http://www.dailymail.co.uk/news/article-1194358/SPECIAL-INVESTIGATION-As-hate-filled-mobs-drive-Romanian-gipsies-Ulster-ask-whos-REALLY-blame.html.

Marcetti, Corrado, Mori, Tiziana, and Solimano, Nicola (eds.) (1993), *Zingari in Toscana. Una ricerca della fondazione Michelucci. 1992–1993*, Firenze: Angelo Pontecorboli editore.

Martin, J. (2010), '"Il n'y a jamais eu de fichier de Roms", selon le général Morel', *Rue 89*, http://www.rue89.com/2010/10/09/il-ny-a-jamais-eu-de-fichiers-de-roms-selon-le-general-morel-170285.

McDonald, H. (2009), 'Romanian Gypsies Beware Beware, Loyalist C18 are Coming to Beat You Like a Baiting Bear', *The Observer*, 21 June, http://www.guardian.co.uk/world/2009/jun/21/race-northern-ireland-romanian-gypsies.

——— (2009), 'Pipe Bomb Threat to Roma Discovered', *The Observer*, 28 June, http://www.guardian.co.uk/uk/2009/jun/28/roma-racist-attacks-pipe-bomb.

McDdonald, Maryon (2006), 'New Nationalism in the EU: Occupying the Available Space', in Gingrich and Banks (eds.) (2006), Neo-Nationalism in Europe and Beyond: Perspectives from Social Anthropology [title in italics please], New York and Oxford: Berghahn Books, pp. 218–36.

Meredith, F. (2009), 'An Easy Target for the Hate Mobs', *The Irish Times*, 20 June,

http://www.irishtimes.com/newspaper/weekend/2009/0620/1224249169 417.
html.

Mirga, Andrzej (2009), 'The Extreme Right and Roma and Sinti in Europe: a New Phase in the Use of Hate Speech and Violence?', *Roma Rights Journal*, 1, pp. 5–9.

Monaghan, R. and McLaughlin, S. (2006), 'Informal Justice in the City', *Space and Polity*, 10 (2), pp. 171–86.

Moffen, P. (2010), 'Entretien avec Laurent Mucchielli. Le tropisme policier du pouvoir actuel a encore franchi un pas', *AfiaviMag.com*, 23 August, http://afiavi.free.fr/e_magazine/spip.php?article1286.

Moisi, Dominique (2009), *The Geopolitics of Emotion*, New York and London: Doubleday.

Moriarty, G. (2009) 'Roma Families Determined to Leave Northern Ireland', *The Irish Times*, 22 June, http://www.irishtimes.com/newspaper/ireland/2009/0622/1224249264383.html.

———— (2009), 'Spate of Racist Attacks Sullies North's Friendly Image', *The Irish Times*, 24 June, http://www.irishtimes.com/newspaper/ireland/2009/0624/1224249416654.html.

———— (2009), 'NI Policing Board Members Question Portrayal of Attack on City Church', *The Irish Times*, 3 July, http://www.irishtimes.com/newspaper/ireland/2009/0703/1224249968331.html.

Morvern, A. (2009), 'Shockwaves: Romanians in Belfast', *Institute of Race Relations*, 25 June, http://www.irr.org.uk/2009/june/ha000051.html.

Mossé, M. (1924), 'Application de la loi du 16 juillet 1912 relative aux marchants ambulants, aux commerçants ou industriels forains et aux nomades', *Journal officiel de la République française. Annexe administrative*, pp. 714–34.

Mouffe, C. (1995), 'Post-Marxism: Democracy and Identity', *Environment and Planning D: Society and Space*, 13, pp. 259–65.

Mudde, Cas (2004), 'The Populist Zeitgeist', in *Government and Opposition*, vol. 39, issue 4, pp. 542–63.

———— (2007) 'Populist Radical Right Parties in Europe', Cambridge: Cambridge University Press.

Mulcahy, G. (2009), 'In defence of anti-racist protest: a reply to Derek Hanway', *Youth Against Fascism*, 24 July, http://youthagainstracism.wordpress.com/2009/07/24/in-defence-of-anti-racist-protest-a-reply-to-derek-hanway/.

Munková, Eva (2008), 'Here come the neo Nazis', in *The New Presence*, 11 (2), pp. 22–25.

Murray Brown, J. (2009), 'Belfast Attacks on Roma Gypsies', *The Financial Times*, 17 June, http://www.ft.com/cms/s/0/915043e6-5b59-11de-be3f-00144 feabdc0.html.

Nagle, J. (2009), 'The Right to Belfast City Centre: from Ethnocracy to Liberal Multiculturalism?', *Political Geography*, 28, pp. 132–41.

REFERENCES

Newsletter (2009), 'Roma Families Leave Ulster', *Newsletter*, 26 June, http://www. newsletter.co.uk/news/Roma-families-leave-Ulster.5404801.jp.

Nézer, F. (2005), *Évolution de la législation belge sur les étrangers indésirables de 1830 à 1914*, Mémoire de licence, Louvain-la-Neuve: Université catholique de Louvain.

Northern Ireland Office (1998), *Good Friday Agreement*, NIO, Belfast, Northern Ireland.

Oberschall, Anthony (2007), *Conflict and Peace Building in Divided Societies: Response to Ethnic Violence*, London & New York: Routledge.

Oesch, Daniel (2008), 'Explaining workers' support for right wing populist parties in western Europe: evidence from Austria, Belgium, France, Norway and Switzerland', in *International Political Science Review*, 29 (3), pp. 349–73.

OSCE (2007), *Guidebook on Democratic Policing by the Senior Police Adviser to the OSCE Secretary General*, 24 January, http://www.osce.org/spmu/item_11_23086. html.

——— (2008) *Good Practices in Building Police-Public Partnerships by the Senior Police Adviser to the OSCE Secretary General*, May, http://www.osce.org/spmu/ item_11_31851.html.

——— (2010) *Police and Roma and Sinti: Good Practices in Building Trust and Understanding*, April, http://polis.osce.org/library/details?doc_id=3682.

OSCE HCNM (2006), *Recommendations on Policing in Multi-Ethnic Societies*, February, http://www.osce.org/documents/hcnm/2006/02/179 82_en.pdf.

OSCE–ODIHR (2010), *Addressing Violence, Promoting Integration. Field Assessment of Violent Incidents against Roma in Hungary: Key Developments, Findings and Recommendations*, June-July 2009, Warsaw: OSCE-ODIHR, 15 June, http:// www.osce.org/documents/odihr/2010/06/44569_en.pdf.

Pálné, Kovács, I. (2001), *Regionális politika és közigazgatás*, Dialóg Campus: Budapest.

Pap, András László (2006), 'Minority Rights and Diaspora Claims: Collision and Interdependence', in Osamu Ieda (ed.), *The Status Law Syndrome: Post-Communist Nation-Building or Post-Modern Citizenship?*, Sapporo: Hungarian Academy of Sciences, Institute for Legal Studies—Hokkaido University.

Papataxiarchis, E. (1988), 'Worlds Apart: Women and Men in the Greek Aegean Household and Coffeeshop', Ph.D. thesis, London: London School of Economics Székelyi, Mária, Örkény, Antal and Csepli, György, (2001), 'Romakép a mai Magyar társadalomban', in *Szociológiai Szemle* 2001/3, pp. 19–46, http://www. mtapti.hu/mszt/20013/szekelyi.htm.

Payne, H.C. (1966), *The Police State of Louis Napoléon Bonaparte, 1851–1860*, Seattle: University of Washington Press.

Pelinka, Anton and Wodak, Ruth (eds.) (2002), *The Haider Phenomenon in Austria*, New Brunswick, New Jersey: Transaction Publishers.

Però, D. (1999), 'Next to the Dog Pound: Institutional Discourses and Practices about Rom Refugees in Left-wing Bologna', *Modern Italy*, 4 (2), pp. 207–24.

REFERENCES

———— (2005) 'The European Left and the New Immigrations: the Case of Italy', in *Crossing European Boundaries: Beyond Conventional Geographical Categories*, Jaro Stacul, C Moutsou, H. Kopnina (eds.), New York and Oxford: Berghahn Books.

———— (2007) *Inclusionary Rhetoric / Exclusionary Practices. Left-wing Politics and Migrants in Italy*, New York and Oxford: Berghahn Books.

Peschanski, D. (1994), *Les Tsiganes en France, 1939–1946*, Paris: CNRS éditions.

PER (2000), *Prevention of Violence and Discrimination Against the Roma in Central and Eastern Europe*.

Petkov, Krastyo (2006), 'The Late Ethno-Nationalisms in Bulgaria: Their Economic and Social Roots', *South-East Europe Review*, 2, pp. 109–28.

Petrova, D. (2009), 'Hardening Attitude Against the Roma', *The Guardian*, 26 June, http://www.guardian.co.uk/world/2009/jun/26/discrimination-roma-families-ireland-prejudice.

Piazza, P. (2002), 'Au cœur de la construction de l'État moderne. Socio-genèse du carnet anthropométrique des nomades', *Les Cahiers de la sécurité*, 48, pp. 207–27.

Pitcher, Ben (2009), 'The Global Politics of Multiculturalism', in *Journal of Development*, 52 (4).

Political Capital Institute (2008), *Országjelentés. Politikai Kockázat Index 2007* (Country Report. Political Risk Index 2007), Budapest, http://www.orszagjelentes.hu/sajto/orszagjelentes_sajtoanyag_polrisk_080429.doc.

Popham, P. and McKittrick, D. (2009), 'Defiance! Meet the Romanian Families Refusing to be Forced Out', *The Independent on Sunday*, 28 June, http://www.independent.co.uk/news/uk/home-news/defiance-meet-the-romanian-families-refusing-to-be-forced-out-1722458.html.

Preda, Marian (1993), 'Conflictul din localitatea Mihail Kogălniceanu' in C. Zamfir; E. Zamfir (eds.), *Ţiganii: între ignorare şi îngrijorare*, Bucureşti: Editura Alternative, pp. 175–200.

Ragaru, Nadeze, (2001), 'Islam in Post-Communist Bulgaria: An Aborted Clash of Civilizations?', *Nationalities Papers*, 29 (2).

Rechel, Bernd, (2007), 'The Bulgarian 'Ethnic Model'—Reality or Ideology?' *Europe-Asia Studies*, 59 (7).

Regione Toscana (1987), *Proposta di legge 175 concernente Interventi per la tutela dell'etnia "rom". Presentata alla Presidenza del Consiglio Regionale della Toscana in data 10.4.1987*, [Typescript].

Reyniers, A., Williams, P. (2000), 'Permanence tsigane et politique de sédentarisation dans la France de l'après-guerre', *Études tsiganes*, 15, pp. 10–25.

Reyniers, A. (1991), 'Pérégrinations des Jénis en France au XIXe siècle', *Études tsiganes*, 2, pp. 19–25.

———— (2006), 'Pérégrination des Manouches en France au XIXème siècle', *Études tsiganes*, 26, pp. 9–17.

373

REFERENCES

RIRNM—RCIER (2008), *Social Cohesion and Interethnic Climate in Romania*, Research Report, Cluj-Napoca: RIRNM.

RIRNM (2009), *Models of Ethnic Segregation. Rural Ghettos in Romania*, Research Report, Cluj-Napoca: RIRNM.

Rivière, L. (1898), 'Le vagabondage et la police des campagnes', *Revue pénitentiaire. Bulletin de la Société Générale des Prisons*, pp. 499–506.

Robert, P. (2004), 'La migration des Sinté piémontais en France au XXème siècle', *Études tsiganes*, pp. 18–19, pp. 29–51.

Rossa, S. (1995), 'Regione e Comuni di fronte al problema degli Zingari in Toscana', Faculty of Political Science, University of Florence, Unpublished MA Thesis.

Rothschild, Donald (1986), 'Hegemonial Exchange: An Alternative Model for Managing Conflict in Middle Africa', in Dennis L. Thompson; Dov Ronen (eds.), *Ethnicity, Politics and Development*, Boulder, CO: Lynne Rienner Publishers.

Rydgren, Jens (2002), 'Radical Right Populism in Sweden: Still a Failure, but for How Long?', *Scandinavian Political Studies*, 25 (1), pp. 27–56.

Sandu, Dumitru (2005), *Roma Social Mapping. Targeting by a Community Poverty Surve*, Research Report, July, Bucureşti: World Bank.

Scioscia, M. (2009), 'L'integrazione fra politiche. Immaginare il futuro tra memoria e presente', in *Politiche possibili. Abitare le città con i rom e i sinti*, Tommaso Vitale (ed.), Roma: Carocci.

Scraton, P. (2009), 'Fear and Loathing in Belfast', *Institute for Race Relations*, 25 June, http://www.irr.org.uk/2009/june/ha000046.html.

Sewell, William. H. R. (1996), 'Three Temporalities: Towards an Eventful Sociology', in Terence J McDonald (ed.), *The Historic Turn in the Human Science*, Ann Arbor: University of Michigan Press, pp. 262–64.

Shirlow, P. (2006), 'Belfast: The 'Post-Conflict' City', *Space and Polity*, 10 (2), pp. 99–107.

Shore, C. (2006), 'Government Without Statehood? Anthropological Perspectives on Governance and Sovereignty in the European Union', *European Law Journal*, 12 (6), pp. 709–24.

Sigona, N. and N. Trehan (2009), *Romani Politics in Contemporary Europe. Politics, Ethnopolitics and the Neo-liberal Order*. London: Palgrave.

Sitou, E. (2008), 'L'affaire des Gitanos: Chronique d'une flambée raciste à Toulouse à la fin du XIXe siècle', *Études tsiganes*, 30, pp. 10–25.

Smith, Anthony (1992), 'Chosen Peoples: Why Ethnic Groups Survive', in *Ethnic and Racial Studies*, 15 (3), pp. 440–49.

Smyth, J. (2009), 'Irish Increase in Racist Crimes Third Highest in EU', *The Irish Times*, 25 June, http://www.irishtimes.com/newspaper/ireland/2009/0625/1224249509793.html.

Stacul, J. (2006) 'Neo-Nationalism or Neo-Localism? Integralist Political Engagements in Italy at the Turn of the Millennium', in *Neo-nationalism in Europe and Beyond. Perspectives from Social Anthropology*, Andreas Gingrich and Markus Banks (eds.), New York and Oxford: Berghahn Books.

Stamatov, Peter (2000), 'The Making of a 'Bad' Public: Ethnonational Mobilization in Post-Communist Bulgaria', *Theory and Society*, 29 (4), pp. 549–72.

Stolcke, V. (1995), 'Talking Culture: New Boundaries, New Rhetorics of Exclusion in Europe', *Current Anthropology*, 36 (1), 1–24.

Szalai, Julia (2008), 'A Few Worrisome Notes on the Formation of the Postcommunist Welfare State', in *Social Policy in a Globalizing World: A North-South Dialogue*, Valeria Fargion (ed.), 'Roma: Redazione la Rivista delle Politiche Sociali', pp. 469–89.

Szalai, Julia (2005), 'A Jóléti Fogda', in Neményi, M., Szalai, J (ed.), *Kisebbségek Kisebbsége. A Magyarországi Cigányok Emberi és Politikai Jogai. Új Mandátum Kiadó*, Budapest, 2005.

Szalai, Julia (1995), 'A Helyi Önkormányzatok Szociálpolitikájáról', in Landau, E., Simonyi, Á., Szalai. J, Vincze, P. (ed.), *Az Államtalanítás Dilemmái: Szociálpolitikai Kényszerek és Választások*, Aktív Társadalom Alapítvány: Budapest.

Szente, V.L. (1997), 'Field Report: Italy', *Roma Rights*, Autumn, 51 (3).

Szlazsánszky, Ferenc (2008), 'A gárda hívásra házhoz megy' (Hungarian Guard for Home Delivery), *Hetek*, 12 (30) (25 July), http://epa.oszk.hu/00800/00804/00543/68659.html.

Tódor, János (2011),'Cigánypénzek, káoszprojektek' (Gypsy moneys, chaotic projects), *Kritika*, 1, pp. 13–15.

Todorova, Maria (2006), 'Language in the Construction of Ethnicity and Nationalism: The Bulgarian Case', CEEOL *Nationalities Affairs*, 28, http://www.ceeol.com/aspx/getdocument.aspx?logid=5&id=b8d7b646-069511db-98280080ad781d9c.

Toma, Stefánia (2006), 'Ethnic Relations and Poverty in a Multi-Ethnic Community in Romania', in Francois Ruegg, Rudolf Poledna, Calin Rus (eds.), *Interculturalism and Discrimination in Romania. Policies, Practices, Identities and Representations*, Berlin: LIT Verlag, pp. 155–72.

Tosi, S. and T. Vitale (2009), 'Explaining How Political Culture Changes: Catholic Activism and the Secular Left in Italian Peace Movements', *Social Movements Studies*, 8 (2), pp. 131–47.

Uerlings, H., Patrut, I.K. (eds.) (2008), *"Zigeuner" und Nation: Repräsentation, Inklusion, Exklusion*, Frankfurt am Main: Peter Lang.

Varró Szilvia (2009), 'A Jobbik mint harmadik erő. I.—Egy sörözőben összejöttek' (The 'Jobbik' Party as the Third Power, Part 1—They Gathered in a Pub), *Magyar Narancs*, 21 (6), p. 10.

——— (2009), 'A Jobbik mint harmadik erő. II.—A tiszták' (The 'Jobbik' Party as the Third Power, Part 2—The Clean Ones), *Magyar Narancs*, 21 (7), p. 10.

REFERENCES

Vassilev, Rossen (2002), 'Bulgaria's Ethnic Problems', *East European Quarterly*, 36 (1).

Vaux de Foletier, F. de. (1973), 'Voyages et migrations des Tsiganes en France au XIXe siècle', *Études tsiganes*, pp. 1–30.

———— (1981), *Les bohémiens en France au 19e siècle*, Paris: Lattès Vaux de Foletier.

———— (1973), 'Voyages et migrations des Tsiganes en France au XIXème siècle', *Études Tsiganes*, 3, pp. 1–30.

Vintileanu, Ioaneta; Ádám, Gábor (eds.), (2003), *Poliţia şi comunităţile multiculturale din România. Prevenirea şi gestionarea conflictelor la nivelul comunităţilor multiculturale*, Cluj-Napoca: Editura CRDE.

Vohl, P.-G. (1937), *Police des ambulants, forains et nomades et des professions connexes*, Paris: Charles-Lavauzelle.

Vörös, K. (1979), *Budapest Legnagyobb Adófizetői 1873–1917*, Budapest: Akadémiai.

Wagniart, J.-F. (1999), *Le vagabond à la fin du XIXe siècle*, Paris: Belin.

Wimmer, Andreas, (2002), *Nationalist Exclusion and Ethnic Conflict: Shadows of Modernity*, Cambridge: Cambridge University Press.

Wright, S. (1998), 'The Politicization of "Culture"', *Anthropology Today*, 14 (1), pp. 7–15.

Zimmermann, M. (ed.) (2007), *Zwischen Erziehung und Vernichtung. Zigeunerpolitik und Zigeunerforschung im Europa des 20. Jahrhunderts*, Stuttgart: Franz Steiner Verlag.

Žižek, S. (2009), *Violence*, London: Profile Books.

Zolnay, J. (2006), 'Kényszerek és Választások. Oktatáspolitika és Etnikai Szegregáció Miskolc és Nyíregyháza Általános Iskoláiban', Esély 4, http://www.esely.org/kiadvanyok/2006_4/ZOLNAY.pdf.

———— (2008), 'A Hiányzó Ágens', Educatio 4, http://www.hier.iif.hu/hu/educatio_reszletes.php?id=71.

INDEX